A POLITICAL AND ECONOMIC DICTIONARY OF EAST ASIA

A POLITICAL AND ECONOMIC DICTIONARY OF EAST ASIA

James E. Hoare
and
Susan Pares

FIRST EDITION

Routledge
Taylor & Francis Group

LONDON AND NEW YORK

First Edition 2005
Routledge
Haines House, 21 John Street, London WC1N 2BP, United Kingdom
(A member of the Taylor & Francis Group)

ISBN 1 85743 258 4

Development Editor: Cathy Hartley
Copy Editor and Proof-reader: Simon Chapman

Typeset in Times New Roman 10/12

The publishers make no representation, express or implied, with regard to the accuracy of the information contained in this book and cannot accept any legal responsibility for any errors or omissions that may take place.

Typeset by AJS Solutions, Huddersfield and Dundee
Printed in the UK by MPG Books, Bodmin, Cornwall

FOREWORD

This publication, A POLITICAL AND ECONOMIC DICTIONARY OF EAST ASIA, takes its place in the Europa series initiated in 2002. East Asia is, by common agreement, one of the most vigorous and fast-changing regions of the world, particularly in the economic sphere. It is also a region with a complicated history and strong political, national and ethnic loyalties. Issues left over by history in many instances bear sharply on the present and require some teasing out. Such complexity cannot easily be seized, but this dictionary attempts to provide some points of reference for the general reader.

The term 'East Asia' as used here covers eight countries or regions—the word 'state' cannot be applied to all of them. They are: the People's Republic of China, its Special Administrative Regions of Hong Kong and Macao, China (Taiwan), the two states on the Korean peninsula, Japan and Mongolia. This last, especially since it freed itself from the former Soviet grip, lies more naturally within the East Asian orbit.

Entries are intended to stand on their own, with coverage of recent developments and, where available, full contact details. The range of entries encompasses political concepts, political parties and groups, political, financial, educational and cultural institutions, main government leaders and prominent individuals, development projects, religious movements and organizations, ethnic groups, administrative divisions and principal cities. The longest entries take the form of short essays on the six major countries or regions within East Asia, followed by entries on those countries' economies and other pertinent issues. Cross-referencing is through the device of highlighting in bold type those words or phrases that have their own entry. For ease of use, the use of bold type for the names of countries in the region has been avoided, with the exception of China and its associated entries, given the complex nature of its history and current affairs.

JAMES E. HOARE
SUSAN PARES
London, January 2005

ACKNOWLEDGEMENTS

The authors are indebted to a number of institutions and individuals whose scholarship has eased their research. In particular, they would like to thank the compilers of *The Annual Register*, the Asian Development Bank, the Institut für Asienkunde Hamburg, the International Institute of Strategic Studies and the World Bank. Their thanks are also due to Robert Ash, J. Dyer Ball, Richard Bowring, Sondra Buckley, Michael Dillon, Janet Hunter, Frederic M. Kaplan, Peter Kornicki, Colin Mackerras, Lynn Pan, David Robertson, Alan Sanders, Julian M. Sobin, Arthur Stockwin, and a host of others whose dictionaries, guides or other works have already covered the ground so thoroughly.

Several publications have been indispensable in helping with the checking of facts and information: the *Encyclopedia Britannica* in both printed and electronic forms, *The Far East and Australasia* (Europa Publications), the *Oxford Dictionary of the World*, the *Oxford Encyclopedia of World History*, '*The Times*' *World Religions* and the Scarecrow Press's series of Historical Dictionaries. The Internet has led us to the essential websites. Any errors and faults of interpretation are the authors' alone.

Finally, we are grateful to the staff of Taylor & Francis, both for advice and assistance, and for waiting patiently for this work to appear.

THE AUTHORS

James E. Hoare and Susan Pares are former Research Analysts in the United Kingdom Foreign and Commonwealth Office, now freelance writers on East Asian affairs. They have spent varying periods in China, Japan and the two Koreas since the mid-1960s. Their final overseas posting was to Pyongyang in 2001–02, where they opened the first ever British Embassy to the Democratic People's Republic of Korea.

James Hoare has published numerous articles/papers and reviews on East Asia, and is the author/editor of a number of books; the most recent are *Embassies in the East: The Story of the British and their Embassies in China, Japan and Korea from 1859 to the present* (Richmond: Curzon Press, 1999); *Britain and Japan: Biographical Portraits*, Vol. III (edited for the Japan Society. Richmond: Japan Library, 1999); (with Andrew Nahm) *Historical Dictionary of the Republic of Korea*, (Lanham, MD: Scarecrow Press, 2nd edition, 2004); and *Culture Smart! Korea* (London: Kuperard 2005).

Susan Pares published *Crosscurrents: Korean-Western Culture in Contrast* (Seoul: Seoul International Publishing House, 1985), and was formerly Editor of *Asian Affairs* (journal of the Royal Society for Asian Affairs, London).

They have also co-authored a number of books, including *Korea: An Introduction* (London: KPI, 1988); *Roots of Modern Conflict: Conflict in Korea: An Encyclopedia* (Oxford, Santa Barbara, CA and Denver, CO: ABC-CLIO, 1999); and *Beijing* (Oxford, Santa Barbara, CA, and Denver, CO: ABC-CLIO 2000) (World Bibliographical Series Vol. 226).

ABBREVIATIONS

Ave	Avenue	Ltd	Limited
Bldg	Building	m	metre(s)
Blvd	Boulevard	m.	million
CA	California	Maj.	Major
c/o	care of	Man.	Manager
Capt.	Captain	MD	Maryland
CEO	Chief Executive Officer	mph	miles per hour
Chair.	Chairman/person/	NGO	Non-governmental
	woman		Organization
cnr	corner	No(.)	Number
Co	Company	NW	North-West
CO	Colorado	NY	New York
Col	Colonel	OECD	Organisation for
Corpn	Corporation		Economic Co-operation
DC	District of Columbia		and Development
Dir	Director	PO(B)	Post Office (Box)
Dist.	District	PPP	purchasing-power parity
Edif.	Edificio (Building)	Pres.	President
esq	esquina (corner)	Prof.	Professor
Exec.	Executive	R.	Reigned
Fr	Father	Rd	Road
GDP	Gross Domestic Product	rtd	retired
Gen.	General	Sec.	Secretary
GNI	Gross National Income	Sgt	Sergeant
GNP	Gross National Product	Sq	Square
Gov.	Governor	St	Street
ha	hectare	Tel	Telephone
HQ	Headquarters	UK	United Kingdom
Km	Kilometre(s)	UN	United Nations
kph	kilometres per hour	US(A)	United States
Lt	Lieutenant		(of America)
Lt.	Lantai (level)	Vol.	Volume

INTERNATIONAL TELEPHONE CODES

The code and relevant telephone number must be preceded by the International Dialling Code of the country from which you are calling.

ROMANIZATION

Romanization has become more complicated in recent years, as governments have moved into an area that scholars once occupied. This is particularly so in East Asia, where the governments of the People's Republic of China and the Republic of Korea have imposed a state-approved system, replacing older systems of romanization. There is a further complication in that most systems display much tolerance for personal choice in the spelling of names. We have not tried to impose conformity where there is none, and have used the systems that are prevalent in the different states and regions that make up East Asia, but without any diacritical marks, as follows:

People's Republic of China – pinyin;
Taiwan, Hong Kong and Macao – Wade-Giles;
Mongolia – standard transliteration;
Korean Peninsula – simplified McCune-Reischauer;
Japan – Hepburn.

In all cases, names are given as they are used in the place concerned. Thus for the Republic of Korea, names are in the form 'Kim Dae-Jung', whereas in the Democratic People's Republic of Korea, names are given as separate words 'Kim Dae Jung'. Names follow the usual East Asian pattern with surname first. Thus 'Kim' is the surname, and 'Dae-Jung' the given names of the former President of the Republic of Korea. The exception is the first Republic of Korea president, Syngman Rhee, who was so widely known by the Western order of his name that we have kept it.

A

Abductees

During the 1970s and early 1980s a number of people went missing in Japan in mysterious circumstances. From the beginning, some families claimed that agents of the Democratic People's Republic of Korea (DPRK) had kidnapped those missing and taken them to the DPRK. Lack of real evidence, however, and the absence of diplomatic relations between Japan and the DPRK meant that successive Japanese governments declined to raise the issue. In 1987–88 the first clear evidence emerged in the testimony of **Kim Hyun Hee**, a DPRK agent convicted of blowing up a **Korean Air** aircraft over the Andaman Sea. She stated that an ethnic Japanese woman had trained her in the DPRK in Japanese practices and customs to prepare her for her mission. She also stated that the woman was in the DPRK against her will.

Following the visit to the DPRK by the delegation led by **Kanemaru Shin**, negotiations began in 1990 between Japan and the DPRK on a possible normalization of relations. During these negotiations the Japanese delegation raised the issue of the alleged abductees. The DPRK delegation vigorously denied the allegations, and broke off the talks. In subsequent years the DPRK continued to deny that it had played any role in the disappearances. However, when Japanese Prime Minister **Koizumi Junichiro** visited the DPRK in September 2002, the DPRK leader **Kim Jong Il** personally admitted that the kidnappings had taken place. He also stated that some of the abductees had died, but others were still alive. He added that the kidnappings had been the work of special units; these had been investigated and those concerned punished. He also pledged that there would be no further kidnappings and agreed that those surviving Japanese who wished to do so might visit Japan.

While Koizumi gained some political credit for his initiative, there was much disquiet in Japan at the DPRK's admissions. When five of those kidnapped visited Japan in the autumn of 2002, the government found it impossible to fulfil its pledge that they would return to the DPRK, and negotiations began to bring out their children. In one case these were complicated by the marriage of Mrs Soga Hitomi to an American, **Charles Jenkins**, whom the US military believed to be a deserter. In May 2004 Koizumi again visited the DPRK, and this time was able to bring back five of the seven children involved. Jenkins and his children at first refused to leave, but in July 2004 they travelled to Indonesia and then to Japan. Further negotiations to seek information on what had happened to the eight abductees who are alleged to have died continued in November 2004, and led to the release to Japan of what were said to be the ashes of one of the abductees. When the ashes were tested, however, this proved not to be the case. The episode continues to arouse much anger in Japan.

Abe Shinzo

Abe Shinzo is the Japanese politician thought most likely to succeed **Koizumi Junichiro** as Prime Minister of Japan in due course.

Abe, born in 1954, is the son of another Abe Shinzo (1924–91), who held various ministerial posts under Prime Minister **Nakasone Yasuhiro,** and is the grandson of Kishi Nobusuke, a former Prime Minister. He thus comes from the heart of Japan's conservative tradition. After graduating in law from Seikei University, Abe worked for a time for Kobe Steel, and may also have attended the University of Southern California. In 1986 he became the private secretary to the then chairman of the ruling **Liberal Democratic Party (LDP)** general council. He entered the **National Diet** in 1993, and was deputy chief cabinet secretary in the Mori Cabinet in 2000, and in the Koizumi Cabinet from 2001. He has established a reputation for being uncompromising towards the Democratic People's Republic of Korea, especially on the **abductees** issue, and on security matters. There has been some scandal about a possible exaggeration of his educational qualifications, and the receipt of funds from the Japan Dental Association, but he has survived.

He became secretary-general of the LDP in 2003, and thus ranked second after Koizumi. When Koizumi reshuffled his team in September 2004, Abe stepped down to deputy secretary-general, but he remains the main contender for the succession to Koizumi.

Academia Sinica

Pinyin: *Zhongyang yanjiuyuan*; Wade-Giles: *Chungyang yenchiu yuan*

Founded originally in **China** at the beginning of the Nationalist **Republic of China (1912–49)** government in 1928, like other such institutions, Academia Sinica moved to **Taiwan** after the Nationalists' defeat in 1949. Today it is probably the most important research centre on Taiwan, reporting directly to the President of the 'Republic of China'. It has 28 research institutes in humanities and sciences, and awards higher degrees in some subjects.

The **Chinese Academy of Sciences** in the **People's Republic of China**, which also claims descent from the original 1928 institution, is sometimes referred to as Academia Sinica.

Pres.: Yuan T. Lee
Address: Academia Sinica
          128–2 Academia Rd
          Nankang
          Taipei 115
          Taiwan
Tel: 886-2-2789-9696
Fax: 886-2-2783-9871
E-mail: aspublic@gate.sinica.edu.tw
Internet: www.sinica.edu.tw

Academy of Korean Studies

Hanguk jungsin munhwa yunguwon

An academic institution established in the Republic of Korea (ROK) in 1978 under President **Park Chung-Hee**, to promote scholarship in the field of Korean studies. From the beginning, however, the Academy's alternative purpose was to improve the international image of the ROK. As well as publishing works on Korea and providing a centre for visiting scholars, the Academy has had a graduate programme since 1980. By 2003 400 masters' degrees and 110 Ph.Ds in Korean studies had been awarded under this programme. The Academy's campus is located just outside of **Seoul**.

Address: Academy of Korean Studies
          50 Unjung-dong
          Bundang-ku
          Seongnam-si
          Kyeonggi-do 463-791
          Republic of Korea
Tel: 82-31-709-8111
E-mail: info@aks.ac.kr
Internet: www.aks.ac.kr

Academy of Sciences

The Academy of Sciences is the principal centre of scientific and technical research in the Democratic People's Republic of Korea (DPRK). Some social science institutes are also attached to it. The Academy was founded in 1952, and is an organization reporting directly to the Cabinet. In 1994–98 its name was 'National Academy of Sciences', but it subsequently reverted to its original title. It has facilities in **Pyongyang**, but much of its work is concentrated in the city of Pyongsong, South Pyongan Province, a short distance from the capital. The Academy has a variety of agencies and organizations under its control, including a number of publishing houses. Some reports state that it has been a centre of the

DPRK nuclear programme since the 1950s. Like all such organizations in the DPRK, the Academy has suffered from lack of funds since the late 1980s.

In addition to the Academy of Sciences, the DPRK has an Academy of Agricultural Sciences, an Academy of Social Sciences, and an Academy of Medical Sciences.

Address: Academy of Sciences
 Gin-Maul 1-dong
 Moranbong District
 Pyongyang
 Democratic People's Republic of Korea
Tel: 850-2-381-8134
Fax: 850-381-4580/381-4410

Agreed Framework

Agreement signed on 21 October 1994 in Geneva, Switzerland, between the USA and the Democratic People's Republic of Korea (DPRK). Talks lasting one month preceded the signature of the Agreed Framework and were aimed at negotiating resolution of the nuclear issue on the **Korean peninsula**. The **DPRK nuclear programme** had been causing international concern for some years. The **International Atomic Energy Agency (IAEA)**, which had already inspected the nuclear facilities at Yongbyon in 1992, found itself thwarted when it tried to inspect further sites. The DPRK's threat in March 1993 to withdraw from the **Nuclear Non-Proliferation Treaty (NPT**—Treaty on the Non-Proliferation of Nuclear Weapons) prompted two rounds of talks with the USA. Its announcement in June 1994 that it would relinquish membership of the IAEA then brought matters to a culmination. A visit to the DPRK in June 1994 by former US President **James (Jimmy) Earl Carter**, who met President **Kim Il Sung**, persuaded the DPRK to resume talks with the USA.

Under the Agreed Framework, the DPRK agreed to freeze all of its activities at Yongbyon, while an international consortium, to be known as the **Korean Peninsula Energy Development Organization**, would supply two light-water reactors (LWRs) to the DPRK to meet its energy needs. Until the LWRs became operational, the USA would supply 500,000 tons annually of heavy oil to the DPRK for heating and electricity production. The USA further undertook to lift trade barriers, to move towards diplomatic relations with the DPRK and to give formal assurances to the DPRK against the threat or use of US nuclear weapons. The DPRK for its part agreed that it would work to implement the Joint Declaration on the Denuclearization of the Korean Peninsula which it and the Republic of Korea had issued in 1991, would remain in the NPT and would continue to accept IAEA inspections. Only when the new LWRs were about to become operational with the delivery of key components would the IAEA verify the accuracy of the DPRK's initial report to the Agency on its nuclear materials.

Adherence to the terms of the Agreed Framework was not always assured by either party. Construction of the LWRs was much delayed and has now been put on hold. The supplies of heavy fuel oil have been suspended. What is regarded as the DPRK's acknowledgement, following a visit by a senior US official to **Pyongyang** in October 2002, that it was engaging in a clandestine uranium enrichment programme is construed as DPRK violation of the Agreed Framework, and the agreement is in abeyance.

Ainu

Name given to the indigenous people of Japan's northern island of Hokkaido. The name means 'human being' in the Ainu language.

Until the mid-19th century the Ainu lived in northern Honshu, southern **Sakhalin**, and in the **Kurile Islands**. They were hunters, fishers and gatherers, with settlements along the rivers and near game trails. Their religion centred on bears, which they worshipped with songs and dances, and on a belief in an all-present spirit world. Ainu numbers were small, in the region of 25,000 in the early 19th century. Even before Japan's opening to the West in the 1850s, they were in decline and their traditional lands were under pressure from Japanese immigrants. This process accelerated after the Russo-Japanese Treaty of 1854 and Japanese insistence that the Japanese were a homogeneous people, with no minority groups.

A determined effort was made to colonize Hokkaido, especially after the **Meiji Restoration** of 1868. In 1869 the Japanese government established a colonization department for Hokkaido, the *Kaitakushi,* and one of its tasks was the suppression of the remnants of Ainu culture. The Japanese made strenuous efforts to assimilate the Ainu. Japanese scholars described them as 'former aborigines' from 1878, studying them as though they were a vanishing race. Ainu culture was confined to museums, as something already dead.

After 1945 the Japanese government continued to insist that Japan did not have minority peoples. However, groups claiming to be Ainu pressed for recognition, and the Ainu Association of Hokkaido, which has campaigned for the restoration of Ainu land, dates from 1946. The struggle for recognition has continued since then. When Prime Minister **Nakasone Yasuhiro** claimed in the mid-1980s that Japan was a monoethnic state, this spurred the Ainu groups into more intense activity, leading eventually to a formal Japanese recognition, in reports to the **United Nations**, of the continued existence of the Ainu. There were legislative changes, while a 1987 lawsuit over a proposed dam led to the legal admission of the Ainu's existence.

Air Koryo

Choson Minhang

Air Koryo is the only airline in the Democratic People's Republic of Korea (DPRK). Originally known as the Civil Aviation Authority of Korea, it appears to date from

1954, when it replaced a **Korean War** period joint DPRK-Soviet Union airline. Details are difficult to obtain, but it reportedly has 2,500 staff and a fleet of 25 Soviet-made aircraft. Air Koryo makes scheduled flights to **Beijing** and Shenyang in the **People's Republic of China**, and to Khabarovsk and Vladivostock in Russia. It also makes occasional charter flights to Japan, **Macao** and Thailand. Domestic routes include **Pyongyang**–Hamhung, and Pyongyang–Samjiyon (for **Mount Paektu**); it is not clear whether these are scheduled or charter flights. Air Koryo joined the **International Air Transport Association** in 1997.

All-China Federation of Trade Unions (ACFTU)

Zhonghua quanguo zonggonghui

Founded in 1925, the All-China Federation of Trade Unions (ACFTU) is the only legal trade union organization in the **People's Republic of China (PRC)**. It claims (July 2004) to have 134m. members in some 1.7m. branches. It held its 14th Congress in September 2003. Although it has begun to be more active on behalf of workers in recent years, its prime role is as a means of passing information between the **Chinese Communist Party** and the labour force. In addition, it is a welfare organization, providing benefits to its members, and it acts as the international representative of the PRC in labour matters.

Chair.: Wang Zhaoguo
Address: ACFTU
        10 Fuxingmen St
        Beijing 100865
        People's Republic of China
Tel: 86-10-6859-2730
Fax: 86-10-6856-2031
E-mail: acftuild@public3.bta.net.cn
Internet: www.acftu.org.cn

Allied Occupation of Japan

Following Japan's defeat in the **Pacific War**, an Allied occupation of the country began from 15 August 1945, the date of Japan's acceptance of the terms of the **Potsdam Conference**. It lasted until the entry into force of the **San Francisco Peace Treaty** on 28 April 1952. In theory, the occupation was a joint allied exercise, controlled by a Far Eastern Commission based in the USA, and in which all of the wartime allies were represented. In practice, apart from a small number of British Commonwealth forces, the occupation was almost entirely an American operation, controlled by the Supreme Commander for the Allied Powers (SCAP) in Japan. From August 1945 until April 1951, SCAP was Gen. **Douglas MacArthur**, and for the last year of the occupation, following MacArthur's dismissal, it was Gen. Matthew Ridgway.

The occupation aimed to demilitarize Japan so that it could not go to war again. The armed forces were demobilized, military bases closed, and ultranationalist groups banned. The allies repatriated millions of Japanese soldiers and civilians from overseas. Many of Japan's wartime leaders, both civilian and military, were placed on trial for war crimes. A new constitution, drawn up under American guidance, and adopted in 1947, abandoned the right to go to war as a state policy. The *zaibatsu*, the large economic conglomerates that were regarded as partly responsible for the Japanese decision to go to war, from which they had profited, were broken up.

The second main thrust of the occupation was the introduction of democracy. Although the imperial system was believed to be closely linked to those groups that had taken Japan to war, the **Japanese Emperor** remained, but now as a symbol of the state, not as an all-powerful ruler. The pre-war political parties were dissolved, and new parties emerged. Power, which in pre-war days had been concentrated in the central government, now devolved to local authorities. Trade unions were encouraged, and major effort went into land and educational reforms.

However, the occupation's reform programme began to falter in 1947–48. The continued civil war in **China** worried the USA, which regarded the **Chinese Communist Party** as a front for the Soviet Union. Japan became less of a threat and, instead, appeared as a possible bulwark against communism. Some of the reforms went into reverse, with the left wing increasingly under pressure from the authorities. Many alleged Communists lost their jobs as a result. By July 1950 even the anti-war sections of the Constitution were undermined, as the paramilitary National Police Reserve came into existence; this would eventually become the **Self-Defence Forces**. Nevertheless, by the time the occupation ended, much in Japan had been changed, and many of the changes still survive today.

Amur river

The Amur river, together with the **Ussuri river**, forms the border between Russia and the **People's Republic of China (PRC)**. The Russian name means 'Black river'. The Chinese sometimes call it the *Heihe* or 'Black river', but the more usual Chinese name is *Heilongjiang*, or 'Black Dragon river'; the river also gives its name to the PRC's Heilongjiang Province. The Amur proper is some 2,800 km in length, and flows into the Sea of Orkhutsk. With its headwaters in the Shilka and Argun rivers, it is more than 4,000 km in length, making it one of Asia's great rivers. The river and its surrounding area is an important ecological site. Before 1858 the Amur river lay within the territory of the Chinese Empire. In that year the northern bank of the river passed to Russian sovereignty under the terms of the Treaty of Aigun, and the present boundary dates from then. After the establishment of the PRC in 1949, the then Soviet Union and the PRC negotiated a series of agreements for the use of the river, and a river commission met regularly. In the late 1960s, however, the Amur, like the Ussuri, was the scene of clashes between Soviet and PRC forces, which became very intense for a time in 1969.

Tensions gradually eased, and after the collapse of the Soviet Union in 1991 the river steadily increased in importance as a centre for Russo-Chinese trade. The value of two-way trade along the Amur amounted to US $9,800m. in 2001. Most remaining border issues were resolved or put aside in a 1997 agreement, and there is now free movement across the river. There are some concerns on the Russian side about the extent of Chinese penetration of the region, and occasionally fears are expressed that the Chinese will either swamp the relatively small population on the Russian side of the river, or demand the return of the northern bank of the Amur to Chinese sovereignty. The Chinese deny any such intentions and the fears seem to have more to do with local politics than any real likelihood of such Chinese irredentism.

Anglo-Japanese Alliance

Nichiei domei

The 1902 Anglo-Japanese Alliance marked the end of the policy of 'splendid isolation', which had dominated British foreign policy for most of the 19th century, and the acceptance of Japan as a major power in East Asia. The Alliance committed each side to protecting the other's interests in **China**, and, in the Japanese case, the **Korean peninsula**, especially against Russia. It also committed each side to neutrality if the other were attacked by a third party, and to intervention if attacked by two assailants. It was, therefore, an important step on the way to the 1904–05 Russo–Japanese War. The two countries revised the treaty in 1905 to include British interests in India and to make more explicit Japan's freedom of action on the Korean peninsula. It was further revised in 1911, when the USA was excluded from the countries covered. The Japanese decision to enter the First World War against Germany in 1914 was based on the Alliance. In 1923 the Washington Four Power Treaty replaced the Anglo-Japanese Alliance. Britain and Japan remember the alliance with affection, but both the Republic of Korea and the Democratic People's Republic of Korea still occasionally denounce it, as well as the US-brokered 1905 Treaty of Portsmouth that ended the Russo–Japanese War, as one of the main factors leading to the Japanese takeover of Korea in 1905–10.

'Army First' policy

Songun

Policy that places the **Korean People's Army (KPA)** in a major leadership role in the Democratic People's Republic of Korea (DPRK).

The 'Army First' policy is in one sense a reflection of the role that the KPA has played since the establishment of the DPRK in 1948. The military have always held an important position, with a strong presence in both state and **Korean Workers' Party (KWP)** organizations. In its current form, however, the policy is associated with the leadership of **Kim Jong Il**, who succeeded his father, **Kim Il Sung**, as leader of the DPRK in 1994. Kim emerged from a period of mourning after Kim Il

Sung's death, but did not assume the state presidency, although he did eventually become secretary-general of the KWP. Instead, he became chairman of the National Defence Commission, later declared the highest organ of the state. In this role, he has emphasized the importance of the KPA as the leading group in the DPRK, thus further undermining Marxist-Leninist orthodoxy. The 'Army First' policy is now presented as the '*songun* policy'—the Korean is no longer translated—a new ideology for the current age, in contrast to the '*juche* policy' of Kim Il Sung's era.

While outsiders sometimes construe the policy as meaning that the KPA should be favoured in receiving food and other resources, this does not seem to be the main intention. Rather, the KPA is the leading organization, not just in military matters but also across a wide range of practical and ideological affairs. People should learn from the KPA and follow its lead. This insight into the way of organizing society is presented as evidence of Kim Jong Il's powerful ability to assess and interpret the needs of the DPRK.

ASEAN Plus Three

Although the **Association of South-East Asian Nations (ASEAN)** is primarily concerned with issues relating to its own region, it clearly has to take account of its neighbours in East Asia. This concern has led to the establishment of a number of structures for dialogue. The most comprehensive of these is the **ASEAN Regional Forum**, but in addition, a separate annual dialogue has existed since 1997 with the **People's Republic of China**, Japan and the Republic of Korea. In November 1999 the leaders of ASEAN and these three countries issued a 'Joint Statement on East Asian Co-operation', which set out the areas of co-operation between them. ASEAN Plus Three not only deals with security matters of common concern, but also envisages closer economic co-operation between the participants.

ASEAN Regional Forum (ARF)

Although the **Association of South-East Asian Nations (ASEAN)**, as its name implies, is concerned with matters relating to south-east Asia, it has also taken account of the fact that the security and well-being of that region is directly affected by the behaviour of the surrounding states. ASEAN has therefore pursued two initiatives to engage those states. One is **ASEAN Plus Three** meetings, involving ASEAN, Japan, the Republic of Korea, and the **People's Republic of China (PRC)**. The other is the ASEAN Regional Forum (ARF).

The ARF draws together 23 countries that have a bearing on the security of the Asia-Pacific region. These are the 10 ASEAN member states, the 10 ASEAN dialogue partners, Mongolia and the Democratic People's Republic of Korea, and Papua New Guinea, which has observer status. The Forum dates from a meeting of the ASEAN foreign ministers in July 1993, when the participants agreed to establish a regular meeting to discuss security matters within the region. The ARF came into being in the following year. The main aim was originally to involve the PRC with

ASEAN, especially since a number of ASEAN countries had territorial disputes with the PRC.

The Forum's original remit has grown since 1993, and it now deals with a much wider range of issues. In 1995 a concept paper envisaged the ARF moving gradually from confidence-building measures to preventative diplomacy and, eventually, to conflict-resolution capability. While there has been some progress towards the first of these, there has been less development of the other areas. The ARF has deliberately avoided creating a formal infrastructure and aims to move only at a pace at which all participants can feel 'comfortable'—a much-favoured ARF term. The Forum meets annually at foreign minister level, and there is an annual Senior Officals' Meeting as well as twice-yearly intersessional support group meetings on confidence-building measures, also at official level. The ARF encourages and finances a wide range of 'Track Two' meetings—i.e. non-official meetings of think-tanks and academic groups. These groups contribute ideas to the main ARF meetings. Both the relative informality of the ARF structure and the Track Two meetings allow consideration of issues that some participating countries would not necessarily wish to have discussed formally.

Asia-Europe Meeting (ASEM)

The Asia-Europe Meeting (ASEM) brings together Brunei, the **People's Republic of China**, Indonesia, Japan, Malaysia, the Philippines, the Republic of Korea, Singapore, Thailand and Viet Nam, and the member states of the European Union, together with the European Commission. ASEM addresses political, economic and social, cultural and intellectual issues, with a view to strengthening relations between the two regions.

The first ASEM summit took place in Bangkok, Thailand, in March 1996, and adopted the fundamental principles of the new group. Subsequent summits have been held in London (1998), **Seoul** (2000), Copenhagen (2002), and Hanoi in the autumn of 2004. Foreign and finance ministers already meet regularly and more such meetings between other ministers are planned. The Asia-Europe Business Forum, which meets in parallel with the summit meetings, provides an opportunity for non-officials to meet for discussions. The Bangkok summit also established the Asia-Europe Foundation, based in Singapore, which is a not-for-profit body, aimed at furthering ASEM's social, cultural and intellectual programme.

ASEM has not so far established a permanent secretariat, but the Philippines proposed in October 2004 that one should be established and has offered to host it.

Asia-Pacific Economic Co-operation (APEC)

Established in 1989 by an Australian initiative at a meeting in **Seoul**, the Asia-Pacific Economic Co-operation (APEC) grouping is a forum for promoting economic growth, co-operation, trade and investment in the Asia-Pacific region. Originally 12, the number of members has subsequently increased to 21. In 1997 the then members agreed that there would be no increase in membership until 2007. Between them, the 21 members account for 50% of current world trade. The present East Asian members of APEC are the **People's Republic of China**, the Republic of Korea (ROK), Japan, **Hong Kong** (as 'Hong Kong, China'), and the **'Republic of China'** (as 'Chinese Taipei').

APEC is unique in world organizations in that it operates by means of non-binding agreements and on a basis of equality. It has generally avoided political issues, although the meetings have sometimes provided opportunities for meetings between senior leaders. In 1994, at its meeting in Bogor, Indonesia, the APEC leaders agreed that developed nations in the grouping would move towards free trade by 2010 and that developing countries would seek the same goal by 2020. There has been little progress towards these aims, and some members have doubted whether the goals are attainable. A Singapore-based secretariat co-ordinates the work of APEC, under a rotating executive director. The 2004 APEC ministerial meeting took place in Chile in November, and the 2005 meeting will be held in the ROK.

Exec. Dir 2004: Ambassador Mario Artaza (Chile)
Address: APEC Secretariat
        35 Heng Mui Keng Terrace
        Singapore 119616
Tel: 65-6775-6012
Fax: 65-6775–6013
E-mail: info@apec.org
Internet: www.apec.org

Asian Development Bank (ADB)

Multilateral financial institution focusing on development in the Asia-Pacific region. The Asian Development Bank (ADB) was established in 1966 with 31 members, or shareholders, to provide loans and advice to its developing member countries and to offer technical assistance with development projects. Membership now stands at 63, of which Japan, the USA and the **People's Republic of China (PRC)** are the largest shareholders. The Bank's headquarters are in the Philippines and it has 24 other offices around the world. The ADB is managed by a board of governors, generally the finance ministers of member states or regions, and a board of directors. Among countries and regions in East Asia, Japan, the Republic of Korea and **Taiwan** are founding members. The PRC, Mongolia and **Hong Kong** joined later.

Pres.: Tadao Chino
Address: 6 ADB Ave
        Mandaluyong City 0401
        Metro Manila
        Philippines

Tel: 632 632 4444
Fax: 632 636 2444
E-mail: information@adb.org
Internet: www.adb.org

Asian financial crisis

In July 1997 a run on the Thai currency, the baht, triggered a major financial crisis in south-east Asia, which rapidly spread throughout the region and into East Asia. The initial cause seems to have been a shortage of foreign currency to meet short-term international debt. Malaysia, the Philippines and Indonesia soon came under similar pressure to Thailand and all devalued their currencies. Before long, the **Hong Kong** dollar was also under threat. However, the Hong Kong government intervened to defend the currency and the pressure moved elsewhere, to the Republic of Korea (ROK), Brazil and Singapore. In November 1997 Japan experienced major problems, including the collapse of the brokers, Sanyo Securities, of the country's third largest securities' firm, Yamaichi Securities, and of its 10th largest bank, Hokkaido Takushoku. However, the underlying economy remained strong, and Japan did not devalue its currency.

The crisis hit the ROK badly, and like Thailand and Indonesia, the ROK government appealed to the **International Monetary Fund (IMF)** for support. In December 1997 the IMF agreed a US $57,000m. package to help the ROK survive the crisis. In January 1998 10 of the ROK's 14 merchant banks closed, and there were widespread layoffs in industry. Further closures in the financial sector followed, as did a major reorganization of the *chaebol*, the big business conglomerates. The ROK finally repaid what it had borrowed from the IMF in August 2001.

The fundamental cause of the crisis seems to have been inadequate supervision of the banking sector, which had allowed the build-up of short-term foreign currency loans without any protection. When these were called in, the crisis erupted. Some reforms have taken place because of the crisis, but in most Asian countries there has been a reluctance to push too hard for reform and banks are still burdened by many non-performing loans. The crisis led to some changes in banking and financial circles but not to the root-and-branch reforms recommended by some commentators.

Association of South-East Asian Nations (ASEAN)

Indonesia, Malaysia, Philippines, Singapore and Thailand established the Association of South-East Asian Nations (ASEAN) on 8 August 1967. Brunei joined in 1984, Viet Nam in 1995, Laos and Myanmar in 1997, and Cambodia in 1999.

Amongst ASEAN's objectives is the promotion of peace and stability throughout the region, and this has led it steadily to an interest in East Asia. This began with concerns about the **People's Republic of China (PRC)**, but soon extended also to Japan, and has since expanded further. Since the early 1990s ASEAN has instituted annual meetings at foreign ministerial level with 10 dialogue partners: Australia,

Canada, the PRC, the European Union, India, Japan, the Republic of Korea (ROK), New Zealand, Russia, and the USA. Discussions with these partners include security issues, but ASEAN has two further structures for discussing security issues, both of which involve East Asian countries. One is the **ASEAN Regional Forum**, dating from 1993–94. The other is the more limited **ASEAN Plus Three**, established in 1997, which brings together the ASEAN countries, the PRC, Japan and the ROK. In November 2004, at a meeting in Laos, the ASEAN countries and the PRC signed an agreement designed to create a free-trade area by 2010 for most ASEAN countries. The four poorest, Viet Nam, Laos, Cambodia and Myanmar (Burma) will not meet the full requirements for membership of this grouping until 2015. In any case, the agreement excludes many items. In addition, the same meeting agreed to put the ASEAN Plus Three arrangements on a more formal footing.

E-mail: public@aseansec.org
Internet: www.aseansec.org

Aum Shinrikyo

This religious cult, whose title can be translated as 'teaching of supreme truth', was responsible for Japan's most notorious terrorist incident, the March 1995 attack on the **Tokyo** subway using the nerve gas, sarin. The attack killed 12 people, and injured more than 5,000. Ten days later the country's chief police officer, who was leading the investigations into the attack, was nearly killed in a shooting incident. This too was believed to have been carried out by Aum Shinrikyo.

The cult dates from 1987. Its founder was Asahara Shoko, who was born Matsumoto Chizuo in 1955. Asahara's teachings, which predicted the end of the world at the end of the 20th century, draw on the traditions of **Buddhism** and Hinduism. He persuaded his followers that, in order to survive, they should create a tight, self-sufficient and hierarchical group that would practise meditation and austerity. At its height, the movement had about 10,000 followers in Japan; abroad, its main adherents were in Russia. Investigations after the Tokyo attack linked the group with a number of murder cases, and an earlier sarin attack in Nagano Prefecture, which killed seven people.

Asahara and several hundred of his followers were arrested in May 1995, and the cult dissolved. In February 2004 Asahara was sentenced to death for masterminding the attack. Eleven other members have also received death sentences. In July 2004 Japanese police charged three former members of the cult with the attempted killing of the country's chief of police in 1995.

The cult continues to exist. In Russia, where its followers changed its name to 'Aleph' in 2000, there are reportedly some 30,000 adherents. Aleph also exists in Japan, where it has 1,600 members. They claim to be peaceable but are the subject of continued police surveillance.

B

Bagabandi, Natsagiyn

Born in 1950, and trained as an engineer in the Soviet Union, Bagabandi became President of Mongolia in 1997. Despite much controversy over his interpretation of the Mongolian Constitution, he was re-elected as President in 2001.

Bagabandi began his political career as a member of the **Mongolian People's Revolutionary Party (MPRP)** from 1980 onwards. Elected to the MPRP Central Committee in 1990, he became a member of parliament in the following year. He was speaker of the **State Great Hural** in 1992–96. In 1996 he became a member of the MPRP Leadership Council, and chairman of the Party in 1997. Elected as state President in 1997, he continued to favour the MPRP and clashed with the Great Hural several times, especially over the appointment of Prime Ministers.

Address: State Palace
              Ulaan Baatar-12
              Mongolia
Fax: 976 31121
E-mail: webmaster@presipmis.gov.mn
Internet: http://gate.pmis.gov.mn/presid

Ban Ki-Moon

Minister of Foreign Affairs and Trade of the Republic of Korea since January 2004.

Ban Ki-Moon is a career diplomat. Immediately before taking up his current post, he served as the chief adviser on foreign affairs to President **Roh Moo-Hyun**. Born in 1944, Ban graduated from the International Relations Department at **Seoul** National University in 1970. After joining the foreign ministry in 1970, he held a variety of diplomatic posts. He has also served twice as a protocol adviser. In 1985 he spent an academic year at Harvard University in the USA, where he took a master's degree.

Address: Ministry of Foreign Affairs and Trade
95-1 Doryeom-dong
Jongno-ku
Seoul
110-051 Republic of Korea
Tel: 82-2-2100-7204
E-mail: web@mofat.go.kr
Internet: www.mofat.go.kr

Bank of China (BOC—People's Republic of China)

The Bank of China (BOC) is the leading bank handling foreign exchange and international settlements for the **People's Republic of China (PRC)**. In 1993 the Bank played an important part in the reform of the PRC's foreign exchange system. In the following year it moved from its former role of specialized foreign exchange bank to operating as a wider-based commercial bank, still in state ownership.

The BOC is the oldest bank in **China**. It was established by Sun Yat-sen, then the provisional President of the new **Republic of China (1912–49)**, from the former Da Qing bank, in whose premises it opened in **Shanghai** in 1912. The BOC was given the functions of a central bank and eventually issued banknotes. In 1928 its status was changed into that of an international exchange bank. In 1929 it opened its first overseas branch and also its London, United Kingdom, agency. In the following years the BOC launched 34 overseas branches. The new Communist regime that asssumed power in the course of 1949 retained the BOC as its foreign exchange bank. It now has 121 branches. In 1979 it was placed under the direct control of the **State Council**.

In the wake of the PRC's economic reforms, the BOC started to issue bonds, beginning with an issue to Japan in 1984, the first overseas bond issue by the PRC. Since 1999 the Bank has operated an asset management corporation (Orient AMC). It had already extended the scope of its operations when, in 1994, it became the third bank in **Hong Kong** to issue Hong Kong dollar notes (after the Hong Kong and Shanghai Bank, now **HSBC Holdings PLC**, and the **Standard Chartered Bank**). In the following year the BOC similarly started to issue **Macao** pataca notes. In 2001 its Hong Kong operation underwent restructuring when 10 member banks of the former BOC Group merged and were incorporated into the Bank of China (Hong Kong) Ltd. In 2002 BOC Hong Kong (Holdings) was listed on the Hong Kong Stock Exchange.

Chair. and Pres.: Liu Mingkang
Address: 1 Fuxingmennei Dajie
Beijing 100818
People's Republic of China
Tel: 86-10-6659-6688
Fax: 86-10-6601-4024
E-mail: info@bank-of-china.com
Internet: www.bank-of-china.com

Bank of Japan

Nippon Ginko

The Bank of Japan (BOJ) was established in 1882 as part of Japan's reform process following the **Meiji Restoration**. Its initial role was to manage the new yen currency, to avoid inflation, and to finance the growth of commerce and industry. The BOJ now performs all of the normal roles of a central bank, issuing coins and notes, and undertaking currency and monetary controls. It is also the banks' bank and the bank of last resort, as well as the bank for the central government. In the past it was very much under the control of the Ministry of Finance, but since the introduction of new legislation in 1998 it has been less tied to the Ministry of Finance, and now reports to the **National Diet** on a twice-yearly basis.

Address: Bank of Japan
2-1-1 Hongoku-cho
Nihonbashi
Chuo-ku
Tokyo 100-8630
Japan
Tel: 81-3-3279-1111
Fax: 81-3-5200-2256
E-mail: webmaster@info.boj.or.jp
Internet: www.boj.or.jp

Bank of Mongolia (BOM)

Since 1991 the Bank of Mongolia has functioned as an independent central bank within a two-tier banking system that includes private commercial banks. In 1954 the Bank was recognized as the state bank of Mongolia when its operations passed into Mongolian hands. From 1924, when Mongolia adopted a Soviet style of government and introduced a system of banking, the Bank had been run as a Mongolian-Soviet joint bank, known variously as the Trade and Industry Bank of Mongolia or the Bank of Mongolia. Russian staff had predominated. The re-organization of 1954 involved the transfer of the former Soviet Union's share of capital and stocks to the new bank and raising the proportion of Mongolian staff to 98% from the 18% it had been in 1924.

Monetary reform in 1925 gave the Bank authority to issue the national currency, the *togrog*, to take the place of foreign currency that had previously circulated. During the unsettled conditions of Mongolia's recent passage from an economy operating within the former Soviet command system to a more open system, the Bank has aimed at a tight monetary policy in the interests of stabilizing the currency and reducing inflation. It also acts as a centre for the compilation and dissemination of statistical data.

Gov.: O. Chuluunbat
Address: 9 Baga Toiruu
Ulaan Baatar 11
Mongolia
Tel: 976 11 324193
Fax: 976 11 311471
E-mail: ad@mongolbank.mn
Internet: www.mongolbank.mn

Bank of Taiwan

The Bank of Taiwan currently ranks as the number one bank in the **'Republic of China' ('ROC') on Taiwan**. The Taiwan Provincial Government established the Bank in May 1946, soon after Chinese forces had occupied Taiwan after the end of the **Pacific War**. The Bank remained under the nominal control of the Taiwan Provincial Government until the phasing out of the latter in December 1998; the Bank then came under the 'ROC' Ministry of Finance. Since 1 July 2003 the Bank has been a corporate organization under 'ROC' company law.

Although in theory only a provincial bank, from 1949, following the departure of **Chiang Kai-shek** and his followers from the mainland, and the relocation of the 'ROC' to Taiwan, it performed many of the roles of a central bank, including the issue of the 'New Taiwan Dollar', and currency management. However, when the **Central Bank of China** was reactivated in 1961, the Bank of Taiwan lost these functions, reverting to the role of a general commercial bank, which it still performs today. At the same time, it continues to play a role in the handling of the New Taiwan Dollar, and has become the bank of choice for the management of military and civil service pension funds.

The Bank, whose headquarters are in **Taipei**, currently has 147 domestic and seven overseas branches, and employs 7,000 personnel.

Leadership: Joseph Lu, appointed 28 June 2004
Address: 120 Section One
Chungking Rd South
Taipei 100
Taiwan
Tel: 886-2-23493556
Fax: 886-2-23315840
E-mail: botservice@mail.bot.com.tw
Internet: www.bot.com.tw

Beijing

Capital of the **People's Republic of China (PRC)** since the founding of the PRC in 1949 and before that a capital or secondary capital of succeeding dynasties of a unified **China** from the 13th until the early 20th century. The name signifies 'northern capital'. The Nationalist Chinese government of **Chiang Kai-shek** had installed its capital at **Nanjing**—'southern capital'—in 1928. Twenty-one years later, after the defeat of the Japanese and then of the Nationalists, Beijing regained its eminence as the political, administrative, educational and cultural centre of the nation. The new Communist government insisted that the capital should become a centre of production rather than consumption and extended the city's industrial base with a range of heavy industry. It also embarked on a process of modernization and redevelopment of the city's fabric that has accelerated since the 1990s. Beijing's hosting of the Asian Games in 2002 and its award of the Summer Olympics for 2008 have spurred yet further development of the capital's infrastructure. The buildings and monuments that for centuries dominated the city's skyline, such as the Forbidden City and the Temple of Heaven, are now overshadowed by high-rise blocks that have replaced the former low houses surrounding them.

The city lies at the northern end of the North China plain, at a point where the mountain ranges of northern China meet the lower land stretching to the south. It is about 160 km from the the the Bay of Bohai to the east. Despite the presence of several rivers, the region around Beijing has always been dry. Reservoirs to the north-east and north-west of the city meet much of its needs, but access to adequate supplies of water has always been a problem, which the demands of a modern economy and modern lifestyles can only exacerbate. Beijing municipality, as finally constituted in 1961, covers a considerable area—16,808 sq km—and comprises central urban, suburban and rural districts and counties. Its population at the 2000 census was 13.82m. Its status as one of the four centrally administered municipalities in China puts it on a par with a province, and the position of mayor of Beijing is a potentially powerful political one. The city proper is served by many buses, trolley buses and two metro lines. Bicycle use, once a distinctive feature of Beijing, is in decline, and the streets are filling rapidly with vehicles and, increasingly, private cars.

Beijing has long acted as a focus for popular demonstration. In 1900 the disaffection with reform and the presence of foreigners in the country that engulfed North China culminated in the siege of the legation quarter in the capital. In 1919 demonstrators gathered in the centre of Beijing on 4 May to protest against renewed infringement of Chinese sovereignty. During the **Cultural Revolution** (1966–76), the biggest rallies of Red Guards were in **Tiananmen** Square, and the square was again the scene of unofficial rallies in 1976 to commemorate **Zhou Enlai** and, in 1989, of a six-week occupation by students.

Blue House

Chong Wa Dae

The 'Blue House' is the official residence in **Seoul** of the President of the Republic of Korea (ROK). The name comes from the colour of the roof tiles. The site was originally that of an old palace, which in 1927 became the residence for the

Japanese governor-general. After the defeat of Japan in 1945, the head of the US occupation forces lived and worked in the Blue House, as have all ROK Presidents after 1948. In 1993 President **Kim Young-Sam** had all the Japanese-era buildings replaced by Korean-style buildings.

The name has come to symbolize the highly centralized system of presidential government that has characterized ROK politics for most of the period since 1948. In everyday parlance, therefore, the 'Blue House' means the presidential secretariat, or sometimes the President himself.

Buddhism

One of the world's leading religions, especially well represented in East and southeast Asia. It follows the teachings of the historical Buddha, Gautama Siddhartha, who was born in 566 BC in what is now Nepal. He sought, and attained, enlightenment and trained a number of disciples to travel and teach to those they met the goal of freedom from the cycle of rebirth and peace of mind through an understanding of suffering, the causes of suffering and the way out of suffering. From its base in north-east India, Buddhism spread in all directions, but eventually lost its vigour in its country of origin, where it was overlaid by Hindu doctrine. Differences in the interpretion and analysis of Buddha's teaching led, in the course of the first century and a half of the new religion's existence, to the emergence of two broad strands: Mahayana, and Therevada or Hinayana Buddhism. Mahayana is the form that has permeated East Asia.

One of its points of difference from Therevada Buddhism is its incorporation of other Buddhas representing various aspects of the historical Buddha's enlightenment, along with belief in Bodhisattvas, figures who have delayed entering into their own enlightenment until all men are freed from suffering. Buddhism came into the various countries of East Asia as a foreign religion, but once accepted passed through a great range of forms. At several times and in different places it received state sponsorship and was given the task of 'protecting the nation', as in the Northern Wei dynasty (4th–6th centuries AD) in **China**, in Koryo-dynasty Korea (10th–14th centuries) and throughout the Nara and Heian periods (8th–14th centuries) in Japan. The width of its scriptures has permitted diverse interpretations, which have led to the formations of many sects, often at the initiative of individual monks. It encompasses both celibate and married orders. It has undergone varying fortunes as it has encountered indigenous beliefs or has been confronted by subsequent religious movements or secular teachings. It has often blended with other religious elements such as **Daoism** or charismatic theology to form **new religions**. Buddhism has had an enormous influence on literature, drama, architecture, calligraphy, painting and sculpture throughout the whole of East Asia.

History: Buddhism is traditionally said to have entered China in the 1st century AD. For a considerable length of time, it was led and supported by missionary monks from India, but gradually incorporated native teachers and increased its adherence.

By the end of the 4th century, its hold, particularly in north-west China, was strong. Chinese pilgrims journeyed to India and brought back religious texts. Buddhism's relations with the various dynastic rulers of China varied from official support to persecution; and different sects were favoured by different emperors. At all times it had to contend with the disapproval of Confucian officials and scholars. In the 6th century the Indian monk Bodhidharma settled in north-west China and founded the Chan sect. Under its Sanskrit, Japanese and Korean names of Dhyana, Zen and Son, this contemplative school of Buddhism has had enormous influence. Its emphasis on meditation as a road to enlightenment is in distinction to the insistence on the importance of scriptures, outward observances and the cult of Buddhist deities that marks other sects. Among these sects, the Pure Land school has been particularly important in China. Buddhism has developed alongside the indigenous institution of Daoism. The two religions have interpenetrated each other, especially in their more popular forms. In common with all religions in China, Buddhism has had to accommodate itself to the ascendancy of an officially atheist movement in the form of Chinese communism and the government of the **People's Republic of China (PRC)** since 1949.

From the 8th century a further form of Buddhism was developing in **Tibet**, Lama Buddhism, characterized by elaborate ritual, a large array of deities and a hierarchical structure of lama leadership. Buddhism had been introduced from India in the 7th century and had mingled with the indigenous Bön religion, in which the placating of spirits was an important preoccupation. The first order of lamas was soon instituted, a monastic system was installed, and a Tibetan translation of the Buddhist canon was ready by the 9th century. In the 15th century further changes in Tibetan Buddhism introduced the concept of the reincarnation of religious leaders from previous leaders or from Bodhisattvas. At the same time, temporal and spiritual leadership were combined in one person, the **Dalai Lama**, regarded as the chief lama of Tibet, with whom the Chinese dealt on political as well as religious matters. Lama Buddhism came to be distinguished by its strict order of priesthood and graduated path to holiness, the extent of its monastic system and the number of its monks, and by its reliance on amulets, chants and prayers as a means of spiritual protection. Again, this form of Buddhism has had to contend with the generally hostile administration of the PRC government since the early 1950s.

The Lama Buddhist model was extended to Mongolia in the 13th century and the Buddhist scriptures were translated from Tibetan into Mongolian by order of Kubilai Khan after his grandfather, the Mongol ruler Ghenghis Khan, had conquered Tibet and seized the Chinese imperial throne. The family ruled China as the Yuan dynasty from 1206 to 1368. Lama Buddhism itself served as a means of binding Tibet and Mongolia into the Chinese Qing empire. It became deeply rooted in Mongolian culture and retained its powerful position until the 20th century, when it was thrust aside on the establishment of a revolutionary, Communist government in 1924.

Buddhism was received from China into the Koguryo and Paekche kingdoms of the **Korean peninsula** in the 4th century AD and the Silla kingdom in the 6th. The willingness of rulers and aristocracy to accept it, particularly in its aspect of protector of the nation, gave it a firm foundation, which lasted until the fall of the Koryo dynasty in 1392. Thereafter Buddhism lost ground as **Confucianism** was incorporated as the guiding principle for government and society and has never recovered its former strong position. Korean Buddhism encompasses both the meditative (Son) and scriptural (Kyo) traditions of the religion. From the 12th century both of these strands have been fused in the main Chogye school. During the period of Japanese colonialism (1910–45), Korean Buddhism was an object of control by Japanese Buddhist orders, abbots were appointed to monasteries by the Japanese administration and the marriage of monks was tolerated.

In a continuing movement eastwards, Korean Buddhist missionaries from the Paekche and Koguryo kingdoms brought the religion to Japan during the 6th and 7th centuries. (Three nuns are said to have travelled earlier from Japan to Paekche to study.) Again, the new religion was accepted at the top of society and prospered for a number of centuries as spiritual guardian of the nation. Contacts with the mainland of north-east Asia, particularly China, ensured the spread of new teaching in Japan. In the 8th century the Pure Land sect, with its emphasis on the Lotus sutra, was introduced from China, as was an esoteric form of Buddhism that took root in Japan as the Shingon sect. Contemplative Chan Buddhism arrived from China in the 12th century. From the 13th century two important strands of Buddhism emerged in Japan: the Zen sect, which looked primarily to meditation to achieve enlightenment and which formed itself into two main schools, Rinzai and Soto, and the Nichiren sect with its belief in the Lotus sutra and the efficacy of chanting propitious words. From an early moment considerable intermingling took place between Buddhism and indigenous **Shinto** beliefs. Japanese Buddhism maintained its important position in Japan into the 19th century, not least as a bulwark against attempts at Christian proselytization by incoming foreigners. With the favouring of State Shinto as the official religion of imperial Japan between 1868 and 1945, however, Buddhism lost much of its former ground. None the less, it played an auxiliary role in the spread of Japanese influence in East Asia in the first half of the 20th century, as in Korea.

Recent developments: Buddhism has experienced some revival in its influence and popularity in its former East Asian stronghold. In the PRC, in common with Daoism, **Islam**, **Catholic** and **Protestant Christianity**, it is accorded a certain protection under the 1982 Constitution, which undertakes to safeguard 'normal religious activities'. The state, however, requires all religious organizations to register with the Bureau of Religious Affairs and defines and regulates many of their functions, including training. From the outset, the Communist government installed in 1949 acted to extend its control over religious organizations and adherents, and in 1953 Buddhists were formed together into the Buddhist Association of China. Only a restricted number of temples remained open and many others were put to secular uses. The **Cultural Revolution** (1966–76) brought almost all religious activity to an end for a while. Buddhist statues and artefacts were destroyed, temples were boarded up or put to secular uses, monks and nuns were forced out of their institutions and Buddhist worship was forbidden. From 1977, however, the Chinese state has followed a more tolerant line and consequently the number of active temples, congregations and monks has risen. Lay Buddhist associations have revived their activities, as have scholarly and research centres. Recent estimates of the number of Buddhist faithful in the PRC stand at 100m.–150m. The two main strands of Buddhism practised in the PRC are Chan and Pure Land Buddhism. Lama Buddhism also has a following, in Tibet and north-west China, and the state supports the Tibetan Institute of Lamaism. Along the far south-western border of China, some minority peoples follow the Therevada Buddhism practised in the neighbouring countries to the south. All Buddhist activity, however, must accept state guidance. Any group that is perceived to act outside of official control, such as the **Falungong** movement, which has a strong Buddhist element, is proscribed. Such severity is not new; for centuries, any Buddhist sect deemed to be heterodox was suppressed by the authorities through fear of subversion. The identification of Tibetan Lama Buddhism with political aspirations and the leadership of the Dalai Lama based outside of the country has made the Chinese state's relationship with Tibetan Buddhism particularly difficult, and there have been recurring reports of destruction of monasteries and imprisonment of Buddhist monks and nuns within Tibet.

Buddhism suffered an eclipse under the Mongolian People's Republic (MPR, 1924–92). Religious instruction of the young was forbidden, temple property was confiscated and monks were persecuted. Only one monastery, in **Ulaan Baatar**, was permitted to function. In 1979 the Dalai Lama, as the spiritual leader of Mongolian lamaism, was allowed to make his first visit to the MPR. The introduction of new forms of government in Mongolia from the early 1990s encouraged a revival of Lama Buddhist activity; training of monks recommenced and temples reopened; and the Dalai Lama has visited again, despite Chinese misgivings. A law of 1993 permits lamaism, Islam and **shamanism** to be propagated, but discourages non-native religions such as Christianity. The number of Buddhist believers in Mongolia may stand at around 1.2m.

Buddhism in the Republic of Korea (ROK) struggled to rid itself of the Japanese influences and practices that pervaded it until 1945. Chief among these had been the introduction of married orders into a previously celibate monastic tradition. The main Chogye order, which contained married priests, reformed itself under official encouragement, but broke into two groups in the process, one celibate, calling itself the Chogye school, the other, the Taego school, married. Strict government supervision of Buddhist leadership, temple management and revenues, student activities and scholarly studies persisted under President **Park Chung-Hee**, and Buddhist monks were drafted into the armed forces. As great a challenge has been the continuing rise of both Catholic and Protestant Christianity in the ROK since the 1950s, sometimes accompanied by considerable hostility towards Buddhism. The popularity of Christianity is partly due to its association with an urban, modern way of living, by contrast with what is viewed as the old, rural traditionalism of Buddhism. In response, Korean Buddhism has worked to make greater contact with students and urban populations and to involve itself in political dissent. It runs the Buddhist Dongguk University in **Seoul**. Buddhism can still claim extensive adherence in the ROK, where more than one-quarter of all believers describe themselves as Buddhists. A newer form of Buddhism, Won Buddhism, developed in the 1920s in the southern part of Korea and formally took its name in 1946. This small sect rejects monasticism, Buddhist images and temple offerings and meets in weekly worship. It too has its own university, Won'gwang University.

The Democratic People's Republic of Korea (DPRK) upholds freedom of belief, and claims around 10,000 Buddhists among its population. Some 60 temples are reported to be open, some of them carefully restored. Monks, who all appear to be married, are in attendance at some of them and claim to officiate at the important Buddhist festivals such as Buddha's birthday. As with the other religions tolerated in the DPRK, Christianity and the indigenous **Chondo-gyo** sect, it is very difficult to judge the true state of belief. From 1945 North Korean Buddhists have been controlled through the Korean Buddhist Federation.

The post-war Constitution (1947) of Japan promulgates both freedom of belief and the separation of state and religion. With the sundering of the former close link between the imperial state and the Shinto religion, Buddhism was able to revive, even if it had lost its earlier pre-Meiji position as an agent of government policies on family registration and family matters. Zen Buddhism is probably the best known practice of Japanese Buddhism and had attracted both followers and interest among foreigners. It has also had considerable influence in the aesthetic and social spheres, both within and without Japan. It has approximately 10m. adherents in Japan. The number of practising Zen monks living in monasteries has, however, declined, a pattern that has marked modern Buddhist activity in general in Japan. Monks may now be married and even follow a hereditary pattern of priesthood. Within the population at large, Buddhist rituals are favoured for funerals; and there is much reliance on Buddhist amulets and charms to gain spiritual protection. Buddhism has fused with other elements in the formation of many new religions, such as **Aum Shinrikyo**. One of its sects, Nichiren Shoshu, was allied indirectly to the political scene through its lay organization Soka Gakkai, which created the political **Clean Government Party** or Komeito. Komeito was active from 1964 until 1994, when it split into two parties. It broke its formal link with Soka Gakkai in 1970.

The **'Republic of China'** on **Taiwan**, **Hong Kong** and **Macao** all have a large Buddhist adherence, though much of their popular religion is centred around local deities. The Buddhist Association of Taiwan claims a membership of more than 9.61m.

Burakumin

The *Burakumin* ('village people') are the largest minority group in Japan.

In practice, the *Burakumin* are indistinguishable from any other group of Japanese. Today, they are concentrated in western Japan, and in total they are believed to number 1.5m.–2m. Their origins lie in groups of people, such as butchers, undertakers and shoemakers, engaged in trades regarded as polluting, and who consequently were excluded from mainstream Japanese society. Such groups lived in separate villages—hence the name—and once identified as outcasts, found it difficult to reintegrate into the mainstream.

In theory, discrimination against all such groups ended with the Liberation Edict of 1871, but in reality many found themselves even more excluded than they had been before. A 'Levellers' Society', established in 1922, tried to improve the lot of the *Burakumin* but with little success. After the **Pacific War**, the Levellers' Society reappeared as the 'Buraku Liberation League' (BLL) in 1955, a group closely associated with the Japan Socialist Party (now the **Social Democratic Party of Japan**) and other left-wing groups. The BLL enjoyed some success in improving the conditions of the *Burakumin*, especially in areas such as housing and education, and Japanese governments have become more responsive to meeting *Burakumin* demands. Discrimination continues, however, with, for example, a thriving detective business in use to check the origins of marriage partners to make sure that one of the parties is not from a *Burakumin* background. The pressure groups demand more action from the government, but also increasingly present the issue of *Burakumin* rights in the wider context of human rights in Japan generally.

C

Cairo Conference 1943

Wartime Allied conference held in the Egyptian capital city in November 1943, and attended by Winston Churchill for Britain, Franklin Roosevelt for the USA, and **Chiang Kai-shek** for the **Republic of China (1912–49)**. The conference marked the acceptance of **China** as a major ally. Chiang pleaded the cause of Korean independence, but the conference decided that the **Korean peninsula** would become independent 'in due course', thus introducing the idea of a period of trusteeship before Korea would be granted independence.

Cao Gangchuan

Cao Gangchuan became Minister of National Defence of the **People's Republic of China (PRC)** in March 2003. He is a vice-chairman of the **Chinese Communist Party (CCP) Central Military Commission (CMC)**. He is therefore in theory at the top of the PRC leadership.

Cao comes from Henan Province, where he was born in 1935. In July 1954 he joined the **People's Liberation Army (PLA)**, and in 1956, the CCP. He studied Russian in the PLA, and spent 1957–63 at the Soviet Union's Military Engineering Corps of the Artillery Corps. This would make him one of the last PLA officers to have studied in the Soviet Union before the **Sino–Soviet dispute** ended such attachments. On his return, Cao spent most of the next 25 years in the equipment and ordnance departments of the PLA, gradually moving up the hierarchy. However, he also appears to have travelled widely on procurement matters, and may well have a better understanding of the outside world than some other military officers.

In 1989 he became director of the military affairs department of the PLA Headquarters of the General Staff, and thus began to operate in the more senior levels of the military. He was deputy chief of the General Staff in 1992–96, and then became the minister heading the Commission for Science and Technology for National Defence (COSTIND). This was an important post, since at the time it represented the link between the PLA and the defence industries. Bureaucratic reforms in 1998 moved the research, development and evaluation and the procurement side of COSTIND to a new General Armaments Department, and Cao has headed this ever since. He has also become the main CCP representative in the department. In 2002 he joined the CCP Political Bureau and became a vice-chairman of the CMC, an important step on the road to becoming Minister of National Defence, which he did in the following year. The Minister of National Defence is, through the CMC structure, subordinate to the civilian leadership of the CCP. Cao is clearly a loyal CCP member and will have no problems in supporting the slightly younger group of leaders that he has now joined.

Address: Ministry of National Defence
20 Jiangshanqiaojie
Beijing 100009
People's Republic of China
Tel: 86-10-6673-0000
Fax: 86-10-6596-2146

Carter, James (Jimmy) Earl, Jr

Thirty-ninth President of the USA, who held office from 1977 until 1981.

Since leaving office, Carter has involved himself through the centre he established in issues of conflict mediation and resolution, and it is against that background that he is remembered for his successful negotiations in June 1994 with the then President of the Democratic People's Republic of Korea (DPRK), **Kim Il Sung**, on the question of the **DPRK nuclear programme**. He was able to persuade the DPRK to halt its programme and begin discussions on the issue with the USA. Although Kim Il Sung died in the following month, Carter's agreement held, and the crisis passed.

This was not Carter's first immersion in Korean issues. At the outset of his single term as a Democratic President, distrustful of the authoritarian policies of the then President of the Republic of Korea (ROK), **Park Chung-Hee**, and of the ROK government's record on human rights, he pledged to remove US ground forces from the **Korean peninsula**. This new approach on the part of a US President was appreciated in the DPRK, and it was reported that Kim Il Sung described Carter in 1977 as 'a man of justice'. However, after a visit to **Seoul** in June 1979, Carter was persuaded not to reduce troop levels in the ROK. In the last days of his presidency he intervened to persuade Park's successor, **Chun Doo-Hwan**, not to execute the dissident opposition leader, **Kim Dae-Jung**, an approach that was continued by his successor, President Ronald Reagan.

Jimmy Carter was born in Plains, Georgia, in 1924. He graduated in 1946 from the US Naval Academy, served in the US Navy from 1946 until 1953, then eventually entered politics. He served as governer of the state of Georgia from 1971 until 1975. In 2002 he was awarded the Nobel Peace Prize.

Address: The Carter Center
Public Information Office
One Copenhill
453 Freedom Parkway
Atlanta
GA 30307
USA
Fax: 1 404 420 5145

Catholic Christianity

One of the three main branches of the Christian church (the other two being **Protestant** and **Orthodox Christianity**).

All Christians accept the divine nature of Jesus Christ (*c.* 6 BC–AD 32) and that he is the Messiah, believe in his birth, death and resurrection and share most, if not all, doctrine and sacraments. All accept the Bible as the word of God. Christ himself was born in what is now Palestine, and the religion developed first in the Eastern Mediterranean, from where it spread eventually to all parts of Europe. European colonization of other areas of the globe from the 15th century led to predominantly Christian societies in South and North America and in Australasia. Missionary activity often accompanied trade and conquest and introduced the religion to many other sections of the world. Catholicism is distinguished from other forms of Christianity by its claim to descent from Peter, one of Christ's disciples. This forms the basis of the office of the papacy, based in Rome, Italy, which is the culmination of the church's hierarchical structure. The Pope claims global authority over all Catholics. The Catholic priesthood is male and celibate. Strong emphasis is placed on the church's sacraments.

Christianity was first introduced into East Asia in the 7th century, when Nestorian Christians were among traders received by the Chinese Tang dynasty (618–906), but the influence of this early church lasted only two centuries in **China**. An initiative by Franciscan monks in the 13th–14th centuries to proselytize in **Beijing** and the south of China under the protection of the Mongol Yuan dynasty (1276–1368) ended at the overthrow of the dynasty. The important waves of Catholic missionary activity in East Asia came in the 16th–18th centuries and again in the 19th–20th centuries. Despite great efforts and perseverance, in numerical terms they achieved relatively little. The number of Catholics in the **People's Republic of China (PRC)** is estimated officially at 4m. (unofficial estimates put it at 10m.). The Chinese-populated island of **Taiwan** recorded 310,218 Catholics in 2000; **Hong Kong** was estimated in 2000 to have 371,327, and **Macao** 29,850 (2000). Japan reported 511,063 Catholics in 2000 (Christians of all denominations account for around 1% of the population of Japan). The Republic of Korea (ROK) numbered 4,228,488 Catholics in 2001, 8.8% of the population. There are thought to be around 3,000 Catholics in the Democratic People's Republic of Korea, where only one church is open, together with a number of 'house' churches, but with no ordained priest. Catholic activity in Mongolia is confined to a single mission, active since 1992, and a handful of converts. The influence that both the Catholic and Protestant strands of Christianity exerted and continue to exert in parts of East Asia is more diffuse. They are agents and symbols of Western learning and of modernization. The earlier Catholic missions were tolerated in part because of the scientific knowledge and new artefacts such as firearms that came with them. The later Catholic and Protestant missionaries introduced modern sytems of education and medicine and initiated social reforms. Over the past century many of the leaders of the new East Asian societies have been Christians, some through receiving a Western education. Against that, the very foreignness of the Christian faith and its links with foreign, potentially hostile, countries has made it suspect. Converts who have formed congregations have been anxious to take control of their own affairs and create an indigenous hierarchy and administration independent of missionary supervision. The universal scope and insistence on allegiance to the papacy that mark the Catholic church have in particular offended the Chinese authorities. The factions within the Catholic church, especially against the Jesuit order, turned host countries against the new religion. One essential difference between the Catholic and Protestant churches in East Asia concerns terminology. Two different phrases are used to indicate, one, Catholic Christianity, known as 'teaching of the heavenly lord', and two, Protestant Christianity, known as 'Jesus teaching'. Moreover, in China and Korea, the term Christian is applied only to Protestant Christianity. Catholic institutions are called simply Catholic. The two denominations appear to be regarded as two separate faiths.

History: The early contacts of the Catholic church in East Asia are inseparable from the general history of European exploration of the region. From the 15th century, papal edicts had enjoined the Portuguese and Spanish monarchies to assist in the conversion of those 'heathen' who came under their control in the course of journeys of exploration. Catholic missionaries thus followed close on the heels of navigators and merchants. The Jesuits were particularly active. In 1549 St Francis Xavier, a member of the order, reached **Nagasaki** in western Japan and spent two years there. (He died in 1552 on an island off the south Chinese coast.) Portuguese Jesuit missionary activity continued in Japan and was augmented in 1593 by Spanish Franciscan missionaries. The two orders had different approaches to proselytizing, the Jesuits preferring to aim at conversion of those in leading positions, the Franciscans seeking to work with the poor. The new religion, though it had some initial success, fairly soon roused doubts among local Japanese leaders over its subversive capabilities and persecution followed from the end of the 16th century. A number of missionaries and several thousand Japanese converts were put to death, the Spanish and then the Portuguese were expelled from Japan and, from 1638, the Christian religion was banned and went underground. For 200 years it survived in remote regions of Japan, especially around the Nagasaki area, developing along its own path, until in 1859 it made contact with Catholic missionaries who had been newly permitted to return to Japan. Only in 1873, with the institution of a policy of religious tolerance, did Catholic proselytizing recommence.

Macao, settled in 1557, was one in a chain of Portuguese bases stretching from Goa in India, via Malacca on the Malaysian peninsula to Macao, on the southern coastline of China, and thence to Nagasaki. A Jesuit seminary was established in 1579 and used as the base for missionary work in Japan and the south of China. Jesuit attempts to gain acceptance from the Ming emperor only succeeded in 1601, when the order was permitted to open a house in Beijing. The Jesuits remained there until 1773. During those years more than 450 Jesuit missionaries lived and worked in China, hoping to convert those at the highest reaches of society, but were tolerated more for their intellectual and practical contributions in introducing new ideas and skills into China than for any spiritual message. The Jesuits were joined by Franciscan and Dominican missionaries, who settled briefly on Taiwan, and who were active in the southern half of China. The three orders were embroiled throughout the 17th and 18th centuries in the rites controversy with the Chinese Qing emperor. This concerned the extent, if any, to which Chinese converts could go in continuing with ancestor worship and sacrifices to Confucius. The Jesuits argued for some accommodation with Chinese practice; the Franciscans and Dominicans would not permit the continuation of such worship. Eventually a papal edict of 1742 forbade such practices, to imperial anger. The Jesuit reluctance to accept the verdict was a contributory factor in the dissolution of the order worldwide in 1773, but on its reconstitution they returned to China in 1842. Their missionary work was taken up immediately by a French lay order, the Lazarists, who maintained an important presence in China into the 19th century. The opening up of the capital and the interior of the country to foreign diplomats, traders and missionaries, forced upon China by the Conventions of Beijing in 1860, greatly increased missionary activity, both Catholic and Protestant. The missionary presence, even when directed towards hospitals and schools, none the less caused constant irritation among the Chinese, which expressed itself in attacks on missionaries and converts alike and culminated in the siege of one of the Catholic cathedrals in Beijing alongside the siege of the legation quarter in 1900. Catholic institutions survived the troubled first half of the 20th century, and in 1949, when they passed under a different regime, Catholics numbered around 3m.

Korea has the distinction in East Asia of having been the only country to initiate itself the propagation of Christianity within its borders. From the late 16th century educated circles in Korea had some knowledge of Catholic teaching through literature brought from China. (The annual delegations to take tribute to Beijing provided opportunities for discussion and purchase of books.) In 1784 a young nobleman participating in the delegation contacted French missionaries in the Chinese capital, was baptised and on his return set up a church in a house. The first converts were often among other noble families; many were women. The new congregation established its own liturgy and clergy but remained without external guidance until 1794, when a Chinese priest arrived. Persecution of the new religion soon started, and in 1801 300 believers were put to death. The church had to survive as an underground organization. In 1829 the Vatican, anxious to bring the new group within its reach, placed it under the care of the Paris Foreign Missions Society, and in the late 1830s three French priests, including a bishop, entered the country. These three perished in further executions in 1839. Periods of toleration alternated with bouts of persecution, as in 1854–56 and in 1866. Korean Catholics went into hiding, working often as itinerant potters. Persecution ceased after 1868, by which time perhaps 8,000 had been killed. In 1984, in a ceremony in **Seoul**, Pope John Paul II canonized 103 martyrs, Korean and French, from the 19th-century purges, almost half of them women. During the first half of the 20th century, Catholic missionaries from Germany, Ireland and the USA also came to Korea.

Recent developments: Since 1949 the Chinese Catholic community has been required to accept certain conditions. Chief among these has been the severing of links with the Vatican, imposed by the Chinese Communist authorities in their desire to break all former contacts with foreign institutions, be they religious, cultural or business. The allegiance of Chinese Catholics is directed to the state, and the claims of a universal church are repudiated. Chinese Catholics recognize the spiritual authority of the Pope but do not accept his ecclesiastical jurisdiction. This position is maintained in the 1982 Constitution, which states that religious organizations and affairs are not subject to any 'foreign domination'. The Chinese Catholic church has its own hierarchy and carries out ordinations, but these are not recognized by the Vatican, and the church is regarded as schismatic. Catholic religious orders and foreign priests were obliged to leave the country after the establishment of the PRC, although a few elderly foreign nuns lingered on, mainly to serve the foreign community, until the **Cultural Revolution** (1966–76). Since 1957 Catholic affairs have been administered through the Chinese Patriotic Catholic Association. The Catholic community came under persecution during the Cultural Revolution and most churches were closed, but since 1977 a greater measure of tolerance has prevailed. Churches and cathedrals have been restored and reopened, and seminaries and convents are again active. The number of faithful remains low, but it is possible that larger numbers are active in informal underground groups.

In the ROK a wholly Korean hierarchy is in place, headed by a cardinal. The Catholic church has from time to time placed itself in opposition to some of the more repressive measures instituted by various presidents, has on occasion opened the cathedral grounds in Seoul to dissidents and has supported labour movements. There is a Catholic university in the capital. The church's most prominent lay member in recent years has been President **Kim Dae-Jung**.

Central Bank of China (CBC—'Republic of China')

The central banking institution of the '**Republic of China**' on **Taiwan**. The CBC enjoys an independent role in the formulation of monetary policy, but has always been close to the government. In 1979, under the terms of the Central Bank of China

Act, it was brought under the control of the **Executive Yuan**. The Act defined the Bank's responsibilities for promoting financial stability, ensuring sound banking practice and maintaining the stable internal and external value of the currency, the New Taiwan (NT) dollar. The CBC manages foreign exchange transactions, supervises payments and settlements services and has the right to issue both paper and metal currency. It shares responsibility for the supervision of financial institutions with the Ministry of Finance and the Central Deposit Insurance Corporation. The CBC acts as the government's banker, compiles and publishes financial data and represents Taiwan in international financial organizations,

The CBC was launched in 1924 in **Guangzhou** at the instigation of Sun Yat-sen, leader of the Chinese Nationalist Chinese government, with the task of financing national development. In 1949 the CBC, in common with other institutions connected with the Nationalist government, followed it to the island of Taiwan after it was ousted from the Chinese mainland by the Communists, but did not resume its operations as a central bank until 1961. Between 1949 and 1961 many of the functions of a central bank were performed instead by the **Bank of Taiwan**.

Gov.: Perng Fai-nan
Address: 2 Roosevelt Rd
      Section1
      Taipei 100
      Taiwan
Tel: 886-2-2393-6161/2396-6253
Fax: 886-2-2357-1971
E-mail: adminrol@mail.cbc.gov.tw
Internet: www.cbc.gov.tw

Central Bank of the Democratic People's Republic of Korea

The leading banking institution in the Democratic People's Republic of Korea (DPRK).

When the banking system was nationalized in 1946, in the early years of the DPRK, the Central Bank and the Farmers' Bank were alone retained. In 1959 the two were merged to form the present Central Bank, and the Foreign Trade Bank was established to handle the Central Bank's international business. The Central Bank has responsibility for the issue of banknotes and the setting of interest rates, controls credit lines, supervises all other banks in the DPRK and is the bank of last resort. It has, moreover, to approve the establishment of new banks. A number of commercial banks have been set up since 1978 to handle the foreign-exchange needs and external payments of North Korean foreign trade enterprises. With the exception of foreign banking institutions, all banks in the DPRK are state-owned. The Central Bank has 227 branches.

Pres.: Kim Wan Su
Address: 58-1 Sungri St
Central District
Pyongyang
Democratic People's Republic of Korea
Tel: 850-2-333-8196
Fax: 850-2-381-4624

Central Military Commission(s)

There are two Central Military Commissions (CMC) in the **People's Republic of China**. The older, and more important, is the **Chinese Communist Party (CCP)** CMC, which dates from the 1930s. The state CMC, which is answerable to the **National People's Congress (NPC)**, dates only from the 1982 Constitution and, given the guiding role of the CCP in state matters, is in fact subordinate to the CCP CMC. In reality, the same people sit on both CMCs.

The party CMC structure provides command authority over the **People's Liberation Army (PLA)**. Although there is a Ministry of National Defence, its role is international liaison, not command of the armed forces. The CMC is made up of serving officers, except for the chairman and senior vice-chairman, who are civilians. In the past, **Mao Zedong**, **Deng Xiaoping** and **Jiang Zemin** have held the chairmanship, while the current holder is **Hu Jintao**, CCP general secretary and state President.

Central News Agency (CNA)

National news agency of the **'Republic of China'** on **Taiwan**.

The Central News Agency (CNA) was established in **Guangzhou** in southern **China** in April 1924 to meet the needs of the **Kuomintang**, the Chinese Nationalist Party, and later of the Chinese Nationalist government. In 1949 the Agency followed the government to the island of Taiwan on its defeat by the Chinese Communists and long served as the state provider of news. In 1996 the CNA was freed from official control when it was constituted as an independent organization in public ownership, but it continues to publicize government policies as well as economic, social and cultural developments within Taiwan. It has both domestic and overseas correspondents, offers news in Chinese, English and Spanish, and targets particularly the **overseas Chinese** community. Since 1994 it has had an online news service.

Leadership: Hui Yuan-hui
Address: 209 Sungkiang Rd
Taipei (104)
Taiwan
Tel: 886-2-2505-8379
Fax: 886-2-2502-3805

E-mail: cnamark@mail.can.com.tw
Internet: www.cna.com.tw

Central Tibetan Administration (CTA)

Government-in-exile of **Tibet**. Its full title is the 'Central Tibetan Administration of His Holiness the Dalai Lama'. In 1959 the **Dalai Lama**, head of state and political as well as religious leader of Tibet, arrived in India after fleeing from Tibet, where an uprising against Chinese control had been militarily suppressed. About 80,000 refugees fled as well. The Tibetan government installed itself first in Musoorie in Uttaranchal in north India, but in 1960 moved to Dharamsala in the north-west Indian state of Himachal Pradesh, where it has remained ever since. Over the past 40 years or so an administration has evolved along classic lines of legislature, judiciary and executive with dependent departments and organizations handling finances, health, education, culture, information, security and so forth. From 1990 the Dalai Lama presided over changes intended to make the administration more representative of **Tibetans** living in exile and more responsive to their wishes. The assembly of deputies was enlarged in 1990 to 46 members elected by Tibetans living not only in India but also in more than 33 other countries. In 1991 a constitutional Charter of the Tibetans in Exile was presented; and in 2001 direct elections to the highest executive authority were introduced. The CTA draws its revenues from annual voluntary contributions and levies on income and salaries from the Tibetan population in exile. It aims at rehabilitative activities and employment, but is apparently closing down the business enterprises it used to run. It provides school education and organizes the reception of refugees from Tibet. The Dalai Lama has said that on independence the government-in-exile would dissolve itself and that a free government would be run in Tibet by Tibetans.

One of the difficulties the government-in-exile has to face is that of accommodating differing views on how to move ahead. The Dalai Lama has sought dialogue with the government of the **People's Republic of China (PRC)**, but less patient elements advocate more aggressive action. There is also a range of differing aims for Tibet, from independence to an autonomous entity under loose Chinese control or a federal union of the three historic provinces. The desire is very strong for a return to a greater Tibet covering the three regions, central Tibet, Amdo in the west and north-west, and Kham to the west, that are regarded as representing the true extent of Tibetan population and culture. Most of the outer areas were absorbed into neighbouring provinces during the 1950s. It is almost inconceivable that the PRC government in its present unyielding mood would agree to such a realignment.

Leadership: His Holiness the Dalai Lama
Address: Office of His Holiness the Dalai Lama Thekchen Choeling
P. O. McLeod Ganj
Dharamsala 176 219
India

Tel: 91-1892-221343
Fax: 91-1892-221813
Internet: www.tibet.com

Chaebol

The big business conglomerates that are a distinctive component of the economy of the Republic of Korea (ROK). Many started out, and continue to operate, as family-run concerns. The largest are familiar international names, such as **Hyundai Corporation**, Samsung and LG. Some of them, such as Samsung, which began in 1938 as a small export firm, have histories reaching back into the Japanese colonial era. Indeed, the Korean *chaebol* are reminiscent of the big Japanese companies, the *zaibatsu*. In the period of economic reconstruction following liberation from Japan in 1945 and then the **Korean War** (1950–53), these new companies often imported or manufactured the consumer goods and provided the services needed by society. During the 1960s and 1970s they moved into heavy manufacturing, shipbuilding, construction (both inside and outside the country), trade and banking, working closely with successive governments, from that of President **Park Chung-Hee** onwards, to push forward the rapid industrialization and fast development of the ROK's economy. Their willingness to co-operate in government plans was eased by the provision of cheap credit and financial and fiscal incentives. Much *chaebol* output is exported, and some of the companies have established overseas manufacturing ventures.

Early success encouraged sometimes excessive expansion and diversification and led to cross-investment between sectors within a *chaebol*, with the aim of enhancing the capital value of a new subsidiary and thus attracting bank loans. During times of economic growth this structure functioned well enough, but could not always withstand harsh financial conditions. The currency devaluations that hit many Asian countries in 1997 and the consequent current-account deficits and debts affected the *chaebol* badly. Some of them, for example, Daewoo, have been forced to sell off companies. Even the giant Hyundai conglomerate has been broken into several components. Successive governments, while prepared to work with the *chaebol*, have always tried to keep them in check and to secure their acceptance of reform, but have not always succeeded. Family ownership and the strong personalities of founding members have also contributed to the resistance of the *chaebol* to change, while exposing them to disintegregation through family rifts and deaths.

Chai Ling

Chai Ling was the self-styled 'commander-in-chief' of the students who remained in **Tiananmen** in the last stages of the 1989 demonstrations. She was born in Shandong Province in the **People's Republic of China** in 1966, and graduated with a degree in psychology from **Beijing** University in 1987. In June 1989 she evaded capture and took refuge in a foreign embassy. From there she escaped to **Hong**

Kong, hidden in a wooden crate. She moved to France, divorced her fellow-student husband and eventually went to the USA, where she attended the Harvard Business School. Chai Ling subsequently remarried and has established a computer business. She was popular with the media in exile, and some of her fellow exiles have criticized her for exploiting her role in 1989 to her own advantage.

Chan, Anson

Anson Maria Elizabeth Chan Fang—Mrs Anson Chan

Anson Chan was chief secretary (i.e. head of the civil service) in **Hong Kong** from 1993 until April 2001. She was born in 1940 in **Shanghai**, where her father was a textile manufacturer. In 1948 the family moved to Hong Kong, where her father died in 1950. She attended the University of Hong Kong, and on graduation in 1962 she joined the Hong Kong Administrative (senior civil service) Branch. She held a variety of posts before becoming director of social welfare in 1980, the first woman to hold such a high position in Hong Kong. She also became involved in the first of many conflicts with the Hong Kong media at that time. In 1987 she became Secretary for Economic Services, an important position that included responsibility for issues such as air services.

In the 1990s, as the last phase of the handover of Hong Kong to the **People's Republic of China (PRC)** began under Governor **Christopher Patten**, Anson Chan became chief secretary or head of the civil service. Her main task was to oversee the final stages of the localization of the civil service before the PRC takeover in 1997. This she accomplished, earning the respect of both the British and the Chinese, and she was asked to stay on under the Chinese-appointed chief executive, **Tung Chee Hwa**, a fellow Shanghainese. However, she did not get on well with Tung, and she distanced herself from him on a number of occasions over issues such as democracy and media freedoms in Hong Kong, to PRC annoyance. The local media also blamed her for the problems that surrounded the opening of the new **Chek Lap Kok—Hong Kong International Airport** in 1998. In 1999 she agreed to delay her retirement until 2002, but she subsequently announced her intention to retire in January 2001, and in fact retired in April 2001. Since retirement she has remained outspoken on matters involving Hong Kong's rights, but has also maintained that the PRC central government has a fundamentally sound approach to Hong Kong. She was awarded the Hong Kong Grand Bahinia decoration in 1999, and was made an Honorary Grand Dame of the British Order of St Michael and St George in 2002.

Cheju Island

Cheju is the **Korean peninsula**'s largest island, 72 km long and 27 km wide. Some 80 km off the south coast, it has a total land area of 1,845 sq km; it is also the peninsula's only island province. It contains the Republic of Korea's highest mountain, Mount Halla, which rises to more than 1,950 m. Cheju was under Mongol control for more than 100 years in the 12th and 13th centuries. During the Choson or Yi dynasty (1392–1910) it was a place of exile. In the colonial period (1910–45) it was administered as part of South Cholla Province, but it became a separate province in 1946. In 1948 it was the scene of a major uprising, involving some Communists, against the growing political dominance of right-wing groups based around President **Syngman Rhee**, and in particular against the elections planned for 10 May in that year. Both sides fought with great ferocity, with thousands killed in the fighting, and about 250 insurgents executed afterwards. Although the postponed elections took place in May 1949, anti-government guerrilla activity continued on the island until after the end of the **Korean War**.

Cheju has a national university, established in 1982. The island's main sources of revenue are agriculture, fisheries and tourism—it has always been a popular Korean honeymoon destination; there is no industry. Its population, 366,000 in 1970, totalled about 530,000 in 2003.

Chek Lap Kok—Hong Kong International Airport

In July 1998 the then President of the **People's Republic of China (PRC)**, **Jiang Zemin**, formally opened the new Hong Kong International Airport at Chek Lap Kok, which replaced Kai Tak, the former airport situated within the urban area. Since then the airport has become one of the world's greatest, with the capacity to handle 89m. passengers daily, and as many as 49 landings and takeoffs per hour.

The need for a new airport in **Hong Kong** had been clear for many years, but the decision to build it, announced in October 1989, came at a particularly difficult time. In 1984 Britain and the PRC had signed an agreement for the return of Hong Kong to the PRC in 1997. Smooth progress in preparing for the handover ended, however, following the suppression of the student demonstrations in **Tiananmen** in June 1989, and the subsequent British (and European Union) sanctions against the PRC. The then governor of Hong Kong, Sir David Wilson, announced new airport and port development projects in October 1989 in order to bolster confidence in Hong Kong's future. The PRC looked upon the move with suspicion, claiming that it was intended to drain Hong Kong's resources in advance of the British departure. The awarding of contracts to British firms, including the architect Norman Foster, increased PRC claims that the project was expensive and doomed to failure. Various negotiations, including a visit by John Major, then British Prime Minister, to the PRC in September 1991, failed to reassure the PRC, which became even more hostile as relations deteriorated after the appointment of **Christopher Patten** as governor of Hong Kong in 1992.

In the event, the project neither bankrupted Hong Kong nor proved a failure. It was completed under budget and was ready for opening somewhat behind schedule; although there were some problems at the beginning with luggage handling, these did not persist. Since the opening PRC criticisms have ceased.

Chen Shui-bian

Politician and President of **Taiwan**—the **'Republic of China'**—since May 2000. He is also chairman of the **Democratic Progressive Party (DPP)**.

Chen was born in 1950 into a poor farming family in Tainan County of Taiwan. In 1974 he graduated from Taiwan National University with a degree in commercial law and had also qualified as a lawyer. From 1976 until 1989 he specialized in maritime insurance as partner in a private law firm. His first involvement in politics came in 1980, as a consequence of defending a group of dissidents arraigned before a military court for their alleged participation in the **Kaohsiung incident** of December 1979. One of the defendants was **Annette Lu**, who now serves as Chen's Vice-President. Chen joined the *Tangwai* ('outside the [KMT] party') movement, and in 1981 was elected to **Taipei** city council as a *Tangwai* candidate. He served on the council until 1985, in which year he was tried and sentenced to a short prison term for libel. After leaving prison, he worked for his wife, Wu Shu-chen, who had been elected to the **Legislative Yuan**. Chen himself was elected to the Legislative Yuan for the DPP in 1989 and was made convener of the Yuan's National Defence Committee.

In 1994 he left these posts on being elected mayor of Taipei. He largely owed his success to a split of the traditional vote between the **Kuomintang (KMT)** and its breakaway party, the **New Party**. None the less, the absence of a sufficient number of experienced non-KMT colleagues meant that he had to co-operate with KMT administrators. He launched a number of clean-up campaigns in the capital against illegal gambling and prostitution, pollution and squatting; but was voted out of office in 1994.

Six years later Chen presented himself as the DPP candidate in the 2000 presidential elections. He won with only 39% of the vote, again benefiting from a split vote within the KMT. Once in office, he again had to rely to some extent on the more experienced KMT elements in government. The Legislative Yuan, moreover, was and remains controlled by his opponents. At the same time, Chen had to meet his party's expectations on such issues as nuclear power and independence for Taiwan. The nuclear question arose early on in his first term when, in October 2000, he found himself caught between DPP protests against the completion of a fourth nuclear power station and KMT support for the project. Ultimately the power station was abandoned, but Chen's handling of the controversy was clumsy and led to the intervention of the island's judicial organs, which pronounced that the legislature rather than the Cabinet was the body empowered to make decisions on such issues.

The independence question is far more divisive. Chen's party, the DPP, and beyond it the **Taiwan Solidarity Union**, favour moves towards independence, thus rebuffing the call of the **People's Republic of China (PRC)** for a one-China policy and with it any possibility of reunification with the mainland. The opposition coalition includes some who still hope for some kind of reconciliation with the PRC, and thus rejects calls for independence as likely to endanger the island's relationship with the PRC. In 2001 the DPP and, by implication, Chen, renounced any formal claim to independence for Taiwan, arguing that the island is already a separate entity. In 2002 Chen expressed his support for a referendum to determine Taiwan's future and spoke of the PRC and Taiwan as two separate countries. In late 2003 he agreed to a referendum bill that allowed for an emergency referendum on independence as a pre-emptive measure in the face of imminent aggression by the PRC. He has also spoken of his wish for constitutional reform, either through a referendum or through the use of existing procedures. His statements on the independence issue have created uncertainty and led his opponents to accuse him of insincerity amid suspicions that independence remains his goal. His stance has, however, so far allowed him to retain the support of his followers and appears, moreover, to have been persuasive in bringing opposition parties such as the KMT to a more centrist position on the issue.

In March 2004, on the day before polling in the presidential elections, Chen and his Vice-President Annette Lu were shot at and slightly wounded. The pair went on to win the election, but by a very small margin. The opposition refused to accept the result and boycotted his inauguration. Two lawsuits pursued after the elections seek to have Chen unseated and the result of the elections overturned. In September 2004 three men were arrested in connection with the March shooting incident, but it has not yet been proved that they were involved in the attack itself.

Address: Office of the President
122 Chungking South Rd
Section 1
Taipei
Taiwan
Tel: 886-2-2311-3731
Fax: 886-2-2331-1604
Internet: www.president.gov.tw

Chiang Ching-kuo

Pinyin: Jiang Jingguo

Politician, Premier of the **'Republic of China' ('ROC')** on **Taiwan** in 1972–78, President of the 'ROC' from 1978 until his death in 1988. Chiang Ching-kuo was the only son of **Chiang Kai-shek**, leader of the **Kuomintang (KMT)** and President of the 'ROC' from 1950 until 1975, and of Chiang Kai-shek's first wife, Mao Fumei. He was born in 1910 in Zhejiang Province in **China**.

Chiang Ching-kuo spent 12 years in the Soviet Union, from 1925 until 1937. Initially he followed political and military studies, first in Moscow, then in Leningrad (now St Petersburg). In the early 1920s the KMT and the **Chinese Communist Party (CCP)** were co-operating, if uneasily, in a United Front at the urging of Soviet advisers. After Chiang Kai-shek turned against the CCP in 1927, the younger Chiang repudiated his father's actions. After his studies he worked in various jobs, including at a Siberian steel factory. There he met and in 1935 married a Russian woman. The couple were permitted to return to China in 1937, by which time a second KMT-CCP United Front had been formed. Chiang held a variety of posts in the Nationalist government and in December 1949 followed his father to Taiwan. His wife took a Chinese name and eventually accompanied him to Taiwan.

Chiang Ching-kuo held a number of posts under the senior Chiang. From 1950 until 1965 he served as head of the security services, coming under criticism for dubious practices, human rights abuses and poor treatment of those targeted by security. In 1965 he was appointed as Minister of Defence and remained in that post until 1969, when he became Vice-Premier. In 1972 he was elevated to the office of Premier, a post he held until he became President in 1978. He was re-elected as President in 1984.

Chiang's second term of office as President was marked by a number of developments that had the effect of loosening longstanding restrictions on both the internal and external political scene in Taiwan. His Vice-President, elected in 1984, was **Lee Teng-hui**, the first Taiwan-born politician to attain high office in both the KMT and the government. Lee was to succeed Chiang when the latter died and was then re-elected as President in 1990, thus breaking the traditional hold of mainland Chinese on the island's leadership. In 1986 various *Tangwai* groups operating 'outside the [KMT] party' were permitted for the first time to form themselves into an unofficial opposition party, the **Democratic Progressive Party (DPP)**. The DPP eventually provided the first non-KMT President of Taiwan, **Chen Shui-bian**, in 2000. In the same year Taiwan and the **People's Republic of China** agreed to negotiate in **Hong Kong** over the fate of a cargo aircraft diverted to the mainland by a defecting Taiwan pilot. These contacts doubtless encouraged Chiang in 1987 to permit Taiwan citizens to visit the mainland. He also lifted martial law in Taiwan, which had been enforced since 1949.

Chiang also concerned himself with promoting the island's economy, particularly its infrastructure. From 1955 until 1960 he was active in building a cross-island highway, and while President launched various large-scale construction projects.

Chiang Kai-shek

Pinyin: Jiang Jieshi

Politician, soldier, leader of the Chinese Nationalist party and government, and President of the '**Republic of China' ('ROC')** on **Taiwan** from 1950 until his death in 1975.

Chiang Kai-shek was born in 1887 in the central east coast province of Zhejiang in **China**. He underwent a military education in China and Japan and while in Japan met fellow Chinese who were already working to overthrow the failing Qing dynasty. He joined in the subsequent republican movement in China and became a member of the **Kuomintang (KMT)** and a protégé of Sun Yat-sen, the temporary President of the new republic. Sun sent him to Moscow in 1923 to study the Soviet political and military system. On Sun's death in 1925 Chiang emerged as head of the Nationalist armed forces and leader of the KMT. From his southern base of **Guangzhou** he embarked in the following year on his Northern Expedition, with the intention of bringing the northern warlord government located in **Beijing** under KMT control. *En route*, in **Shanghai**, in 1927, Chiang turned against the local members of the **Chinese Communist Party (CCP)**, massacring large numbers of them. From 1923 the CCP and the KMT had liaised uneasily in the first United Front, but rivalries within the Front between right and left elements led to a split. Chiang imposed his own rule, established his capital in **Nanjing** in 1928 and captured Beijing in the same year.

From 1928 until 1937 Chiang led the Nationalist government from Nanjing. He presided over a programme of modernization and reform in the economy, the legal system, public welfare, education and communications, but was constantly embroiled with challenges to his authority, not least from the Chinese Communists. Despite the growing threat from Japan, which occupied the north-east portion of China in 1931, Chiang gave his attention primarily to eradication of the Communist threat. In 1937 he was forced into a second United Front with the CCP that sought to promote a joint struggle against the Japanese invaders, but later returned to fighting the Communists as well as the Japanese. Japan and China were at war from July 1937. In the face of spreading Japanese control of the country, Chiang moved his capital from Nanjing first to Guangzhou, then to **Chongqing** in western China. When Japan and the USA opened hostilities in 1941 following the Japanese attack on Pearl Harbor, Nationalist China was brought into the Allied cause and received considerable military and financial support from the USA. In his capacity as head of the Chinese government, Chiang participated as one of the 'Big Four' in the **Cairo Conference** of 1943, which met to consider Allied war aims against Japan. After the Japanese defeat in 1945, Chiang prepared for further confrontation with the Communists, and civil war broke out in 1946. The end came in defeat for the Nationalist cause, and in December 1949 Chiang fled to Taiwan.

Chiang had been elected President of the Republic of China in 1947. On arrival in Taiwan he reinstated the republic and resumed the office of President. He was re-elected as President in consecutive elections. He upheld the ROC's claim to be the legitimate government of the whole of China, preserved the goal of retaking the mainland, kept Taiwan under martial law and maintained the country was living in a period of 'Communist rebellion' during which special temporary measures were required. Political life was effectively stifled. The economy by contrast was set on the road to expansion. On his death Chiang was succeeded first by the country's Vice-President, then, in 1978, by his son **Chiang Ching-kuo**. Chiang Kai-shek was married twice, the second time, in 1927, to Soong Mei-ling. To meet the wishes of her family, he converted to Methodist Christianity in 1929.

Chien, Eugene

Chien You-hsin

Engineer, diplomat and politician, who served as Minister for Foreign Affairs of the **'Republic of China' ('ROC')** on **Taiwan** from 2002 until 2004. 'Eugene' is his adopted Western name.

Eugene Chien was born in 1946. He studied mechanical engineering at Taiwan National University, then aeronautics and astronautics at New York University. On his return to Taiwan, he held various teaching posts in the engineering faculty at Tamkang University until 1984. Thereafter he worked in government and politics.

From 1984 until 1987 Chien was a member of the **Legislative Yuan**, then held administrative and ministerial posts until 1993. In that year he was appointed Representative of the **Taipei** Economic and Cultural Office in the United Kingdom (which represents Taiwan's interests in Britain), a post he held until 1998. On his return to Taiwan, he joined the Consultative Committee of the National Security Council, then was chosen in 2000 by President **Chen Shui-bian** to serve as deputy secretary-general in the office of the President, despite his adherence to the **Kuomintang**. In 2002 he was appointed as Minister of Foreign Affairs, a position he resigned in April 2004 after the then director of the American Institute in Taiwan left her post amidst contention over her favourable recognition of Chen Shui-bian's victory in the 2004 presidential elections while the outcome was still disputed. Chien was due to take up a post as the next Taipei Representative to Belgium and the European Union, but his appointment was cancelled in August 2004 after it was alleged that the Taipei Representative Office in London had issued a passport and a legal document to the wife of a fugitive Taiwan arms dealer. This procedure was said to have occurred in February 2003 during Chien's term of office at the foreign ministry.

China

Zhongguo

Country occupying the south-east portion of the Asian landmass before it narrows into the south-east Asian peninsula. Since 1949 it has been governed as the **People's Republic of China (PRC)**, but in the past was described simply as China. The name 'China' is now generally applied to the PRC, particularly after the majority of states had by 1975 accorded recognition to the PRC rather than to the **'Republic of China'** on **Taiwan**.

The evidence of artefacts and remains of settlements in central and western areas along the **Yellow river** and its tributary the Wei, and in eastern and south-eastern coastal regions of China, indicates the existence of Neolithic farming societies from around the 7th millennium BC. By approximately 1500 BC the first of the early dynasties, Shang, distinguished by its fine bronzes, had emerged in the Yellow river basin. Its successor, Zhou (1050–221 BC), eventually broke up into smaller kingdoms under the impact of attacks by nomadic peoples from the north and west. Out of this fragmentation came the state of Qin (221–207 BC), which for the first time achieved a unified Chinese state (and which provided the name adopted by foreigners to describe the whole of China). The Han dynasty (206 BC–AD 220), described as the first of the imperial dynasties, built successfully on this unity to expand its authority into Central Asia, the **Korean peninsula** and what is now Viet Nam, before collapsing itself. This sequence of developments illustrates recurring patterns in the course of dynastic China: raids from without on settled agricultural communities; internal unrest; disintegration of once powerful states into smaller, often warring units; (re)unification by one stronger state that bequeathes a well-ordered administration to its successor; and the initial success of the beneficiary before its own eventual decline. Purely Chinese dynasties alternated with non-Chinese ones (Liao, Jin, Yuan, Qing among others) imposed by victorious invaders coming from regions to the north-west or north-east of China proper and resented as aliens. In the unsettled conditions following the break-up of the Han empire in 220, **Buddhism**, itself a foreign religion, won much acceptance. The area occupied by China during periods of expansion was sometimes considerable, as when the Qing (1644–1911) brought **Inner Mongolia** and Outer Mongolia (now Mongolia), **Xinjiang** and **Tibet** under their control during the 17th to 19th centuries.

The imperial dynastic system was sustained by the concept of the mandate of heaven which the emperor and his successors might hold for as long as they continued in virtuous ways. The empire was served by a well-educated élite of bureaucrats and buttressed by the teachings of **Confucianism** on statecraft and generally strict codes of punishment. The basis of the economy was agriculture, established on the cultivation of rice and grain, and professional activities and commerce were judged lowly occupations unworthy of an official. Trade did none the less go on, conducted through the tribute system which brought annual missions to the capital from neighbouring countries with goods to offer. Sea trade also flourished intermittently, especially in the 15th century during the Ming, often as a means of replenishing state revenues. In many areas of science and technology the Chinese were far ahead of Europe. Among their achievements were the invention of paper and printing, porcelain, gunpowder and the magnetic compass, bronze and iron casting, advances in civil and mechanical engineering, in agricultural, marine and textile technology and in astronomy. Distance from Europe, coupled with suspicion of foreign intentions, kept China's contacts with the outside world to a minimum, although the Silk Route through Central Asia was travelled for centuries from Han times and brought Arabs and Europeans such as Marco Polo and several Catholic priests to the Mongol, later Yuan court in the 13th and 14th centuries. From the 16th century Portuguese traders and missionaries of **Catholic Christianity** started to arrive by sea in the south of the country via **Macao**. These foreign priests were able to secure permission to travel to the capital, by then the northern city of **Beijing**. They maintained a presence there throughout much of the 17th and 18th centuries. Their hopes of converting leading members of the Chinese court and society were disappointed, but they acted as a conduit for the transmission of Western culture to the imperial court and of Chinese civilization to the West. The Portuguese were followed in the 17th century by Dutch traders and in the 18th century by British merchants.

For the greater part of the 19th century the twin threats of pressure from without the country and dissent within severely tested the resilience of the Qing dynasty and demonstrated its weakness in the face of opponents who came with strong demands and, this time, superior technical abilities. British demands that China open up to trade, including trade in opium, were backed by force in the two Anglo–Chinese wars of 1839–42 and 1856–60. The first war ended for the Chinese in the cession of **Hong Kong** to the British in 1842 and the opening of five coastal treaty ports. By the mid-1850s the foremost of these ports, **Shanghai**, had established its own administration. The French then joined the British in renewing warfare to press for further concessions. In 1860 the two countries won the right to have diplomatic representation in Beijing and to expand trade and missionary activities inland. Other European powers, together with the USA, Russia and Japan, exacted similar concessions through treaties still regarded by the Chinese as 'unequal'. By 1885 29 treaty ports existed, some of them inland. The Chinese Imperial Customs and postal service were run by foreigners on behalf of the Chinese government. Towards the end of the 19th century foreign interests acquired concessions for the development of railways, mining, shipping, banking and manufacturing, which lasted until the end of the Second World War. The various foreign powers had arrived at the point of competing 'spheres of influence' over China.

The inability of the Qing dynasty to ward off foreign intrusion was matched by its failures in controlling internal rebellion and economic and social difficulties. Peasant revolts in the south of China in the 1840s, exacerbated by the effects of the first Anglo–Chinese war, prepared the way for the Taiping Rebellion that started in 1851 in the south and moved as far north as **Nanjing**. Its demands for social and economic reform were rejected, and the rebellion itself was finally suppressed in 1864 with foreign assistance. From the 1860s one faction within the Qing court began to advocate a measure of economic, technical and educational modernization in imitation of Western material advances, but any change in the social and political framework of the country or reform of the imperial system of administration was resisted. The resentment of foreign privileges and encroachment, aggravated by drought, culminated in the popular assault on the foreign legation quarter in Beijing in 1900. China had already been humiliated when Japan defeated it in a short war (1894–95) over supremacy in Korea and annexed the island of Taiwan.

The Qing dynasty's failing hold on power was further weakened by growing nationalist and anti-**Manzhou** sentiment in the first decade of the 20th century. Sections of Chinese society that had received a Western education or had absorbed the lessons of Western activity in China began to use such experience to work in China's favour. Thus, a new class of Chinese entrepreneurs bought back loans and concessions from foreigners and raised capital for Chinese ventures. The leader of the developing nationalist movement was Sun Yat-sen, whose education had been partly Western. Drawing on suppport among Chinese both inside and outside the country, he became the provisional head of the first **Republic of China** when, finally, the Qing dynasty came to an end in 1912. In the same year he founded the Chinese Nationalist Party (**Kuomintang—KMT**) on the Three People's Principles of nationalism, democracy and the people's livelihood; but both republic and party fell foul of a cruder form of authority when Yuan Shikai, a former imperial officer, seized control. Yuan died in 1916, but China thereafter disintegrated into a period of warlord rule in the provinces under an impotent central government. Foreign concessions and businesses continued in existence. Japan, which had annexed Korea in 1910, was starting to press China for further privileges. When the Paris Conference and Versailles Peace Treaty of 1919 that followed the First World War awarded the former German concessions in Shandong Province to Japan, Chinese anger burst out in demonstrations in Beijing on 4 May 1919. Students played a large part in the protests, which spread into strikes and anti-Japanese boycotts. The demonstrations coalesced into the May Fourth Movement that took on wider proportions as it campaigned for fresh values in society, culture and literature.

In the wake of the May Fourth Movement, a new political party emerged, the **Chinese Communist Party**, established in 1921 in Shanghai. Among the founding members was **Mao Zedong**. Its formation reflected in part Chinese disillusionment with Western political models and their failure to bring improvement to China, a disillusionment shared by Sun Yat-sen. Two years before, in 1919, Sun had revived the KMT. The two parties, with Soviet support, agreed in 1923 to work together in a United Front with the aim of first securing national liberation. It was short-lived. Sun Yat-sen died in the following year and leadership of the KMT passed to **Chiang Kai-shek**. In 1926 a joint Northern Expedition was launched to oust the warlord-controlled government in Beijing, but before it had concluded Chiang had joined with the right-wing element in his party to suppress the Communists in Shanghai. Further attacks on Communists in other cities occurred. Chiang established a Nationalist government in Nanjing in 1928 under his leadership as President of the Republic of China and continued to harry the Communists in the rural areas to which they had retreated. Mao's interest had turned to encouraging revolution among the vast rural population rather than among the many fewer industrial workers. In 1934 around 100,000 Communist followers broke out of the Nationalist encirclement to start the **Long March** of 9,600 km (5,965 miles) from their base in Jiangxi Province in south-east China, through the mountainous western regions, to **Yanan** in the north-western province of Shaanxi. Only about 10,000 survived the year-long ordeal. By the time they reached Yanan in 1935 Mao's leadership of the Chinese Communist movement was assured. Chiang continued to pursue the Communists, even though by 1931 Japan had seized **Manchuria** in north-east China and was extending its occupation of the country from 1937. In that year the Nationalists and Communists agreed to form a second United Front to resist Japan. The Nationalist government received considerable aid from the USA after 1941, and Chiang represented China at the **Cairo Conference** held in 1943 to discuss post-war dispositions. The Communists used the war years to consolidate their position in the country, so that on liberation in August 1945 they were in a stronger position to offer a political challenge to the Nationalists.

For six months after the end of war, the United Front held and a measure of co-operation was possible. In March 1946, however, the consensus broke and the two parties launched into a civil war, in the course of which the Communists moved south, gaining control over progressively larger tracts of territory until, on 1 October 1949, they were able to establish the second Chinese republic, the People's Republic of China. Chiang Kai-shek fled to Taiwan, where he installed the rival 'Republic of China'.

China, People's Republic of (PRC)

Zhonghua renmin gongheguo

Independent republic, established in 1949 on the greater part of the territory of the first Chinese republic and the former empire of **China**.

A long land border makes the PRC a neighbour of the Democratic People's Republic of Korea (DPRK), the Russian Federation, Mongolia, Kazakhstan, Kyrgyzstan, Tajikistan, Afghanistan, Pakistan, India, Nepal, Bhutan, Myanmar, Laos and Viet Nam. The country is bounded to the east by the Yellow Sea, which separates it from the Republic of Korea (ROK), and the East China Sea, beyond which lies Japan. The Taiwan Strait divides the PRC from the island of **Taiwan**. The southern coastline of the PRC is bounded by the South China Sea. The country is divided into 22 provinces that include Hainan Island, five autonomous regions and four special municipalities directly under the central government that have the status of provinces. **Hong Kong** and **Macao** are administered as **Special Administrative Regions (SARs)**. More than one-third of the population is urban-based; just under two-thirds live in the rural areas.

Area: 9,562,904 sq km; *capital:* **Beijing**; *population:* mainland China 1,265,830,000 (2000 census), Hong Kong SAR 6,780,000 (2000), Macao SAR 440,000 (2000); *official language:* Chinese—52 national minority languages are recognized, of which six have official status in their respective autonomous areas; *religion:* none, but five mainstream religious affiliations are recognized: **Buddhism, Daoism, Islam, Catholic Christianity,** and **Protestant Christianity**.

The PRC is headed by a President, who is elected by the **National People's Congress (NPC)**, the highest organ of state power. The NPC also elects the chairman of the **Central Military Commission (CMC)**. The NPC's term of office is five years. It meets once a year. When not in session, its rights are exercised by its permanent body, the Standing Committee of the NPC, under its chairman. The 10th and most recent NPC was convened in March 2003 and was attended by 2,951 deputies. Deputies to the NPC are elected by the provincial-level people's congresses, which are the local organs of state power, by the armed forces and by representatives of **overseas Chinese** and from Hong Kong and Macao. Deputies to provincial-level congresses are elected by people's congresses at the next lower level. Only at county level are deputies elected directly by the electorate.

The President of the PRC must be at least 45 years of age. His (or her) term of office is the same as that of the NPC and no more than two consecutive terms may be served. The President nominates the Premier, Vice-Premiers and ministers of the **State Council**, the highest organ of state administration and the executive organ of the Central People's Government. Each office in the State Council is held for five years. A maximum of two successive terms of office is permitted.

State power is paralleled by the structure of the **Chinese Communist Party (CCP)**, headed by the Politburo and its Standing Committee and supported by the Central Committee. A descending system of local committees and secretariats ensures a CCP presence at all levels of society, including the armed forces. National and local leaders generally have a party function as well as an administrative one, and there has been at times intense interaction between the two spheres. The current President of the PRC, **Hu Jintao**, is also the general secretary of the CCP Central Committee.

History: Even before **Mao Zedong** proclaimed the establishment of the PRC on 1 October 1949, the Chinese Communists had already embarked on programmes of land redistribution and administrative measures in areas that had been won from the Chinese Nationalists in the course of the civil war (1946–49). In 1948 they proposed the convening of a consultative conference representing a wide range of political interests with a view to forming a coalition government. In late September 1949 this group, the **Chinese People's Political Consultative Conference (CPPCC)**, announced the founding of the PRC and authorized the Central People's Government. During the years of campaigning against the Nationalists and the Japanese, Mao had had the opportunity and, from 1935, the time at his base in **Yanan** in Shaanxi Province, to reflect and write extensively on the kind of society he wished to achieve for China. Foremost was to be a style of mass politics that would draw its legitimacy from the people. The period from the inception of the PRC until his death in 1976 was strongly marked by Mao's views and policies. His was not the only voice, however, and he had to persuade, and if necessary outmanoeuvre, his colleagues to secure acceptance of his line. The implementation of Mao's vision had to be accompanied by pragmatic measures, a task often undertaken by the Premier, **Zhou Enlai**, but on occasion the extremity of Mao's views overrode more prudent policies.

Many pressing problems faced the new administration in 1949. It had to secure the country's boundaries, which it completed with the incorporation of **Tibet** in 1951. (Hong Kong and Macao were not tackled at this stage, and Taiwan was left for later liberation.) Within the country, it had to restore order, with the disbanding of private armies and the incorporation of former Nationalist soldiers into its own forces. Non-Communist elements in the population had to be brought into a United Front and urban residents reassured by a movement that had gained its greatest support and experience in rural areas. Inflation had to be controlled. Reform of social relations was enacted through measures against former landlords and, within the family, a new marriage law. Literacy and education were boosted. The outlines of a new order began to appear: centralized political control and economic planning, nationalization of resources and industry, moves towards rural collectivization. Soviet models were influential in the early years and Soviet aid was crucial in vitalizing the Chinese economy.

Not all Chinese were won over, however, to the new regime. In 1957 an exercise in inviting critical views—the One Hundred Flowers campaign—backfired on all concerned. Mao was dismayed at the extent of opposition expressed to the Party and to socialism, and an anti-rightist movement ensued that made clear the narrow limits of tolerance for dissenting ideas. The incident illustrated too the ambivalent relationship Mao had with intellectuals and experts. From the late 1950s the Soviet centralized model in administration and planning was gradually being modified in favour of more provincial-level responsibility. Mao and his associates were anxious to hasten the pace of China's advance towards its own form of socialism, if not communism. In their desire to free what they regarded as the people's energies and initiative from bureaucratic restraints, they launched the Great Leap Forward in 1958 as a campaign of mass political mobilization that would achieve collectivization and expand industrial production through the utilization of marginal resources. The rural communes date from this period and for a number of years functioned as the basic administrative units in the countryside. Their comparatively large size allowed them to support activities such as land reclamation and irrigation projects that would have been beyond the capacity of smaller units. The effects of the Great Leap Forward, however, were generally negative and sometimes disastrous. Uncoordinated local decisions that led to peasants abandoning agriculture to engage in small-scale industrial production disrupted farm output, which, combined with poor weather, led to shortfalls in food production and, it is now known, famine and many deaths. The leadership was divided. Mao was exposed to criticism and in 1959 relinquished the position of head of state, while retaining his leadership of the CCP. The Great Leap Forward ended in 1960, replaced by more cautious policies intended to restore the economy. Another casualty of the experiment was the PRC's alliance with the Soviet Union. Angered by China's 'adventurism' and claims to be advancing towards communism, it withdrew its technical advisers in 1960.

Mao's fears that Soviet-style revisionism and the ascendancy of the bureaucracy in China would blunt and dominate the zeal with which the PRC had been founded drove him to an even more extreme campaign. From **Shanghai** he launched the **Cultural Revolution**, calling on the nation's youth to be successors to the first revolution. For two years from 1966 a violent struggle spread across China as the Red Guards attacked those in positions of authority in the Party and state bureaucracy, work units, universities and the arts, or fought with each other. Several highly placed veteran leaders were ousted, including the head of state Liu Shaoqi and **Deng Xiaoping**, secretary-general of the CCP. Many lives were lost, and education and research were disrupted in many areas, though not in all. In 1964 the PRC had tested its first atomic bomb, and in 1967 followed this with its first test of a hydrogen bomb. The army did not participate in the criticism campaigns and in 1968 was ordered to intervene to end the chaos.

By 1969 the worst phase of the Cultural Revolution was over and the Red Guards were sent to the countryside to learn from the peasants. Right up to the time of Mao's death, in 1976, a struggle continued between his supporters who, like him, wanted political fervour to be the leading element in national life, and those, like Zhou and Deng Xiaoping (reinstated in 1973 as Vice-Premier), who sought to steer the country towards a more profitable course. In early 1975, one year before his death, Zhou Enlai proposed a modernizing programme in agriculture, industry, national defence, and science and technology. It was not taken up. In the April following his death in January 1976, demonstrations in **Tiananmen** Square in Beijing to mourn Zhou were dispersed, and Deng Xiaoping was demoted for the second time.

Mao died on 9 September 1976 and almost immediately thereafter moves were made to close the era associated with him. His closest supporters, who included his widow, were arrested. **Hua Guofeng**, chosen by Mao as his successor after his earlier choice **Lin Biao** had apparently defected and perished in 1971 in an air crash, assumed all top posts, but from 1977 had to contend with Deng Xiaoping, who was restored to the post of Vice-Premier in that year. Between 1978 and 1981 necessary processes of 'reversing verdicts' on events earlier judged harmful, of rehabilitating individuals who had been persecuted, of 'removing labels' from formerly discredited social groups and of reassessing Mao's contribution all took place. Mao was held to have led the PRC well in the early stages of its history, but to have failed it in the last 20 years of his life. The Cultural Revolution was denounced as 10 lost years and its arch supporters were tried and executed or sentenced to prison. The 'four modernizations' proposed by Zhou Enlai were revived and became the basis of a far-reaching programme of change in the country's economic and social life that was formally endorsed by the CCP in December 1978. Indeed, the PRC over the past 25 years has been largely occupied with implementing economic reform and with coping with the new situations and problems that reform has given rise to.

The change in the country's course was not welcomed by all when it was first proposed, and differences have continued to surface between those in the leadership who want to move ahead rapidly with modernization and those who resist too fast a pace. The uneven results of economic reforms have added to such doubts. The rationale of economic modernization is to raise the people's living standards and ensure the state's security. Many people, especially those living in the eastern coastal provinces, have benefited greatly, particularly those who have been able to engage in some form of private enterprise; but those living in the inland regions and rural areas or working in the state sector have not fared so well. The current leadership under Hu Jintao is thought to favour a more balanced approach that sets the gains of economic progress against the need to redress disparities in income and in access to health care.

Changes in the material and social life of many Chinese have been profound, but have not been accompanied by equivalent movement in the country's political strcucture. The leadership that embarked on economic modernization in the late 1970s was resolved that it should proceed under Party control. There was to be no corresponding enlargement of political activity. Thus, the campaign that began in late 1978 through posters on 'Democracy Wall' in central Beijing was tolerated so long as it confined itself to criticism of the excesses of the Cultural Revolution, but was suppressed when it started to challenge the socialist system as a whole. The theme of a more democratic form of government for China as a 'fifth moderniza-tion' re-emerged in the late 1980s, both at a high level among factions in the leadership and in the form of student demonstrations in various parts of China in 1986–87. It was suppressed in a campaign against 'bourgeois liberalization' that brought down the Party general secretary, **Hu Yaobang**, in 1987. The call for democracy was taken up again, together with complaints over corruption and demands for a dialogue with leaders, by students in Beijing in April–June 1989. Again, some elements in the leadership, notably Hu's successor **Zhao Ziyang**, expressed some sympathy with the students; but on the night of 3–4 June tanks and soldiers cleared Tiananmen Square, which the demonstrators had occupied, killing an undetermined number of people. Zhao lost all of his positions, and a harder political line prevailed under the new CCP general secretary **Jiang Zemin** and the new Premier **Li Peng**. The power of the state has been challenged again more recently by proponents of the Chinese Democratic Party in 1998, by the quasi-religious movement **Falungong** between 1999 and 2002, and by threats of Muslim secessionism in **Xinjiang**.

The CCP, while insisting on its leading role, has in fact undergone a certain amount of change. During the Cultural Revolution CCP structures were dismantled and only in 1980 were the Central Committee secretariat and the post of secretary-general restored. Moves were made thereafter to promote the participation of younger, more professionally qualified Party members. In 1987 the CCP's then secretary-general, Zhao Ziyang, urged a separation of Party and state functions to allow a more professional approach in work situations. Aware that the Party, although retaining its hold on power, might no longer command the support it once had, Jiang Zemin launched a campaign in 2000 to make the CCP more representative of the interests of all Chinese. In 2001 it took the step of allowing business people to apply for membership and thereby moved away from its basic role of champion of the peasants and proletariat.

Recent developments: An abiding concern in recent years has been to ensure a smooth transition of power from older to younger generations of powerholders. In 2002 the 16th Party Congress allowed Jiang Zemin to relinquish his post of secretary-general of the CCP Central Committee in favour of Hu Jintao, a member of the group known as the 'fourth generation'. Since 2003 Hu has also been chairman of the PRC, i.e. head of state. Another 'fourth generation' official, **Wen Jiabao**, became Premier in 2003. In September 2004 Jiang Zemin finally stepped down from his last remaining post, that of chairman of the CMC (the organ directing the armed forces). His place was taken by Hu Jintao, who thus now holds the highest Party, state and military offices. In October 2003 China succeeded in putting its first astronaut, Yang Liwei, an airforce pilot, into space in the Shenzhou 5 spacecraft. The PRC had first embarked on a space programme in the 1970s, relaunched it in 1992 and plans further space missions. It is the third country after the USA and Russia to send a manned spacecraft into orbit. The award of the 2008 Summer Olympics to Beijing can be expected to boost the country's economic activity and its international profile.

International relations and defence: In the 55 years of its existence the PRC's relations with the rest of the world have passed through several phases. Chinese foreign policy has sometimes been reactive, but the PRC, while largely avoiding 'foreign adventures', has also contributed by its actions to the evolution of international events. It has done so in response to several basic, interrelated requirements: defence of the PRC's borders; its rivalry with the **'Republic of China'** on Taiwan; and its desire for independence and respect. The memory of past humiliations at the hands of foreign powers has to some extent shaped its attitudes towards the rest of the world. A further element in the PRC's style of foreign policy is the formal nature in which it may be expressed. A decision is made in support of a principle, such as the **Five Principles of Peaceful Co-existence**, or of a theory or world view, such as the three worlds theory and the theory of multipolarity. At the same time, much skilful diplomacy goes on behind the scenes to keep an important relationship alive. With others, especially in the 1950s–1970s, the PRC cultivated a dual approach of official and informal contacts that allowed state-to-state dealings to be pursued while support was given to revolutionary and anti-colonial movements in many parts of the world. PRC aid was directed, for instance, towards countries in Africa where the Tan-Zam railway became an aid project in 1967, despite the upheaval of the Cultural Revolution within the PRC that impinged even on foreign relations. (All but one of the PRC's ambassadors were recalled during those years.)

The PRC's defence of its national integrity and interests has sometimes led it into confrontation with its neighbours. Thus it pre-empted any hostile advance on its border with the **Korean peninsula** by its participation in the **Korean War** (1950–53). In 1962 it fought with India over the demarcation of disputed frontiers at the western and eastern ends of the Himalayas. Similar border clashes with the then Soviet Union occurred in 1969 on the **Ussuri river**. Irritation with Viet Nam's invasion of the PRC's ally Cambodia in 1978 led it into a limited invasion of Viet Nam in 1979. The PRC maintains an active presence in various **islands in the South China Sea** that are also claimed by Taiwan and several of its south-east Asian neighbours. It has warned Britain against any 'interference' in its management of Hong Kong since the former colony's reversion to China in 1997. (The former Portuguese-administered region of Macao reverted in 1999.) In 1999 Chinese anger at the US bombing of the country's embassy in Belgrade manifested itself in demonstrations.

The installation of a rival government on Taiwan in 1949 under the Nationalist leader **Chiang Kai-shek**, in the retained name of the 'Republic of China', has remained a constant affront to the PRC. It maintains the right to reunite Taiwan with the mainland, if necessary by force, but has to judge the feasibility of doing this in the light of possible international reaction, particularly from the USA. As in many situations, the PRC has mounted a dual strategy of persuasion and threat. From 1954 until 1979 it shelled the **offshore islands** attached to Taiwan, and in 1996 fired missiles into the seas around Taiwan to show its displeasure at the first direct presidential elections held on Taiwan; but in recent years has used the concept of 'one country, two systems' as applied in Hong Kong and Macao in an attempt to reassure Taiwan Chinese. On the diplomatic front the PRC has lobbied hard, since it was accorded the 'China' seat in the **United Nations** in 1971, to have the 'ROC' excluded from membership of international organizations; and the majority of states now recognize only the PRC. In a few areas, such as representation at the Olympic Games, a formula acceptable to both countries has been devised.

The PRC's most intense relations, aside from Taiwan, have been with the former Soviet Union, the USA and Japan. From the 1920s the Chinese Communists had dealt with the Soviet Communist apparatus, not always harmoniously. In 1949, as the USA and many other Western countries, though not all, refused to recognize the new regime, the PRC was obliged to turn to the Soviet Union and Eastern Europe for material support and professional advice, and a Sino-Soviet friendship treaty was signed in 1950. The relationship was never easy and by the late 1950s was foundering amid disagreement over policies towards US imperialism and progress towards socialism/communism and over Khrushchev's attack on Stalin at the 20th Soviet Party Congress in 1956. The **Sino–Soviet dispute** became entrenched in 1960 and the relationship, although sustained by unpublicized negotiations, deteriorated considerably into a PRC fear of Soviet military aggression after the Soviet invasion of Czechoslovakia in 1968 and actual border clashes in 1969. The collapse of communism in Eastern Europe and the Soviet Union by 1991, although it unsettled the Chinese, did remove the threat of a strong Soviet Union and led eventually to a more relaxed relationship between the PRC and the Soviet Union's successor state, the Russian Federation. Border demarcation issues were largely settled, and in 2001 the two countries signed a new treaty of partnership and friendship.

The PRC's relations with the USA have to some extent been a function of its relationship with the Soviet Union, and the PRC has probably benefited most when a three-way strategy prevailed. In 1949 China had hoped to receive American understanding, but the violent US anti-communism of the early 1950s, together with the Korean War, militated against that, and the USA renewed its commitment to the 'ROC'. In 1955 the PRC's offer of bilateral talks with the USA at ambassadorial level was followed up for a while in Geneva, Switzerland. Such discussions were initiated again in Warsaw, Poland, in 1968. In 1972 the then US President, Richard Nixon, visited the PRC. The communiqué issued confirmed the view held on both sides of the Taiwan Straits that Taiwan was part of China. Full diplomatic relations between the PRC and the USA were established in 1979 and formal US links with the 'ROC' were broken. The PRC and the USA have maintained a mutually watchful line on Taiwan ever since. The PRC's firing of missiles towards Taiwan in 1996 was matched by the dispatch of US aircraft carriers into the area. A collision in April 2001 between a US surveillance aircraft operating not far from the Chinese coast and a PRC plane that was monitoring it, together with the willingness of the Bush Administration to meet the 'ROC''s request for weaponry, led to a strained period in the Sino-US relationship. There is also no doubt that the PRC is wary of US supremacy and resentful of US insistence on making an issue of human rights. At the same time, it recognizes the value of the USA as a restraining presence in the Asia-Pacific region and as an export market.

The PRC's relationship with Japan has, perhaps, remained the most uneasy of its international contacts. Diplomatic relations were established in 1972 and a peace treaty was signed between the two countries in 1978. The PRC shares, however, in the general apprehension among East and south-east Asian countries over a possible resurgence of Japanese militarism. At the same time, Japan's technical expertise has been a lure for the PRC, and a large element in Sino-Japanese dealings has been trade. Indeed, it would be fair to say that the PRC's foreign policies as a whole over the past 25 years have been heavily weighted by issues of trade and modernization.

The PRC's defence expenditure is estimated to have been 3.9% of its gross domestic product in 2003. Following high-level decisions taken in 2002 and 2003, it is reducing its vast armed forces, whose strength is currently estimated at 2,255,000, by approximately one-fifth, to assist a programme of modernization. Around 1m. are thought to be conscripts, who are chosen selectively and serve two years. Reserve militia forces may number 800,000. The PRC navy is formed of three fleets. The PRC's strategic defence capability includes about 450 ballistic missiles, many of them short-range. Testing of missiles was first announced in 1980. Substantial purchases have been made of Russian equipment in recent years to boost modernization, and domestic production is proceeding. The PRC has also supplied arms and equipment to countries in North Africa, the Persian (Arabian) Gulf region and the Middle East and, it is thought, nuclear technology to several countries, including Pakistan and Iran.

China, People's Republic of, Economy

Political and economic life have been closely entwined in the **People's Republic of China (PRC)**, where, in Marxist terms, people were long defined by their work and social category, and economic policy was a function of political theory. State intervention in all aspects of the nation's life, including economic activity, was, moreover, a feature of the imperial system in **China**. Tradition thus combined with ideology to ensure that the PRC had a centrally planned economy directed by the **Chinese Communist Party (CCP)** when the new republic was established in 1949.

Since 1978 the extent of central planning has diminished in favour of increasing private enterprise, and the state no longer involves itself directly in all branches of economic activity but generally takes a supervisory role. The CCP continues none the less to oversee the gradual transformation, often through experimental channels, of the economy, with the aim of providing a measure of stability. The PRC still has a mixed economy, with a continuing state sector alongside a non-state sector. The country is implementing its Tenth Five-Year Plan (2001–05). It is currently enjoying a period of sustained growth in gross domestic product (GDP), the rate of which in 2003 was 9.1%.

GNI: US $1,400,000m. (2003); *GNI per caput:* US $1,100 (2003); *GDP:* US $1,400,000m. (2003); *GDP per caput:* US $1,115 (2003); *exports:* US $249,131m. (2000); *imports:* US $214,657m. (2000); *currency:* renminbi (plural: renminbi; commonly known as the yuan; US $1 = 8.28 yuan).

For nearly three decades from 1949 the economy of the PRC was run as a command economy, with public ownership of the means of production and centralization of decisions. The First Five-Year Plan was introduced in 1953. Soviet patterns were influential during the 1950s, leading to an emphasis on heavy industry, with new projects often located in inland areas, and the creation of ministries to direct various industries. Land reform was a preliminary to the gradual collectivization of agricultural production, but output remained insufficient. In 1958 **Mao Zedong** broke with the principle of central planning and management and the Soviet model to place the initiative for improving both agricultural and industrial productivity in local hands. The country was to 'walk on two legs', one of them modern technology and heavy industry, the other local responsibility and innova-tion. Mao's Great Leap Forward, however, could not be sustained, and in 1960 direction of the economy passed back to the professional technocrats. In the early 1960s greater emphasis was placed on development of the agricultural sector. The **Cultural Revolution**, launched in 1966, was not primarily aimed against the economy, but it disrupted transport and the production of raw materials and seriously damaged the research sector as intellectuals and specialists were targeted. (The big exception was the nuclear programme, which was clearly shielded against Red Guard attack.) By 1969 the most violent phase of the Cultural Revolution was over, and the Fourth Five-Year Plan (1971–75) called for a return to central economic planning.

Two years after Mao's death in 1976 the CCP Central Committee, in a plenary session held in December 1978, indicated a new direction for the country of modernization and economic reform and an end to political campaigns. A number of reforms had been proposed by the mid-1980s, even if they were only imple-mented over a number of years. Rises in state purchase prices for agricultural products and the introduction of greater monetary incentives for workers were soon enacted. Agriculture was placed on a family basis instead of being carried out collectively, and a contract responsibility system was implemented for farmers, who agreed to meet a state-imposed quota in return for being able to sell any surplus at local free markets. Agricultural land is now owned by villages, which contract it out to individual families. Diversification of the rural economy was proposed in the form of rural collective enterprises producing light industrial goods, a model taken up a few years later by urban collective enterprises. Responsibility for much economic planning was devolved down to provincial level and enterprise managers acquired more authority as well as responsibility for the prosperity of their business. Labour recruitment moved from a system of allocation to one of contracts for new workers, and the possibility of dismissal materialized. Experiments to raise state revenue involved the issue of government bonds and the payment of taxes by state-owned enterprises in place of turning over all profits to the state. In a move to encourage investment from overseas, a law permitting the formation of joint ventures was enacted in 1979, and four **Special Economic Zones** were set up from 1980. These early initiatives led to rapid annual growth rates in both agriculture and manufacturing in the period from the late 1970s until the mid-1980s, improved productivity and an increase in incomes and the value of retail sales. They also brought problems of inflation and difficult adjustments in the price system as prices in the planned sector were gradually brought into line with market prices. Other constraints became apparent in difficulties in the supply and transport of raw materials. By the late 1980s the economic growth rate was slowing and recession loomed. The events of June 1989 in **Tiananmen** Square further unsettled the domestic scene.

In a bid to stimulate the economy **Deng Xiaoping**, although technically retired from political life, pushed for the implementation of a 'socialist market economy' against more conservative opposition. In 1992 his proposals for continuing economic reform were accepted by the 14th Congress of the CCP. Deng's insistence on rapid economic development is still being discussed, but more in terms of its impact on society and the environment. In the short term the ensuing overheating of the economy had to be brought under control, and the PRC then found itself embroiled in the **Asian financial crisis** of 1997–98. Its export markets in Asia shrank under the impact of the crisis and foreign direct investment from Asian sources temporarily ceased. It did not, however, devalue its currency. The economy none the less continued to decelerate, prompting further restructuring. In 1998, in a move to further loosen direct central control, corporate state-controlled institutions replaced the central ministries that had regulated whole industries. Such corporate bodies and other big companies now offer shares on the stock market that first emerged in the PRC in 1990. Measures to stimulate the economy have taken the form of proactive fiscal policies, a willingness to record a budget deficit, and government spending on large infrastructure projects, especially in the less-favoured western regions in a 'Great opening of the west', as well as continued spending on state-owned enterprises (SOEs). Party and state congresses in 2002 and 2003 have brought in new leaders from the top levels downwards and authorized continuing privatization and further reforms in the taxation and banking sectors. In 2001 the PRC was admitted to the **World Trade Organization**. Membership will oblige it to open up its internal markets, services and distribution networks. It will take further time for the effect on the internal economy to become clear, but the expectation is that it will induce greater competition and less protectionism among domestic enterprises and will integrate domestic markets into the international economy.

One of the biggest problems for the PRC in managing the transition to a mixed economy continues to be the SOEs. From an early point it was clear that the state-owned sector would present a problem to reformers. The enterprises, varying greatly in size and scope, still employ large numbers of people—up to one-half of the urban workforce—but now contribute less than the non-state sector of the economy to the value of industrial output. They often serve heavy industry or industries of strategic state importance or produce goods not offered by the private sector. They retain considerable fixed assets, in the form of housing, nursery schools and clinics for their employees, for whom they also provide pensions. It is this social aspect of their functioning that makes it so difficult to dismantle them rapidly, since any contraction in their functioning threatens to bring with it unemployment and social dislocation. At the same time, they are costly to retain and, when failing, deprive the state of revenues. The banking sector has been obliged to provide financial support for SOEs through the provision of loans. Many of these, however, are non-performing and consequently a burden on the banks; and the government still has to subsidize the state-owned sector heavily. A law permitting bankruptcy was introduced in the mid-1980s but does not appear to have been widely used. In 1988 independent managers were put into the SOEs to improve their administration. A number of smaller enterprises have been privatized or converted to joint ownership. In 1998 a three-year programme of reform for the sector was initiated, involving the restructuring of a number of large and medium-sized SOEs operating mainly in industries considered to be of strategic value. The aim is that a limited number of such concerns should operate on a commercial basis under state control. Effective reform of the state-owned sector is dependent on successful reorganization of such social elements as housing, health-care and pensions, and on the effective containment of unemployment brought about by any shrinkage in the SOEs.

The health of the PRC's economy is becoming more dependent on its foreign trade. This has now attained a volume of US \$474,300m. (2001). Until the 1980s the pattern of the PRC's foreign trade followed the former Soviet model of large foreign trade corporations that interacted between foreign clients and domestic buyers or producers. Such a system protected the domestic market from competition, but at the same time isolated it from new technical developments that might have allowed heavy industry in particular to advance. By the early 1980s an alternative model had been adopted, that of export-led economic growth such as other East Asian countries had followed. Foreign direct investment was also welcomed. Many foreign-funded enterprises are active in the export-import market. The PRC initially took the traditional route of light industrial goods, textiles and clothing, processed foodstuffs and craft products as the basis of its trade drive, and is still an important producer of cheap consumer goods. It also exports raw materials and minerals, as well as luxury goods such as furs. Provincial administrations and some enterprises now have authority to conduct their own foreign trade. More recently, the shift has been away from traditional export lines towards manufactured goods such as machinery and electronic equipment, a course followed earlier by the PRC's neighbours Japan and the Republic of Korea. In 2000 the PRC's principal trading partners were, in descending order, Japan, the USA, the European Union and **Hong Kong**.

The size and diversity of the PRC's economy makes the country a major player on the global scene. It is a big recipient of inward investment. The vitality of the non-state or alternative sector, built on rural and urban collective enterprises, free-market trade, private businesses and now state-controlled corporations and foreign-funded enterprises, accounts for much of the PRC's economic health. Price controls have almost all been lifted. New industries, such as information technology, electronics and automobiles, are starting to replace the former heavy industries that were once the mainstay of the economy. Other important industries remain those engaged in machine-building, petroleum extraction and refining, and construction. Energy is still a problem area, as there is much dependence on coal, and the state-run media issued warnings in mid-November 2004 of coming power shortages during the winter months. The country's transport and communications systems are further weak points. Differences in development between the prosperous coastal areas and the more poorly endowed inland regions are a cause of concern to the government and a subject of unofficial anxiety. For the time being the government will also have to continue to run a budget deficit and absorb the costs of the unprofitable state-owned sector. Growth, however it can be stimulated, would appear to remain a necessity if the PRC is to carry the country with its economic reforms. At the same time, it must guard against the economy overheating and to that end has raised interest rates.

China, Republic of (ROC, 1912–49)

Da chung-hua min-kuo/Da zhonghua minguo

Name given to the republic established on the mainland of **China** in 1912 following the overthrow in 1911 of the Qing dynasty that had ruled China since 1644.

The provisional President of the first republic was Sun Yat-sen, who was also a co-founder of the Nationalist **Kuomintang (KMT)** party. In 1913 the warlord Yuan Shih-kai seized and held control of the new republic until his death in 1916, and dissolved the KMT. Nationalist leadership was slowly restored in the face of the rival warlord government in the capital, **Beijing**. Sun Yat-sen died in 1925. The KMT's new head, **Chiang Kai-shek**, moved against his northern rivals in 1926, turning in the process against the **Chinese Communist Party**, his erstwhile partners in a United Front, establishing his new capital at **Nanjing** and subduing Beijing in 1928. From that year the Republic of China (ROC), under the leadership of Chiang

Kai-shek and the Nationalist government, represented China to the world. It was continually challenged by the Chinese Communists and from 1931 had to contend with Japan's growing encroachment on the mainland. None the less, it was the ROC that joined the Allies from 1941 during the Second World War and was represented at the 1943 **Cairo Conference**. Under Japanese invasion, the ROC had to move its capital from Nanjing, first to **Guangzhou**, then to **Chongqing**. In 1949 impending Communist victory in the civil war that had been fought out between the Communists and the Nationalists since 1946 compelled Chiang to remove his forces and followers, numbering around 2m., to the island of **Taiwan**. There he reinstalled the **'Republic of China' ('ROC')** as a rival administration to the **People's Republic of China (PRC)**.

The PRC has no objection to the use of the title Republic of China to describe the government that, with some interruptions, administered China between 1912 and 1949. It does, however, lobby against the continued application of the formula 'ROC' to the authorities currently installed on Taiwan. Until 1971 the 'ROC' held the 'China' seat at the **United Nations**, when it was replaced by the PRC, which has since resisted all attempts by the regime on Taiwan to be readmitted to world organizations as an independent state. At the same time, the PRC objects to the concept of an independent 'Republic of Taiwan', preferring some formula such as 'Chinese Taipei' or 'China-Taiwan'. In practice, the name Taiwan is frequently applied to the society and government existing on the island.

'China, Republic of' ('ROC', 1949–)

Regime established in 1949 on the island of **Taiwan** and a few smaller islands by the Chinese Nationalist leader, **Chiang Kai-shek**.

Area (island of Taiwan, Penghu (Pescadores) Islands, **offshore islands** of Kinmen (Jinmen, also known as Quemoy) and Matsu (Mazu) and several smaller islands): 36,000 sq km; *capital:* **Taipei** (Taibei); *population:* 22,405,568 (2001), more than 98% **Han Chinese**, less than 2% aboriginal peoples; *official language:* Chinese; *religion:* **Daoism** (42%), **Buddhism** (36%), I-Kuan Tao (7.8%), **Catholic** and **Protestant Christianity** (3.6%), **Islam**.

The Constitution of the 'ROC' was first adopted in late 1946, but has been amended several times since 1991. The government displays characteristics of both the presidential and cabinet systems of administration and functions through five *yuan* or councils. The President, who is head of state and commander of the armed forces, has since 1996 been elected by direct vote for a four-year term and is eligible for re-election to a second term. He or she is also empowered to nominate the Premier and convene the National Assembly. This latter body, an elected organ, consists of 300 delegates elected by proportional representation. It is now convened in a limited number of circumstances of national importance to consider and vote upon amendments to the Constitution, proposals to alter the national territory or calls for the impeachment of the President or Vice-President. The National Assembly's term of office is confined to no more than one month. The state's highest legislative organ and other elected body is the **Legislative Yuan**. It is empowered to change government policy and comprises 225 members elected through a combination of direct voting and proportional representation. Eight members are elected from and by each of two further groups: aborigines and **overseas Chinese**. Members of the Legislative Yuan serve for three years and are eligible for re-election. The **Executive Yuan**, the state's highest administrative organ, reports to the Legislative Yuan and supervises the ministries and commissions. The Judicial Yuan has responsibility for the administration of justice. Its 15 Grand Justices have powers of judicial review and are nominated and appointed by the President for a period of nine years. The Examination Yuan administers recruitment into the civil service. The Control Yuan has powers of impeachment, censure and audit over public functionaries. It comprises 29 members nominated and appointed by the President for a term of six years.

The 'ROC' is administered as 16 counties, two special municipalities, Taipei and **Kaohsiung**, and five other municipalities.

The 'ROC', or more simply Taiwan, has passed through two broad political phases since Chiang Kai-shek re-established the Nationalist government on the island in 1949, declaring it the legitimate government of the whole of China with Taipei the temporary capital, and resumed the office of President in 1950. His death in 1975 did not lead to immediate change, but since the mid-1980s the political scene has become increasingly active. Today, in place of the former single authority of the **Kuomintang (KMT)** or Nationalist Party, a wide range of parties represent a spectrum of objectives. The diversity of views is in part the outcome of a drive towards greater popular participation in political activity and fuller accountability in political institutions. It also reflects the particular composition of Taiwan society, its experiences during the past 50 years and the ever-present rivalry with the **People's Republic of China (PRC)**. In 1949 a national government dominated by mainland Chinese was imposed on the provincial Taiwan administration. Today the population is to some extent still divided by mainland/island identification. The need to respond to the PRC's insistence on reunification, on terms that do not rule out the use of force, has developed into a broad debate on the desire of some for reunification, the wish of others for some sort of accommodation with the mainland, and that of others again for independence for Taiwan. This expresses itself in such issues as how to refer to the island, as the 'ROC' or as an independent state of Taiwan. Trading companies on Taiwan, which are now able to deal with the PRC, find the political debate unsettling for business.

The Nationalist Chinese administration in Taiwan began inauspiciously with heavy-handed government that culminated in the 1947 massacre of islanders who had rebelled against mainland control. The KMT admitted responsibility for the incident only in 1992. Although mainlanders were and remain in a minority (they and their descendants account for around 15% of Taiwan's present population), they succeeded in imposing a national government on the island that acted as if still confronted by the enemy. Martial law remained in force from 1949 until 1987;

and the island was subject to Temporary Provisions attached to the Constitution in 1948 and effective during 'the period of mobilization for the suppression of the Communist rebellion'. These measures were rescinded only in 1991. Political representation was for long dominated by KMT members who had been elected to national bodies in 1947 on the mainland and who remained in office with indefinitely extended terms since they could not be replaced, outnumbering Taiwanese representatives. In 1969 supplementary lists brought in new elected representatives who were Taiwanese; but the ageing mainland members were only made to retire in 1991. Underneath this national government a provincial Taiwan government administered what was regarded as a province of China, until it was brought to an end in 1998. Starting with the election of **Lee Teng-hui**, the Taiwan-born governor of Taiwan, as Vice-President in 1984, native Taiwanese began to move into the higher echelons of the KMT and the administration. After the death in 1988 of **Chiang Ching-kuo**, Chiang Kai-shek's son, who became President three years after his father died, Lee assumed the presidency. In 1990 he was re-elected president for the KMT, the first native Taiwanese to be returned to the office.

The KMT retained its monopoly as a political party until the formation of the **Democratic Progressive Party (DPP)** in 1986 from a number of *'Tangwai'* opposition groups active 'outside the [KMT] party' and representing Taiwanese interests. Although it was illegal at the time (the ban on opposition parties was lifted in 1989), the DPP was allowed to contest partial elections for the Legislative Yuan and the National Assembly, winning about one-quarter of the votes cast. The arrival of opposition parties in 1989 prompted the KMT to seek ways of rejuvenating itself and of widening its appeal among the electorate. The DPP from the outset pushed for an independent Taiwan, a concept that the KMT, dedicated to some form of reunification with the mainland, could not tolerate. As the electoral process moved in the first half of the 1990s towards direct elections to legislative bodies and the presidency, the DPP held its position. Lee Teng-hui was returned in 1996 as the first directly elected President, but in the 2000 presidential elections was replaced by **Chen Shui-bian** of the DPP; and in the 2001 elections for the Legislative Yuan, the DPP emerged as the largest single party, though without an overall majority, pushing the KMT into second place. The KMT's long hold on Taiwan politics had been broken.

In the approach to the 2000 presidential elections Chen Shui-bian undertook not to declare formal independence for Taiwan unless the PRC launched an attack and in office appears to have softened somewhat his stance on independence. The DPP itself publicly favours self-determination for the people of Taiwan, membership in the **United Nations (UN)** and the establishment of an independent Taiwan following a referendum. Chen has lost some popularity for his muted line on independence, but also for his wavering commitment on retaining Taiwan's nuclear power-free status and for his handling of the economy. None the less, he was re-elected as President in March 2004.

Domestic issues and the behaviour of political parties, especially complaints of corruption, occupy much of the political ground together with concerns over the appropriate response to the PRC. In the freer atmosphere since 1989, when the formation of political parties became legitimate, the number of registered parties has multiplied and old allegiances have been terminated as new parties have been formed. In the early 1990s the KMT lost its unity on the issue of Taiwan's identity and in 1993 a faction broke away from Lee Teng-hui's leadership to form the **New Party**. This favours reconciliation with the mainland. The Taiwan Independence Party was established in 1996 after breaking with the DPP. In the 2000 presidential campaign **James Soong** contested the presidential election as an independent after having failed to obtain the KMT nomination. He secured second place and immediately established his own party, the **People First Party**. It works closely with the KMT. Lee Teng-hui himself moved away from the KMT after 2000 to offer his backing to President Chen Shui-bian and his support for a new group, the **Taiwan Solidarity Union (TSU)**, that attracted members from both the KMT and the DPP. These various parties have grouped into two broad coalitions, the **Pan-Blue coalition** made up of the KMT, the People First Party and the New Party; and the **Pan-Green coalition**, grouping the DPP, the TSU and the Taiwan Independence Party. On the issue of relations with the PRC, the two coalitions favour differing policies. The Pan-Blue Coalition takes a softer line on reunification and supports greater economic interaction with the mainland. The Pan-Greens tend to favour the cause of Taiwan independence over a Chinese solution. The line separating the two groups appears to be following mainland/island identities. The Pan-Blues draw their support in the main from those who left the mainland in 1949 and their descendants; the Pan-Greens enjoy more support from native Taiwanese.

Relations with the PRC: Relations between the two states that confront each other across the Taiwan Straits have always been uneasy. Between 1954 and 1979 the PRC reinforced its political and diplomatic hostility by regular shelling of the offshore islands, and has refused to renounce the threat of military force against Taiwan if the island were to declare independence or refuse to co-operate. From time to time the relationship expands into a triangular affair that includes the USA, and the issue of Chinese representation in world bodies gives it a global dimension. Since the mid-1980s a more complicated situation has emerged as politics in Taiwan have developed into a multi-party activity that has given rise to a number of responses to the single mainland position of one China that should be reunified on the PRC's terms. For long the KMT maintained the mirror position: the 'ROC' alone was the legitimate government of China and would pursue reunification under its aegis. Any talk of independence for Taiwan was as repellent to the 'ROC' as it was, and still is, to the PRC. The PRC's successful campaign in 1971 to have the 'China' seat in the UN reassigned away from the 'ROC' to itself has undermined the claim of the 'ROC', but it has taken longer for some elements in the KMT to accept the situation. Now the relationship with the mainland is no longer expresssed in terms of action against a rebellious faction and the PRC's existence is admitted, even if the legitimacy of its government may not be recognized. More irritating to the PRC is the emergence of an independence faction in Taiwan that insists relations should be on a state-to-state basis.

The PRC has not shifted from its basic position of one China under its control, but has deployed a number of tactics to win Taiwan's acceptance of that position, so far without success. From 1978 it started to suggest various ideas on a possible future relationship that involved forms of autonomy. Among these was a proposal, suggested in 1981, that Taiwan should become a **Special Administrative Region** of the PRC similar to what was being advocated for **Hong Kong** and **Macao** in discussion of those territories' future. Proposals put forward in the early 1980s offered a high degree of autonomy such that the island would retain its own armed forces and flag, exercise the power of legal decisions and issue its own passports among other freedoms. The PRC's conditions were that it alone should speak for China in international affairs and that Taiwan should be renamed Chinese-Taipei or China-Taiwan. In 1984, following the conclusion of the Sino-UK Joint Agreement on Hong Kong, the PRC promoted the concept of 'one country, two systems'. The KMT, still in control of the island's politics, refused to abandon its long-held principles on reunification. In 1986, however, the two regimes found themselves negotiating in Hong Kong over the return of a cargo plane that had been diverted to the mainland by a defecting Taiwan pilot. The following year, 1987, marked the first relaxation on visits by Taiwan citizens to the mainland, which led to visits in both directions. The introduction, in 1986, of a measure of political plurality in Taiwan marked the beginning of a range of counter-proposals to the mainland Chinese position. In 1987 the DPP opposition party first openly addressed the issue of independence. Lee Teng-hui of the KMT, who by 1989 had succeeded as President, proposed a 'one China, two governments' formula and in 1990 offered government-to-government discussions with the PRC. The PRC refused these, insisting it would only negotiate on a party-to-party basis with the KMT. In a bid to reduce tension, Lee Teng-hui in 1991 formally terminated the continuing state of war with the mainland, but also intimated that Taiwan should be considered a *de facto* sovereign and autonomous country. In response, the PRC warned that it might resort to the use of force if Taiwan tried to establish itself as a separate state. Neither the PRC nor Taiwan was prepared to move from its basic position and continued, throughout the remainder of the 1990s, to restate and reformulate their proposals. By 1999 the KMT had itself adopted the 'two-state' approach to intra-Chinese relations. The PRC made it clear that it did not favour any kind of confederal solution to the problem. On three occasions during the decade the PRC conducted military exercises and missile tests in the areas surrounding Taiwan in shows of displeasure and intimidation. At the same time, discussions proceeded between the two states, in **Beijing**, Taiwan and Singapore, on matters of trade and social and 'consular' issues. Dedicated organizations were established to handle these discussions, on the Taiwan side the National Unification Council, the Mainland Affairs Council and the Straits Exchange Foundation, all set up in 1990; and on the PRC side the

Association for Relations across the Taiwan Straits, founded in 1991. Trade and investment links seem well established.

Recent developments: The PRC has not withdrawn its threat to use force against Taiwan if the island declares secession or seeks to postpone discussion of reunification. It is now confronted by a situation where its old rival, the KMT, has lost its hold on power and trails the main party in government, the DPP. The increasing multiplicity of political parties in Taiwan, it may be assumed, must oblige the PRC to reconsider its insistence on dealing only with the KMT on a party-to-party basis. The mainland has criticized the current President, Chen Shui-bian, as a troublemaker intent on promoting a separate Taiwan identity. Shortly before Chen's inauguration in May 2004 as re-elected President it issued a statement that threatened war if Chen continued to seek independence, but offered concessions if he accepted the one-China policy. The PRC's intention is doubtless to try to isolate Chen in the political scene. The advent of **Hu Jintao** to the PRC's three top posts in 2003 and 2004 and the withdrawal of **Jiang Zemin** from the scene have been welcomed in Taiwan, since it is thought that Hu may take a less confrontational line towards cross-straits relations than his predecessor did. This hope may lie behind President Chen Shui-bian's invitation in October 2004 to the leadership of the PRC to enter into talks.

Chen Shui-bian was re-elected as President in March 2004 by a narrow margin of 30,000 votes. He and his Vice-President **Annette Lu** were shot at and slightly wounded while campaigning the day before the election. In September 2004 three men were charged with weapons offences in connection with the incident, but have not been linked conclusively with the shooting. Chen's re-election was challenged in the High Court in November 2004 by opposition parties who accuse him of irregularities, including staging the attack on himself. Elections to the Legislative Yuan in early December 2004 led to a set-back for the Pan-Green coalition, which failed to secure a majority.

International relations and defence: The most important external relations of the 'ROC' after its manoeuvring with the PRC, are with the USA. Indeed, a kind of triangular relationship may be said to exist between the two Chinas and the USA. Throughout the 1950s and 1960s the USA provided essential diplomatic, military and economic support to the 'ROC', recognizing the validity of its existence. The PRC's preparations in June 1950 to invade Taiwan were thwarted by the dispatch of the US Seventh Fleet to the Taiwan Straits, and US commitment to the island's protection was reinforced by a mutual security treaty signed in 1954 in the wake of the **Korean War**. By the early 1970s American policies were veering towards recognition of the PRC, a process that culminated in the establishment of full diplomatic relations with the PRC in 1978, the withdrawal of recognition from the 'ROC' and the termination of the mutual security treaty. The USA defined its new relationship with the island in the **Taiwan Relations Act** of 1979. This aimed to give the USA a large measure of flexibility in maintaining active relations with Taiwan, including the provision of military equipment and services 'of a defensive character' and the continuation of investment. The USA also undertook to maintain its capacity to resist any recourse to force that would threaten the security of Taiwan—a clear warning to the PRC. In 1996 President Clinton, invoking the 1979 Act, sent an aircraft carrier into the waters around Taiwan in response to China's decision to conduct missile tests in the Taiwan Straits. The tests marked the PRC's displeasure at the first direct presidential elections on the island. China has since tried to limit the extent of the US contribution to Taiwan's defence capabilities, but has not been able to prevent the delivery of US F-16 fighter aircraft and missile systems to Taiwan during the 1990s and early 2000s, nor continuing US sales of equipment intended to enhance the island's naval and air defence capacity. The USA has repeated its commitment to support Taiwan in the event of Chinese military action against the island, but has, however, declined to provoke the PRC too far and has, for instance, refused to support attempts by the 'ROC' to be readmitted to the UN and has drawn back from sales of equipment with a combat capability. Both Presidents Lee Teng-hui and Chen Shui-bian have visited the USA.

With the change in regime in the late 1980s the 'ROC' assumed a more proactive diplomatic policy of extending or at least maintaining relations with a wide range of countries, sometimes using the offer of aid and investment as an inducement. It has had only varying success in securing diplomatic recognition among a number of small states. The USA keeps an informal presence on the island through the American Institute of Taiwan, and other countries have set up trade and/or cultural centres. In 1997 and 2001 the **Dalai Lama** visited Taiwan. The 'ROC' broke off diplomatic relations with its close neighbour Japan in 1972 when Japan recognized the PRC and did not seek a *rapprochement* until the early 1990s. The relationship became difficult in the mid-1990s with disputes over ownership of the **Diaoyu-Tai/Senkaku islands**, fishing rights and the issue of **comfort women**. In 1998 the 'ROC', in its first legal definition of its sea boundaries, claimed the Diaoyu-Tai islands and Spratly Islands among the **islands in the South China Sea**. It maintains satellite communications and a coastguard presence on Taiping island, the largest of the Spratlys.

The defence budget of the 'ROC' accounted for 2.4% of its gross domestic product in 2003. This was to be augmented by a supplementary 15-year budget announced later in the same year. The island's armed forces total around 290,000, with reserves numbering 1,657,000. Of the 200,000-strong army, between 23,000 and 30,000 are deployed on the offshore islands of Kinmen and Matsu. The navy, numbering 45,000, has one of its bases in the Penghu Islands. The air force (45,000) includes among its fighters French *Mirage* and US F-16 aircraft. Paramilitary groups include 22,000 civilian coastguards, with responsibility for guarding out-lying islands to which Taiwan lays claim.

'China, Republic of', Economy

The 'Republic of China' ('ROC') has managed to counter the political and diplomatic reverses of the past three decades through maintaining a buoyant economy that is still recording positive growth, even if the rate of growth has slowed down. Per caput income stood at US $12,941 in 2001. Largely oriented towards the external world, the economy has prospered through exports and trade. Its trading and investment contacts with the **People's Republic of China (PRC)** have grown considerably since they were first opened up in 1987. In January 2002 the 'ROC' was admitted to the **World Trade Organization (WTO)** as Taiwan.

GNP: US $280,000m. (2003); *GNP per caput:* US $12,410 (2003); *GDP:* US $290,039.5m. (2001); *GDP per caput (at PPP):* US $24,500 (2003); *exports:* US $122,866.4m. (2001); *imports:* US $107,237.4m. (2001); *currency:* New Taiwan dollar (US $1 = NT $33.5 as of 2004).

The agriculture, industry and infrastructure of Taiwan had already been developed to some extent during the Japanese colonial period (1895–1945). US aid and financial support from 1949, when the Chinese Nationalists reinstalled the 'ROC' on the island, allowed the economy to recover rapidly. (US aid between 1951 and 1965 has been estimated at US $1,440m.) An early programme of land reform encouraged increased production among the farmers to whom the land had been largely redistributed and had the effect of pushing former landowners to direct the compensation they had received towards urban entrepreneurship. Economic policy in the 1950s was to favour industrialization through import substitution, which took the form of labour-intensive manufacturing involving low levels of technology. This approach gave way at the end of the decade to a strategy of export-led growth, supported by a variety of government measures, such as fiscal encouragement, and by foreign direct investment. Rather than being entrusted to a few dominant firms, as happened in the Republic of Korea (ROK) with the formation of *chaebol*, Taiwan's industrial base lay, and continues to lie, in the hands of many small- and medium-scale enterprises (SMEs). These account for around 97% of manufacturing enterprises. In the 1970s, in an attempt to deepen the economy, industrialization through the promotion of the heavy industry and chemical sectors was undertaken, but less effectively than in, for example, the ROK, and labour-intensive production of textiles, garments and consumer electrical goods continued to predominate. From the early 1980s machinery and machine tools and information technology were promoted as strategic sectors in a programme of upgrading and diversification. Further high-technology sectors were added later. By the end of the 1990s Taiwan was in third place behind the USA and Japan among manufacturers of information technology products', which became the country's single most important source of foreign exchange. Production is led by specialized research companies, but is still largely undertaken by SMEs; and advanced technology and key components have to be imported from the USA and Japan.

Each stage of Taiwan's development has been supported and to some extent directed by the government, not least through the nurture of a well-educated and skilled workforce. For many decades the country's economic policies succeeded in achieving sustained annual rates of growth that in 1952–1990 fluctuated between 7.9% and 9.8%. During the 1990s the annual growth rate fell to 6.4% and it declined further, to 2.8%, in 2002; but it has since risen slightly, to 3.2% in 2003. Taiwan was not severely affected by the **Asian financial crisis** of 1997–98, but the economy did none the less recede in 2000–2001. The biggest change in the country's economic direction has been its increasingly close interaction with the PRC. Since 1987, when private visits to mainland China were first permitted, trade across the Straits of Taiwan, largely directed through **Hong Kong**, has grown, as reflected in the rise in its value from US $8,100m. in 1991 to US $32,400m. in 2000. 'ROC' investment in enterprises in the PRC has also risen, and 'ROC' businesses now reportedly employ some 5m. Chinese workers. The present fear is that the economy of the 'ROC', already heavily reliant on foreign trade, may be becoming too dependent on its connection with the mainland. The PRC's accession in December 2001 to the WTO, followed by that of the 'ROC' in January 2002, is expected to reinforce this interdependence. In preparation for accession the 'ROC' liberalized its domestic markets and addressed some of the issues, such as protection of intellectual property rights, that had earned it criticism for copyright infringement and pirating. The USA, however, not the PRC, is the biggest trading partner of the 'ROC', followed by Japan. The USA is important as an export market for 'ROC' goods, but trade with Japan includes a large element of high-tech imports from that country. None the less, the foreign trade of the 'ROC' continues to display a surplus. Industrial goods form the chief component in the country's exports— 98% in 2001. 'ROC' businesses have also invested in south-east Asia and in the European Union.

The economy of the 'ROC' has to operate in the almost complete absence of natural resources. In 2000, for instance, it had to import 97% of its total energy supplies. Energy from nuclear sources was developed in the late 1970s–mid-1980s, when it met more than one-half of the country's energy requirements, but since then reliance on nuclear power has become a controversial issue, the share of nuclear energy in power generation has declined, and construction of a fourth nuclear plant has been abandoned. The country's defence needs also place a heavy burden on the economy. Domestic production meets some of the requirements, but much is purchased from foreign suppliers that have included France, and the Netherlands, but primarily from the USA, operating under the terms of the **Taiwan Relations Act** of 1979. The value of US arms deliveries to Taiwan in 2002 was estimated at US $1,100m. Another sector that requires constant attention is the country's infrastructure, which in 1991 was made the subject of a six-year development plan.

The former agricultural base of the economy has shrunk enormously to provide no more than 1.9% of total output in 2001. The land is cultivated intensively, mainly for rice, peanuts and maize. Fruit and sugarcane are further crops and livestock is also reared. Industry's share in output has fallen from a peak of 47.1% in 1986 to just under 31% in 2001. In that year the service sector contributed more than two-thirds of national output and employed 56.5% of the workforce. It is currently the most buoyant sector in the economy.

China Association of Science and Technology (CAST)

Zhongguo kexue jishuxiehui

The China Association of Science and Technology (CAST) owes its origins to the meetings planning the World Council of Scientific Workers' Conference in **Beijing** in 1950, soon after the establishment of the **People's Republic of China (PRC)**. Two organizations developed out of these meetings and the conference: the National Scientific Society and the National Association for the Popularization of Science and Technology. In 1958 these two merged to form CAST. Like all such academic and scientific bodies, CAST came under attack during the **Cultural Revolution**, and only revived in the late 1970s.

CAST is now the most important national institution of scientific and technological workers in the PRC. Its main roles are to encourage academic exchanges in the field of science and technology, to conduct education and training in these fields, to represent the views and concerns of scholars, and to manage national learned societies. It also provides guidance to local science and technology societies. It has 167 affiliated national societies, and nearly 5m. members.

> *Address:* CAST
> 3 Fuxing Rd
> Beijing 100863
> People's Republic of China
> *Tel:* 86-10-6857-1898
> *Fax:* 86-10-6857-1897
> *E-mail:* castint@cast.org.cn
> *Internet:* www.cast.org.cn

China Institute for Contemporary International Relations (CICIR)

Zhongguo xiandai guoji guanxi yanjiusuo

The China Institute for Contemporary International Relations (CICIR) is one of the most important foreign policy think-tanks in the **People's Republic of China (PRC)**. It traces its origins to the 1940s, but in its present form it dates from 1960. Like other academic institutions it closed down almost completely during the **Cultural Revolution**, but revived at the end of the 1970s. The staff are drawn from the Ministry of Foreign Affairs, universities, and other bodies associated with international affairs, and number about 300. They carry out research studies on the politics, economics and strategies of areas of the world of particular interest to the PRC. CICIR reports directly to the **State Council**, but is also believed to have links with the Ministry of State Security, established in the early

1980s. It publishes a journal, *Contemporary International Relations*, in Chinese and English.

Address: A-2 Wanshousi
Haidian District
Beijing 10081
People's Republic of China
Tel: 86-10-6841-8640
Fax: 86-10-6841-8641

Chinese Academy of Sciences (CAS)

Zhongguo kexueyuan

The leading science and technology research institute in the **People's Republic of China (PRC)**.

Founded in 1949 and based on the former **Academia Sinica** and the Peiping (now **Beijing**) Academy of Sciences as well as Soviet models, the Chinese Academy of Sciences (CAS) played a major role in Chinese scientific advances in subsequent years, including the development of the nuclear bomb. Like all such institutions, it suffered badly in the **Cultural Revolution**. Its budget was drastically reduced and many of its staff dispersed to the countryside. Its fortunes revived in the early 1970s, and in 1975 **Hu Yaobang** took over its leadership.

In the late 1970s a programme was implemented to recreate CAS's earlier pre-eminence. It admitted its first post-Cultural Revolution graduate classes in 1978, and began to establish international links in the 1980s. In 1978 also the social science sections became the **Chinese Academy of Social Sciences**, a separate institution. Today, CAS has five research divisions, 108 scientific and technical research bodies, and some 200 science- and technology-related institutions, including universities and publishing houses. It has linked institutions in most PRC provinces. In 2000 it had 58,000 staff, of whom 39,000 were scientific personnel and 34% were women. It awards higher degrees. While in theory subordinate to the State Science and Technology Commission, in practice it reports directly to the PRC's Cabinet, the **State Council**.

Pres.: Prof. Dr Ing. Lu Yongxiang
Address: Chinese Academy of Sciences
52 Sanlihe Rd
Beijing 100864
People's Republic of China
Tel: 86-10-6859-7289
Fax: 86-10-6851-2458
E-mail: info@mail.casipm.ac.cn
Internet: www.cas.ac.cn

Chinese Academy of Social Sciences (CASS)

Zhongguo shehui kexueyuan

The Chinese Academy of Social Sciences (CASS) dates from 1978. The institutions that made up the new academy were originally part of the **Chinese Academy of Sciences**, but all had suffered badly during the **Cultural Revolution**. The creation of CASS, and a meeting held in March 1979 at which the discipline of sociology was formally revived, marked a return to scholarship in the social sciences in **China**. CASS, which is directly under the **State Council**, consists of independent research bodies concentrating on economics and politics, but also including subjects such as sociology and archaeology. It occupies modern premises not far from the centre of **Beijing**, close to the Jiangguomenwai diplomatic quarter, on the site of the old imperial examination halls. During the student demonstrations of 1989 many CASS staff sided with the student demonstrators, and anti-regime banners appeared on the building. For a time after the suppression of the demonstrations units of the **People's Liberation Army** occupied CASS, while many staff members had to write confessions. CASS and most of its staff weathered the storm, however, and it is once again at the forefront of intellectual activity in the **People's Republic of China**.

Address: Chinese Academy of Social Sciences
Jianguomennei dajie 5
Beijing
People's Republic of China
Tel: 86-10-8519-5999
E-mail: wangzhan-wlzx@cass.org.cn
Internet: www.cass.net.cn

Chinese Communist Party (CCP)

Zhongguo gongchangdang

The ruling political party in the **People's Republic of China (PRC)**. The Chinese Communist Party (CCP) has held exclusive power since the establishment of the PRC in 1949 and is closely intermeshed with the country's administration and military. The current secretary-general of the CCP Central Committee, **Hu Jintao**, for instance, also holds the offices of President—head of state—and chairman of the **Central Military Commission**, the top military post. Eight other small political parties, the **democratic parties**, are permitted to function under CCP leadership. Membership of the CCP stood at 66,355,000 at the time of the 16th National Congress of the party in 2002.

The CCP is pyramidal in structure, rising from small 'primary organizations' active in enterprises, government departments, educational establishments, research institutes, villages, army companies and so on, up through county and municipal branches to the provincial and special city (**Beijing**, **Shanghai**, **Tianjin** and

Chongqing) apparatus and finally to the national organization. At each level party committees are elected by general membership meetings for primary organizations, or by party congresses. A similar pyramid exists in the military. At the apex, the national party Congress, meeting once every five years, elects a Central Committee, which in turn produces a smaller Political Bureau or Politburo and its Standing Committee. Day-to-day power resides in the Politburo Standing Committee. The single most powerful party post is that of secretary-general (the post of party chairman was abolished in 1982). The current, 16th Central Committee, elected in 2002, numbers 198 members. From it were elected a 24-strong Politburo and a nine-member Standing Committee of the Politburo. The Central Committee is predominantly male and **Han Chinese** in its composition. The 15 members from national minorities make up 7.5% of the Central Committee, a figure not far removed from the minorities' share of 8.4% of the general population; but the five female members in no way reflect the true proportion of women in the country.

Membership of the CCP is open to those aged 18 years and over among workers, farmers, members of the armed forces, intellectuals (a term that covers a wide range of white-collar jobs) and 'advanced elements of other social strata', but is in practice highly selective. In 2001 **Jiang Zemin**, the then secretary-general of the CCP Central Committee, opened up membership to the 'new classes' of private entrepreneurs and professional people. The Party has attempted to raise the educational and vocational standards of its cadres and to attract younger members. It is aware of the charges of corruption and degeneration among its members that tarnish its image.

The CCP was founded in 1921 in Shanghai at a meeting hailed as the first party Congress and attended by 13 delegates representing 57 Party members. (These appear to be the official figures; other sources give slightly varying statistics.) A branch was active for a while in France, where Chinese students had gone to study. Its founding members were influenced by the success of the 1917 Bolshevik Revolution in Russia and by the May Fourth movement of 1919 in **China**. For the first six years of its existence the CCP allied itself with Chinese workers and, under the influence of Soviet advisers, formed a United Front with the Nationalist **Kuomintang (KMT)**; but when the KMT turned against the Communists in 1927 they retreated into the rural areas and started political work among the peasants. KMT military harassment forced the CCP into the **Long March** of 1934–35, which brought it to **Yanan** in the north-western province of Shaanxi. By the time that the Party had reached its new base, **Mao Zedong**, a founding member, had emerged as its leader and chief ideologue. The years in Yanan allowed him to prepare and refine the new Party to meet the particular needs of China and eventually to take power.

During the first 10 years of the new PRC Mao effected a number of political, economic and social changes and established beyond doubt both his own and the Party's pre-eminence. In 1966, however, he turned against the CCP, which he viewed as bureaucracy-ridden and effete, and through the Red Guard movement of the **Cultural Revolution** mobilized young people to criticize and for a while supplant the working of the Party with revolutionary committees. The sequence of Party congresses was broken between 1956 and 1969 and the CCP structure disrupted. Following Mao's death in 1976 the CCP gradually restored its mechanism and authority. At the third plenum of the 11th CCP Congress in 1978 **Deng Xiaoping** shifted the focus of the Party's work on to economic development and opening up to the outside world, policies the CCP has pursued ever since. The Constitution adopted at the 16th CCP Congress in November 2002 emphasized the urgency of achieving socialist modernization. In place of class struggle, which had featured in the 1969 Party Constitution as the 'principal contradiction' in society, the new Constitution insisted that the gap between the 'ever-growing material and cultural needs of the people and the low level of production' was the 'principal contradiction' of today. It warned that in the process of working towards common prosperity, some areas and some people might 'become rich first', a development that has manifestly come to pass. As a concession to the Party's origins, the Constitution claims that, none the less, China is at the 'primary stage of socialism and will remain so for a long period'. The country is to continue to be guided by Marxism-Leninism, Mao Zedong Thought, Deng Xiaoping Theory and future continuations of the ideology that these three sources represent. While lacking in firm guidance, this prescription will presumably permit maximum flexibility in meeting new situations.

Sec.-Gen of the CCP Central Committee: Hu Jintao
Internet: www.ccponline.net

Chinese language

The largest element in the Sino-Tibetan family of languages, now spoken by around 95% of the population of the **People's Republic of China (PRC)**, in **Taiwan**, **Hong Kong**, **Macao** and Singapore, all of which have predominantly Chinese populations, and by many Chinese emigrant communities. The multiplicity of forms of spoken Chinese leads some to use the term 'Chinese languages'; others refer to 'dialects'. It is a tonal language, consisting of single-syllable words that are uninflected, i.e are without number, case, gender and tense, and which rely often on syntax and context to convey meaning. The elements of the language—structure, grammar, syntax, vocabulary—are largely the same among all Chinese speakers.

The broad distinction in spoken Chinese is between what is now termed standard Chinese, sometimes still Mandarin, spoken north of the **Yangzi river** and west of Hunan Province, and seven other dialects spoken in the south-east of **China**. Standard Chinese can be divided into the northern dialect spoken around the capital **Beijing** and in north-east China, the north-western and south-western dialects and that spoken in eastern areas around **Nanjing**. **Shanghai** and the surrounding region has its own dialect (Wu); Fujian Province has north and south variants of the Min dialect, spoken also in Taiwan and among many emigrant Chinese communities in south-east Asia; the central-south provinces of Jiangxi and Hunan have their own dialects (Gan and Xiang respectively); the **Hakka** people speak their own form of Chinese; and in

Guangdong and Guangxi provinces Yue or Cantonese is spoken. Guangdong has been an area of great migration, and Cantonese is consequently the form of Chinese found in Hong Kong and Macao and among many **overseas Chinese**.

Modern standard Chinese is used as the official language and lingua franca throughout the country. Known as *putonghua*, or 'common words', it is based on the northern dialect, takes Beijing speech as its phonetic standard and uses the grammatical norms of representative modern literature. An older term *guoyu*, 'national language', is used on Taiwan.

The unifying element in Chinese is its written form, which is invariable and comprehensible to all literate Chinese. Chinese is written in characters, each of which corresponds to a single-syllable word. The written language is of great antiquity and is known to have been in use since *c.* 1300 BC. By the 6th century AD the form of script still most commonly used was already emerging. The Chinese written language was used extensively by the educated classes in Japan, the **Korean peninsula** and Viet Nam. In 1956 simplified characters were introduced into the PRC to speed literacy and comprehension. Taiwan has retained the longer characters. Pinyin romanization has been the standard in the PRC since the 1970s. The older Wade-Giles (second half of the 19th century) and Yale (1940s) systems, devised for native English speakers, are still used in Taiwan and other areas outside of the PRC.

Chinese People's Political Consultative Conference (CPPCC)

Zhongguo renmin zhengzhi xieshang huiyi

The Chinese People's Political Consultative Conference (CPPCC), sometimes referred to as 'China's House of Lords', dates from the period of the establishment of the **People's Republic of China (PRC)** in the autumn of 1949. Before the creation of the **National People's Congress (NPC)** in 1954, the CPPCC acted as a legislative body for the new state. Even then it had no real power, being subordinate to the **Chinese Communist Party (CCP)**, as both it and the NPC remain to this day. However, as a broadly based organization with representatives of parties and organizations other than the CCP, it can be presented as evidence that the PRC takes account of a wide range of views. Like the NPC, it did not meet during the **Cultural Revolution**, but resumed its activities in 1978. It 'invites' participants, whose term of office is five years. The current CPPCC, the 10th, has 2,196 members.

Chair.: Jia Qinglin
Address: 10th CPPCC National Committee
   23 Taipingqiao dajie
   West City
   Beijing
   People's Republic of China
E-mail: info@cppcc.gov.cn
Internet: www.cppcc.gov.cn

Choe Kyu-Ha

Born to the family of a Confucian scholar in 1919, Choe was a career Republic of Korea (ROK) diplomat who briefly played an important role after the assassination of President **Park Chung-Hee** in 1979. He graduated from the High Normal School in **Tokyo** in 1941, taught at National Taitung Institute in **Manzhouguo** from 1943 until 1945, and at **Seoul** National University from 1945 until 1950. In 1952–59 he served in the semi-official ROK mission to Japan. After the 1961 military coup that brought Park to power, Choe held a variety of senior administrative and diplomatic posts. Prime Minister when Park was killed, he became acting President from October to December 1979, and then President. He resigned in August 1980, paving the way for **Chun Doo-Hwan** to become President. Choe then virtually disappeared from public life. In 1996, when Chun and his successor, **Roh Tae-Woo,** were tried for treason, Choe refused to testify despite his pivotal role at the time, a position he has maintained ever since.

Choe Tae Bok

Choe Tae Bok is chairman of the **Supreme People's Assembly**, the parliament of the Democratic People's Republic of Korea. Choe was born in 1930 in the port city of **Nampo**. He was educated at **Kim Il Sung University**, and in 1980 was Minister of Higher Education; he has also held a number of other party and government education-related portfolios. First elected to the SPA in 1986, he became chairman in 1998.

Chondo-gyo

Teaching of the Heavenly Way

Chondo-gyo is a religious group that exists in both the Democratic People's Republic of Korea (DPRK) and in the Republic of Korea (ROK). It appears to have no followers outside the **Korean peninsula**. Its origins lie in the Tonghak ('Eastern Learning') movement founded in 1860. This was an eclectic religion, which drew on traditional **shamanism** and hopes for a better future, on the concept of the unity of god and man, and on a belief in the equality of man. Exploiting contemporary concerns, it soon became an anti-establishment and anti-foreign (particularly anti-Christian) force in the late 19th century. Its followers took part in the 1893–94 Tonghak Uprising against foreign influences regarded as detrimental to Korea. The rebellion had the opposite effect from what the Tonghaks intended. It led **China** and Japan to intervene in Korea, to the Sino–Japanese War of 1894–95, and ultimately to the Japanese domination and takeover of the peninsula.

The movement survived, however, and in 1906 its leaders changed the name to Chondo-gyo. The group claimed that, through self-discipline and the cultivation of the mind, one could obtain the divine virtue of being able to influence everything without conscious effort. Chondo-gyo leaders played an important part in the anti-Japanese demonstrations known as the 1 March Movement in 1919, and in later independence movements. Its followers were active in the opposition to the division of the peninsula in 1945, insisting that Korea was one nation. The division of the peninsula affected its membership since in 1945 the majority of its followers were in the northern half of the peninsula.

Today it is a minor religion in the ROK. The governing body of Chondo-gyo claims that its followers number hundreds of thousands. Official figures indicate that there were in reality about 53,000 followers in 1985, and that the number had fallen to 28,184 by 1995. Since the end of military rule in the ROK, the Tonghak Rebellion has become less of a taboo subject than it was in the past, and some of the sites of the various battles in the 1890s have become national monuments.

A Chondo-gyo church and political party also exists in the DPRK. The party supposedly represents the interests of those of peasant origin, but, like all DPRK political parties, its main task is to support the **Korean Workers' Party**. There is also a Chondo-gyo temple in **Pyongyang**, but it is difficult to establish the number of those who attend it.

Chong Dong-Chea

A former journalist turned politician, Chong Dong-Chea became the culture and tourism minister of the Republic of Korea in June 2004.

Chong was born in **Kwangju** in 1950, and graduated from Kyunghee University in 1977. He joined the then Hapdong News Agency, but was one of the many journalists purged under **Chun Doo-Hwan**. In 1988 he joined the radical *Hankyoreh Shinmun*. In 1995 he became a member of **Kim Dae-Jung**'s **National Congress for New Politics**, and in the following year was elected to the **National Assembly**. He was Kim Dae-Jung's chief of staff for the 1997 presidential election, and he performed the same successful role for **Roh Moo-Hyun** in 2002.

Chong Sung-Hwa

Born in 1926, Chong Sung-Hwa was the army chief of staff of the Republic of Korea in October 1979, when the head of the Korean Central Intelligence Agency (now the National Intelligence Service) assassinated President **Park Chung-Hee**. To maintain order, acting President **Choe Kyu-Ha** appointed Chong as martial law commander. However, when **Chun Doo-Hwan** staged his December 1979 coup, he had Chong arrested and charged with complicity in Park's murder. Chong was imprisoned but later released. In 1993 Chong brought a charge of mutiny against Chun and his accomplice and successor as President, **Roh Tae-Woo**. The court agreed that their actions in 1979 had been mutinous, but declined to take the issue further. Nevertheless, Chong's action sparked a wave of popular protest that led to the arrest and eventual conviction of Chun and Roh in 1996.

Chongqing

A major city in the **People's Republic of China**, Chongqing is an autonomous municipality, surrounded by Sichuan Province. It stands on a promontory on the confluence of the **Yangzi** and Jialing rivers. It was opened to foreign trade in 1890. During the **Pacific War**, it was the capital of the **Republic of China** in 1937–45. Today it is an important transportation centre and a major city for heavy industries. It became an autonomous city in 1996. Its population, including those living in its large hinterland, numbers approximately 30m.

Chosen soren

Chochongnyon (Korean); *Chosen Soren* (Japanese)

The full name in Japanese is *Zainichi chosenjin sorenggokai,* and in Korean, *Chae ilbon chosonin chongyonhaphoe*; both mean General Association of Korean Residents in Japan.

A pro-Democratic People's Republic of Korea (DPRK) organization in Japan.

Founded in May 1955, today it has about 200,000 members. It has a dual role. Since the DPRK has no diplomatic or other official presence in Japan, *Chosen soren* has attempted to act as an unofficial channel between the governments of the two countries. It is also a pressure group for Korean interests in Japan, and it administers schools and a private university. It has also been a major supporter of the DPRK over the years. *Chosen soren* runs joint venture companies in the DPRK, for example, but probably its most important role has been in supplying funds to the DPRK. These derive from its various business interests, including the running of *pachinko* (one-armed bandit) halls. Estimates vary of the amount of remittances sent annually, from US $400m. to $2,000m., but there is general agreement that such remittances have declined since the 1960s and 1970s.

In recent years the Japanese government has curbed some of its activities, because of concern over issues such as the **DPRK nuclear programme** and the **abductees** issue. *Chosen soren* also faces a problem as younger Koreans desert it, either because its education is of little use in modern Japan or because they no longer regard themselves as linked with the DPRK.

There is also a pro-Republic of Korea group in Japan, generally known as *Mindan*, but this is of less political importance.

Chou, Susana

President of the **Legislative Assembly** of the **Special Administrative Region (SAR)** of **Macao** of the **People's Republic of China** since its establishment in December 1999.

Born in **Shanghai** in 1941, Susana Chou graduated in electronic physics at Anhui University and studied French in Paris. She served in the colonial-era Legislative Assembly continuously from 1976, following the introduction of direct elections.

She also made a name for herself in Macao business circles, becoming president of the Macao World Trade Centre. She was honorary consul for France in Macao for many years.

From 1987 onwards, following the signing of the Sino-Portuguese Joint Declaration on Macao, she was involved with the various drafting and preparatory committees leading up to the establishment of the Macao SAR on 20 December 1999.

Address: c/o Legislative Assembly (see entry)

'Chrysanthemum Club'

Disparaging term used by some Western revisionist scholars in the 1980s to describe academic and other writers regarded as being too pro-Japanese, or who were thought to have in some way allied themselves with Japan. It was also used to describe anybody who attempted to see the Japanese point of view. The term refers to the chrysanthemum flower that symbolizes both the **Japanese Emperor** and the State of Japan. The comparable term for those thought to be supporters of the **People's Republic of China** is 'panda-huggers'.

Chun Doo-Hwan

A soldier turned politician, Chun Doo-Hwan seized power in a military coup in December 1979, and became President of the Republic of Korea (ROK) in the following year.

Born in a small village in South Kyongsang Province in 1931, Chun graduated from the Korean Military Academy in 1955. Following the 1961 coup led by **Park Chung-Hee**, Chun was a member of the Supreme Council for National Reconstruction in 1961, and held various security-related positions in 1963–69. Between 1969 and 1970 he was senior aide to the army chief of staff. In 1970–71 he served in Viet Nam. Returning home in 1971, he held a number of important military posts until in March 1979 he became commander of the Defense Security Command.

Following Park's assassination in October 1979, Chun and his colleagues seized power from the civilian government on 12 December 1979. They arrested **Chong Sung-Hwa**, the army chief of staff and martial law commander and others on charges of treason connected with Park's murder. In 1980 Chun became acting director of the Korean Central Intelligence Agency (now the National Intelligence Service) and chairman of the Standing Committee of the Special Committee for National Security Measures. When President **Choe Kyu-Ha** resigned in August 1980, Chun became President. In February 1981 a newly-created electoral college elected him as President of the Fifth Republic. When his supporters formed the **Democratic Justice Party** he became its leader until June 1987.

Under the terms of a constitutional amendment, Chun was limited to a single term as President. His presidency began with a purge of political figures from Park's day, including veteran opposition leaders **Kim Young-Sam** and **Kim Dae-Jung**, and a wide-ranging attack on the media. Chun spent much time travelling and taking part in summit meetings. In 1983 he negotiated a major aid and loan agreement with Japan. He attempted to open a dialogue with the Democratic People's Republic of Korea (DPRK), without much success. He was the presumed target of the 1983 Rangoon bomb attack, apparently carried out by DPRK agents. Despite this attack, Chun accepted a 1984 offer from the DPRK of materials for flood relief. This rare imaginative gesture came to nothing.

In the latter part of Chun's presidency, there was some relaxation of the tight controls. He freed Kim Young-Sam from house arrest in 1984 and allowed Kim Dae-Jung to return from the USA in 1985. Following demands for political reform, Chun agreed in April 1986 to a debate on constitutional revision. This failed to produce quick results, and Chun suspended the debate in April 1987. He then insisted that the existing arrangements for indirect presidential elections would apply to the 1987 election. He also made it clear that his preferred successor was his fellow conspirator in 1979, **Roh Tae-Woo**. A series of protests, which seemed to threaten the 1988 Olympic Games, led Roh to announce that he would not consider standing for presidential office unless Chun accepted political reforms, including a direct presidential election. Chun agreed, and the crisis passed.

Chun's term of office expired on 25 February 1988 but he received little credit for this peaceful transfer of power. A wave of criticism of the former President and his family for corruption led him to make a nation-wide television appearance in which he admitted many wrongdoings during his administration. He and his wife then retired to a Buddhist temple until December 1991. The issue of how Chun had come to power would not go away, however. Renewed calls for an investigation of the December 1979 coup and of the **Kwangju uprising** followed Kim Young-Sam's election as President in 1992. In December 1993 Chong Sung-Hwa brought a case of mutiny in the courts against both Chun and Roh. It failed, but pressure continued, and in December 1995 Chun and Roh were arrested on charges of bribery and corruption, soon followed by charges of treason and mutiny. Both were convicted in 1996. Chun was fined and sentenced to death, although the death sentence was reduced to life imprisonment on appeal. Both Chun and Roh were released after the 1997 presidential election. Chun has occasionally appeared in public since then, but he now commands little respect. Allegations of corruption involving his family continue to surface.

Chung Dong-Yong

A student activist turned political journalist, Chung Dong-Yong became the unification minister of the Republic of Korea (ROK) in June 2004.

Born in 1953 in South Cholla Province, he attended **Seoul** National University from 1972. In 1974 he was arrested for student activism and imprisoned under the ROK's National Security Laws. Released, he resumed his studies and, on graduation, joined the Munhwa Broadcasting Corporation in 1980. In 1989 he became the

Corporation's Los Angeles correspondent. In 1996 he entered the **ROK National Assembly**, receiving the largest number of votes for a single candidate. Under President **Kim Dae-Jung** he was spokesman for the **National Congress for New Politics**, and then for the **Millennium Democratic Party (MDP)**. When the **Uri Party** replaced the MDP as the ruling party, he became its chairman. In April 2004 he led the Uri Party to victory in the National Assembly elections, in spite of a reference to people in their 60s and 70s having no need to vote, since their political day had passed. He resigned as Uri Party leader on 16 May 2004, and took up his ministerial position on 30 June 2004. In addition to his own talents, he has the advantage of an impeccable family background; during the **Korean War** guerrillas fighting for the Democratic People's Republic of Korea killed his three elder brothers.

Citizens' Party

Minchuantang

This small **Hong Kong** political party dates from May 1997. Its founder was **Christine Loh**, a businesswoman. She was its only representative in the **Legislative Council** at the 1998 elections, but did not stand again in 2000. The Party aims to promote policies for the benefit of Hong Kong citizens, and to train future leaders. It has a young leadership, mainly from professional backgrounds, and describes itself as favouring 'green policies'.

> *Chair.:* Alex Chan
> *Address:* Hong Kong Citizens' Party
> GPO Box 321 Central
> Hong Kong SAR
> People's Republic of China
> *Tel:* 852-2893-0029
> *Fax:* 852-2147-5796
> *E-mail:* enquiry@citizensparty.org
> *Internet:* www.citizensparty.org

Clean Government Party

Komeito

Japanese political party.

The Clean Government Party is unusual in that it developed originally from a religious group, derived from **Buddhism**, known as the *Sokka Gakkai* or 'Value Creation Society'. This is one of the most successful of Japan's **new religions**, with several million followers. Members of the group began to contest local elections on an anti-corruption ticket from 1955, and in the following year three *Sokka Gakkai* candidates were elected to the upper house of the **National Diet**.

It was only in 1964, however, that the *Sokka Gakkai* organized the *Komeito*, or Clean Government Party. While it was conservative in its outlook, the main concern of the Party, as its name implies, was the corruption associated with the ruling **Liberal Democratic Party (LDP)**. In 1967 all 25 of its candidates were elected to the House of Representatives, while in the 1969 elections 47 of its 76 candidates were successful. The Party continued to grow during the 1970s, although in those years it broke its formal links with *Sokka Gakkai*. In 1983 it achieved its best parliamentary result, winning 58 seats. In the political upheavals of the 1990s, when centrist policies appeared to predominate, the Party seemed to lose direction, and in 1994 it merged with the 'New Frontier Party', or *Shinshinto*. This link lasted until 1998, but the *Komeito* elements always retained some independence from the *Shinshinto*. These broke away in 1998 to form first the 'New Peace Party'—*Shinto Heiwa*—and, later, the 'New Komeito' (*Shinkomeito*). Since November 1998 New Komeito has been in a somewhat uneasy coalition with the ruling LDP. It objects, for example, to visits to the **Yasukuni Shrine** and to other indications of what are regarded as the right-wing tendencies of the LDP. Nevertheless, it remains in the coalition.

Closed Country Policy

Sakoku

A term used to describe the policy adopted in the 1630s by Japan's then rulers, the Tokugawa shoganate, towards foreigners. In practice, there never was a closed country policy, because Japan continued to have trade relations with **China**, the **Korean peninsula**, and even, to a more limited extent, with the Dutch through **Nagasaki**. The term itself is an early 19th century coinage. The exclusion policy came under heavy Western pressure from the beginning of the 19th century, and collapsed with the signing of the first **unequal treaties** in the 1850s.

COMECON

COMECON was the term generally used in the West for the Council for Mutual Economic Assistance, founded in 1949, which was the economic equivalent of the Warsaw Pact. It linked the Soviet Union and the Communist countries of Eastern Europe in a mutual trading community. The Mongolian People's Republic (now Mongolia) joined in 1962, and its economy became heavily involved with the COMECON system. While the Democratic People's Republic of Korea (DPRK) was never a member, its economy was also closely tied to COMECON. With the end of the socialist states in Eastern Europe, the council was dissolved in June 1991. Its disappearance contributed to economic problems in Mongolia and in the DPRK during the 1990s.

Comfort women

Japanese: *jugan ianfu*; Korean *jungun wianbu*

The 'comfort women' question has been an issue between Japan and several other countries since a number of women from the Republic of Korea (ROK) came forward in the late 1980s, claiming that they had been used as 'sex slaves' by the Japanese military during the **Pacific War**. They demanded that Japan should apologize and provide compensation for what had happened to them

'Comfort women' was a term used by the Japanese military in the various East Asian theatres of war from the early 1930s onwards. It referred to women drafted to provide sexual services to Japanese troops. The practice appears to have begun in **Shanghai** in the early 1930s, and became widespread after the outbreak of the Sino–Japanese War in 1937. The issue received some attention after the end of the war; in 1948 the Netherlands authorities tried a group of Japanese officers for forcing Dutch women into prostitution in the Dutch East Indies. In general, however, both the Japanese military and the victorious allies ignored the question. The real status of many of the women was hidden. Some were categorized by the Japanese as 'auxiliary nurses' or by other means of hiding their status, while many were just turned loose to find their own way back to where they came from. Occasional references surfaced in Japan and elsewhere, but there were no systematic studies of the issue. The women themselves seem to have kept quiet. There are no reliable figures for those involved; estimates vary from 80,000 to 200,000. On the basis of incomplete figures, it is estimated that 80% were from Korea, and that about the same proportion were between 14–18 years of age when they were drafted.

During the late 1970s a protest movement developed among women in the ROK over what became known as prostitution tourism, or sometimes *kisaeng* tourism, after the Korean word for an accomplished hostess. This led some into further examinations of prostitution in the ROK, and it was in this context that information about the 'comfort women' started to appear. There were demands that Japan acknowledge that the programme had been under official auspices, and that the Japanese government should formally apologize. The Japanese reaction was a denial in the **National Diet** in June 1990 that the comfort women had been anything more than privately organized camp followers of the Japanese armies.

This denial prompted further action by women in the ROK, and women in Malaysia, the Philippines, and the Netherlands began to raise the issue. In December 1990 a group of women in the ROK founded the 'Korean Council for the Women Drafted for Military Sexual Slavery by Japan'. They demanded that Japan provide acknowledgement, compensation, and a memorial for the 'comfort women'. In 1991 the protests reached new heights, as a number of Korean women, led by Kim Hak-Sun (1924–97), came forward to testify about what had happened to them. In December 1991 Kim and others took a test case to the Japanese courts.

In January 1992, while on a visit to **Seoul**, the then Japanese Prime Minister, Miyazawa Kiichi, admitted that the 'comfort women' programme had been officially sanctioned during the Pacific War, and expressed regret. The Japanese government declined to pay compensation, however, arguing that the 1965 Normalization Treaty between the ROK and Japan had settled all such issues. This was similar to the arguments used to refuse to pay compensation to former **prisoners of war of the Japanese**. The issue now acquired a higher international profile, with the Human Rights' Commission of the **United Nations** taking it up, and both the ROK and the Democratic People's Republic of Korea issuing official dossiers on the subject. Under pressure, the Japanese government eventually admitted that the comfort women programme had been under official auspices, and that it had involved coercion and deception.

In July 1994 Japan's Socialist Prime Minister, **Murayama Tomiichi**, again apologized, and, as with the prisoner of war issue, offered, 'measures in lieu of compensation'. This was a reference to a privately funded 'Asian Women's Fund' that the Japanese government had set up and had encouraged companies to support. The women's groups and the two Korean governments rejected this fund; the governments stated that they would provide compensation to those who wanted it. Kim Hak-Sun died in 1997, but a class action case continued in the Japanese courts, and in 1998 a district court found in favour of three Korean comfort women. The court awarded them compensation of US $2,453 each. Following an appeal, however, in March 2001, the High Court overturned this judgment. It has again gone to appeal. There have been further apologies from Japan. The most recent was in December 2004, when the chief secretary to the Cabinet personally apologized to two women, one from the ROK and one from the Philippines.

Like the prisoner of war issue, the comfort women question remains a complication in Japan's relations with a number of countries, and it has become a factor in the **history textbooks controversy**.

Commission of the Ministry of Foreign Affairs in Macao

An office of the Ministry of Foreign Affairs of the **People's Republic of China (PRC)** established in **Macao** in December 1999, following the return of Macao to the PRC. It interacts with the local government of the **Special Administrative Region** of Macao on foreign policy matters, including the establishment of consular and foreign business offices.

Confucianism

A system of political and social morality based on and developed from the teachings of the Chinese scholar and philosopher Confucius (551–479 BC). Confucianism cannot be described as a religion; though it speaks of the will of heaven, it is not focused on worship of a deity or deities and does not claim divine revelation. It is concerned with life in, not after, this world. Its importance has been enormous in **China** and in neighbouring societies influenced by the Chinese model, in particular Korea, Japan and Viet Nam. From an early point Confucianism became identified with ancestor worship, but the practice of honouring the spirits of deceased ancestors predated Confucius. It was incorporated into the rituals associated with his teaching but was not a practice devised by him. Even though Confucianism does not enshrine any deity, Confucius himself became the object of a state cult in China in the 1st century AD and even today is commemorated in regular ceremonies at temples of Confucius in **Beijing, Seoul, Taipei** and Hanoi. A small number of people in the Republic of Korea (ROK) describe their religious affiliation as Confucianism. Popular Chinese religion may include an altar to Confucius in its temples in places such as **Hong Kong**, and elements of Confucianism are blended with **Buddhism** and **Daoism** in many of the new syncretic religions that have developed in **Taiwan**, Japan and the ROK. Much greater numbers of people in many parts of East Asia (and south-east Asia) decribe themselves as still influenced by Confucian principles.

Confucius is the Latinized form of the term Kong Fuzi, meaning 'Master Kong', the title accorded to Kong Qiu. He was born at Qufu in what is now Shandong Province of the **People's Republic of China (PRC)**. Unsuccessful as a public servant, he is remembered as a scholar who sought to return the standards of political behaviour of his day to the golden norm of an earlier age. After his death, his teachings were complied into the *Analects*. Confucius himself was versed in the classical texts of his time. Preoccupied with the qualities essential to achieve a harmonious balance within society, he encouraged the virtues of benevolence, reciprocity in human dealings, and righteousness in the ruling élite, and of loyalty among those ruled. Unmoved by considerations of class, he accepted students on merit. In succeeding centuries his teachings were interpreted, developed and applied to meet the needs of changing situations, such as the rise of Buddhist and Daoist influence in China. The most far-reaching re-evaluation of Confucian doctrine was that undertaken by the official and scholar Zhu Xi (1130–1200), whose commentaries on Confucian texts, building on the work of earlier teachers, inserted a metaphysical element into Confucianism and reinvigorated its principles and application under the rubric of Neo-Confucianism. For centuries both Confucian and Neo-Confucian texts provided the content of education and the examinations for state service in China and neighbouring countries.

In China Confucianism formed the basis for government from the early Han dynasty (3rd century BC) right up to the first years of the 20th century. In its international diplomacy, imperial China extended the principle of ruler and subject to its dealings with its neighbours, whom it regarded as lesser entities. From China Confucianism was introduced during the 4th century AD into the **Korean peninsula**, where it was absorbed as an essential element in the formation of state bureaucracy amid a general willingness to accept Chinese models. The Koryo dynasty's enthusiasm for Buddhism was replaced, in the succeeding Choson dynasty (1392–1910), by a strict adherence to Neo-Confucianist teaching, again adopted from China, which endured up to the end of the dynasty. Korea in turn provided a stepping stone for the introduction of Confucianism into Japan from the 5th century. As in China and Korea, the emphasis on the relationship between ruler and ruled was used as a means of enhancing the legitimacy of those in positions of authority. Indeed, in all three countries Confucianist teaching at its various stages seems to have provided a framework for tendencies that may have already been inherent in these societies, such as the power of family and clan, the elevation of the male principle, and the subordination of individual needs to the common good. It encouraged a respect for the value of education throughout East Asia, but, at least in its later stages, reduced the status of women. It conferred enormous authority, but also great responsibilities on the ruler. In Japan it supported the eminence given to the **Japanese Emperor** in the late 19th–early 20th century. In both the ROK and the Democratic People's Republic of Korea it has encouraged autocratic styles of leadership well into the 20th century. Although Chinese communism has at times moved to discredit both Confucius and Confucianism, leaders of the PRC have shown little sign of modifying a generally imperious approach to government.

Confucianist doctrines and practices have declined in East Asia over the past century. What has remained is a devotion to 'Confucian values', especially as a bulwark against Western influences. The underlying understanding of society lies in the cardinal relations between leader and led, father and son, elder sibling and younger, husband and wife. In each relationship the first expects obedience from the second, but must in turn give protection and guidance. Only in the last of the 'five relationships', that between friends, is a measure of equality accepted. Confucian values embrace a willingness for hard work, together with loyalty to family and group and sometimes leaders. Though often not achieved, the maintenance of social harmony and stability remains an ideal.

'Cow walking'

Gyuho

'Cow walking' is a filibustering technique used in Japan, designed to delay the passage of a bill through the **National Diet**. The aim was to walk very slowly through the lobbies, imitating the slow gait of a cow, thus preventing the passage of a bill. The **Social Democratic Party of Japan** used the technique with some success in the 1960s, since a bill held up in this fashion tended to be abandoned. Eventually, in order to avoid such disruptive tactics, the two main parties reached agreement on management techniques for parliamentary business that took account of both sides' interests. 'Cow walking' enjoyed a brief revival in the more fluid Japanese politics of the 1990s, but the electorate reacted adversely against such delaying tactics, and the practice ceased.

Cultural Revolution

Term applied to the last major political campaign initiated by **Mao Zedong** in the **People's Republic of China (PRC)**. Launched in the spring of 1966, its full name was the Great Proletarian Cultural Revolution.

There are disagreements about its exact dates, but in 1981 the **Chinese Communist Party (CCP)** declared that it lasted from March 1966 until Mao's death in October 1976. Despite its title, the Cultural Revolution was not really about culture but about the direction in which both the PRC and the CCP should develop. Mao, the chairman of the CCP, was impatient at the slow pace of economic reforms after the failure of the 1958 Great Leap Forward, and believed that the leadership of the CCP was marginalizing him. A major power struggle between Mao and his supporters and more orthodox party leaders such as Liu Shaoqi and **Deng Xiaoping** became a nation-wide upheaval. Mao called on students and the **People's Liberation Army (PLA)** under the control of Mao's designated successor, **Lin Biao,** to struggle against what he described as the 'capitalist roaders'—those whose policies would lead to a restoration of capitalism in the PRC—in the Party and government. Liu and Deng both lost their positions; only the Premier, Mao's long-time lieutenant, **Zhou Enlai**, escaped, although he periodically came under attack for the duration of the Cultural Revolution.

From August 1966 student groups, organized as Red Guards, conducted campaigns against leaders in all areas of the Party and state. Schools and universities closed. The Red Guards denounced and humiliated teachers and other symbols of authority. They destroyed historic buildings and artefacts. Religious believers and **minority nationalities** suffered particularly badly. As radicalism increased, the Cultural Revolution spilled over into foreign affairs, exacerbating a number of existing problems, such as the **Sino-Soviet dispute**. The Red Guards attacked several diplomatic premises in **Beijing** and **Shanghai,** and sacked the British mission in Beijing. Abroad, Chinese diplomats' attempts to promulgate 'Mao Zedong Thought', a simplified synthesis of Mao's ideas, especially among **overseas Chinese** communities, and their reaction to perceived slights to Mao or the PRC, led to clashes in a number of countries. There were also Cultural Revolution-related demonstrations in **Hong Kong** and **Macao.**

To preserve order, Mao gave the PLA a considerable role in running the country's civilian institutions, a role it would maintain well into the 1970s. By autumn 1967 the clashes between various groups of Red Guards and the damage done to the PRC's international reputation led Mao to disperse the Red Guards to the countryside. By 1969, when the CCP held its Ninth Party Congress, there was a steady move away from the radicalism of the early years. The CCP now began to rebuild, and the PRC returned to normal diplomatic behaviour. Officials who had disappeared from view, including Deng Xiaoping, reappeared and took office once more. At the same time, severe infighting continued between pro- and anti-Mao groups right up to the chairman's death in October 1976. Then, led by his widow,

Jiang Qing, the extreme radicals made one final bid for control. They failed and were arrested.

Verdicts on the Cultural Revolution are mixed, but there is no doubt that it damaged the PRC in several ways. A whole generation suffered disruption to their education. Although Zhou Enlai attempted to prevent too much disruption in some fields, the economic damage was great. Priceless buildings, books and artefacts have gone forever. The Cultural Revolution pitted neighbour against neighbour, but after 1976 they had to live together, which caused friction. Even today the Cultural Revolution remains a topic best avoided in the PRC.

D

Daesong Bank

Leading commercial bank in the Democratic People's Republic of Korea (DPRK).

Daesong Bank, founded in 1978, is supervised by the Daesong Trading Company, the largest trading company in the DPRK, whose transactions it processes. This company in turn is reportedly controlled by the **Korean Workers' Party**. (Foreign trade in the DPRK is largely conducted through trading companies, which are themselves affiliated to the Party, government ministries or the armed forces.) The Daesong venture is reported to have connections with the DPRK leader **Kim Jong Il**. In 1982 a subsidiary of the Daesong Bank, the Golden State Bank, was set up in Vienna, Austria, as the sole North Korean bank in Europe. It ceased operations in July 2004.

Pres.: Ri Hong
Address: Kyonghung St
            Potonggang District
            Pyongyang
            Democratic People's Republic of Korea
Tel: 850-2-381-8221
Fax: 850-2-381-4576

Dai

Minority nationality living in southern Yunnan Province in the south-west of the **People's Republic of China (PRC)**. They numbered 1,025,400 in the 1990 population census.

The term Dai is that officially given in the PRC to this ethnic group and to their language, but they are also known by other names. The Dai form part of an ethnic people also settled in Viet Nam, Laos, Thailand and Myanmar, like them follow Therevada **Buddhism** and share many of their customs and festivals. They are mainly farmers, cultivating rice and tropical crops, and are concentrated in the Dai autonomous prefecture near the Mekong river where it flows through the south of Yunnan. They are famed as dancers and artists and particularly for the water-splashing festival they hold in mid-April to mark the advent of the Dai year.

Although known collectively as the Dai, they subdivide into distinct cultural and linguistic groups. Their two main languages are both Tai languages, part of the Kam-Tai linguistic group of the Sino-Tibetan family, and are related to Thai, Lao and **Zhuang**. These two languages have distinct scripts derived from the Thai alphabet. Other varieties of writing systems are also reported to exist. Dai has the status of an official language in its autonomous areas, but it is not clear which form of Dai is preferred; nor is it clear why the language of this small minority has been elevated in this way, unless it is intended to serve as a lingua franca in a province that numbers 22 separate ethnic minorities or as a link with the peoples living in neighbouring countries.

Dalai Lama

Title accorded to the political and spiritual leader of the **Tibetan** people.

Transmission of the authority of the office is by recognition of the reincarnation of the recently deceased Dalai Lama in the form of a young boy. The term 'Dalai Lama', signifying 'ocean of wisdom', was first conferred in 1578 by the **Mongol** leader Altan Khan on Sonam Gyantso, the abbot of Drepung monastery in **Tibet**. Altan Khan also applied the title posthumously to two earlier leaders of the Gelugpa 'yellow hat' order of Tibetan **Buddhism**. Sonam Gyantso was thus the third Dalai Lama. By the 17th century the independence and authority of the office were secured in Tibet through the energies of the fifth Dalai Lama, who created the office of **Panchen Lama** and decreed that the Dalai Lama was a manifestation of the Bodhisattva of Compassion. From the end of the 19th century the holders of the office of Dalai Lama have had to confront difficult political situations. In 1904 the 13th Dalai Lama fled **Lhasa** when a British expeditionary force entered the city, an intervention that prompted **China** to reassert its sovereignty over Tibet. In 1910 he fled again when a Chinese warlord invaded Tibet. The 14th and present Dalai Lama had to contend with renewed Chinese invasion in 1950, when the government of the newly established **People's Republic of China** extended its control over the whole of the Chinese mainland and made it clear that it intended to oversee all religious activity. In 1959, after an uprising in Tibet had been suppressed by the Chinese army, he fled to India.

The present Dalai Lama, Tenzin Gyatso, was born in July 1935 in north-east Tibet with the name Lhamo Dhondrub. At the age of two he was recognized as the reincarnation of the deceased 13th Dalai Lama and was enthroned in Lhasa in February 1940. He began his education when he was six years old. In November 1950 he was called upon to assume full political authority as head of the state and the government after the Chinese invasion. In 1954 he travelled to **Beijing** to meet the Chinese leader **Mao Zedong** to discuss ways of improving the situation in Tibet, and in 1956 visited India on a similar mission. Following the Chinese crackdown in Tibet in 1959 he fled to India, where he was granted political asylum. Since 1960 the Dalai Lama has been based at Dharamsala in the north-west Indian state of

Himachal Pradesh, where he presides over the **Central Tibetan Administration**. In 1989 the Dalai Lama was awarded the Nobel Peace Prize. He writes and travels widely.

Address: Office of His Holiness the Dalai Lama
Thekchen Choeling
P. O. McLeod Ganj
Dharamsala 176 219
India
Tel: 91-1892-221343
Fax: 91-1892-221813
Internet: www.tibet.com

Daoism

Indigenous Chinese belief that expresses itself in a philosophical form and also as an organized religion with its own temples, clergy, liturgy, sacred texts and range of deities, of which the most widely known in the West are probably the Eight Immortals. In its organized form it still has a following—officially estimated at 5.5m.—in the **People's Republic of China (PRC)**, and is strong in **Hong Kong** and in **Taiwan**, where the number of adherents was recently estimated at 4.54m. It has also spread in the various **overseas Chinese** communities, but has never gained a foothold in Japan or in the **Korean peninsula**, where it was known from the Koryo period (918–1392) but met with opposition from both **Buddhism** and later **Confucianism**. The fluid nature of its organization has led to local variants and to its coexistence with the popular forms of Buddhism. Elements of Daoism, such as its preoccupation with longevity and immortality and its use of exorcism and of exercises and regimes, have been incorporated into some of the **new religions**. Popular Daoism shares some characteristics, for instance, with the **Falungong** movement.

The teaching of the Way, or *Dao*, originated in the ancient state of Chu (which flourished in central-south **China** for several centuries from the 8th–7th century BC). It is associated with the sage Lao Zi. Its principal text is the *Daodejing*, of which an edition dating to around 300–250 BC exists. The Way is the constant principle, the primal source of all unity and existence, an expression of the universal creative force. To live by the Dao is to accept the natural laws of the universe with their ceaseless round of change. The concept of *yin/yang*, the interplay of polarizing forces, is associated with Daoism, but is even older than the philosophy. The emergence of an organized religion is dated to the 2nd century AD and is ascribed to Zhang Daoling. At times, it enjoyed imperial support. During the **Cultural Revolution** (1966–76) in the PRC, Daoist temples were destroyed, priests were persecuted and worship came to an end. Daoism has survived, however, and is now accepted as one of the five 'legitimate' forms of religion in the PRC.

Demilitarized Zone (DMZ)

The Demilitarized Zone (DMZ) is a strip of land 4 km wide that cuts across the entire width of the **Korean peninsula,** separating the Democratic People's Republic of Korea (DPRK) to the north from the Republic of Korea (ROK) to the south. The Zone follows the line of actual control at the end of the **Korean War** in 1953, not the **38th parallel** that more commonly symbolizes the division of Korea. It stretches 240 km on land, with an additional 60 km extending into the Han river estuary on the west side of the peninsula. Starting from this estuary, the DMZ pursues a line running north-east–east–north-east to end at the East Sea coast. It extends 2 km on each side of the Military Demarcation Line that stretches along the middle and forms the boundary between the two Korean states.

The DMZ was established under the first article of the 1953 Korean armistice agreement. The agreement stipulates strict control of the movement of soldiers, police and civilians into the Zone and of the introduction of weapons and the construction of military installations, conditions that have not always been observed. The DMZ is fortified on each side by mine fields, barbed wire entanglements and anti-tank walls constructed within the Zone and by civilian control lines north and south of the Zone. Between 1974 and 1990 the government of the ROK announced that it had discovered the existence of four tunnels which, it claimed, had been dug beneath the DMZ from the northern side for purposes of infiltration. The DPRK government rebutted such claims. Since 1991 responsibility for the security of the DMZ has been in the hands of forces of the DPRK and the ROK. The Zone is constantly patrolled. The reduction of violent episodes and armed intrusions in recent years has been followed by agreements between the ROK and the DPRK, only partly implemented, to open rail links and two roads across the DMZ and to terminate the broadcasting of propaganda messages at each other across the Zone.

Paradoxically, the DMZ forms a kind of wildlife reserve, since shooting is prohibited there. Farming is still permitted within both the southern and northern sections of the Zone. Visitors from either side may make escorted trips to their respective section of the Joint Security Area at **Panmunjom** within the DMZ.

Democratic Alliance for the Betterment of Hong Kong

A political party in **Hong Kong,** dating from 1992 and always closely identified with the **People's Republic of China (PRC).**

The founder of the Democratic Alliance was Tsang Yok Sing, headmaster of a school regarded as pro-PRC, and a staunch critic of British policies, especially those pursued under **Christopher Patten,** the last British governor of Hong Kong. Today the party has 10 seats in the Hong Kong **Legislative Council,** and is well represented in the district councils. It also sends four representatives to the PRC's **National People's Congress.** It still claims to act as a bridge between the PRC and Hong Kong, but also is active on Hong Kong issues.

Chair.: Ma Lik
Address: 12th Floor
         SUP Tower
         83 Kings Rd
         Hong Kong
Tel: 852-2528-0136
Fax: 852-2528-4339
E-mail: info@dab.org.hk
Internet: www.dab.org.hk

Democratic Justice Party (DJP)

Minju chongudang

In January 1981 the supporters of President **Chun Doo-Hwan** of the Republic of Korea (ROK) formed a new political party, the Democratic Justice Party (DJP), with Chun as its president. It was a highly conservative organization, and at once became the ruling party in the **ROK National Assembly**. In April 1988 Chun's successor as President, **Roh Tae-Woo**, replaced Chun as head of the party. In February 1990 the DJP merged with the Reunification Democratic Party and the New Democratic Republican Party to become the **Democratic Liberal Party**.

Democratic Labour Party (DLP)

Minju nodondang

In January 2000 the newly formed Democratic Labour Party (DLP) became the Republic of Korea's (ROK) first genuinely left-wing political party since 1948.

By October 2002 the Party claimed 30,000 members, of whom 13,000 were trade unionists. It brings together various 'progressive forces', and claims to represent labour, students, peasants, and other dispossessed groups. The Party enjoyed some success in the 2002 local elections, winning two mayoral positions in the industrial city of Ulsan. It was formed too late to make an impact in the 2000 **ROK National Assembly** elections, but in the 2004 elections it won 10 seats. It is close to the Korean Confederation of Trade Unions.

Chair.: Kim Hyegyeong
Address: Democratic Labour Party
         Hanyang Bldg
         14–31 Yoido-dong
         Youngdongpo-gu
         Seoul 150-748
         Republic of Korea
Tel: 82-2-761-1333
Fax: 82-2-761-4115
E-mail: kdlp@kdlp.org
Internet: www.kdlp.org

Democratic Liberal Party (DLP)

Minju chayudang

On 22 January 1990 the ruling **Democratic Justice Party** in the Republic of Korea (ROK) and two other parties, the Reunification Democratic Party (RDP) and the New Democratic Republican Party (NDRP), announced that they would merge in a 'grand alliance', to form the Democratic Liberal Party (DLP). The merger gave the new party an absolute majority in the **ROK National Assembly**, with 18 more seats than the opposition, thus allowing the government to enact any legislation. Only five lawmakers of the former RDP refused to join the new party. When the representatives of the three parties met on 9 February 1990, they chose **Roh Tae-Woo**, **Kim Young-Sam**, and **Kim Jong-Pil** as supreme representatives of the new party. In 1996 the Party was renamed the New Korea Party.

Democratic parties (People's Republic of China)

Eight small political parties permitted to exist in the **People's Republic of China (PRC)** alongside the all-powerful **Chinese Communist Party (CCP)**.

They emerged between the 1920s and the 1940s as alternative political groupings to both the CCP and the Nationalist Chinese **Kuomintang (KMT)** and are particularly associated with professional sections of society or with special-interest groups. After the establishment of the PRC in 1949, the CCP, through its United Front Department, co-opted them as part of its drive to widen acceptance of the new regime, create an impression of political plurality, and neutralize alternative focuses of political activity.

Several of the groups started off under different names. In 1949 they were reorganized into the following eight 'democratic parties': the China Democratic League (membership in 2003: 131,300); Jiu San [3 September] Society (membership in 2003: 68,400); China Association for Promoting Democracy (membership not known); Chinese Peasants' and Workers' Democratic Party (membership in 2003: more than 65,000); China National Democratic Construction Association (membership in 2003: 85,105); China Zhi Gong Dang [Party for Public Interest] (membership not known); Revolutionary Committee of the Chinese Guomindang (membership not known); and the Taiwan Democratic Self-Government League (membership not known). Of the eight, the first four draw their members primarily from among intellectuals and professionals working in the fields of literature, science, culture, education, technology, medicine and public health. To some extent they function as much as professional associations working in the interests of their members as they do as political parties. The China Democratic League is especially popular with high-level intellectuals. The China National Democratic Construction Association represents the interests of industrialists, businesspeople and those working on economic affairs. The three remaining parties speak respectively for returned **overseas Chinese**, former KMT members and Taiwanese living on the mainland.

The democratic parties have always been held on a tight rein by the CCP, which has regulated their numbers and indicated the constituencies among which they might recruit members. They suffered in the aftermath of the One Hundred Flowers campaign of 1956–57, when, at **Mao Zedong**'s urging to criticize the CCP, they were judged too sharp in their comments and were purged. The parties survived, however, and since Mao's death in 1976 have been treated more favourably. They did not associate themselves too closely with the protest movements of 1989 and, possibly as a consequence, were invited into closer consultation with the CCP as 'parties participating in government affairs'. More government posts and more seats in the **National People's Congress** were to be open to them. Their place in a 'system of multiparty co-operation and political consultation' under the leadership of the CCP, in the interests of a 'patriotic united front', was confirmed in the revised CCP Constitution adopted at the 16th party Congress in November 2002.

Democratic Party (DP—Hong Kong)

Minshutang

The Democratic Party (DP) dates from 1994. Its predecessor was the United Democrats, **Hong Kong**'s first ever political party, organized by **Martin Lee** and others in 1991 to campaign for greater freedom and democracy than seemed to be allowed under the terms of the **Hong Kong Basic Law**.

The United Democrats had won a sweeping victory in the 1991 **Legislative Council (LegCo)** elections, taking 17 out of 18 seats. The United Democrats had been a rather flexible group, but the DP was better organized, a sign of the growing political development of Hong Kong. Martin Lee was chairman of the new party and remained so until 2002. He remains a member, as do other veteran campaigners for democracy in Hong Kong.

Despite fears that the incoming administration of **Tung Chee Hwa** would muzzle the party after July 1997, it survived. However, the undoing of the reforms introduced by **Christopher Patten**, the last British governor of Hong Kong, denied it the sweeping electoral successes of the past. It accepts that Hong Kong is now part of the **People's Republic of China**, but continues to campaign for greater democracy. It had a total membership of 632 in July 2004, and held 11 LegCo seats in the 2000 elections. It also has 94 district councillors.

Chair.: Yeung Sum
Address: 4th Floor
　　　　　Hanley Commercial Bldg
　　　　　Nathan Rd
　　　　　Kowloon
　　　　　Hong Kong
Tel: 852-2397-7033
Fax: 852-2397-7033 *or* 2397-4801

E-mail: dphk@dphk.org
Internet: www.dphk.org

Democratic Party (DP—Republic of Korea)

Minjudang

The name Democratic Party has become synonymous with the opposition in the Republic of Korea (ROK) since the beginning of the state in 1948, and the title has been used as the English name of a number of opposition parties. Other opposition parties have often included 'Democratic' somewhere in their titles.

Shortly after a series of constitutional amendments in November 1954 designed to increase the President's powers, the members of the Democratic Nationalist Party formed the 'Society of the Comrades for the Protection of the Constitution', which in September 1955 became an enlarged DP with Shin Ik-Hui, Cho Pyong-Ok and Chang Myon as leaders. After the fall of **Syngman Rhee**, and the introduction of the brief Second Republic, this DP was the majority party. The **ROK National Assembly** elected its then leaders, Yun Po-Son and Chang Myon, as the President and Prime Minister respectively of the Second Republic.

Even at that stage, the Party was divided into an 'old' and a 'new' faction. When the new faction gained prominence under Chang Myon's leadership, the old faction broke away, forming the New Democratic Party in October 1960. The military coup in May 1961 led to the dissolution of all political parties. However, when new political parties emerged in the spring and summer of 1963, Pak Sun-Chon established a new DP in July. In May 1965 this party and the Civil Rule Party (*Minjongdang*) merged to become the Masses Party (*Minjungdang*). In order to strengthen the opposition group, in February 1967 the Masses Party and the New Korea Party (*Shin Hankukdang*—formed in May 1966) were united into another New Democratic Party (*Shin minjudang*), which became the main opposition party against President **Park Chung-Hee** until the suppression of all political activity in 1980.

Yi Ki-Taek and others formed a third Democratic Party in June 1990. In September 1991 Yi Ki-Taek and **Kim Dae-Jung** of the New Democratic Party agreed to merge their parties, bringing the fourth DP into existence with Kim and Yi as co-presidents. This lasted until Kim Dae-Jung created another new party, the **National Congress for New Politics**, in 1996.

Democratic Party (DP—Japan)

Minshuto

Japanese political party that emerged from the break-up of the **Liberal Democratic Party (LDP)** in the mid-1990s to become the main opposition party.

The Democratic Party (DP) began as a small splinter party led by **Kan Naoto** and **Hatoyama Yukio** in 1996. In April 1998 the collapse of the New Frontier Party brought many new members, and the Party was relaunched. Ninety-seven members of the lower house and 41 members of the upper house of the **National Diet** registered themselves as members of this new party, which held its first convention on 27 April 1998. At the convention Kan Naoto was elected as president and former Premier Hata Tsutomo became secretary-general. After the July 1998 upper house elections, the Party had 141 registered members, 92 in the lower house and 49 in the upper house; these numbers had increased to 93 and 51 respectively by April 1999. In September 1999 Hatoyama became president, a post he held until December 2002, when Kan replaced him. Hata lost the position of secretary-general to **Okada Katsuya** at the same time. The Party received a boost in membership when the Liberal Party dissolved in September 2003. It then had 137 registered lower house and 67 upper house members. At the November 2003 lower house elections, the Party's representation increased to 177 members. In May 2004 Okada became president. The Party experienced something of a reverse in the July 2004 upper house elections, after which it had 55 members. This did not affect Okada, who was re-elected unopposed as president in September 2004.

Despite its electoral success, and its position as the main opposition party, the DP remains a somewhat uneasy coalition of left and right, more a vehicle for gaining office than a party of principle. The divisions are particularly strong, as might be expected, on defence and foreign policy matters, where the difference between the left and the right in Japanese politics has always been sharpest.

Pres.: Okada Katsuya
Address: Democratic Party of Japan
　　　　　 1-11-1 Nagato-cho
　　　　　 Chiyoda-ku
　　　　　 Tokyo 100-0014
　　　　　 Japan
Tel: 81-3-3595-9960/3-3995-7312
Fax: 81-3-3595-7318
E-mail: dpjenews@dpj.or.jp
Internet: www.dpj.or.jp

Democratic Progressive Party (DPP—Taiwan)

Minzhu jinutang

The Democratic Progressive Party (DPP) dates from September 1986, some three years before political parties became legal on **Taiwan**. It has since developed into the main opponent of the **Kuomintang**. It enjoyed some success in local elections but its first big breakthrough came in 1994, when **Chen Shui-bian** became mayor of **Taipei**. In 2000 Chen and his running mate **Annette Lu** became President and Vice-President respectively, and the DPP retained these positions in the 2004 presidential elections.

The Party has avoided the issue of Taiwan's independence, although resolutions adopted in 1999 declared that Taiwan was a sovereign state whose official name was the **'Republic of China' ('ROC')**, and that the 'ROC' was not part of the **People's Republic of China**. The resolution also made clear that any change in the *status quo* would require a plebiscite. The Party had some 20,000 registered members in 2003.

Address: Democratic Progressive Party
        10th Floor
        No. 3 Peiping East Rd
        Taipei
        Taiwan
Tel: 886-2-2392-9989
Fax: 886-2-2393-0342
E-mail: foreign@dpp.org.tw
Internet: www.dpp.org.tw

Democratic Republican Party (DRP)

Minju konghwadang

A political party established in the Republic of Korea in February 1963 by the leaders of the 1961 military coup. The coup leader, Gen. **Park Chung-Hee**, was its president. It remained the governing party until 1979. Following Park's assassination in October 1979, it was dissolved along with other political organizations in May 1980. In 1987 **Kim Jong-Pil** revived it as the New Democratic Republican Party.

Deng Xiaoping (1904–97)

When Deng Xiaoping died in February 1997 he held no formal position in either the **Chinese Communist Party (CCP)** or the government of the **People's Republic of China (PRC)**, but there was no doubt in anybody's mind that, until that moment, he had been the country's paramount leader since 1978.

Deng was born in Sichuan Province in 1904. He worked and studied in France with other Chinese students, including **Zhou Enlai**, and joined the CCP in 1924. Thereafter, he spent some time in Moscow, and on his return was active in CCP circles. He joined **Mao Zedong** and Zhu De in the Jiangxi Soviet, and when that was closed down in 1934, he joined the **Long March**. During the war against Japan and the civil war that followed, Deng served as a political commissar with various Communist forces. After the establishment of the PRC in 1949, Deng worked for a time in Sichuan, but in 1952 he moved to **Beijing**, becoming Deputy Prime Minister to Zhou Enlai and, in 1956, CCP secretary-general. From then until the outbreak of the **Cultural Revolution** in 1966, Deng was closely associated with the pragmatic policies of Zhou Enlai and **Liu Shaoqi**, the PRC President, rather than the increasingly quixotic paths favoured by Mao Zedong. Criticized as the second most important person taking the capitalist road, Deng retired to Sichuan.

As the Cultural Revolution waned in the early 1970s, Deng returned to office, at first secretly, but eventually openly. Once again, he was Deputy Premier to the now ailing Zhou Enlai, and rapidly became associated with a programme of economic reform. He fell from power briefly after Mao's death in 1976, but after the fall of the Gang of Four quickly resumed his position of authority. He masterminded the ousting of **Hua Guofeng** in 1980–81, and manoeuvred his protégés, **Zhao Ziyang** and **Hu Yaobang**, into the premiership and the CCP secretary-general posts respectively, while retaining real power behind the scenes. In 1979 he visited the USA (and appeared on the cover of *Time Magazine*), thus cementing Sino-US relations. He failed to solve the **Taiwan** issue, but concluded the 1984 Sino-British agreement on the reversion of **Hong Kong** and the 1987 Sino-Portuguese agreement on the reversion of **Macao**.

Deng became dissatisfied with Hu Yaobang, and forced his resignation in 1987. When the student demonstrations began in Beijing following Hu's death in 1989, Deng took an increasingly hard line. He favoured the decision to declare martial law, and to send in the troops on 4 June 1989. However, while he condemned the students, and backed the dismissal of Zhao as CCP secretary-general, he continued to favour a programme of reform and opening up. In particular, his visit to the south of the country in 1992 made clear his continued commitment to such policies. He died in February 1997, just before the return of Hong Kong to Chinese sovereignty.

Diaoyu-Tai/Senkaku islands dispute

The Diaoyu-Tai (Chinese) or Senkaku (Japanese) islands are a small group of uninhabited islands that lie between **Okinawa** and **Taiwan**. Until 1972 the USA administered them as part of the Ryukyu Islands, apparently without any dispute until the late 1960s. The situation changed, however, with the signing of the agreement between Japan and the USA for the return of the Ryukyu Islands to Japan, and reports that there might be oil in the area. Both the **People's Republic of China (PRC)** and the **'Republic of China'** on Taiwan then claimed that the islands were historically part of Taiwan, and therefore belonged to **'China'**. The dispute has waxed and waned ever since, with the islands actually occupied by Japanese forces. In 1978 the government of the PRC formally agreed to set aside the issue as one to be resolved at some future date, but from time to time groups from the PRC or Taiwan attempt to land on the islands. In 1996 a **Hong Kong** protester drowned during an attempt to land on the islands, and in March 2004 the Japanese arrested and deported a small group of PRC citizens who had landed on them.

Doi Takako

Leading Japanese politician, and the first woman to head a major political party, now chairperson of the **Social Democratic Party of Japan (SDPJ)** for the second time.

Doi Takako was born in **Kobe** in 1928. After graduating from the Doshisha University in **Tokyo**, she became a university lecturer in constitutional law. She entered the Lower House of the **National Diet** in 1969 as a member of the Japan Socialist Party (JSP—now the SDPJ). In 1986 she became leader of the Party, which had suffered a major electoral setback in the July 1986 Lower House elections. Despite facing the popular **Liberal Democratic Party** leader, **Nakasone Yasuhiro**, Doi succeeded in improving the JSP's image, and led it to a successful campaign in the 1989 Upper House elections, winning seats in rural areas in a way that the JSP had not done before. This electoral success continued at the 1990 Lower House elections, when the JSP won some 50 additional seats.

However, the 1991 Gulf crisis touched on difficult issues for the JSP, such as the legality of the **Self-Defence Forces**, and the Party's candidate in the Tokyo mayoral election performed very badly. Doi resigned as chairperson. Her political fortunes revived as the LDP began to fall apart, and in 1993 she became speaker of the Lower House. When the JSP, by now calling itself the SDP, split in 1996, she again became its leader, a post she has held ever since. However, the Party is now much reduced, holding only 19 seats—most of them occupied by women—in the Diet. Instead of the wide range of issues on which it has campaigned in the past, it now concentrates on peace and women's issues. Doi remains a respected figure in Japanese politics, but has not fulfilled the promise of the 1980s.

E

East Sea/Sea of Japan controversy

The 'East Sea' and 'Sea of Japan' are names used for the stretch of water that lies between the east coast of the **Korean peninsula** and Japan. During the Japanese colonial period in Korea in respect of 'sea of Japan' (1910–45), Japan registered 'Sea of Japan' with the International Hydrographic Organization in 1929. Since the establishment of the Republic of Korea (ROK) in 1948, successive ROK governments have sought at least to have both names accepted, although the Korean preference is for East Sea. The ROK argues that 'East Sea' or even 'Sea of Korea' has a pedigree dating back to the beginning of the Three Kingdoms period in 37 BC, and that 'Sea of Japan' only came into general use from the end of the 18th century. As well as taking its case to the Sixth (and subsequent) **United Nations** Conference on the Standardization of Geographical Names in 1992, and to the Fifteenth International Hydrographic Conference in 1997, the ROK has conducted a campaign to persuade commercial map publishers and others to use 'East Sea'. Japan conducts a similar campaign. The Democratic People's Republic of Korea also claims that 'East Sea' is the correct name, using much the same material as the ROK to support this position.

Elbegdorj, Tsakiagiin

Prime Minister of Mongolia in 1998, and again from August 2004.

Born in 1963, Elbegdorj was for a time a worker and then a soldier. In 1988 he graduated as a journalist after training in the Ukraine, and worked on the **Mongolian armed forces'** newspaper, *Red Star*. Later he studied at Harvard University in the USA. With the beginning of Mongolian democracy in the early 1990s, he became an opposition politician and a member of parliament. In April–December 1998 he was Prime Minister. He became an adviser to the newly formed Democratic Party in 2000, but left soon after to continue his studies in the USA. His appointment in 2004 followed two months of parliamentary deadlock. Eventually, the Democratic Coalition, which Elbegdorj represented, agreed to share power with the **Mongolian People's Revolutionary Party**.

Executive Council (ExCo)

The Executive Council (ExCo) began as an advisory body of officials to the governor when **Hong Kong** was a British colony. It gradually developed to include non-official and, later, Chinese members. Under the last British governor of Hong Kong, **Christopher Patten**, it became more like a Cabinet of the senior civil service officials, although there were still unofficial members.

Since 1997 and the establishment of the Hong Kong **Special Administrative Region** of the **People's Republic of China**, the **Hong Kong Basic Law** governs the composition and functions of ExCo. ExCo now assists the chief executive in making policy. The latter should consult it before introducing legislation or dissolving the **Legislative Council**. ExCo consists of the 14 principal officers of the Hong Kong government, plus five non-official members. The chief executive appoints the non-official members, and their term of office lasts as long as that of the chief executive who appoints them. ExCo meets approximately once a week, with the chief executive presiding.

Address: Executive Council Section
    Chief Executive's Office
    1st Floor
    Main Wing
    Central Government Offices
    Lower Albert Rd
    Central
    Hong Kong
Tel: 852-2810-2581
Fax: 852-2845-0176
E-mail: maisiemscheng@ceo.gov.hk (Clerk to ExCo)
Internet: www.ceo.gov.hk

Executive Yuan

The Executive Yuan is the highest administrative organ of the **'Republic of China'** on **Taiwan**. It acts as the government's 'Cabinet' and reports to the **Legislative Yuan**. It is an appointed body headed by the Prime Minister and oversees a policy-making council, the ministries and commissions, and a number of subordinate organizations.

Address: Executive Yuan
    1 Chunghsiao East Rd
    Section 1
    Taipei
    Taiwan
Tel: 886-2-2356-1500/886-2-3356-6500
Internet: www.ey.gov.tw

F

Falungong/Falun Dafa

Practice of self-cultivation based on bodily exercises and meditation, which aims to promote physical well-being and spiritual elevation.

Falungong is a form of the ancient Chinese system of *qigong*, a set of exercises based on deep breathing which are intended to release the flow of vital energy through the body. The term 'Falungong' signifies '*qigong* based on the Wheel of the Law'; Falun Dafa 'the great law of the Wheel of the Law'. The practice of Falungong was founded in the **People's Republic of China (PRC)** in 1992 by Li Hongzhi (born Li Lai, 1952), a native of Jilin Province in north-east **China**. It contains elements of popular **Buddhism** and **Daoism** and claims to offer followers a means of salvation. Li has made some extreme statements, hinting at the possibility for practitioners to acquire supernatural powers and suggesting apocalyptic developments for society. For the first two years of its existence the movement was accepted as part of the wider *qigong* scene in the PRC, but eventually broke with the official *qigong* association. It sought to have itself registered as a social organization, but was denied this, and its publications were banned in 1996 and 1998–99. Li Hongzhi himself emigrated to the USA in 1998. The movement came under challenge in the late 1990s from academics and journalists over its beliefs and quasi-religious nature, to which it responded by mass protests. Peaceful, large-scale gatherings, often in front of government and Party offices, have been Falungong's main means of protesting and of petitioning for legitimacy. Its biggest demonstration was in April 1999, when 10,000 people gathered outside **Zhongnanhai**, the compound in central **Beijing** housing Party and state organs, to protest against earlier police harassment of Falungong followers in the nearby city of **Tianjin**. The size of the demonstration and its occupation of such a sensitive site prompted harsh official reaction, and the movement was declared illegal in July 1999. Since then a regime of repression and discrediting has been in place and many Falungong members have been imprisoned. A number of deaths in detention have been reported, as many as 980 since 1999, according to some sources.

The movement has fallen foul of the authorities in the PRC for a number of reasons. Its beliefs, dismissed by some critics as superstition, run counter to the professed atheism of the Chinese regime. Falungong does not claim to be a religion, but even if it did make such a claim, it could not easily be fitted alongside the five religious affiliations that the Chinese state tolerates, but also controls: Buddhism, Daoism, **Islam**, **Catholic** and **Protestant Christianity**. The greatest threat it presents has been its ability and willingness to muster large numbers of people in a challenge to state power. The government claims the movement had become a hierarchical structure organized on a regional basis and as such was plotting its overthrow. Falungong has denied such intentions. Much of its membership is found among the more elderly sections of society and among women and lower-income groups in both urban and rural areas. It appears to have received particular support among those who have been marginalized in the economic restructuring of recent years. A few of its members are drawn from the higher ranks of the establishment. The movement's appeal would seem to be in part to those who feel they have become disadvantaged in recent years. It enters thus into the long tradition of heterodox belief groups articulating a sense of grievance that have clashed with state authority in China over centuries.

Falungong's membership inside the PRC has been estimated variously as between 40m.–70m. during the late 1990s. Official sources now claim it is much less. Support outside China is estimated at around 40m., spread over some 50 countries.

Five Principles of Peaceful Coexistence

The Five Principles of Peaceful Coexistence have been an important feature of the foreign policy of the **People's Republic of China (PRC)** since the 1950s. The principles are: mutual respect for territorial integrity and sovereignty; mutual non-aggression; non-interference in each other's internal affairs; equality and mutual benefit; and peaceful co-existence.

They first appeared in an April 1954 agreement between the PRC and India relating to **Tibet**. They were spelled out in more detail at the April 1955 Afro-Asian Conference held in Bandung, Indonesia. Thereafter, they became one of the key features of PRC foreign policy statements. At first the PRC stressed them as the basis for relations with non-communist countries, but with the development of the **Sino–Soviet dispute**, a willingness to adhere to the principles was regarded as a key to good relations with any country. PRC diplomats still use the five principles in their negotiations.

Foreign settlements

From the end of the first Anglo–Chinese War in 1842 until 1943, Westerners in **China**, Japan and the **Korean peninsula** largely lived in foreign settlements established at a number of ports. The settlements were places established by treaty—hence the alternative name of treaty ports—where foreigners had the right to reside. Here they could live under their own jurisdiction, build houses and follow their own religious practices. In China they included **Shanghai**, always the largest and most important, **Guangzhou** (Canton) and **Tianjin**, as well as many others. The principal Japanese foreign settlements were **Yokohama, Kobe** and **Nagasaki**. In Korea only Inchon really developed into a foreign settlement. The Japanese foreign settlements, and with them foreigners' special privileges, ended in 1899, when revised treaties took effect. In Korea the establishment of Japanese colonial rule in 1910 produced the same result. In China the formal end of the foreign settlements was not until 1943, when Britain and the USA signed treaties for the abolition of extra-territoriality in China. By that stage the major foreign settlements were actually under Japanese control, so this was mainly a symbolic gesture. Many of these foreign settlements laid the foundation for modern port and industrial cities.

Fukuda Yasuo

Until his resignation on 6 May 2004, Fukuda Yasuo, a long-standing member of the **Liberal Democratic Party (LDP)**, had been Japan's longest serving chief Cabinet secretary, a post he assumed in October 2000.

Fukuda is the son of Fukuda Takeo, Japan's Prime Minister in 1977–79, and thus comes from the centre of the LDP political élite. He was born in 1936, graduated from Waseda University in **Tokyo** in 1959, and for almost 20 years worked in the petroleum business. In 1977–78 he was his father's chief secretary while the latter was Prime Minister, and continued as his private secretary until 1989. In 1990 he became a member of the House of Representatives of the **National Diet** for his father's former constituency. Thereafter he held a number of party and parliamentary posts before he took up the position of chief secretary.

In this role he became the essential right-hand man to successive Prime Ministers, and it was widely expected that he would in due course become Prime Minister himself. Although noted as a steady rather than brilliant politician, with a flair for good public relations, he could be outspoken on some issues. In May 2002, for example, he speculated that the Japanese Constitution did not prohibit Japan from developing nuclear weapons. The remark caused some concern among Japan's neighbours and he did not repeat it. His political career came to an abrupt end, at least temporarily, when he admitted in May 2004 that he had failed to pay mandatory pension premiums from February 1990 until September 1992, and in August–December 1995. However, as the scandal not only affected the LDP but also opposition politicians, and other ministers who had not paid did not feel the need to resign, Fukuda may well return to politics in the future.

G

G20—Group of Twenty

Multilateral forum comprising 19 countries and the European Union that seeks to promote dialogue between industrial states and so-called 'emerging-market countries'.

The Group was set up in 1999 at the instigation of the then Group of Seven (G7), now the Group of Eight (G8), to strengthen the working of the international monetary and financial system. It has focused on issues such as the encouragement of internationally recognized standards in such areas as combating 'money-laundering' and the financing of terrorist activities, and closer co-operation in the prevention and handling of financial crises such as that of the late 1990s. The **International Monetary Fund** and the **World Bank** attend meetings of the G20.

Member countries are represented by their finance ministers and central bank governors. The Group has no permanent staff of its own and is chaired and administered on a rotating basis. Germany currently holds the chairmanship. Among East Asian members of the G20 are the **People's Republic of China**, Japan and the Republic of Korea.

Chair. (2004): Hans Eichel (finance minister of the Federal German Republic)

Geneva Conference 1954

The Geneva Conference met from 26 April to 20 June 1954. The origins of the conference lay in Article 4 of the Korean armistice agreement, in which the two military commanders recommended that a political conference should be held to negotiate the withdrawal of foreign troops from the **Korean peninsula**. The participants included the 16 nations that had contributed troops to the **United Nations** forces in the **Korean War**, together with the Soviet Union, the **People's Republic of China**, and the two Koreas. By the time the conference met, however, events in Indo-China overshadowed Korean issues, and no attempt was made to reconcile the mutually incompatible proposals tabled by the two Korean states. While the conference made some progress on Indo-China issues, it broke up in mid-June having achieved none on Korean matters, and did not reconvene.

Goh Kun

For a brief period in the spring of 2004 Goh Kun, then Prime Minister, was also the interim head of state of the Republic of Korea (ROK), following the impeachment of President **Roh Moo-Hyun** on 12 March 2004.

Goh, born in 1938, comes from a family linked with opposition politics. However, after graduating from Seoul National University and a period as a university teacher, he became a civil servant under Presidents **Park Chung-Hee** and **Chun Doo-Hwan**. Under the latter, he was appointed successively as Minister of Transport and then as Minister of Agriculture. Later, after he entered the **ROK National Assembly** in 1985 as a member of the then ruling **Democratic Justice Party**, he was Minister of Home Affairs. He was mayor of **Seoul** in 1988–90. He then spent some time as president of the private Myonji University, before becoming Prime Minister under President **Kim Dae-Jung** in 1997–98, and was then again mayor of Seoul in 1998–2002. He was Roh Moo-Hyun's first Prime Minister from 2003 until his resignation in May 2004.

Goh has a reputation for both a steady approach and incorruptibility. His last period as mayor of Seoul is associated with the determined pursuit of accountability, including the use of the internet to track planning and similar applications.

Grand National Party (GNP)

Hannara-dang

The Grand National Party (GNP), formed by a merger between the New Korea Party and one of the many Democratic Parties in the Republic of Korea (ROK), dates from November 1997.

The Party, which has campaigned on a platform of 'progressive conservatism', became the main opposition party following **Kim Dae-Jung**'s election as President in 1998. It performed well in parliamentary and local elections, but its candidate (and party president), **Lee Hoi-Chang**, failed to win in both the 1997 and the 2002 presidential elections. In June 2003 Choe Byung-Yul, a former lawyer, journalist, and mayor of **Seoul**, became the party chairman following Lee Hoi-Chang's resignation from politics; in March 2004 Choe gave way to **Park Geun-Hye**. Although the GNP lost some ground in the April 2004 **National Assembly** elections, it still emerged as the second largest single party, after the new pro-government **Uri Party**, with 121 seats. It thus remains a credible opposition to President **Roh Moo-Hyun**. However, the Party may face some difficulties if the Uri Party persists with a campaign begun in July 2004 to identify those with known links to the Japanese during the colonial period (1910–45), given the role of the former President, Ms Park's father, **Park Chung-Hee**, who was once a Japanese military officer.

Chair.: Park Geun-Hye
Address: Grand National Party
17-7 Yoido-dong
Youngdoengpo-ku
Seoul 150-874
Republic of Korea
Tel: 82-2-3786-3000
Fax: 82-2-3786-3610
E-mail: webmaster@hannara.org.kr
Internet: www.hannara.org.kr

Greater East Asia Coprosperity Sphere

Daioa kyoeiken

During the **Pacific War** Japan attempted to establish an economically self-sufficient area in East and south-east Asia made up of Japan, **China**, **Manzhouguo** and, after the attack on Pearl Harbor in 1941, captured British, Dutch, French and US colonial territories. There was some economic integration in the region, and a Greater East Asian Ministry operated for a time. The reality was, however, that Japan's wartime needs overrode every other consideration, and the sphere never functioned as intended. Some commentators describe Japan's post-war economic successes as the achievement of the Greater East Asian Coprosperity Scheme by other means.

Guangzhou

Capital of Guangdong Province of the **People's Republic of China (PRC)**, Guangzhou is better known internationally as Canton, the local pronunciation of the Chinese characters with which it is written.

Guangzhou is a subtropical city that lies on the Pearl river (*Zhenzhujiang*) estuary, some 145 km from the South China Sea. Because of this strategic position, linking the waterways of southern **China** with the sea, Guangzhou has been a major trading port since at least the 3rd century AD, with far-reaching links. It has China's oldest mosque. In the late 18th century it became a centre of the opium trade, and was thus heavily involved in the wars to which that trade gave rise. After the 1842 Treaty of **Nanjing**, **Shanghai** came to overshadow Guangzhou's new **foreign settlement**, but the city played a major role in the revolutionary developments of the early 20th century. In 1938–45 it was under Japanese occupation. After the establishment of the PRC, Guangzhou benefited from the **Chinese Communist Party's (CCP)** suspicions of Shanghai, and from 1957 it became the site of the twice-yearly Chinese Export Commodities' Fair. During some periods, such as the **Cultural Revolution**, the Fair became the PRC's virtually sole outlet to the outside world. After **Deng Xiaoping** introduced the policy of reform and opening up in the late 1970s, Guangzhou again gained from its strategic position. (Deng may also have favoured the city, where he took refuge when he was under attack.) It has close links with **Shenzhen, Hong Kong, Macao** and other towns in the Pearl river delta, and together they have become a major centre for economic development. In addition to its traditional role as a transit port for tea, silks and other products of South China, Guangzhou now also has a shipbuilding industry, produces textiles and is a growing centre for modern light industries, including electronics. It has also become a popular tourist centre.

Guangzhou covers some 7,500 sq km, and has a population of 3.95m. in the inner urban area. This rises to 6.7m. in greater Guangzhou. It has good transport links with the rest of the PRC and with the world; it has its own international airport but also benefits from its close proximity to the other airports in the Pearl river area, including the new **Chek Lap Kok—Hong Kong International Airport**.

H

Hakka

Hakka is the name given to a Chinese ethnic group found mainly in southern China. The term is of relatively recent origin, and translates as 'Guest People'. They speak Mandarin rather than Cantonese, and have a number of customs that differentiate them from their neighbours. They did not bind women's feet, for example. They also have their own, Hakka language. They probably migrated from northern China about 1,000 years ago. Hakka are prominent among the **overseas Chinese**, and many of them have been active in political movements since the mid-19th century. They are estimated to total between 50m.–75m. world-wide, with the majority in South China.

Han Chinese

A term used in **China** to describe the vast majority of people of the country. It covers about 95% of the population, but hides great variations in language and culture. The name comes from that of the first great imperial dynasty, which ruled China from 206 BC until AD 221.

Han Sung-Joo

Han Sung-Joo has been the Republic of Korea's (ROK) ambassador at the **United Nations (UN)** since 2003, and is a distinguished political scientist.

Born in 1940, he studied at **Seoul** National University and took a Ph.D. at the University of California, Berkeley. He taught at the City University of New York in 1970–78, and then returned to the ROK, taking the chair of international relations at Korea University. From 1993–94 he was foreign minister under President **Kim Young-Sam**. He later spent some time as the UN special representative on Cyprus. Before taking up his present appointment, Han was acting president of Korea University, as well as director of the Ilmin Institute of International Relations. He has published several books, and in 1984–93 was a regular contributor to *Newsweek* magazine.

Hang Seng Index

Stock Exchange Index in **Hong Kong**, which started in 1969, named after the Hang Seng Bank.

The Index appears daily, compiled by HIS Services Ltd, a wholly owned subsidiary of the Hang Seng Bank. **HSBC Holdings PLC** has owned the latter bank, originally established in 1933, since 1965. The Hang Seng Index is a market value weighted index of the 33 largest Hong Kong companies. It is one of the two generally recognized and quoted Asian Stock Exchange indexes, the other being the **Nikkei Index** in Japan.

Hangul

Alphabet used for the written form of the Korean language.

Hangul, meaning 'Korean writing', was devised under the supervision of the Choson king Sejong (r. 1418–50), who commissioned a team of scholars to study ways of representing accurately the sounds of Korean. Until then Chinese characters, in either full or truncated form, had been used as the written form of the language, even though the differences between Chinese and Korean in phonology and grammar made them unsuitable for that purpose. Sejong presented his alphabet in 1443–44 under the title of *Hunmin chongum*, or 'Correct sounds to be taught to the people', and his intention was to make the written language accessible to a greater number of people as well as to facilitate record-keeping. The phonetic principles of the new alphabet came largely from contemporary Chinese studies, which in turn drew on Sanskrit phonetics. The shape of the new letters seems to have derived in part from the square script elaborated by Lama Buddhists in Mongolia in the 13th century, which was known in Korea. Despite Sejong's recommendation of *hangul*, it was shunned by scholars and officials, who sought to preserve their position as an élite educated in the Chinese classics and writing. Only in the 19th and early 20th century did *hangul* come to replace wholly or in part the use of Chinese characters in newspapers and official documents.

Hangul is a carefully constructed script, meeting the needs of spoken Korean. With a few exceptions, it can also generally convey the sounds of foreign languages.

Hanshin earthquake

On 17 January 1995 a major earthquake, measuring 7.2 on the Richter scale, struck the **Kobe-Osaka** area (also known as the Hanshin region) of western Japan. It occurred at 05.46 hours, when many people were still in bed, and caused some 5,500 deaths, injured 41,500 and left more than 300,000 homeless. It was the most destructive earthquake in Japan since the 1923 **Kanto earthquake** in the **Tokyo-Yokohama** region. In addition to housing, the earthquake destroyed many modern high-rise buildings, part of the Hanshin expressway, and many of Kobe's port facilities.

The authorities were slow to react and rescue services proved inadequate. It took 24 hours to mobilize the **Self-Defence Forces**, and information was generally lacking at first. Gradually, however, rescue operations began and the surviving population was moved to safety. In order to rehabilitate the city quickly, rebuilding efforts concentrated on the port facilities. Despite some initial loss of shipping, by 1998 Kobe had restored its economy to 80% of its pre-earthquake level.

Hatoyama Yukio

Japanese politician, a scion of a long-established political family, who was prominent in the **Democratic Party of Japan (DPJ)** until ousted by **Kan Naoto** in December 2002.

Hatoyama was born in **Tokyo** in 1947. His great-grandfather had been speaker of the **National Diet**, while his grandfather was Prime Minister in 1954–55 and first president of the newly created **Liberal Democratic Party (LDP)** in 1955. His father was foreign minister in the 1970s. Hatoyama studied engineering at Tokyo and Stanford Universities, and entered the Diet as an LDP member in 1986. However, he defected to the New Party Harbinger in 1993, and increased his electoral majority in the 1993 elections. He held a number of junior Cabinet posts, and in 1996 joined the Democratic Party, which became the DPJ in 1998. For some time he and Kan Naoto shared the leadership, but in December 2002 Kan ousted Hatoyama after the latter had attempted to merge the DPJ with the Liberal Party.

Hiroshima

On 6 August 1945 Hiroshima became the first city in the world to be attacked with an atomic bomb.

Hiroshima is the capital city of the prefecture of the same name on Japan's main island of Honshu. The city developed around a castle town in the Edo period (1600–1867) and by 1940 it was Japan's seventh largest city, with a large military population. It was thus considered to be a legitimate target for the use of the first atomic bomb. The bomb killed at least 200,000 people and destroyed about 90% of the city. Today the site of the epicentre of the bomb is a Peace Park. In this stands the Atomic Bomb Dome, the ruins of one of the few buildings to survive the attack. The commemoration of the attack on 6 August is now the city's main festival.

Today Hiroshima has been completely rebuilt and is a centre for machinery manufacturing, automobile production and food processing. In 1994 the city hosted the Asian Games. It occupies some 741 sq km and the greater Hiroshima area had a population of some 2.9m. in 2003.

History textbooks controversy

Japan has had a system for formal government approval of textbooks used in schools for civics and history teaching since the Meiji era (1868–1912). This continued under the post-war **Allied Occupation of Japan**, when the authorities insisted on screening out comments or information that supported Japan's pre-war political system, including the role of the **Japanese Emperor**. When Japan regained its independence in 1952, the new government continued the occupation arrangements.

New textbooks appear every four years. While commercial firms prepare and publish the textbooks, schools cannot use them until the Ministry of Education (now the Ministry of Education, Culture, Sports, Science and Technology) has formally approved them. The ministry only issues such approval after the removal or rewriting of what officials regard as controversial or negative points.

Japanese domestic problems with these arrangements date at least from 1965, when a historian, Ienaga Saburo (1913–2002), filed a lawsuit against the Ministry of Education which had refused to endorse one of his textbooks, because Ienaga had concentrated on the negative aspects of Japan's past. In response, Ienaga argued that the process of approving textbooks was illegal and unconstitutional. His legal challenge failed, but he went to court on two more occasions to contest the point. At the third attempt, before the Supreme Court in 1997, Ienaga's legal action once again failed. However, although the court ruled that the Ministry of Education did have the authority to vet textbooks, it added that such vetting should avoid interfering in the educational content of textbooks. By that stage, conservative historians had entered the battle, arguing that the culture of apologizing for Japan's past had gone too far, and that Japanese children were being taught to despise their country's history. Under the leadership of Fujioka Nobukatsu, a Professor of Education at **Tokyo** University, the conservatives organized the 'Japanese Society for History Textbook Reform', and produced their own textbook, which reflected nationalist traditions. When schools failed to adopt this for classroom use, the conservatives claimed that they were the victims of left-wing bias.

In 1982 the issue took on an international dimension. The Ministry of Education demanded the toning down of references to Japanese wartime behaviour in **China** and the colonial period in Korea. These attempts to 'excuse' Japan's past behaviour led to private and public protests from the **People's Republic of China (PRC)**, from the **'Republic of China'**, and from the Republic of Korea (ROK). Other countries that had experienced Japan's wartime rule also raised the issue. In the face of these protests, the Japanese authorities allowed the use of somewhat more robust language about Japanese wartime behaviour.

The issue did not abate, however, and it has resurfaced each time a new textbook has been issued. In 2000 the conservative *New History Textbook* caused controversy both at home and abroad, since it was deemed to have minimized not only earlier matters of controversy, but also the issue of **comfort women**. On this occasion the

Democratic People's Republic of Korea joined forces with the PRC and the ROK in accusing Japan of distorting history.

HIV/AIDS in East Asia

The first cases of human immunodeficiency virus (HIV) appeared in East Asia in the early 1980s, soon after international recognition of the virus. They seem to have originated outside the region. Acquired immunodeficiency syndrome (AIDS) followed the standard pattern of emerging about two years after HIV. Despite the large number of people who live in this area, the incidence of both HIV and AIDS remains relatively low in East Asian countries and regions. However, the social stigmas attached to HIV/AIDS are considerable throughout the region.

The **People's Republic of China (PRC)**, with the largest population, inevitably has the largest numbers of those with HIV/AIDS in the region. When HIV/AIDS first appeared in the early 1980s, the authorities tended to dismiss it as something that only concerned foreigners. This approach seemed to be vindicated when the first person to die of AIDS in the PRC, in 1985, was a foreign national. In the following year the PRC began testing for HIV foreigners who proposed to spend more than six months in the country. Some effort was also made to ban the import of blood and blood products. Gradually, however, it became clear that this was a problem that was not confined to foreigners, and that the economic and social changes in the 1980s were helping the spread of HIV/AIDS. The earlier restrictions on international and domestic travel were eased, and the state relaxed the tight social controls of the early years of Communist rule, thus creating conditions in which HIV/AIDS could spread. The re-emergence of a drugs problem in the PRC also contributed to its spread. By 1987, when the first PRC national died, the government could no longer ignore the prevalence of HIV/AIDS and introduced a National Programme for Prevention and Control. At the end of the 1990s HIV/AIDS was present in all of the PRC's provinces, with particularly strong concentrations in areas with high drugs usage. Estimates then put the number of those suffering from HIV/AIDS at around 500,000 out of a population of more than 1,200m., but later estimates put the figure as high as one million. Efforts at control are spasmodic, however, and there has been international criticism on human rights' grounds of some of the more draconian measures adopted. Even in April 2004 a Vice-Minister of Health could still point to a lack of awareness in the PRC of the problem, accompanied by a lack of openness and an unwillingness to spend money to resolve it.

Both the Chinese **Special Administrative Regions** of **Hong Kong** and **Macao** have low numbers of HIV/AIDS sufferers. In Hong Kong the first known HIV case dates from 1984. The main reason for the spread of HIV/AIDS seems to be sharing of needles by drugs users. Contaminated blood has also been a factor. By 2000 the number of those with HIV was estimated at 1,500, of which 500 could be expected to progress to AIDS. In Macao, where the first HIV cases were diagnosed in 1986, the main means of spreading infection appears to be overwhelmingly sexual. The precise number of those affected is not available, but is likely to be small.

Little is known about the prevalence of HIV/AIDS in **Taiwan**; the World Health Organization (WHO) and other **United Nations** bodies do not collect statistics for the **'Republic of China'**, and there are few other sources. So far, however, the authorities do not appear to regard HIV/AIDS as a matter for much concern.

Japan is unusual in that the origins of HIV/AIDS infection in the country lie in the importation of contaminated blood for haemophilic patients between the mid-1980s and the early 1990s. The incidence of HIV/AIDS remains very low, at less than 0.01% of the 15–49 age group.

HIV/AIDS in the Republic of Korea (ROK) seems to be 93% sexually-related. However, numbers remain low; in 2000 3,800, or fewer than 0.1% of the population, were thought to be HIV-positive. The ROK Ministry of Health stated in May 2004 that, as of March of that year, since the first case in 1985 about 2,679 people had been diagnosed as HIV-positive, 550 people had died of AIDS, and 411 then had AIDS. The HIV infection rate is thought to have increased by, on average, 18% annually since 1999.

Mongolia has a very low incidence of HIV/AIDS—only three cases had been reported by the end of 2001, and the total number of infected patients in the whole country is believed to be no more than 100. The first instance of HIV/AIDS in Mongolia was found in a male prostitute in 1992.

No information is available for the Democratic People's Republic of Korea (DPRK), which denies that HIV/AIDS exists in the country. However, WHO and other international bodies believe that as more DPRK citizens have travelled abroad in recent years, there is the possibility that HIV/AIDS has already entered the DPRK, and there may be as many as 100 HIV/AIDS sufferers in the country.

Ho, Edmund

Edmund Ho Hau Wah

A businessman turned politician, Edmond Ho has been chief executive of the **Special Administrative Region (SAR)** of **Macao** since 20 December 1999, when the former Portuguese colony reverted to the **People's Republic of China (PRC)**.

Born in Macao in 1955, Ho attended university in Canada, where he received a degree in business administration from York University. He then qualified as a chartered accountant and auditor. In 1982–83 he worked in **Hong Kong**, returning to Macao in 1983. He held a variety of business appointments and was also prominent in social and educational activities. From 1986 he was a member of the **Chinese People's Political Consultative Conference**, and was elected to the PRC's **National People's Congress** in 1988. He also became active in local politics, joining the Macao legislature in 1988. From then until 1999 he was vice-president of the Macao **Legislative Assembly**. After the signing of the Sino-Portuguese Joint Declaration in 1987 Ho played an important role in the drafting of the **Macao Basic Law**, and participated in the various preparatory bodies established to facilitate the handover. In May 1999 the Selection Committee for the Chief Executive of the Macao SAR nominated him for the position of chief executive, and Premier **Zhu Rongji** confirmed this appointment on 20 May 1999. In August 2004 Ho won a second term as Macao's chief executive, receiving 296 votes out of a possible 300.

> *Address:* Office of the Chief Executive
> Headquarters of Macao SAR Government
> Avenida da Praia Grande
> Macao
> *Tel:* 853-726-886
> *Fax:* 853-726-168
> *E-mail:* inf@macau.gov.mo
> *Internet:* www.macau.gov.mo

Hong Kong

Xianggang

A **Special Administrative Region** of the **People's Republic of China (PRC)** since July 1997, and before that, from 1842, a British colony.

Hong Kong lies on the Pearl river estuary not far from the PRC's **Guangzhou** (Canton) city. It occupies 1,100 sq km, and it had a population of 6.8m. in 2002, of whom 95% are of Chinese origin. Per caput gross domestic product (GDP) reached more than US \$25,000 in 2003, which puts Hong Kong on a level with most advanced countries.

Britain acquired Hong Kong in three stages. Hong Kong island, on which the capital, Victoria, is situated, became British after the 1842 Treaty of **Nanjing**, which ended the first Anglo–Chinese or Opium War. **China** ceded the Kowloon peninsula, on the mainland opposite the island, in 1860, after the end of the second Opium War. The final stage of acquisition came in 1898, when Britain joined in the scramble for concessions in China, and obtained the New Territories on a 99-year lease. In this last development lay the seeds of the 1997 reversion to the PRC.

From the beginning, other ports on the China coast overshadowed Hong Kong in importance until the **Pacific War**. At first Guangzhou and then **Shanghai** dominated China's foreign trade, leaving Hong Kong behind as something of a backwater. Hong Kong fell to the Japanese in 1942, and although there had been some pressure for its return to China during the war, it reverted to British rule in 1945. Despite this, Hong Kong's future appeared uncertain. There was concern, as the Chinese civil war developed, that the victorious Communist forces would neither respect the old treaties nor stop at the undefendable Hong Kong border. They did stop, however, and Hong Kong remained under British rule after 1949. The PRC made it clear from time to time, none the less, that it expected Hong Kong to revert to Chinese control in due course, and that the pattern elsewhere in the British Empire of a progress from colonial status to independence was not to apply to Hong Kong.

Hong Kong benefited from the restrictions that the PRC placed on foreign trade. Its old rivals, Guangzhou and Shanghai, could no longer compete, and many Chinese capitalists re-established themselves in the colony. Its population also grew as refugees flooded in from the PRC. Economically, Hong Kong would develop within 30 years from a low-cost, low-quality manufacturing centre into a source of high-quality goods and, increasingly, a service-oriented economy. The colony had low taxes, minimal government interference, and a British-based legal system, all of which encouraged its development.

The question of Hong Kong's future become urgent in the late 1970s, because of the issue of the validity of land leases that went beyond 1997, the date of return of the New Territories. Discussions began with the Chinese. The British at first hoped that some form of continued British administration would be permitted, but when British Prime Minister Margaret Thatcher visited **Beijing** in 1982, the Chinese ruled out anything except a complete reversion to Chinese sovereignty. However, the Chinese leader, **Deng Xiaoping**, accepted that circumstances were different in Hong Kong, and agreed that the formula 'One country, two systems', originally devised for **Taiwan**, should apply to Hong Kong. On this basis, negotiations continued, with agreement reached in 1984 on the Sino-British Joint Declaration. This document, registered as a treaty at the **United Nations**, provided for the people of Hong Kong to continue to enjoy their own administration, with a high degree of autonomy in legal, economic and social matters, for 50 years after the reversion. A Sino-British Joint Liaison Group would monitor arrangements until 1997 and also the early years of the new system. Hong Kong reluctantly endorsed these proposals.

The people of Hong Kong reacted with shock to the events in **Tiananmen** in 1989. Large demonstrations expressed much criticism of the PRC and there were widespread fears about the prospect of Chinese rule and demands for greater democracy in Hong Kong. In an attempt to restore confidence, the Hong Kong Government began a number of economic confidence-building measures, including the new **Chek Lap Kok—Hong Kong International Airport**. The appointment of **Christopher Patten** as governor of Hong Kong in 1992 resulted in a greater willingness to move towards structures that were more democratic to replace the colonial apparatus, but this led to increasing criticism from the PRC.

The Patten reforms did not survive after 1997. Yet, despite the fears of many of the PRC's intentions, the transition to Chinese rule has been relatively successful. Although the PRC has remained unwilling to countenance an increase in democracy, there has been no attempt to undermine the principles laid down in the 1984 Joint Declaration. The new chief executive, **Tung Chee Hwa,** was a well-known Hong Kong businessman, and many members of the old civil service remained in place. Although the **People's Liberation Army (PLA)** has a presence in Hong Kong, this has generally been low-key. It was not until 2004, for example, that it staged its first major parade. There has been no influx of people from the PRC, and the border controls that were in place before 1997 remain in force. Economically, Hong Kong continues to perform well, although it was affected by the **Asian financial crisis** of 1997 and the outbreak in 2003 of **Severe Acute Respiratory Syndrome**.

Hong Kong Basic Law

The Hong Kong Basic Law, formally promulgated on 4 April 1990, has served as the fundamental Constitution of the **Special Administrative Region (SAR)** of **Hong Kong** of the **People's Republic of China (PRC)** since 1 July 1997. Some consider the Law to have derived from the Sino-British Joint Declaration of 1984. Most PRC lawyers, however, link it to the PRC Constitution.

Responsibility for the Basic Law lay with the Basic Law Drafting Committee, which the PRC established in 1985. This committee, made up wholly of people from Hong Kong, had the task of canvassing opinions and then drafting the Law based on the views expressed to it. The committee's first draft, produced in April 1988, was followed by a five-month consultation period. The second draft appeared in February 1989, and was followed by an eight-month consultation period.

The aim of the Basic Law is to give formal implementation to the concept, expressed by **Deng Xiaoping**, that Hong Kong people would have a high degree of autonomy after Hong Kong reverted to the PRC. Under its provisions, the rights and freedoms of Hong Kong people are protected. Socialism will not be practised in the SAR, which will continue to operate within a capitalist system for 50 years after 1997. Common law will continue in use, together with freedom from arbitrary arrest or imprisonment, freedom of the press, freedom of association and assembly, and trade union rights. Hong Kong's adherence to international covenants on a variety of human rights would also be guaranteed. While defence and international affairs generally are reserved to the PRC, Hong Kong continues to have the right to separate international representation in a number of areas, such as trade and aviation matters.

One problem area has been the power of interpreting the Basic Law where there are differences of opinion. Despite attempts by Hong Kong political activists to argue that this should lie within the Hong Kong judicial system, so far the PRC has insisted that such powers lie with the Standing Committee of the PRC's **National People's Congress**. Since 1997 a number of issues have arisen, including the question of right of abode in the SAR in 1999, and, in April 2004, the issue of the selection of the SAR chief executive.

The SAR maintains a webpage that gives information about the Basic Law and about the legal challenges that have been mounted against it in the Hong Kong courts since 1 July 1997.

Internet: www.info.gov.hk/basic_law

Hong Kong Economy

Although affected by the **Asian financial crisis** of 1997, avian influenza, which remains an ongoing concern, and the 2003 onslaught of **Severe Acute Respiratory Syndrome (SARS)**, Hong Kong's economy, regarded as the freest in the world, has come through the region's transformation from a British colony to a **Special Administrative Region (SAR)** of the **People's Republic of China (PRC)** in good shape. According to the territory's financial secretary, speaking in autumn 2004, it is now in the process of moving from an industrial to a knowledge economy.

GNP: US $312,100m. (first quarter 2004 estimate); *GNP per caput:* US $25,430 (2003 estimate); *GDP at PPP:* US $213,000m. (2003 estimate); *GDP per caput at PPP:* US $28,000 (2003 estimate); *exports:* US $225,900m. (2003); *imports:* US $203,300m.; *currency:* Hong Kong dollar (US $1 = Hong Kong $7.7868 (2004)).

The Hong Kong economy has gone through several stages since Britain first acquired the island of Hong Kong in 1842. For the first 100 years of its existence, Hong Kong was in essence another **foreign settlement** along the **China** coast. It was a centre for the transhipment of goods from the West for south China and from south China to the West. Hong Kong was important as a naval centre, but nearby **Guangzhou**, and even more **Shanghai**, overshadowed it as a trading centre. After the end of the **Pacific War**, it looked at first as though Shanghai would regain its former predominance. The victory of the **Chinese Communist Party** in the Chinese civil war, however, soon led to Shanghai's eclipse.

Hong Kong's advantage was that it was now the only fully open port on the China coast. It also gained through the influx of Shanghai merchants escaping the Communists, and began to develop as both an international port and a manufacturing centre. New markets in Asia and further afield replaced the loss of trade with the PRC. Economic development, as in Japan, received a further impetus from the **Korean War**. The influx of large numbers of workers from the PRC provided a labour force. A series of fires and natural disasters eventually forced the Hong Kong government to intervene in areas such as housing development, but, in general, government in the colony was low-key and *laissez-faire* in economic and social matters. Government expenditure was low, as was taxation. At the same time, the rule of law and the stable political structure favoured business development. There was a free flow of information, including financial information. Hong Kong began to develop as an industrial centre. It specialized mainly in light industry, such as toy production and electrical and electronic goods, but it also undertook shipbuilding and other engineering works. As the PRC began to resume contacts with the rest of the world, Hong Kong also began to take on a role in the PRC's trade.

Although the **Cultural Revolution** in the PRC had some effect on the Hong Kong economy, with strikes, demonstrations, and disruption of trade with the PRC, the colonial authorities held firm, and did not lose control as happened in **Macao**. As the PRC began to come out of the most intensive phase of the Cultural

Revolution, Hong Kong resumed its role in the China trade. It also benefited from being a rest and recreation centre for US forces during the Viet Nam War. In the early 1970s Hong Kong's economy began to change. It remained an important manufacturing centre, as it still does. Now, however, the emphasis was on more technologically advanced products, and the territory's former reputation as a producer of low-quality goods was superseded. Cheaper air transport and the growth of international tourism benefited Hong Kong, and led to the construction of new facilities to cope with the influx of tourists. As the PRC under **Deng Xiaoping** set itself on a new course of reform and opening to the outside world from 1978 onwards, Hong Kong began to gain. Trade increased and many of those visiting the PRC visited Hong Kong. Rail links improved, and the development of the **Special Economic Zone** at **Shenzhen**, just across the Hong Kong border, had a positive impact on the Hong Kong economy.

The PRC cast one shadow over Hong Kong's development in the 1970s. The lease on the New Territories, acquired from China in 1898, was due to expire in 1997, at which point the New Territories would revert to the PRC. Without the New Territories, there was a question of the viability of the rest of the territory, especially as the PRC had made it clear that it would seek the return of the whole of Hong Kong in 1997. By the late 1970s this issue was beginning to affect the issue of leases in the colony, and therefore its economic well-being. The 1984 Sino-British agreement on the return of Hong Kong in its entirety in 1997 thus had a positive effect on economic development.

From 1978 onwards the Hong Kong economy steadily became part of a wider Hong Kong-Macao-Shenzhen-Guangzhou economic area, with high growth and fast development. The more the PRC opened up, the more Hong Kong gained. From the early 1980s onwards Hong Kong's economy grew by an average annual rate of 5%, so that between 1982 and 2002 the size of the economy doubled. By 2002 per caput gross domestic product (GDP) stood at US $23,800, making Hong Kong second only to Japan in Asia. During the same period Hong Kong's trade in goods expanded by eight times, and trade in services by three. By 2002 the total value of visible trade was US $3,164,000m., or some 251% of GDP. Adding in exports and imports of services, the figure was equivalent to 295% of GDP, compared to 173% in 1982. Hong Kong also benefited from a high volume of inward investment, totalling US $3,270,000m. at the end of 2001.

The figures do not reveal the whole story, however. Hong Kong's economic development has not been entirely smooth. Confidence in Hong Kong dipped in 1989, especially after the suppression of the student demonstrations in **Tiananmen**. The dispute between the PRC and the last British governor of Hong Kong, **Christopher Patten**, also affected the economy from time to time, especially when the PRC attacked policies such as the building of **Chek Lap Kok—Hong Kong International Airport**, and a new container terminal. The Asian financial crisis struck the SAR soon after its reversion to the PRC. The Hong Kong government stood firm against the attack on the Hong Kong dollar, aided by the PRC's decision not to devalue its currency. More recently the 1993 SARS epidemic harmed an economy that had already suffered a downturn in 2000–2001.

The Hong Kong economy has recovered after SARS, and once again is set on a path of growth. SARS harmed the tourist industry, as the PRC restricted traffic across its borders. Tourism began to recover by the end of 2003, and in 2004 there was a notable increase in numbers arriving from the PRC and further afield. The British decision to build a new airport proved to be the right one, and PRC criticism has ceased. Hong Kong's closer integration into the South China economic area has been further emphasized by the conclusion of an agreement on closer economic co-operation, signed in June 2003, and registered with the **World Trade Organization** in December 2003. The current structure of the economy also reflects the PRC's importance. Primary production, such as agricultural and fishing, has practically disappeared as a factor. Even secondary production, chiefly the manufacturing of goods, which accounted for nearly 32% of economic activity in 1981, has declined to about 13%. What has grown, and continues to grow, is the tertiary sector. This, comprising wholesale and retail trade, financial and similar services, transport, communications and tourism-related business, now accounts for more than 85% of GDP, compared with 67% in the early 1980s.

Hong Kong's main trading partners in 2003 were the PRC, the USA, Japan and **Taiwan**. Of these, the PRC was responsible for about 43% of total trade, and the USA for considerably less—11.9%. Great Britain, the former colonial power, has long since fallen behind; its share of Hong Kong's trade, at 2.3%, ranked eighth in importance.

Hong Kong's continued economic development is still based on the factors that accounted for its initial success: the rule of law, a relatively *laissez-faire* government, the free flow of information, and openness to the outside world. Although it was predicted that the resumption of Chinese sovereignty would erode these basic building blocks, this has not happened in the economic sphere, and Hong Kong continues to benefit. The selection of **Tung Chee Hwa**, a man with a business back-ground, as the first chief executive of the SAR provided reassurance that the new rulers of Hong Kong wanted it to continue to develop economically, whatever other signals it may have sent. There are challenges, however. The changes in the PRC since the late 1980s have unleashed local competitors for Hong Kong's position. Shanghai is anxious to regain its pre-war position as the China coast's dominant trading centre. Beyond the PRC, there is competition from Singapore and new centres such as **Seoul**. For the present, however, Hong Kong's pre-eminence seems assured.

Hong Kong Independent Commission against Corruption (HKICAC)

Body established in 1974 in an attempt to combat corruption in **Hong Kong**.

The rapid development of the **Hong Kong economy** in the 1960s and early 1970s led to a major increase in corruption, especially in the Hong Kong civil service and in the police force. A celebrated case in 1973, arising from the investigation of an expatriate police superintendent, Peter Godber, over large sums for which he could not account, brought matters to a culmination. Godber fled the colony, which added to the outrage. The colonial authorities, which had hitherto ignored evidence of corruption, now acted, and in February 1974 the HKICAC began working. It was from the start, and has remained, a separate organization from the Hong Kong police force. The HKICAC successfully sought Godber's extradition from the United Kingdom, and he was eventually imprisoned. The fact that Godber was an expatriate and a police officer did much to establish the HKICAC as an independent and resolute body.

Since then, and even after the reversion of Hong Kong to the **People's Republic of China** in 1997, the HKICAC has pursued the fight against corruption in what is now the Hong Kong **Special Administrative Region**. Some suspect that it is not quite as active as in the past, but it continues the fight to eradicate corruption wherever it is found in Hong Kong. Other anti-corruption organizations in East Asia have followed the HKICAC approach, although not all have enjoyed the same high reputation as their Hong Kong counterpart.

E-mail: general@icac.org.hk
Internet: www.icac.org.hk

Hong Kong Liaison Office of the Central People's Government

In January 2000 the **Xinhua News Agency** branch in **Hong Kong** formally changed its name to the Hong Kong Liaison Office of the Central People's Government of the **People's Republic of China (PRC)**. The then head of the Xinhua branch, Jiang Enzhu, a senior diplomat with long experience of working with Britain, became head of the new liaison office. In August 2002 Gao Siren, another senior diplomat, replaced Jiang. The office is viewed with suspicion by many in Hong Kong, who consider its role to be that of checking democratic tendencies in the Hong Kong **Special Administrative Region** and undermining the principle that Hong Kong people should govern Hong Kong.

A branch of the Xinhua News Agency operated in Hong Kong from 1947. From the start it had a wider role than the mere collection and dissemination of news. In addition to its news-gathering function, the Xinhua office was the **Chinese Communist Party**'s unacknowledged Hong Kong branch, controlling party affairs in the British colony. After the Communist victory in 1949 and Britain's decision to establish diplomatic relations with the PRC, the latter sought to have formal representation in Hong Kong, as the previous **Republic of China (1912–49)** government had done. Britain refused, fearing that any PRC-linked office would became a focal point for opposition to colonial rule. In the absence of formal representation, Xinhua became the unofficial presence of the PRC in the colony.

Over the years the office grew in size, so that by the 1990s it had several hundred staff; of these, according to press reports, about 80–90 were concerned with normal news agency work. During the **Cultural Revolution** the detention of Xinhua 'journalists' led to the house arrest of the Reuters **Beijing** correspondent, Anthony Grey. As Britain's relations with China improved after 1972, the Hong Kong government's dealings with Xinhua became more formalized and regular, although the agency was still only an unofficial channel. In 1990, following the 1989 **Tiananmen** incident, the then head of the Hong Kong branch, Xu Jiatun fled to the USA. His memoirs, published in 1993, revealed much about the workings of the agency in Hong Kong. Relations between the British authorities and Xinhua were poor for most of **Christopher Patten**'s governorship. It was also during this period that local suspicions in Hong Kong grew about the exact role of the agency.

Hong Kong Progressive Alliance

Xianggang xiejinlianmeng

Formed in 1994, this **Hong Kong** political party has the reputation of being pro-**People's Republic of China (PRC)** and pro-business.

The Progressive Alliance's membership comes from the business and professional classes. The party has sent a number of delegates to the PRC's **National People's Congress** and to the **Chinese People's Political Consultative Conference**. The chairman, Ambrose Lau, is a British-trained solicitor. The Alliance won five seats in the 1998 **Legislative Council** elections, and four in the 2000 elections.

> *Chair.:* Ambrose Lau Hon-chuen
> *Address:* Hong Kong Progressive Alliance
> c/o Legislative Council
> Hong Kong
> *Tel:* 852-5262-2316
> *Fax:* 852-2845-0127
> *E-mail:* info@hkpa.org.hk
> *Internet:* www.hkpa.org.hk

Hong Song Nam

Hong Song Nam was Premier of the Democratic People's Republic of Korea (DPRK) in 1998–2003, when Pak Pong Ju replaced him. Hong was born in 1929, and educated at **Kim Il Sung University** and in Czechoslovakia. In 1971 he was director of the heavy industry department of the **Korean Workers' Party (KWP)**. Two years later he was noted as the Vice-Prime Minister and chairman of the State Planning Commission. He then held a variety of state and KWP posts until his appointment as Prime Minister. After losing his post as Prime Minister, he re-emerged in the same year as the head of the KWP in South Hamgyong Province.

Hosokawa Morihiro

In 1993 Hosokawa Morihiro became the first non-**Liberal Democratic Party (LDP)** Prime Minister of Japan for 38 years. Although he was only Prime Minister from August 1993 until April 1994, he instituted a reform agenda that has dominated Japanese politics ever since.

Hosokawa was born in Kumamoto in 1938 into a long-established aristocratic family. After a brief spell as a journalist, he was elected to the upper house of the **National Diet** in 1971 on an LDP ticket. In 1983–91 he was governor of Kumamoto Prefecture, where he found central government control particularly irksome. In 1992 he founded the Japan New Party (JNP—*Nihon Shinto*). Despite its recent foundation, the JNP won 35 seats at the July 1992 general election, in which Hosokawa was also returned to a seat in the lower house of the Diet. Following the election the LDP Cabinet fell in August, and Hosokawa became Prime Minister, heading a multi-party coalition. He had a radical agenda, including decentralization, anti-corruption and tax reforms. However, it was not easy to introduce such measures in the face of bureaucratic opposition, and little of the agenda had been implemented when Hosokawa suddenly resigned in April 1994.

After his resignation, Hosokawa continued in politics, joining first the New Frontier Party (*Shinshinto*), and then, in 1998, the **Democratic Party** of Japan (JDP—*Nihon minshuto*). In 2000 he abandoned politics in favour of pottery.

HSBC Holdings PLC

Created in 1991, HSBC Holdings PLC is one of the largest banking groups in the world, second only to Citigroup. The group owes its origins to the Hong Kong and Shanghai Bank (HSBC) first established in **Hong Kong** in March 1865 and in **Shanghai** in April 1865. The founder was a Scottish clerk, Thomas Sutherland, originally with the P&O Line. The Bank was incorporated in Hong Kong by the Hong Kong and Shanghai Bank Ordinance of 1866. Branches of the Bank were rapidly established throughout the East Asian **foreign settlements**.

From the beginning the Bank was involved in financial matters, and it handled **China**'s first public loan in 1874. Since then the HSBC has been involved in most Chinese public loans. By 1900 it was widely regarded as Asia's main financial institution. During the **Pacific War** most of its branches had to close, but it resumed business in 1945. The Communist victories in China led eventually to an attack on all foreign banks, but the HSBC managed to keep its Shanghai branch open until, in the 1970s, a change of approach on the part of China's leaders occurred.

In the mean time the Bank had begun to expand into other areas. In 1959 it acquired The British Bank of the Middle East and the Indian-based Mercantile Bank. In the same year it also acquired a controlling interest in the Hang Seng Bank, a sign of its continued involvement in Hong Kong. In the 1980s it began operations in Canada and Australia, and in 1992 it acquired Britain's Midland Bank. This policy of adding new areas continues, but the HSBC is still an important financial institution in Hong Kong, and elsewhere in East Asia. Together with the **Bank of China** and the **Standard Chartered Bank**, it retains the right to issue banknotes in Hong Kong. The focus of its activities in Hong Kong is the HSBC Tower in Hong Kong's Central District, a building designed by the British architect Norman Foster. In Shanghai, where its offices were once on the Bund, it now occupies the HSBC Tower in the new district of Pudong. Its British headquarters are at Canary Wharf in London's East End.

Hu Jintao

Hu Jintao became secretary-general of the **Chinese Communist Party (CCP)** in 2002 and President of the **People's Republic of China (PRC)** in March 2003.

He was born in 1942, probably in **Shanghai**, where his family owned a shop. Like many others in the PRC's current leadership, he is an engineer by training, having studied hydraulic engineering at Qinghua University in **Beijing**. While at Qinghua he joined the Communist Youth League (CYL), and later the CCP. He was briefly involved, as a party member, in the struggles at Qinghua during the **Cultural Revolution**, but avoided serious difficulties. From 1968 until 1982 Hu worked in Gansu Province, a remote and backward area, but one that kept him away from the centre in the later stages of the Cultural Revolution. In 1981 he returned to Beijing, first to attend a cadre (officials') training school, and then as an alternate member of the Central Committee of the CCP. He returned briefly to Gansu in 1982 to head the local CYL, but before long was back in the centre as number two in the national CYL. In 1984 he became first secretary, or leader, of the CYL. In the following year he moved to Guizhou Province as party secretary. This was both a promotion—he was the youngest party secretary in the country—and also something of a set-back. However, it meant he was away from the centre when **Hu Yaobang** lost the position of CCP general secretary in 1987. Since he was close to Hu, a more central position might have affected his prospects for further promotion.

Instead, his career continued upwards. In 1988 he became party secretary in the **Tibet** Autonomous Region (TAR). This was not an easy appointment since there was much unrest in Tibet and Hu felt compelled to declare martial law. At the same time, he attempted to meet some of the **Tibetans'** grievances, while learning more about the area by regular tours. However, he was prone to altitude sickness and as a result had to spend long periods outside the region. This placed him in Beijing at an opportune moment, and at the 14th **National People's Congress** Hu was elected to the Politburo. His progress was now rapid. In 1994 he became head of the CCP Central School, Vice-President of the PRC in 1998, and, a sure sign of his importance, a vice-chairman of the CCP **Central Military Commission (CMC)** in 1999. When **Jiang Zemin** stepped down as CCP general-secretary in 2002, Hu took over. In the following year he succeeded Jiang as head of state and in 2004 assumed the leadership of both CMCs.

Hu's elevation marks a departure in PRC politics from the heavily Shanghai-based leadership of the immediate past. He is regarded as reform-minded, linked to Hu Yaobang and other relatively liberal figures, but he has hitherto been careful not to be too far ahead of Jiang Zemin and his colleagues. Now that he is the official paramount leader, he may try new ways, although so far there has been no sign of this.

Hu Yaobang (1915–1989)

Born in 1915, Hu Yaobang joined the **Chinese Communist Party (CCP)** in the late 1920s. He took part in the **Long March** and was a political officer with the **People's Liberation Army** during the Chinese civil war. After the establishment of the **People's Republic of China** in 1949, Hu occupied a number of party posts, mostly connected with the youth movement, but he disappeared from view at the start of the **Cultural Revolution** in 1966. He reappeared in 1972. He worked with **Deng Xiaoping** when the latter reappeared in 1975, and again after his second reappearance in 1977. In 1980 Hu joined the Politburo Standing Committee and became secretary-general of the CCP in 1982. Before long his enthusiasm for reform outran not only that of many of the conservatives within the party leadership, but also that of Deng and Premier **Zhao Ziyang**. As a result, Hu resigned his position as secretary-general early in 1987. Although he remained on the Politburo, he had no influence. He remained popular among students and others as a symbol of reform.

Hu died on 15 April 1989, and on the following day mourning altars began to appear at Beijing University. Before long this spontaneous expression of sorrow at Hu's death developed into major student demonstrations against the government, leading ultimately to the demonstrations in **Tiananmen** in June 1989.

Hua Guofeng

A political leader in the **People's Republic of China**, born in Shanxi in 1920 or 1921, Hua Guofeng fought with the Eighth Route Army (a forerunner of the **People's Liberation Army**) against the Japanese and in the Chinese civil war. After 1949 he became a provincial official and, as deputy governor of Hunan Province (**Mao Zedong**'s home province), was the highest-ranking local official to survive the **Cultural Revolution**. He played an important role in investigating the **Lin Biao** affair in 1971, and became a Vice-Premier in 1975. When Premier **Zhou Enlai** died in 1976 Hua became acting Premier. Following Mao's death in October 1976, Hua succeeded him as chairman of the **Chinese Communist Party (CCP)** and also as chairman of the Party's **Central Military Commission**; Mao was supposed to have endorsed these appointments by telling Hua, 'With you in charge, I am at ease'.

Hua successfully fought off the challenge to his leadership from Mao's widow and other members of the Gang of Four, but **Deng Xiaoping**, with whom he had worked for a time as Vice-Premier, eventually outmanoeuvred him to become the paramount leader. Hua resigned as Premier in 1980 and as chairman of the CCP Central Committee in 1981. He continued to serve on the CCP Politburo until the 1990s, but never regained his former importance.

Hui

Accounted the fourth largest minority nationality in the **People's Republic of China (PRC)**. In the 1990 population census they numbered 8,612,000.

In appearance and language they are almost indistinguishable from the **Han Chinese** and are, in fact, defined by their Muslim religion alone. (No other religious group in the PRC has claimed minority status on the basis of faith.) The Ningxia Hui Autonomous Region, a small north-western area surrounded by the **Inner Mongolia** Autonomous Region and Gansu and Shaanxi Provinces and watered by the **Yellow river**, was designated for the Hui in 1958. It capital is Yinchuan. The region's economy is based on agriculture, which is dependent on irrigation, and on coal-mining. Approximately one-third of the population of Ningxia Hui Autonomous Region is Hui. They are particularly concentrated in the southern part of the Autonomous Region. Large communities also exist in Gansu Province, where they form the biggest minority group, and in Yunnan. They are, however, found in many other parts of **China** and in **Beijing** and **Tianjin**. In a rare reported instance of communal fighting, Hui in the central province of Henan clashed with their Han neighbours in October 2004.

Although the Hui much resemble the Han around them, they are not Chinese in their origins. **Islam** was first brought into China in the early 7th century through travellers, often merchants from Arabia and Persia seeking trade with the Tang court (618–907), who came overland across Central Asia to the north-west areas of the country or by sea to ports in the south-east coastal regions. The second and greater wave of Muslim immigrants were introduced forcibly by the Mongol armies who, from their invasions westwards in the 13th century into Central Asia, brought back workers and craftsmen but also women and children to serve the Mongol administration and aristocracy. Intermarriage with local people and processes of adoption and conversion brought them into closer contact with the Chinese population. They live now in compact communities centred on the mosque and observe the required Muslim festivals and dietary laws. Hui cuisine, with its replacement of pork with mutton, is a distinctive feature of some restaurants in, for example, Beijing.

Hwang Jang-Yop

In February 1997 Hwang Jang-Yop, born in 1923, a secretary of the Central Committee of the **Korean Workers' Party (KWP)** in the Democratic People's Republic of Korea (DPRK), became the highest-ranking DPRK defector to the Republic of Korea (ROK) since the 1950–53 **Korean War**. In addition to his KWP role, Hwang was widely credited with being the main theorist of the KWP's *juche* (self-reliance) philosophy, and had been a tutor to **Kim Jong Il**, the son and heir of the DPRK's first leader, **Kim Il Sung**. Hwang's defection, which took place in **Beijing** following a visit to Japan, appears to have been arranged by the ROK Agency for National Security Planning (now the National Intelligence Service) and was at first regarded as a sign of problems within the DPRK regime.

The DPRK denounced the defection. Hwang became the centre of much activity by intelligence agencies, but he revealed little beyond details of how the DPRK political structure operates, and it became clear that personal as much as political reasons had played a part in his defection, and that he had long been away from the DPRK centres of political power. Hwang has complained that his views are ignored and that he has not been allowed to travel abroad.

Hyundai Corporation

Among the largest of the big business conglomerates or *chaebol* in the Republic of Korea (ROK).

Hyundai was founded by Chung Ju-Yung (1915–2001), who was born in what is now the Democratic People's Republic of Korea (DPRK). He set up his first company, a small car-repair workshop, in 1946. Hyundai subsequently diversified into heavy industry, cement, construction, engineering, shipbuilding, insurance, pharmaceuticals and motor cars, and by the early 1990s it accounted for 16% of the ROK's gross domestic product and 12% of its total exports. Its most recent ventures have been overseas, into the exploitation of oil and natural gas resources and into gold and coal extraction, with the intention of securing vital raw materials. Control of Hyundai subsidiaries is frequently vested in members of the Chung family.

As well as his industrial interests, Chung Ju-Yung was active in many other areas of ROK life, and stood, unsuccessfully, as a presidential candidate in 1992. He also took his company into the area of **Korean North-South relations**, moved by sentiment as well as by business aspirations. From the late 1980s, as the ROK revised its former hostile policies on contacts with the DPRK and its Communist allies in favour of a less confrontational position, Chung began to make approaches to the DPRK, in the hope of extending Hyundai's operations into the North. He made his first visit to **Pyongyang** in 1989, when he proposed various business projects, including one for tourist development of the scenic Kumgang mountains on the east coast of the country (the region straddles the **Demilitarized Zone** dividing the DPRK and the ROK and lies just south of Chung's birthplace). After protracted negotiations, the Kumgang mountains tourist project was finally initiated in late 1998, and in 1999 Hyundai Asan, the subsidiary set up to run the company's DPRK ventures, was established under the direction of Chung Mong-Hun, Chung Ju-Yung's fifth son. Hyundai Asan is also involved in the proposed development of an industrial park at **Kaesong** on the west side of the DPRK.

Hyundai's intervention in North-South relations has come at a price. The tourist project is consuming vast amounts of money and is now being underwritten by the ROK government. Furthermore, it now appears that Hyundai, whether or not acting with official knowledge, transferred some US $500m. to the DPRK before the June 2000 summit between the then President of the ROK, **Kim Dae-Jung**, and the DPRK leader, **Kim Jong Il**, by way of inducement or at DPRK insistence. Following prosecution for this payment, Chung Mong-Hun, who took over as head of the Hyundai Group in 2000, committed suicide in August 2003. His widow is attempting to assume control of the group. The Hyundai conglomerate has faced financial difficulties and pressure to restructure and has been broken into several companies, all sharing the same name.

CEO and Pres.: Mark Juhn
Address: Hyundai Corporation
         226, 1-ga, Sinmunno
         Jongno-gu
         Seoul 110 786
         Republic of Korea
Tel: 82-2-390-1114
E-mail: webmaster@hyundaicorp.com
Internet: www.hyundaicorp.com

I

Inner Mongolia

Territory of northern **China**, 1.18m. sq km in area, bordered on the north by Mongolia and the Russian Federation and on the west, south and east by a number of Chinese provinces and by Ningxia Hui Autonomous Region. It is administered as the Inner Mongolia Autonomous Region (IMAR). The **Yellow river** traverses part of Inner Mongolia, but much of the terrain is high plateau supporting extensive grasslands. The climate is harsh, varying between winter and summer extremes, and often dry. To the north, into Mongolia, the land becomes the Gobi desert, and much of Inner Mongolia is also described as desert. One of the branches of the **Trans-Siberian Railway** runs from the Chinese capital **Beijing** through Inner Mongolia and Mongolia up to Siberia.

The area south of the Gobi was brought under Chinese imperial control in the 17th century and was settled by **Han Chinese**. It remained so until the fall of the Qing dynasty in 1911. Thereafter, it was absorbed into other administrative regions until, in the confused conditions of the 1930s, a movement aimed at autonomy for Inner Mongolia was initiated, but with little eventual success. Soviet determination at the end of the Second World War to retain a hold on Outer Mongolia meant an end to any hope of reunification of the two Mongolias. As the Chinese Communists progressively took control of the north-east region of China after 1945 they created an autonomous region in 1947 out of the Mongol populations of the north-east. As their authority expanded westwards they incorporated other areas with Mongol populations and in 1954 sited the capital of the IMAR at Höhhot. The boundaries of the IMAR have been changed several times since its creation. The present region had a population of 23.76m. in the 2000 population census. The majority are Han Chinese, and the **Mongol** minority, 3,379,738 in the 1990 census, probably account now for around 3.5m. The IMAR's largest city is Baotou, an industrial centre with an important iron and steel complex. The region is rich in coal, oil and minerals. The areas around the Yellow river produce considerable quantities of grain, and the northern grasslands support extensive herds of sheep, cattle, horses and camels, largely tended by the Mongol population.

International Air Transport Association (IATA)

Canada-based international organization aimed at making air travel safe, reliable and efficient. Founded in 1945 in Havana, Cuba, it has been a two-tier organization since 1979. As a trade association, it handles technical, financial, legal and traffic services issues between airlines. Some 270 airlines world-wide, including all East Asian airlines, belong to this tier. The second tier is concerned with traffic co-ordination, and covers matters such as fares and cargo rates. The international take-up of this aspect of membership is much lower, at about 100 airlines. Some East Asian airlines, such as Japan Airlines, Air China, **Korean Air** and Asiana, participate at this level, but others do not.

CEO/Dir-Gen.: Giovanni Bisignani
Address: IATA Main Office
        800 Place Victoria
        POB 113
        Montreal H42 1MI
        Quebec
        Canada
Tel: 1-514-874-0202
Fax: 1-514-874-9632
E-mail: partnership@iata.org
Internet: www.iata.org

International Atomic Energy Agency (IAEA)

Established in 1957, this **United Nations (UN)** organization has the role of promoting and monitoring the peaceful uses of atomic energy. It has a director-general, six deputy directors-general, and a staff of 2,200, drawn from 90 countries. There are 137 member states and the International Atomic Energy Agency (IAEA) periodically reports to the UN General Assembly or to the Security Council. All of the East Asian states, except for the **'Republic of China'**, are members of the IAEA, although there has been an unresolved dispute since late 2002 over the **Democratic People's Republic of Korea nuclear programme**. In 2004 the IAEA investigated the Republic of Korea's alleged experiments with an enriched uranium programme.

Dir-Gen.: Dr Mohammad el-Bardei
Address: POB 100
        Wagramstrasse 5
        1400 Vienna
        Austria
Tel: 43-1-26000
Fax: 43-1-26007
E-mail: officialmail@iaea.org
Internet: www.iaea.org/worldatom

International Civil Aviation Organization (ICAO)

The International Civil Aviation Organization (ICAO), created in Chicago, USA, in 1944, formally came into existence in 1947. Its purpose is to encourage the orderly development of civil aviation by setting international standards for the safety, security, efficiency and regularity of air services. It is a special agency of the **United Nations (UN)**, linked to the UN Economic and Social Council. It now has some 183 members. All of the East Asian countries belong to it, except the **'Republic of China'**, and **Hong Kong** and **Macao** are also members. There is an Asia-Pacific Office, based in Bangkok, Thailand.

The ICAO played an important role during the crisis that followed the shooting down of the Korean Airlines (now **Korean Air**) flight KE007 by Soviet fighter aircraft in September 1983.

President of the Council: Dr Assad Kotaite
Address: ICAO
999 University St
Montreal
Quebec H3C 5H7
Canada
Tel: 1-514-954-8219
Fax: 1-514-954-6077
E-mail: icaohq@icao.net
Internet: www.icao.mt

International Maritime Organization (IMO)

The International Maritime Organization (IMO) is a London-based **United Nations (UN)** organization, which began as the Inter-governmental Maritime Consultative Organization (IMCO), following a conference on safety at sea held in Geneva, Switzerland, in 1948. The conference drew up a convention, which entered into force in 1958, and the IMCO came into existence in the following year. It changed its name to the IMO in 1982. Although the original aim of the IMO was safety at sea, its role has much expanded to cover pollution and many other areas. Except for the **'Republic of China'** all of the East Asian states are members of IMO, including land-locked **Mongolia**, which joined in 1996. In addition, **Hong Kong** (since 1967) and **Macao** (since 1990) are associate members of IMO.

Sec.-Gen.: Efthimios Mitropoulos (since 1 January 2004)
Address: IMO
4 Albert Embankment
London SE1 7SR
United Kingdom
Tel: 44-20-7735-7611
Fax: 44-20-7587-3210
E-mail: info@imo.org
Internet: www.imo.org

International Military Tribunal for the Far East (IMTFE)

Kyokuto kokusai gunji

Military court established by the Allies in Japan to try alleged Japanese war criminals at the end of the **Pacific War**.

In the declaration following the July 1945 **Potsdam Conference**, the wartime Allies stated that Japanese war criminals would be punished. Accordingly, in January 1946, the Supreme Commander for the Allied Powers in **Tokyo** established the International Military Tribune for the Far East (IMTFE), a military court to try 28 senior civil and military officials who had led Japan since 1931. These, described as Class A war criminals, were charged with planning and initiating aggressive war; the **Japanese Emperor** was not charged. The Tribunal had 11 judges, one each from the nine countries that had signed the surrender document, one from the Philippines and one from India. The presiding judge was an Australian, Sir William Webb. The Tribunal operated under a modified form of Anglo-American law, using English as its official language. During the course of the trials, which began in May 1946, one of the defendants was declared unfit to stand, and two died. In November 1948 the remainder were found guilty. Seven were sentenced to death, 16 to life imprisonment, one to 20 years' imprisonment, and one to a term of seven years. The death sentences were carried out in December 1948.

Those imprisoned were paroled when the **San Francisco Peace Treaty** became effective in April 1952, and all were unconditionally released in April 1958. Other tribunals, held in areas once occupied by Japan, tried civil and military officials for a variety of conventional war crimes, including offences against **prisoners of war of the Japanese**. There was no formal link between the IMTFE and these local courts.

Even at the time, the IMTFE was controversial, and both the Tribunal and its decisions have remained so ever since. Many in Japan view the IMTFE as an example of 'victors' justice', rather than an impartial court of law. However, as with the Nuremberg trials of Germans charged with war crimes, it helped set the precedent that the senior leadership of a country cannot escape responsibility for actions that it has authorized.

International Monetary Fund (IMF)

Specialized agency of the **United Nations (UN)** charged with ensuring the stability of the international monetary and financial system. The International Monetary Fund (IMF) strives to achieve this through the promotion of international monetary co-operation, the balanced growth of international trade, exchange stability and the establishment of a multilateral system of payments. The IMF also lends its resources under appropriate safeguards to members facing balance-of-payments difficulties, a provision that was much drawn upon during the oil price crisis of the mid-1970s and the financial markets crisis of the late 1990s, which affected several countries in east and other parts of Asia. The Fund furthermore offers training and technical assistance in such areas as financial analysis and policy, and reform and management of tax, banking and financial systems, and collects and analyses the national economic data that members are required to submit regularly as a condition of membership.

The IMF, together with the **World Bank**, originated in a conference convened by the UN in 1944 at Bretton Woods in New Hampshire, USA, to examine ways of achieving a framework for post-war economic co-operation. (This gathering is sometimes referred to as the Bretton Woods conference, and the IMF and the World Bank as the Bretton Woods institutions.) The Fund itself was brought officially into existence on 27 December 1945 and began operations on 1 March 1947. Its funds are provided by its members, primarily through payment of their quotas, which are broadly determined by each member's economic size. Member countries are each represented by a governor on the Board of Governors. As of June 2004, membership of the IMF stood at 184. Among countries in East Asia, the following are members (with their date of accession): Japan (August 1952), Republic of Korea (August 1955), Mongolia (February 1991). **China** was among those countries signing the Articles of Agreement in December 1945. The **People's Republic of China** did not accede to the IMF until 1980. **Hong Kong** subscribes to the Fund's Special Data Dissemination Standard but is not a separate member.

Man. Dir: Rodrigo Rato
Address: 700 19th Street NW
　　　　　　Washington, DC, 20431
　　　　　　USA
Tel: 1-202-623-7000
Fax: 1-202-623-4661
Internet: www.imf.org

International Whaling Commission (IWC)

The International Whaling Commission (IWC) dates from 1946, and supervises the conduct of **whaling** throughout the world. It has 43 members, including the **People's Republic of China**, Japan, Mongolia, and the Republic of Korea (ROK). Of these countries, only Japan has an active whaling tradition, which has frequently brought it into dispute with the IWC. Several meetings of the Commission have been held in **Tokyo**, and the 2005 meeting will be held in Ulsan in the ROK.

Chair.: Commander Henrick Fischer
Address: The Red House
　　　　　　135 Station Rd
　　　　　　Impington
　　　　　　Cambridge CB4 9NP
　　　　　　United Kingdom
Tel: 44-1223-233971
Fax: 44-1223-232876
E-mail: iwc@iwcoffice.org.
Internet: www.iwcoffice.org

Inter-Parliamentary Union (IPU)

The Inter-Parliamentary Union (IPU) dates from 1889 and is today an international organization linking the parliaments of 140 independent states. Its independence allows parliamentarians to meet even when their governments are hostile to each other. Japan joined the IPU in 1910, and the country's **National Diet** is therefore the oldest East Asian member; today, all of the East Asian parliaments are members, except for that of the **'Republic of China'**. The IPU holds regular conferences. **Tokyo** was the first East Asian capital to host a conference, the 49th, held in 1960. It also hosted the 61st in 1974. **Seoul** was the venue of the 70th conference in 1983, while the 85th took place in **Pyongyang** in 1991. **Beijing** hosted the 96th conference in 1996.

Pres.: Sergio Páez
Sec.-Gen.: Anders B. Johnsson
Address: 5 chemin du Pommier
        Case postale 330
        CH 1218 Le Grand-Sacconex/Geneva
        Switzerland
Tel: 41-22-919450
Fax: 41-22-9194160
E-mail: postbox@mail.ipu.org
Internet: www.ipu.org

Islam

One of the world's leading religions, from whose origins in the 6th century AD in the Arabian peninsula a global following has developed. It is a monotheistic religion, based on the teaching of Muhammad (570–633), regarded as the Prophet and Final Messenger of Allah. Its sacred text is the Koran, whose 30 sections were revealed to Muhammad. The rapid spread of Islam was in part due to Arab conquests of surrounding regions, but also in part to the far-reaching travels of traders, who took it into many parts of Asia.

Islam has adherents in all of the countries and regions of East Asia, with the exception of the Democratic People's Republic of Korea. Its largest presence is in the **People's Republic of China (PRC)**, where Muslims number 18m.–20m. Somewhat fewer than one-half of these are included in the **Hui** minority of Chinese-speaking Muslims (estimated at 8.6m.), who are dispersed throughout the country but are particularly represented in the north-west and south-west regions of the country. Long-settled Hui communities are found, together with sometimes ancient mosques, in **Beijing**, Xi'an and **Guangzhou**. Altogether 10 minorities are described as Muslim: the Hui, the Turkic **Uygur** and **Kazak** minorities living in the north-west border areas of the PRC, and seven smaller ones. During the **Cultural Revolution** (1966–76), in common with other religious denominations, Muslim activities and practices came under attack, but in recent years the faithful have been able to resume their functions, including making the pilgrimage to Mecca. Islam is accepted in the PRC as one of the five 'organized' religions and is administered though the China Islam Association. In Mongolia, the Kazak minority of around 103,000, living in the westernmost province of the country where it approaches Kazakhstan, is Muslim. Islam suffered persecution in the 1930s together with **Buddhism**, but has now been reinstated as one of the country's three native religions.

The Muslim Hui element in the Chinese population undoubtedly accounts for the presence of small Muslim communities and mosques in **Taiwan** (around 53,000 adherents), **Macao** and **Hong Kong**. The open, global connections of these last two will have also exposed them to Muslims arriving from other parts of the world. Hong Kong has a Muslim community of about 80,000 and its old mosque dates back to the 1840s. It has in addition a small number of Hindus, Sikhs and Jews. Islam has had a foothold in Japan since the late 19th century and maintains a small presence, along with an Islamic Centre and an Arabic Islamic Institute. Islam first entered the **Korean peninsula** with **Koreans** returning at the end of the **Pacific War** after years spent in north-east China, where they had come into contact with Muslims and converted to Islam. This small community was able to join the Turkish forces fighting under the **United Nations** Command in the **Korean War** (1950–53) in worship under the imams accompanying the Turkish troops. With this reinforcement, the Muslim community in the Republic of Korea (ROK) was put on a formal footing. Korean workers travelling to the Middle East and the Persian (Arabian) Gulf in the 1970s maintained these contacts with the rest of Islam; while foreign workers in the ROK, some from Muslim countries, have added to the numbers inside the country.

History: Islam was first introduced into East Asia in the early 7th century through travellers to **China**, often merchants from Arabia and Persia seeking trade with the Tang dynasty (618–907). Such travellers (who included Jews and Nestorian Christians as well as Muslims) came overland across Central Asia to the north-west areas of China or by sea to ports in the country's south-east coastal regions. Some settled permanently and through intermarrige with **Han Chinese** women, adoption and conversions formed the first Muslim communities in China. Their numbers were greatly augmented through the Mongol incursions westwards in the 13th century into Central Asia, from where the Mongol armies brought back sections of the population by force—craftsmen and skilled workers, but also women and children—to serve the Mongol administration and aristocracy. These involuntary settlers formed the second wave of Muslim immigrants.

Recent developments: The government of the PRC, while prepared to accept regulated religious activity, is undoubtedly nervous over any attempts to foster transnational religious links and has repeatedly claimed that there exist 'separatist' movements in the Uygur minority border region of **Xinjiang**. The north-western frontier of Xinjiang (and of China) adjoins the Central Asian republics of Kazakhstan, Kyrgyzstan and Tajikistan, with which the region shares ethnic and religious affinities. Fear of a more strident form of Islam taking hold in this frontier zone has prompted the PRC to pursue an active role in the **Shanghai Co-operation Organization**, formally established in 2001 with these three republics and other participants. The Organization has set up a shared anti-terrorist structure to contain any spread of Muslim fundamentalism in the region.

Islands in the South China Sea

Rocky outcrops, subject to numerous conflicting claims, in a region potentially rich in resources.

The South China Sea is a vast stretch of water bounded by the **People's Republic of China (PRC)**, mainland south-east Asia, Indonesia and the Philippines. Within this area are numerous rocks, shoals, reefs and two groups of islands that are just above the high water mark. These are known in the West as the Paracel Islands, which lie about equidistant from the PRC's Hainan Island and the Vietnamese mainland, and the Spratly (or Spratley) Islands, which lie much further south. There are also Chinese, Vietnamese, Malaysian, Indonesian and Filipino names for the islands. The area is rich in fish and a number of shipping lanes pass through it. Since the 1950s it has been identified as, possibly, a good source of oil and gas.

There have long been conflicting claims to the islands and to the seas around them. In the 19th century both Britain and France—the latter as the colonial power in Viet Nam—raised flags on the islands, but it was only in 1932 that France opened a weather station in the Paracel Islands. **China** began to claim them in the late 19th century. The **Republic of China (1912–1949)**, Britain and France all protested when Japan occupied them in 1939. In the **San Francisco Peace Treaty**, Japan gave up all entitlement to the islands, but they were not assigned to any other country. At the signing of the Treaty, both the PRC and the **'Republic of China' ('ROC')** on **Taiwan** claimed the islands, as part of the historic territory of China. In addition, the 'ROC' had garrisons on some islands, dating from the Japanese surrender at the end of the **Pacific War** in 1945.

During the 1950s the Philippines began to claim part of the Spratly group, while the other claimants restated their position from time to time. In 1974 the PRC, taking advantage of the weakness of the South Vietnamese garrison in the Paracel Islands because of the Viet Nam War, occupied the whole archipelago. Viet Nam regularly reasserts its claim, but the PRC still occupies the islands. In the late 1970s Malaysia established a presence in the Spratlys, arguing that the islands it claimed lie on Malaysia's continental shelf. Brunei has a fishing zone that covers part of the Spratlys. In 1988 there was a serious naval clash between PRC and Vietnamese naval forces in the Spratlys. Some commentators argue that such action by the PRC is evidence of its aggressive foreign policy. The 'ROC' maintains satellite communications facilities and has a coastguard unit in the Spratlys.

The issue of the South China Sea claims has long concerned the **Association of South-East Asian Nations (ASEAN)**. With the establishment of the **ASEAN**

Regional Forum there were some attempts to discuss the issue, but these were abandoned in the face of PRC opposition. However, prompted by Indonesia, the various claimants, with the exception of the 'ROC', signed a 'Declaration on the Conduct of Parties in the South China Sea' in November 2002. While not solving all problems, the Declaration has reduced tension.

J

Japan

Dai Nihon koku/Dai Nippon koku

An independent constitutional monarchy in East Asia, entirely surrounded by sea.

The Japanese archipelago stretches some 2,400 km off the coast of East Asia. The Sea of Okhotsk and the Nemuro Straits separate it from Russia. It is separated from the **Korean peninsula** by the **East Sea**, known in Japan as the Sea of Japan, and the Tsushima or Korea Strait, which runs between the Republic of Korea and Japan's Kyushu Island. There are four main islands, Hokkaido, Honshu, Shikoku and Kyushu, plus a number of island groups including the **Ogasawara Islands** (the Bonin Islands) and **Okinawa** (the Ryukyu Islands). Administratively, Japan is divided into 47 prefectures.

Area: 377,635 sq km; *capital:* **Tokyo**; *population:* 126,824,166 (March 2004 census), Japanese 99.4%, Korean 0.5%, Chinese and other 0.1%; *official language:* Japanese; *religion:* joint **Shinto** and **Buddhist** 80%; **Catholic and Protestant Christian** 1.2%.

Since 1946 Japan has been a constitutional monarchy. The **Japanese Emperor** is the formal symbol of the nation, but exercises no political power. This lies with the Prime Minister and the **National Diet**. The Constitution lays down that the Prime Minister should command a majority in the Diet, which formally elects him. The Prime Minister appoints the Cabinet. The Diet is a bicameral legislature, with both houses chosen by popular vote. All citizens aged 20 years of age and over are permitted to vote. The upper house is the House of Councillors (*Sangiin*), which has 252 seats, and one-half of whose members are elected every three years. Seventy-six seats are filled from the 47 multi-seat prefectural districts, and 50 from a nation-wide proportional representation single list, allocated on a party basis. Members of the *Sangiin* who come from the prefectural seats serve six-year terms. The lower house is the House of Representatives (*Shugiin*). This has 500 members, 200 of whom are elected from 11 regional blocks by proportional representation, in a reform introduced in 1993, and 300 from single-seat constituencies. The latter serve four-year terms.

History: The origins of the Japanese people are obscure. The earliest occupants seem to have been the **Ainu**, a people now largely found in the northernmost island of Hokkaido. The present-day Japanese are descendants of a mixture of peoples from the Pacific islands, south-east Asia and, especially, the Asian mainland. Archaeological evidence points to the presence of hunter gatherers, perhaps as early as 50,000 BC, on the archipelago; the Japanese claim these as their ancestors, but they are more closely related to the Ainu than they are to modern Japanese. Japanese foundation myths trace the origins of the imperial system to these distant dates, but, in reality, recognizable political structures only appeared in the islands around 300 BC, in the Yayoi period; during this time, rice cultivation came to Japan from the Asian mainland. Clearer still is the existence of the Yamato state, based near modern **Osaka** around AD 300, although even this was but one of a number of states on the peninsula. Chinese and Korean influence was strong, bringing Buddhism, which coexisted beside the native Shinto religion, and later **Confucianism**, writing and political and economic structures from the mainland to Japan. Yamato eventually subdued the other political groups, establishing its imperial capital at **Kyoto** in 794, where it would remain until 1868.

Fujiwara family control eclipsed imperial power in the 9th century, establishing a pattern that would also last until 1868. From 1192 onwards Japan came under a succession of military rulers, or *shogun*. A succession of shogunates wielded effective power, interspersed by periods of civil war, while the emperors lived in seclusion in Kyoto. Tokugawa Ieasu established what proved to be the last shogunate at the beginning of the 17th century. The Tokugawa shogunate (or *Bakufu*) provided Japan with stable but repressive government for the next 250 years. While formally imposing a rigid social hierarchy, in which the military warriors, or samurai, occupied the highest social positions, and merchants were at the bottom, the Tokugawa also created opportunities for the latter to develop and expand their real influence in society.

The first Europeans reached Japan in the 16th century. For a time the country seemed open to the possibility of a widespread conversion to Christianity, despite occasional periods of persecution. The Tokugawa shogunate, however, became suspicious of these outsiders and, from 1639, banned Japanese from going abroad and expelled all foreigners, with the exception of a small number of Chinese and Dutch traders, who were confined to the southern port of **Nagasaki**. Formal diplomatic relations were maintained with the Korean court, but, in general, Japan turned its back on the outside world. Some countries tried to penetrate this isolation, but the Japanese rebuffed all such efforts until the 1850s. Then, under strong pressure from Europe and the USA, and mindful of what had happened in **China**, the Tokugawa gave way. Between 1854 and 1869 the shogun signed what were later known as **unequal treaties** that allowed Western trade and the establishment of **foreign settlements** in Japan. Among these settlements, **Yokohama**, **Kobe** and Nagasaki would all become important trading and industrial cities.

The signing of the treaties would prove to be the undoing of the Tokugawa shogunate, which had negotiated them as though it was the sovereign power in Japan. This usurpation of imperial power and the consequent admission of foreigners into Japan provoked great opposition. Assassins attacked foreigners and leading members of the Tokugawa government, leading in turn to punitive attacks by the Western powers. Domestic pressures for political and social change added to the pressures on the government. The result was civil war in 1867–69, which led to the overthrow of the Tokugawa shogunate, and power was 'restored' to the emperor in the **Meiji Restoration**. (Meiji designates the reign of the Emperor Mutsuhito who came to the throne in 1867.)

In the following 30 years Japan was transformed from an isolated, agricultural country into a modern centralized state, with a growing industrial economy. As a symbol of change, the capital was moved from Kyoto to Edo, the former castle town of the Tokugawa, now renamed Tokyo, or Eastern Capital. Tough measures disarmed the samurai and dismantled the quasi-feudal structure that had existed, albeit much modified, since the 9th century. Theoretically, the emperor ruled, but in practice power rested with an oligarchy of those who had overthrown the shogunate in the 1860s. A highly restricted constitution, introduced in 1889, did not alter the real balance of power within the country. It also gave much power to the ministers for army and naval affairs. In the 1890s the revision of the early treaties ended all restrictions on Japan's sovereignty.

At the end of the 19th century Japan began to acquire an overseas empire. It ended the ambiguous status of the Ryukyu Islands in 1879, incorporating them into the empire as Okinawa Prefecture. The 1894–95 Sino–Japanese War led to the acquisition of **Taiwan**. The 1902 **Anglo-Japanese Alliance** acknowledged Japan's international recognition as one of the world powers. The Alliance, and Japan's defeat of Russia in 1904–05, paved the way for the declaration of a Japanese protectorate over Korea in 1905, and for the outright annexation of that country in 1910. These developments also led to a substantial increase in Japanese possessions and influence in China. When the Meiji emperor died in 1912 Japan enjoyed a high international reputation.

Japan joined the Allied side in the First World War, but its forces were little involved. The Japanese were disappointed when the 1919 Versailles Peace Treaty refused to consider their demands for an end to racial discrimination. They were further disappointed when Britain abandoned the Anglo-Japanese Alliance. Domestically, in the 1920s such developments as the departure of the last of the Meiji-era oligarchs, tentative moves towards greater democracy, with party government, and, from 1925, universal manhood suffrage, occurred. Such moves were steadily undermined following the 1929 Wall Street collapse, which damaged the Japanese economy. In China, the Japanese military began a forward policy that led to the takeover of **Manchuria** in 1931, followed by the establishment of the puppet state of **Manzhouguo** in 1932. Faced by international criticism, Japan walked out of the League of Nations in 1933. Expansion in China increased the power of the Japanese military both at home and abroad, eventually leading to all-out war in China in 1937 following the relatively minor clash known as the **Marco Polo Bridge Incident**. Domestically, the steady move towards a war footing and the growing power of the military led to the forced amalgamation of all political parties into the Imperial Rule Assistance Association, created in 1940.

Japan's decision to join the Germans in the Anti-Comintern Pact in 1936 linked concerns in Europe with those in Asia. Japanese actions in China increasingly created tension with Britain and the USA, whose interests they threatened. By mid-1941 Japan had decided that its only hope of breaking out of the increasing Anglo-US stranglehold was a swift war. On 7 December 1941 the Japanese navy struck at the US naval base at Pearl Harbor in the Philippines, thus beginning the **Pacific War**. Japan followed Pearl Harbor with the rapid occupation of Malaya, Singapore, **Hong Kong** and Burma, followed by Borneo, the Dutch East Indies, the Philippines and northern New Guinea by mid-1942. Japan attempted to organize these captured territories into an economic and political unit, including the creation of a **Greater East Asian Coprosperity Sphere** and promises of independence. The reality was, however, that Japan in most cases behaved just like other imperialist states, and sometimes more harshly, so that it received little credit for such moves.

From the beginning Japan's forces were overstretched. With the Battle of Midway Island in June 1942, the Allies' counter-offensive, led by the USA, began to push back the Japanese advance. By November 1944 Tokyo was within range of land-based bombers. In the autumn of that year the US navy destroyed the Japanese navy at the Battle of Leyte Gulf, and British forces began to push the Japanese army out of Burma. US forces captured Manila in the Philippines in March 1945. The battle then shifted to Okinawa, which was captured at huge cost. Invasion plans were now in preparation for the attack on the Japanese mainland. The US air force dropped atomic bombs on **Hiroshima** and Nagasaki on 6 and 9 August 1945. This development, and the Soviet Union's decision to enter the war on 8 August, led the Japanese Emperor to cast his vote against continuing the war. The war ended with Japan's unconditional surrender on 15 August 1945, with the formal signing of the act of surrender on the *USS Missouri* in Tokyo Bay on 2 September 1945.

Japan was in a desperate position. Military losses included more than 1.5m. dead and millions of sick and wounded. The intense bombing as Allied forces drew closer to the mainland killed nearly 400,000, wounded more than 300,000, and destroyed more than 2m. The road and rail infrastructure suffered not only because of the bombing, but also because of intensive wartime demands and lack of repairs. Much of the Japanese merchant fleet was at the bottom of the Pacific Ocean. Food rations had dropped steadily as the war progressed. In addition, large numbers of Japanese previously settled in the colonial empire or in its informal attachments in China were now due to return to Japan.

Although the period that followed is known as the **Allied Occupation of Japan**, only the USA had any substantial role from September 1945 until the formal end of the Occupation in April 1952. Gen. **Douglas MacArthur**, appointed Supreme

Commander for the Allied Powers (SCAP), was determined to keep control for himself, and especially to keep the Soviet Union out of Japan. There was token Allied representation and no more. At first, the Occupation authorities began a major programme of reform. They dissolved some of the giant business conglomerates known as *zaibatsu*. The Constitution of 1946—in force from May 1947—removed the emperor from the political stage, emphasized democracy and abandoned the right to the use of military force except in self-defence. Trials of those deemed responsible for the war were held, while lesser officials and politicians were purged. There were also practical matters to consider. Early thoughts of reducing Japan to an agricultural economy were quickly revised owing to the need to feed and house large numbers of people. Even so, as late as 1949, many Japanese still suffered hunger from time to time.

By then, the reforming zeal of the Occupation had been exhausted. The spread of communism in China led to concern that Japan might go the same way. The major transformation, however, came with the **Korean War**. In order to free US forces for Korea, the Japanese were encouraged to establish a reserve police force, the forerunner of today's **Self-Defence Forces**. The Japanese economy also benefited from war-related work. The war also led to an intensification of a campaign against Communists in government employment, a campaign later extended to other areas, including the media.

Japan regained its full independence under the terms of the **San Francisco Peace Treaty**, which came into force in April 1952. Although there was talk of a 'reverse course', there was no sustained attempt to overthrow the work of the Occupation; in particular, Japan retained Article 9, the 'no war' clause, of the Constitution, although the reserve police force now became the Self-Defence Forces. Conservative parties had dominated the Diet, except for a brief period, during the Occupation, and they continued to do so after April 1952. In 1955 the two largest groups merged to form the **Liberal Democratic Party (LDP)**, which would rule Japan until 1993. The main opposition party was the Marxist Japan Socialist Party (JSP—now the **Social Democratic Party of Japan**), joined in 1960 by a dissident faction from within its own ranks, the Democratic Socialist Party (DSP), and the Buddhist-derived **Clean Government Party** or *Komeito*, founded in 1964. The Marxist-Leninist **Japan Communist Party** did not normally co-operate with the other opposition parties.

Under a succession of powerful Prime Ministers, the LDP concentrated on economic development at home and maintained close ties with the USA abroad. By the mid-1950s Japan's production levels and standard of living had returned to pre-war levels, and in the 1960s and the early 1970s, when annual growth rates of more than 10% were achieved, the country became a major economic power. Japan's admission to the **United Nations** in December 1956 and the 1964 Tokyo Olympic Games were important stages on the country's road to post-war rehabilitation.

There were of course problems. The ties with the USA led to protests at the continued US military presence in the country. These were particularly violent at the time of the renewal of the 1954 US-Japan Security Treaty in 1960, and led to the resignation of Prime Minister Kishi and to the cancellation of a planned visit by US President Dwight Eisenhower. The US link also complicated Japan's relations with the **People's Republic of China**, which were not normalized until 1972. The Viet Nam War benefited Japan as the Korean War had done earlier, but it also proved very divisive in Japanese society, giving rise to violent student demonstrations. The economy continued to grow, however, and Japan, in a famous phrase coined by the US academic Ezra Vogel, was widely seen as 'Number One'.

The death of the Showa Emperor in 1989 seemed to many to mark the end of an era. The economy had begun to slow down in the 1980s, and was badly damaged by a world-wide recession in the 1990s, from which it has never fully recovered. The LDP's domination of the political scene began to weaken. The Party's fortunes recovered somewhat under **Nakasone Yasuhiro**, Prime Minister in 1982–87, but thereafter again went into decline. In the 1990s there was a major political upheaval. Scandal had never been far from the LDP, and had contributed to the fall of more than one Prime Minister. In June 1993 the then LDP Government was defeated in a vote of no confidence in the House of Representatives, following splits within the Party. In the subsequent general election, the rump of the LDP performed reasonably well, but the opposition parties in combination outnumbered it. These managed to combine to form a government and the LDP found itself out of office for the first time since 1955. Since then new parties have regularly emerged as the old political certainties have gradually eroded.

The 1993 coalition did not last long, and in 1994 the JSP and the LDP formed a government under the JSP leader **Murayama Tomiichi**. Murayama managed the difficult period, which included the **Hanshin earthquake**, the **Aum Shinrikyo** Tokyo gas attack and the 50th anniversary of the end of the Pacific War, reasonably well, but destroyed the JSP in the process. Following Murayama's resignation in January 1996, leadership of the coalition reverted to the LDP.

Recent developments: It was only with the election of **Koizumi Junichiro** as Prime Minister in April 2001 that a more dynamic leadership emerged. Koizumi has led the LDP and Japan ever since, emphasizing—but not always delivering—reform and privatization policies, although his parliamentary position has gradually weakened, and he incurred losses in the lower house elections in November 2003 and in the upper house in July 2004. His main achievement has been a breakthrough in relations with the Democratic People's Republic of Korea, which he visited in 2002 and 2004. Although many important issues, including security matters, between the two countries have not been resolved, Koizumi has gone further than any previous Japanese leader in tackling the difficult problems between the two. By sending non-combatant Japanese troops to Iraq, he has also moved forward the debate on the role of the Self-Defence Forces. However, he failed to revitalize the economy, which remained in stagnation until late 2003, and has not tackled issues such as the ageing population, with its implications for the labour force and pensions' payments.

Recent Elections: Lower House, 8 November 2003	Seats
Democratic Party	177
Liberal Democratic Party	237
Clean Government Party	34
Japan Communist Party	9
Democratic Socialist Party	6
Conservative Party	4
Liberal League	1
Mushuzoku-no-kai (independent)	1
Non party	11

Upper House, 11 July 2004	
Democratic Party	50
Liberal Democratic Party	49
Clean Government Party	13
Japan Communist Party	4
Social Democratic Party	2
Others	5

Japan, Economic Development

The origins of Japan's post-war economic development lie in the rapid industrialization that followed the **Meiji Restoration** in 1868, although that too had solid foundations in the social and economic system that it replaced. Japan was in a parlous state at the end of the **Pacific War** in 1945 and if the **Allied Occupation of Japan** had carried out its original intention to punish the country for going to war, economic recovery would not have been easy. However, whatever had originally been planned was soon replaced by the USA's willingness to aid Japan's recovery, a process much helped by the **Korean War**. By the mid-1960s, when Japan had long since passed pre-war levels of production and consumption, the country seemed well on the way to becoming the world's greatest economic power. If the rapid pace of development has flagged since 1991, the Japanese economy is still a major force in the world, and, in particular, it has shown a strong capacity to adapt to changing demands.

GNP: US $4,383,000m. (2003 estimate); *GNP per caput* US $34,510 (2003 estimate); *GDP at PPP:* US $3,582,000m. (2003 estimate); *GDP real growth rate:* 2.7% (2003 estimate); *GDP per caput at PPP:* US $28,200 (2003 estimate); *exports:* US $448,000m.; *imports:* US $342,000m. (2003); *current account balance:* US $136,000m. (2003); *reserves:* US $664,600m. (2003 estimate); *currency:* freely convertible yen (US $1 = 115.933 yen (end 2003); 105.356 (Nov. 2004)).

Despite wartime devastation, a run-down infrastructure, and the loss of its overseas territories, Japan still possessed some economic advantages in 1945. Chief among these was a well-disciplined and educated workforce. Wartime needs had led to some innovation and development. Even the destruction had advantages, in that it provided a clean slate and it gave opportunities for new thinking. Yet, the task of reconstruction was daunting. Without massive US assistance, the boost provided by the Korean War, and the relatively non-punitive terms of the 1952 **San Francisco Peace Treaty**, it would have been hard to achieve. The low percentage of Japan's expenditure on defence was another important factor. Production, which in 1946 was about 30% of that in 1936, reached 114.4% of the 1936 level in 1951. It would take longer for consumption to reach pre-war levels, but by the mid-1950s Japan's economy was growing fast. By 1965 the manufacturing economy was four times greater than its pre-war counterpart, and the average family was consuming 75% more than its pre-war counterpart. Annual growth rates averaged 9.3% from 1953, and from 1958 until 1973, 15%. Gross national product was US $10,900m. in 1950, and $202,000m. in 1970. Industries such as textiles, which had been very important pre-war, played a major role at first, sometimes to the consternation of old competitors such as Britain, but increasingly steel and steel-related fields, such as shipbuilding and automobiles, predominated. By 1969 Japan manufactured 48.2% of the world's ships, and with the production of more than 2.5m. passenger cars had become, from a negligible starting point, the third largest producer in the world. There was also a steady increase in high-tech industries, especially cameras and electronic goods. Japan's main market was the USA, but its impact was world-wide. The one area where Japan did not make much impact, for political reasons, was the **People's Republic of China (PRC)**.

In the early 1970s a number of set-backs occurred. In 1971 the so-called 'Nixon shocks' took place. The USA began the process of normalizing relations with the PRC without any advance warning to Japan, raised tariffs against Japanese goods, and suspended the convertibility of gold against the dollar, thus forcing Japan to revalue the yen. Japan resisted for a time, but eventually gave in, thus increasing the price of Japanese goods in the USA. Then came the oil crisis of 1973 and a general increase in commodity prices. Although the Japanese economy faltered for a short time, it soon revived. In the 1970s a resurgence took place in the Japanese shipbuilding industry, for example, so that it was still producing close to 50% of world output well into the 1980s. Per caput income was greater than that of the USA by the mid-1980s, and Japan was the world's largest creditor nation.

In the late 1980s spectacular rises in land prices and other speculative developments occurred. For several years this 'bubble economy' continued to grow, but it collapsed in 1991, leaving many loans outstanding. For almost the first time in 40 years Japan faced a major recession in 1992–93, the effects of which lingered on until the turn of the century. Even in recession, however, the Japanese economy has remained one of the largest in the world, and the international demand for Japanese goods remains high. Japan faces competition from some countries, such as the Republic of Korea (ROK), in computer chips, and, increasingly, the PRC across a wide range of industries, but its manufacturing base is still strong. Japan produced more than 8.4m. automobiles in 2003, compared with Germany's 5.2m. and the

USA's 4.5m. Income levels remain high. The strong yen has allowed Japanese companies and individuals to invest heavily abroad, especially in real estate. Much Japanese manufacturing now takes place off shore, and even apparent competitors such as the PRC and the ROK often have a heavy dependency on Japanese components.

Japan does face problems. While unemployment rates are low by international standards, they are high by Japanese standards, and rising. The population is ageing; the 2004 census shows 19.24% over 65. Non-performing loans from the early 1990s are still affecting the banking system, which also suffered in the 1997 **Asian financial crisis**. Prime Minister **Koizumi Junichiro** has not so far delivered the banking and other reforms that he promised on taking office in 2001. At the same time, in early 2004 there was an economic rebound, with improvements in the corporate and banking sectors. Gross domestic product figures for the final quarter of 2003 were the best for 13 years, and the trend continues. Japanese exports fell, but so did imports, and the current account surplus amounted to $136,000m.

Japan Communist Party (JCP)

Nihon kyosanto

The Japan Communist Party (JCP), which currently has some 400,000 members, is primarily an urban party. It is also Japan's oldest political party.

Founded in 1922, the JCP operated as an underground organization with a small following during the 1920s and 1930s, re-emerging as a legal party in 1945. In 1946 a veteran Communist, Nosaka Sanzo (1892–1994), who had spent time in Moscow and with the **Chinese Communist Party**, became the party leader, a position he would hold until 1982. Under Nosaka, the JCP called for a united front. Since it had opposed the militarists before the **Pacific War**, it enjoyed some popularity, winning 39 seats in the 1949 lower house elections. However, its closeness to Moscow told against it. Purged by the occupation authorities, it effectively went underground again. It reappeared in the mid-1950s, but suffered factionalism and divisions. One group joined the Japan Socialist Party (now the **Democratic Socialist Party of Japan**), while in 1964 another group established a pro-Soviet Union 'Voice of Japan' Communist Party. The mainstream JCP under Miyamoto Kenji (secretary-general from 1958 and chairman of the Central Committee in 1982–97) was for a time pro-Chinese. The two parties quarrelled, however, at the onset of the **Cultural Revolution** and remained estranged until the 1980s.

Freed of links to either the Soviet Union or **China**, the JCP increased its membership, while its newspaper *Akahata* (Red Flag) sold well, with a readership much wider than the party faithful. The Party also performed well in elections, winning 38 seats in the 1972 lower house elections, and 39 in 1979. To counter this growing popularity, the ruling **Liberal Democratic Party** revived stories of Miyamoto's past, which included the killing of a police informer. This tactic was successful, and the JCP's electoral support declined in the 1980s. Further scandal harmed the Party when it was revealed in 1992 that its former leader, the then 100-year old Nosaka Sanzo, had denounced Yamamoto Kenzo, one of his companions in Moscow in the 1930s, who was shot on Stalin's orders.

Miyamato gave way to Fuwa Tetsuzo in 1997. Fuwa and his colleagues have not succeeded in improving the Party's position; in the most recent elections for the lower house, in November 2003, it won only nine seats. In elections to the upper house in July 2004 it retained four seats. Although the various upheavals that have marked the Japanese political scene since the early 1990s have pushed other former opposition parties into government, the JCP firmly remains an opposition party.

Chair. of the Central Committee: Fuwa Tetsuzo
Address: Japan Communist Party
          4-26-7 Sendagaya
          Setagawa-ku
          Tokyo 151-8586
          Japan
Tel: 81-3-3403-6111
Fax: 81-3-3746-0767
E-mail: intl@jcp.jp
Internet: www.jcp.or.jp

Japan Foundation

Nihon kokusai koryu kikin

Originally established in 1972 as a legal entity under Japan's Ministry of Foreign Affairs, the Japan Foundation became an independent administrative institute in October 2003.

The aims of the Japan Foundation are to promote international exchanges, to increase appreciation of Japan's culture and arts overseas, to encourage Japanese language learning, and to encourage the building of collections of Japanese literature. To do this, it conducts a world-wide programme, with offices in many countries.

Address: Japan Foundation Headquarters
          20th-21st Floor
          ARK Bldg
          1-12-32 Akasaka
          Minato-ku
          Tokyo 107-6021
          Japan
Tel: 81-3-5562-3511
Fax: 3-5562-3494
E-mail: info@jpf.org.jp
Internet: www.jpf.go.jp

Japan Institute of International Affairs (JIIA)

Nihon kokusai mondai kenkyujo

A private, non-profit-making organization, the Japan Institute of International Affairs (JIIA) dates from 1959, and was originally an initiative by former Prime Minister Yoshida Shigeru. In 1960 the Japanese Ministry of Foreign Affairs (MFA) accredited it as a foundation, and it has effectively become the MFA's think-tank. A large part of its funding comes from the MFA. In 1976 it absorbed the Euro-Asian Association, which had been primarily concerned with the study of Communist countries. JIIA's purpose is to encourage the academic study of international relations, exchange research findings and to organize study groups, seminars and conferences on international issues. It has a small permanent staff, but relies mainly on academic researchers from other institutions. The JIIA's main fields of interest are Russia, the Asia-Pacific region, the Americas, and Europe, but it also studies global issues outside of these areas. It has a wide range of international links but they are particularly strong with institutions in the **People's Republic of China** and in south-east Asian countries.

> *Pres.:* Satoh Yukio
> *Address:* JIIA
> 11th Floor
> Kasumigaseki Bldg
> 3-2-5 Kasumigaseki
> Chiyoda-ku
> Tokyo 100-6011
> Japan
> *Tel:* 81-3-3503-7263
> *Fax:* 81-3-3503-7168
> *E-mail:* info@jiia.or.jp
> *Internet:* www.jia.or.jp

Japanese Emperor

Of all the East Asian countries, only Japan remains a monarchy. Since 1989 the monarch has been the Heisei Emperor, whose given name is Akihito. The emperor's given name is rarely used in Japan, however; instead, people use the name selected on an emperor's accession by which he will be known after his death. Heisei is the name of the present emperor; this name is also used for dating the years; thus, 2004 is Heisei 16.

In theory the Japanese imperial lineage stretches back unbroken for thousands of years. The reality is that the origins of the imperial line are lost in the mists of time. What is certain is that for most of the last 1,000 years the emperor lived in seclusion in **Kyoto**, while real power rested elsewhere. Only with the 1868 **Meiji Restoration** did power revert to the emperor. Even that was a myth, since the Meiji

Emperor, while much honoured, was under the tight control of the oligarchy that had carried out the 1868 Restoration. Under his son, the Taisho Emperor (r. 1912–26), imperial rule was even more of a fiction, since Taisho suffered long periods of mental incapacity. His son, Hirohito, was regent for much of his reign before becoming the Showa Emperor in 1926, but real power continued to lie elsewhere. At the same time, a cult of loyalty developed around the emperor, reaching a peak during the **Pacific War**. Whatever the theoretical position, before 1945 the Imperial Household Ministry, which controlled access to the emperor, was one of the most powerful government ministries, and kept a tight control over imperial matters.

Japan went to war in the emperor's name, but there is still debate about what role, if any, the emperor played or could have played in the events leading up to war. What is clear is that when he did intervene to recommend surrender in August 1945, his wishes prevailed. Japan had by then suffered heavily and faced certain defeat, and it is not clear that if he had intervened earlier he could have stopped the war. The matter remains one of controversy.

The emperor was not tried before the **International Military Tribunal for the Far East**, despite pressure from some Allied countries. In Japan's post-war Constitution, drawn up under US guidance, the emperor became the symbol of the state. Japan thus became a constitutional monarchy. Outside of Japan there was debate about the emperor's wartime role, but within Japan neither that issue nor the wider one, of what exactly the emperor symbolized, received much public attention. After Japan regained its independence in 1952, the emperor and his family kept a low profile.

The occupation authorities downgraded the status of the Imperial Household Ministry to an agency answering to the Prime Minister. Although subsequent reorganizations have restored some of its power, it remains part of the Japanese Cabinet Office system. While the agency has nothing like its predecessor's pre-war control over the imperial family, it has acquired a reputation for secrecy about the emperor's religious position, and for adopting an unimaginative approach to the role of the emperor and his family. The former was particularly marked when the Showa Emperor died in 1989 and his son succeeded him. The latter has become a public issue because of the alleged unhappiness of the crown princess, a former diplomat, over the restrictive regime to which she is subjected, and because of concern at her inability to produce a male heir. The crown prince has indicated dissatisfaction with the way the agency performs.

Most Japanese do not display much interest in these issues, although the crown princess and her troubles have made some impact, perhaps because of the precedent of Princess Diana in Britain. The lack of a male heir has also led to more attention being focused on the imperial family than is usual, and there are reports that the government is studying the issue of female succession. The discussion of such issues has perhaps made the imperial family appear more human, but has so far revealed no wish to replace them by any other form of representation.

Japanese Red Army

Rengo sekigun

Japanese terrorist organization that emerged in the late 1960s, formed from among various extreme left-wing groups that had been active in the student and anti-Viet Nam War demonstrations of the 1960s.

One of these groups began attacking police boxes in November 1969, leading to the arrest of more than 50 of its members. In 1970 another group, calling itself the Red Army Group, hijacked a Japan Airlines passenger aircraft and directed it first to the Republic of Korea, where the the passengers were released, and then to the Democratic People's Republic of Korea (DPRK). The DPRK repatriated the crew of the aircraft but allowed the hijackers to remain. In 1971 other members of the group continued a campaign of robbery and bomb attacks, with the stated aims of overthrowing the Japanese monarchy and government, and creating world revolution. These various groups merged to form the 'United Red Army' in 1971. From then onwards the Red Army launched attacks on embassies in various countries. Under the leadership of Ms Shigenobu Fusako it also developed links with the Popular Front for the Liberation of Palestine, which led to its most violent act, a grenade and machine gun attack at Tel-Aviv's Lod Airport in May 1972, in which 24 people died. Meanwhile, following a siege near the resort of Karuiza in February 1972, the Japanese police captured a number of Red Army members. They also found the graves of 14 former members who had been tortured and killed by their companions. These discoveries prompted a major police campaign against the group, but, while it remained small, it continued to carry out terrorist attacks on embassies and other targets into the 1990s.

Shigenobu returned to Japan at the end of the 1990s, and was arrested near **Osaka** in March 2000. One year later she announced that the group was disbanding. In 2001 Lebanon expelled some members of the group who had taken refuge there. They then took refuge in Jordan, but the Jordanian authorities handed them over to the Japanese. Four remain in the DPRK. Three others died there, and one, who returned to Japan, was sentenced to 12 years' imprisonment in 2004. In November 2004 Japan formally demanded that the DPRK return the remaining hijackers for trial. The DPRK's refusal to do so up to now has been one reason why the US Department of State lists that country as a supporter of terrorism.

Jenkins, Charles

In 1965, while serving with the US army in the Republic of Korea, Charles Jenkins, then a 23-year old sergeant, disappeared while on duty at the **Demilitarized Zone** between the two Koreas. Later, he surfaced in the Democratic People's Republic of Korea (DPRK), where he remained in obscurity until 2002, together with a small group of other former US military personnel who had defected. It then became apparent that he had married Soga Hitomi, one of the **abductees** from Japan, and that they had two children. Ms Soga returned to Japan in the autumn of 2002, but Jenkins, who faced a possible US court martial, and their children remained in **Pyongyang**. Following Japanese Prime Minister **Koizumi Junichiro**'s second visit to Pyongyang in May 2004, the Jenkins family met in Indonesia, and eventually travelled to Japan.

The US authorities insisted that Jenkins be handed over under the terms of the Japan-US Status of Forces' Agreement, and he was detained on charges of desertion. When tried, he pleaded guilty, stating that he had been frightened of going to Viet Nam. He received a sentence of 30 days' detention and a dishonourable discharge from the army. On his release he expressed the hope that he might be able to revisit the USA. He and his family have now moved to Sado, the island in northern Japan that was his wife's home.

One other US serviceman, Private First Class James Joseph Dresnok went to the DPRK in 1962 and still lives there. A further two are said to have died of natural causes.

Jiang Zemin

Former head of state of the **People's Republic of China (PRC)** and secretary-general of the **Chinese Communist Party (CCP)**.

Deng Xiaoping, the former paramount leader of the PRC, described Jiang Zemin as the 'core of the third generation' of the PRC leadership, after **Mao Zedong**, the first generation, and Deng himself, representing the second. That third generation is now giving way to a fourth generation, centred on **Hu Jintao**, who took over as CCP secretary-general in 2002 and as state President in the following year. Jiang was born in Jiangsu Province in 1926. He joined the CCP in 1946, while studying at the Communications University in **Shanghai**. After 1949 he held various industrial and government posts, before spending a year training at the Stalin Automobile Works in Moscow in 1955. On his return to the PRC he again held a series of posts until he appeared as the deputy director of the foreign affairs bureau of the First Ministry of Machine Building in 1974. In 1982 he became the electronics industry minister and, concurrently, CCP secretary in the ministry. In the same year he joined the CCP Central Committee.

In 1985 Jiang became mayor of the PRC's second most important city, Shanghai. Two years later, while remaining mayor, he became the CCP secretary-general for the city, and was promoted to the CCP Political Bureau (Politburo). When the student demonstrations that followed the death of **Hu Yaobang** in April 1989 spread to Shanghai, Jiang handled the issue carefully and was able to avoid the loss of control that occurred in **Beijing**. Shanghai thus avoided the confrontation and bloodshed that took place in the capital.

Following the dismissal of the CCP secretary-general, **Zhao Ziyang**, for siding with the demonstrators, Deng Xiaoping summoned Jiang to the capital to take over the post. It was an unexpected decision. Despite Jiang's success in Shanghai, he seemed a relatively slight figure when compared to Zhao or Zhao's predecessor, Hu Yaobang. In the event, Jiang remained in the top positions until 2002 and 2003, seeing off all who might have challenged him and putting his own men in place. As Deng relinquished his **Central Military Commission (CMC)** roles, Jiang took them over too, thus increasing his influence, and in 1993 he replaced Yang Shangkun as state President. To many outside the PRC he continued to appear a less than serious figure, fond of quoting Shakespeare in English and singing songs, but there was nobody to challenge him.

How long he will be able to exert influence now that he has given up his party and state roles is difficult to determine. Although he kept the CMC positions until 2004, he does not have a real base in the military, unlike Deng, and he has never been a soldier. However, he is a survivor, and has avoided making too many enemies.

Jo Myong Rok

A vice-marshal in the **Korean People's Army** of the Democratic People's Republic of Korea (DPRK) since 1995, and the first vice-chairman of the National Defence Committee since 1978.

Born in 1930 (some sources say 1928) in **China**, Jo Myong Rok was educated at the Mangyongdae Revolutionary School. He was a member of the central committee of the **Korean Workers' Party** in 1974 and was commander of the air force in 1978. In 1986 he became a delegate to the **Supreme People's Assembly**. In October 2000 he visited the USA as a DPRK special envoy, but his visit failed to lead to the expected reciprocal visit by US President Clinton to the DPRK.

Juche

Term denoting the policies of self-reliance and independence that have guided the Democratic People's Republic of Korea (DPRK) for half a century.

The word was introduced into the country's political vocabulary by the DPRK leader **Kim Il Sung** in late 1955, with the connotation of self-sufficiency and independence in devising solutions to the problems facing the DPRK. The word is composed of two parts: *ju*, signifying 'master', 'the main element'; and *che*, meaning 'the whole' or 'essence'. As a word it signifies the 'basic constituent' or 'basis of action'. Kim Il Sung used the concept in the first instance to underline the desirability of not becoming involved in the sharpening ideological dispute between the DPRK's two chief allies at that time, the **People's Republic of China** and the Soviet Union. From there he extended its application into other areas of activity, such as the economy, and developed the *juche* doctrine, which has remained the basis of the DPRK's official philosophy and is enshrined in the Constitution as the country's 'guiding principle'. *Juche* revolves around two concepts: the people are the masters of their destiny, and they should remain independent of all outside influences. External contacts and the acceptance of assistance are permitted, but the nation should avoid spiritual and psychological dependence and any sense of deference to stronger powers. While *juche* stresses the central role of human beings, people can play out this role only through subordination to a leader. The doctrine, which was developed further by **Hwang Jang-Hyop**, who later defected to the Republic of Korea, thus supported the rule of Kim Il Sung and the succession of his son, **Kim Jong Il**—Hwang tutored the latter. *Juche* has survived as the basis of the DPRK's philosophy and policies despite the country's visible dependence on outside assistance over the past decade. So intimately is the concept associated with Kim Il Sung that in 1997, on the occasion of the third anniversary of his death, both the term *juche* and Kim's year of birth—1912—were incorporated into the DPRK's official chronology. Thus, 2004 is expressed as Juche 93 (the initial year being included).

K

Kaesong

Kaesong is the southernmost city of the Democratic People's Republic of Korea (DPRK), and has an estimated population of 200,000–300,000. It was the capital of the unified **Korean peninsula** during the Koryo dynasty (918–1392). Like other DPRK cities, it has suffered from the decline of the **DPRK economy**, but it produces porcelain and ginseng. Visitors can see an old residential quarter, a rare such survival in the DPRK, and a museum of the Koryo period. There are also Koryo royal tombs nearby.

The city was just on the southern side of the **38th parallel** at the division of Korea in 1945. Swiftly captured at the beginning of the **Korean War**, it has remained in the DPRK ever since, the only major South Korean city to do so. It was the site of the first truce talks in 1951, but the **United Nations** considered that this gave too much control to the DPRK-**People's Republic of China** side, and abandoned it in favour of the nearby village of **Panmunjom**. Since the late 1990s the South Korean **Hyundai Corporation** has been interested in developing an industrial free-trade park at Kaesong. A ground-breaking ceremony for this park took place in July 2003, and the enterprise was formally launched in June 2004. There are also plans to develop Kaesong as a tourist centre, and, possibly, to apply for the status of World Heritage site.

Kan Naoto

A Japanese politician who at one time had the reputation of being a political mould-breaker, Kan Naoto's career seemed to have come to a halt when he resigned as leader of the **Democratic Party of Japan (DPJ)** in June 2004 for having failed to pay mandatory pension premiums for 10 months in 1996.

Kan was born in 1946 in Yamaguchi Prefecture and studied at the Tokyo Institute of Technology. After graduation he worked as a lawyer, but also became involved in urban and anti-corruption issues in **Tokyo** during the 1970s. After a number of unsuccessful attempts, he was elected to the Lower House of the **National Diet** in 1980. He was a member of the Social Democratic League (SDL) during the 1980s, but as **Hosokawa Morihiro** began his move towards the premiership, Kan became associated with the policy-making group around him. In 1993 Kan withdrew from the SDL, and joined the New Party Harbinger. In January 1996 he became Minister of Health and Welfare in the first Hashimoto coalition government. In this role he made an unprecedented apology for a Japanese politician to victims and families of a long-standing scandal concerning contaminated blood.

This action helped him to become one of the two leaders of the Democratic Party on its foundation in September 1996. At first he and **Hatoyama Yukio** were 'joint representatives' of the Party, but this dual leadership was not workable, and in September 1997 Kan became the sole 'representative' and Hatoyama secretary-general. In September 1999, after the Democratic Party had absorbed some of the other parties and had relaunched itself as the DPJ, Hatoyama challenged Kan for the leadership position, and won. Hatoyama won again in September 2002, but in December 2002 Kan replaced Hatoyama. In July 2003 the DPJ agreed to a merger with the **Liberal Party** to challenge Prime Minister **Koizumi Junichiro**, but the attempt failed.

When the pensions issue arose early in 2004, Kan, who had criticized government ministers who had also admitted failing to pay, admitted his own failure to pay the required premiums during his time as a minister. At first he refused to resign. Pressure built up, however, and he resigned on 10 May 2004, to be succeeded on 20 May as leader by **Okada Katsuya**, the Party's secretary-general.

Kanemaru Shin

A prominent Japanese politician, Kanemaru Shin had by the time of his death in 1996 come to symbolize all that was wrong with politics in Japan.

Born in 1914, he was educated at Tokyo Agricultural University, and entered the **National Diet** in 1958 on the **Liberal Democratic Party (LDP)** ticket. From the early 1970s he held a variety of party and government posts, but his real influence began when Takeshita Noburu took over the former **Tanaka Kakuei** faction within the LDP. Kanemaru's son was married to Takeshita's daughter, and before long Kanemaru effectively ran what was now the Takeshita faction along traditional 'boss' lines. In the process he amassed huge funds. This led to his downfall as he became involved in a scandal with a company called Sagawa Kyobin. He had also shown himself politically inept during a visit to the Democratic People's Republic of Korea (DPRK), where he far exceeded his brief in promising compensation for Japan's alleged damage to the DPRK since the end of the **Pacific War**. A police raid on his house in 1992 revealed vast sums of money collected for political purposes, and Kanemaru resigned from parliament. He died just before he was due to be tried on corruption and other charges.

Kang Sok Ju

Kang Sok Ju is first vice-minister in the Ministry of Foreign Affairs of the Democratic People's Republic of Korea (DPRK). In this role he has played a prominent part in the negotiations relating to the **DPRK nuclear programme**.

Born in **Pyongyang** in 1939, he attended the Pyongyang University of Foreign Studies. He appeared as a Vice-Minister of Foreign Affairs in 1983, and took up his present post in 1998. He is a member of the Central Committee of the **Korean Workers' Party** and a delegate to the **Supreme People's Assembly**. He has a reputation for being a tough, confident, and inflexible negotiator.

Kanto earthquake

A major earthquake that struck **Tokyo** and **Yokohama**, both situated on the Kanto plain, just before noon on 1 September 1923. Yokohama was close to the epicentre and suffered particularly badly, with the old **foreign settlement** disappearing. The earthquake killed more than 100,000, and both it and the subsequent fires and explosions destroyed a vast amount of property. Rumours that foreigners had started the fires led to the deaths of thousands of **Koreans** and other foreigners; these killings remain a cause of bitterness in the **Korean peninsula**. Although there were grandiose plans for rebuilding Tokyo, there were no funds available, and the opportunity was lost.

Kaohsiung

Kaohsiung, on **Taiwan**'s south-west coast, is the chief industrial city and port of the island. The city began in 1661 as a Chinese Qing-dynasty county government centre. It was called Takao under the Qing. In the Japanese colonial period (1895–1945) it was renamed Kaohsiung in 1920, and became a city in 1924. In 1979 it became a special municipality under the **Executive Yuan**. The harbour, begun by the Japanese in 1908, now has dry dock, container and ship-breaking facilities, and its 116 wharves can handle vessels of up to 100,000 metric tons. In 2002 Kaohsiung was the world's fourth largest port complex. The city has a total land area of 153.6 sq km, and a population of 1.5m. There are 327 educational establishments, including nine junior colleges and university-level institutions.

Kaohsiung incident

Demonstrations held in the Taiwan port city of Kaohsiung on 10 December 1979 to commemorate Human Rights Day. They are now acclaimed as one of the first moves in the democratization of Taiwan politics and brought to prominence a number of people later active in the ranks of the opposition and now in mainstream politics.

The incident was sparked by a police raid on the offices of an illegal publication that had criticized the monopolization of power in Taiwan by the **Kuomintang**. On the instructions of the Government Information Office under its then director **James Soong**, police confronted protesters and arrested several of their leaders. Among the eight who were brought to trial before a military court in 1980 was **Annette Lu**, now Vice-President of Taiwan. The team of lawyers defending the eight accused included **Chen Shui-bian**, currently President and head of the **Democratic Progressive Party**. The defence highlighted charges of the use of torture by the police to extract confessions. In the course of police interrogations the mother and young twin daughters of one of the accused were murdered. The case remains unsolved.

Kashgar

A market and garrison town in the **People's Republic of China**'s **Xinjiang** province; its Chinese name is Kashi. It is a mainly Muslim, **Uygur**-speaking area, and although it has been under Chinese rule since 1759, it has a long tradition of independence. In 1870–77 it was the centre of an independent khanate under Yakub Beg. In the 1930s and 1940s the independent Republic of East Turkestan centred on Kashgar. Its population is some 200,000. The main products are agricultural, but manufacturing includes carpets and other handicrafts.

Kasumigaseki

Kasumigaseki is the name of a district in **Tokyo**'s Chiyoda-ku. After the **Meiji Restoration** in 1868 several new central government offices were established in the area. Today it is the home of the Ministry of Finance, the Ministry of Foreign Affairs and several other senior ministries, and the name is synonymous with Japan's central government. The area is also regularly targeted for demonstrations by right-wing groups.

Kawaguchi Yoriko

Kawaguchi Yoriko became Japan's first ever 'special adviser to the Prime Minister on diplomatic affairs' in September 2004. She had previously been Minister of Foreign Affairs, but **Machimura Nobutaka** replaced her in that office in September 2004.

Born in **Tokyo** in 1941, she attended Tokyo University, graduating in international relations in 1965. She then joined the Ministry of International Trade and Industry (MITI), where she spent most of her career, apart from spells at Yale, where she was awarded an M.Phil. in economics in 1972, and in Washington, DC, USA, where she was minister at the Japanese embassy in 1990–92. In 1993 she became managing director at Suntory, a drinks company. In January 2001 she returned to government as Minister for the Environment in **Koizumi Junichiro**'s first ministry. She became foreign minister after Koizumi dismissed **Tanaka Makiko** in February 2002.

Kazak

One of the smaller minority nationalities, numbering 1,110,800 in the 1990 population census, of the **People's Republic of China (PRC)**.

The Kazaks are a Turkic-speaking group living in the north-west of the country, predominantly in the **Xinjiang** Uygur Autonomous Region and in Gansu and Qinghai Provinces, where they have traditionally led a nomadic life as pastoralists. They are one of the 10 Muslim minority nationalities in the PRC. In Xinjiang, where they form the second largest minority group, they are concentrated in the Zhungar basin in the extreme north of the region, which has a border with the Central Asian republic of Kazakhstan. The Chinese Kazaks share ethnic links with the Kazak population of Kazakhstan. Attempts by the Chinese authorities to collectivize Kazak herds as part of the PRC's rapid drive towards industrialization and communalization under the impetus of the Great Leap Forward (initiated in 1958) led to the departure of 60,000 Kazaks across the frontier into what was then the Kazakh Republic of the Soviet Union. Family and ethnic contacts were only renewed after the collapse of the Soviet Union in 1991. The sensitive nature of cross-border ethnic and religious links in the whole Xinjiang region, together with a desire to retain Kazak loyalties, may account for the relatively high profile the Chinese government accords to the Kazak language. This has official status in the Kazak autonomous areas. Only six minority languages—**Uygur**, Mongolian, **Tibetan**, **Korean**, Kazak and **Dai**, all spoken in border regions—enjoy this standing.

Kim Dae-Jung

In December 1997, after three previous attempts, Kim Dae-Jung became President of the Republic of Korea (ROK).

Born in 1924 in **Kwangju**, South Cholla Province, Kim graduated from high school in 1943 and became a clerk in a Japanese-owned shipping company of which he took control in 1945. In 1950 he became president of a daily newspaper in Mokpo, in South Cholla. He graduated from Konguk University in 1953, and later earned graduate degrees from Korea and Kyunghee Universities. He entered the **ROK National Assembly** in 1960. Re-elected in 1963, Kim became spokesman for the newly formed Masses Party in 1965, and when the **Democratic Party** and the Masses Party merged into the New Democratic Party (NDP) in 1967, he became its spokesman.

Having narrowly lost the 1971 presidential election to **Park Chung-Hee**, Kim became a vocal critic of Park and his Government. In August 1973 the Korean Central Intelligence Agency (KCIA, now the National Intelligence Service) abducted Kim from **Tokyo**, Japan. Kim claimed that the KCIA intended to kill him, and that US intervention saved him. Thereafter, he was arrested many times for anti-government activities. In 1979 he was sentenced to death for alleged espionage activity; the sentence was reduced to life imprisonment. After **Chun Doo-Hwan** came to power, Kim was purged in May 1980, tried, and again sentenced to death for his alleged instigation of the **Kwangju uprising**. Following intense international pressure, the sentence was reduced to life imprisonment, and in December 1982 Kim went to the USA for medical treatment.

Returning to Korea in February 1985, Kim served as co-chairman of the Council for the Promotion of Democracy. He collaborated with **Kim Young-Sam** in the Reunification Democratic Party, and then organized his own Party of Peace and Democracy in 1987. Both Kims contested the 1987 presidential election, thus allowing **Roh Tae-Woo** to win. Kim Dae-Jung returned to the National Assembly in 1988. A series of party mergers led, in September 1991, to the emergence of the New Democratic Party, whose presidential candidate Kim became for the 1992 elections.

Kim was defeated, this time by Kim Young-Sam. He announced his retirement from politics, and left Korea to study in Britain. However, on his return to Korea in 1993, he resumed his political career, founding the **National Congress for New Politics**. In 1997 he and his long-time opponent, **Kim Jong-Pil**, joined forces to fight the presidential election. Kim Dae-Jung became the candidate, winning the election by a narrow majority; Kim Jong-Pil eventually became Premier. Despite the narrow margin of the victory, it had great symbolic importance as the first ever peaceful transfer of political power from government to opposition in the ROK.

Kim's first task was to tackle the **Asian financial crisis** that had struck the ROK in the autumn of 1997, but he also introduced a new approach to relations with the Democratic People's Republic of Korea (DPRK), the so-called **'sunshine policy'**. In 1999 the NCNP changed its name to the **Millennium Democratic Party**. Following a quarrel with Kim Jong-Pil, the coalition split in 2000, but after both parties had performed badly in the April 2000 elections, it reformed in May.

The 'sunshine policy' seemed vindicated in June 2000, when Kim Dae-Jung and the DPRK leader, **Kim Jong Il**, met for the first ever summit between the two Koreas in **Pyongyang**, the DPRK capital. Kim Dae-Jung briefly enjoyed huge domestic and international prestige, winning the 2000 Nobel Peace Prize. The high hopes of June 2000 faded, however, and during 2001 Kim's domestic popularity steadily declined, as did that of his party. Corruption scandals involving his sons and lack of progress in relations with the DPRK added to his problems. When he left office in January 2003 Kim was a sick man, with a badly scarred political reputation. Revelations about clandestine payments made to the DPRK in order to bring about the 2000 summit further tarnished his reputation.

Kim Geun-Tae

In June 2004 Kim Geun-Tae, once one of the country's most prominent anti-government student leaders, became the Republic of Korea's (ROK) Minister of Health and Welfare. Born in Kyonggi Province in 1947, Kim graduated in economics from **Seoul** National University in 1972. He was then already wanted by the police on charges under the draconian anti-communist laws, and by 1974 he was on the police 'most wanted' list. He continued as an activist under President **Chun Doo-Hwan**, founding the Association of Young People for Democracy in 1983. By then he was known as the 'godfather of student activism'. Arrested in 1985, he spent three years in prison. He entered the **ROK National Assembly** in 1996, and was floor leader first for the **Millennium Democratic Party** in 2000 and then, from 2003, for the **Uri Party**. He is regarded as close to President **Roh Moo-Hyun**, who was also an anti-government political activist in the 1970s. One problem he faces, however, is that it has been alleged that his three brothers defected to the Democratic People's Republic of Korea (DPRK) during the **Korean War**. If the Uri Party and the government continue to pursue their current policy of investigating the past conduct of family members of prominent politicians, such allegations could affect Kim's future political career.

Kim Hyun Hee

In November 1987 Kim Sung Il and Kim Hyun Hee, travelling as father and daughter on Japanese passports, were arrested at Bahrain airport on suspicion that they had earlier planted a bomb on **Korean Air** Flight 858, which had just exploded over the Andaman Sea. Kim Sung Il committed suicide, but Kim Hyun Hee was taken alive. She claimed to be a Japanese called Mayumi Hachiya, but later confessed that she was from the Democratic People's Republic of Korea (DPRK), and that she and her partner were on a mission to destroy the flight to disrupt the 1988 **Seoul** Olympic Games. She also claimed that **Kim Jong Il**, son of the DPRK leader, **Kim Il Sung**, had planned the attack. The Republic of Korea (ROK) placed her on trial and she was sentenced to death. While awaiting execution, Kim became a Christian and expressed repentance for her actions. The ROK government later pardoned her. She wrote an autobiography, *The Tears of My Soul*, published in 1993, and in 1997 she married an officer from the ROK National Intelligence Service. In her autobiography she stated that she was born in **Kaesong** in 1962, lived abroad while her father was on a diplomatic posting, and had been recruited as an agent after university. She also claimed that a Japanese woman had coached her in the DPRK. This was the first substantive evidence in support of Japanese claims regarding the issue of **abductees**.

There have always been some doubts about Kim's story, and in 2004 relatives in the ROK of those killed in the 1987 attack demanded that the case be reopened. They argued that the Government of President **Chun Doo-Hwan** could have staged the attack in order to win support for **Roh Tae-Woo** in the 1987 presidential election campaign. So far, this claim has not been pursued.

Kim Il Chol

Kim Il Chol became the Democratic People's Republic of Korea's Minister of the People's Armed Forces in 1998. He was born in **Pyongyang** in 1933, and attended the Mangyongdae Revolutionary School. This indicates that his father either fought against the Japanese or died in the **Korean War**. By 1974 Kim was a naval vice-commodore, becoming commodore in 1978. He was also an alternate member of the Central Committee of the **Korean Workers' Party (KWP)**. Two years later he became a full member of the KWP Central Committee and a member of the Central

Military Committee. In 1998 he became a vice-marshal in the **Korean People's Army**, was elected to the 10th **Supreme People's Assembly**, and became a vice-chairman of the **National Defence Committee**.

Kim Il Sung

Leader and ruler of the Democratic People's Republic of Korea (DPRK) from its foundation in 1948 until his death in July 1994. From the post of Premier, which he occupied in 1948 with the formation of the new state and its first administration, he was elevated in 1972 to the position of President and head of state. A party structure was already in place in the northern half of the **Korean peninsula** from late 1945. Kim Il Sung came to dominate it from mid-1946 and thereafter moved upwards through successive party positions to become general secretary of the **Korean Workers' Party**, the leading party post, in 1966. In his later years he was referred to as the Great Leader.

His attempt to unify through the **Korean War** (1950–53) the two states that had emerged on the Korean peninsula ended in failure and the continued division of the country. He concentrated thereafter on building up his own position and that of his family through shrewd and ruthless elimination of political rivals and those judged unreliable, and on turning the DPRK into an independent socialist entity. The philosophical foundation of the new state was provided by his doctrine of *juche*, which emphasized self-sufficiency and self-reliance and the value of man as the master of his destiny. The economic course he proposed for the DPRK, of agricultural collectivization and rapid industrialization, met with considerable domestic support and initial success, but could not sustain its momentum and from the 1980s began to decline. The need for national reconstruction and his international supporters' discouragement of renewed military action, not to mention the substantial US military presence in the southern half of the peninsula, diverted policy away from the pursuit of reunification. Instead, a sporadic campaign of terrorism was pursued, aimed at destabilizing the Republic of Korea. In 1960, and again in 1980, Kim proposed a '**Democratic Confederal Republic of Koryo**', in which both Korean political systems would coexist in one state. This remained his model for unification until his death. From 1972 until 1973 the two Koreas engaged in a ministerial-level dialogue to discuss ways of moving towards reunification, but the contact petered out. In international affairs Kim steered skilfully between larger regional forces, in particular the Soviet Union and the **People's Republic of China**. His ability to identify the advantages to the DPRK in various contemporary international trends, such as anti-colonialism and the **Non-Aligned Movement**, coupled with his talent for personal rapport, allowed him to strike up friendships with a number of world leaders, especially in the Third World. Eventually, however, he antagonized the USA and others in the world community by his willingness to allow the DPRK to pursue its own nuclear programme. He died before the DPRK was reduced to appealing for international food aid by the disasters of the mid-1990s.

Kim Il Sung was born in 1912 into a peasant family in the village of Mangyongdae in the outskirts of **Pyongyang** (his birthplace is now a national shrine). His original name was Kim Song Ju. From 1919 until 1929 his education appears to have been divided between schools in north-east **China** and Korea as his family moved between the two countries. It seems likely that he was expelled from school in China in 1929 for unlawful student activities, was imprisoned and on release joined one of the Korean anti-Japanese guerrilla bands operating from north-east China. There was some liaison between these bands and Chinese Communist groups. Around this period he is thought to have changed his name from Kim Song Ju to Kim Il Sung. Much has been made of his achievements in political organization and guerrilla activity against the Japanese, but he did rise to some prominence and was the subject of special attention by the Japanese gendarmerie. Under Japanese presssure from 1941, the guerrilla groups, including Kim Il Sung, retreated into the Soviet Union. There is no clear record of his activities during the **Pacific War**. In 1945, following the division of Korea, he returned with many of his former guerrilla colleagues and a number of Soviet **Koreans**, who together helped to establish the administration in the Soviet-run northern part of the peninsula. Kim does not appear to have been especially chosen for this role; rather, as an able organizer and administrator, he appealed to the Soviet forces.

His abilities carried him forward to the reconstruction and reorientation of his country. He appears to have been genuinely welcomed by his people for his vigour, vision and undoubted popular touch. No detail of people's lives seems to have been deemed too insignificant for his comment. The reverse of this quasi-personal interest was a readiness to dominate and control, often in an isolationist and highly individual direction. The question of a successor concerned him greatly. After several false starts, he selected his eldest son, **Kim Jong Il**. The younger Kim remained in the background until the 1980s, then appeared as the designated successor. On his death in 1994 Kim Il Sung left a country facing multiple problems. Many of these had come about as a result of policies Kim had insisted on following over the years; but there is no doubt that he largely fashioned the DPRK and made it what it is today.

Kim Il Sung University

Kim Il Sung University in **Pyongyang** is the most prestigious educational institute in the Democratic People's Republic of Korea (DPRK).

It began in 1946 as the North Korean People's University, but changed its name after the establishment of the DPRK in September 1948. Today it has 14 departments and some 12,000 students, and it is the only full university in the country. It is built on an attractive site not far from the Kumsusan Memorial Palace, which was DPRK President **Kim Il Sung**'s workplace in life and is now his mausoleum. Students are selected on the basis of background and qualifying tests, but there are rumours that children of the top leadership are guaranteed places whatever their educational standards. Its graduates, who include the current DPRK leader, **Kim Jong Il**, occupy senior positions in party and government.

Kim Jong Il

Leader of the Democratic People's Republic of Korea (DPRK) since July 1994, when he succeeded his father, **Kim Il Sung**. His formal titles are general secretary of the **Korean Workers' Party (KWP)**, a post to which he was elevated in October 1997, commander-in-chief of the armed forces (since 1991) and chairman of the National Defence Commission (since 1992). Although long anticipated as his father's successor, he has taken only one of his father's formal titles, that of party general secretary. In September 1998, after a change to the Constitution, his position of chairman of the National Defence Commission was redefined as the highest post. He has not been named President, assumption of that office having been pre-empted by the decision in 1998 to designate Kim Il Sung 'President in perpetuity'. State ceremonial functions have passed to the chairman of the presidium of the **Supreme People's Assembly**, and there are thus no routine opportunities for foreigners such as ambassadors to meet Kim.

Kim Jong Il was born in 1941. According to official DPRK accounts, his birthplace was a guerrilla camp on **Mount Paektu** on the Sino-Korean border, in an area traditionally regarded as sacred. In reality, he was probably born in the Soviet Union, where his father lived from 1941 until 1945. (Khabarovsk has been named as possibly his place of birth.) During the **Korean War** he was sent to north-east **China** for safety. He was educated at **Kim Il Sung University** in **Pyongyang**, graduating in 1963. He then worked in the secretariat of the KWP, eventually becoming his father's secretary and assisting him in the purges of cadres accused of insufficient loyalty and enthusiasm in 1967. In 1973 Kim Jong Il became party secretary in charge of organization and propaganda. His treatise *On the Art of the Cinema*, which appeared in that year, confirmed his close interest in the use of cinema as a didactic tool in propagating the appropriate ideological message. During the early 1970s he is reported to have been involved in film and stage productions. Throughout the following years his father worked to have him accepted as his successor, sometimes against domestic resistance and foreign doubts. Until he was formally designated as his father's successor in 1980, he was not named but was referred to as 'the party centre'.

Kim Jong Il faced a series of daunting problems after his father's death. The dispute with the USA over the **DPRK nuclear programme** had been settled for the time being through the signing of the **Agreed Framework** in October 1994. From that year, however, the DPRK was struck by a series of natural disasters that caused widespread damage and disruption to the land and the economy and led the DPRK government to appeal in September 1995 to the **United Nations** for food relief. The resulting modest influx of foreign aid workers into the country has been unwelcome to the DPRK authorities and, it appears, to Kim Jong Il himself; and Kim has likewise made clear his opposition to the introduction of economic reforms that might take the country away from the socialist model. None the less, in 2002 he agreed to price and wage restructuring and to the improvement of managerial skills in production and marketing.

In foreign affairs, Kim Jong Il has moved away from his father's former alliances and towards grappling with the issues of the country's relations with the Republic of Korea (ROK), with regional neighbours such as the **People's Republic of China**, the Russian Federation and Japan, and with the USA. In 2000, after considerable groundwork, Kim Jong Il and the then President of the ROK, **Kim Dae-Jung**, met in Pyongyang. No further summit meetings have yet followed, but contacts between the two Koreas continue at various levels and in a number of fields. In 2000–02 Kim exchanged several visits with the Chinese and Russian leaders. In 2000 he received the then US Secretary of State for discussions on an agreement concerning North Korean missiles and regional security. Since President George W. Bush's assumption of office in 2001, US policies towards the DPRK have hardened. In response, the DPRK has withdrawn from international nuclear agreements, although it still maintains a moratorium on missile tests. Whatever the nature of the decision-making process in the DPRK, it must be assumed that Kim Jong Il has the final say on important questions and that he therefore backs the current North Korean line on the USA. His decision to meet the Japanese Premier **Koizumi Junichiro** in 2002 to discuss issues dividing the DPRK and Japan was a bold move, even if the talks became largely concerned with the fate of Japanese **abductees**. The DPRK's admission of responsibility for the abductions would seem to reflect its desire to unfreeze DPRK-Japan relations and thereby press its claim for compensation from Japan.

Not a great deal is known about Kim Jong Il's abilities, though he has largely managed to shake off the former unflattering image of his being a playboy. Since his father's death many of his public appearances have been with the military, leading to speculation that he is dependent on them for support—or may feel more at ease in a military atmosphere. His private life is reported to be complicated, involving children by several mothers. Rumours surface of one son or another whom Kim may be seeking to foster as a potential successor, but nothing definite has been established.

Kim Jong Suk

First wife of the Democratic People's Republic of Korea (DPRK) leader, **Kim Il Sung**, and mother of his successor, **Kim Jong Il**.

She was born in North Hamyong Province in the far north of the **Korean peninsula** on 24 December 1917. Her family were peasants who moved to **China** when she was still a child. She joined the anti-Japanese guerrillas and eventually met Kim Il Sung. Accounts of her life, mostly published since Kim Jong Il's designation as his father's successor in the 1980s, relate that she was a markswoman who devoted much of her time to protecting Kim Il Sung.

According to official accounts, Kim Jong Il was born on **Mount Paektu**, the Korean sacred mountain on the Sino-Korean border, on 16 February 1942. In fact, the Japanese had driven Kim Il Sung and his guerrillas out of Korea well before then, and the birth probably took place in Khabarovsk in the Soviet Union in 1941. Kim Jong Suk returned to Korea some time in late 1945, and is reported to have been active in the Korean Women's League and other organizations. She died in childbirth in 1949.

Little was heard of her until Kim Jong Il began to make acknowledged public appearances in the 1980s. Since the death of Kim Il Sung in July 1994, however, a cult of personality has been created around her, entailing statues, pictures and several hagiographical biographies. Her titles include 'Mother of the Nation', 'Indomitable Revolutionary Fighter', and one of the 'Three Generals of Mount Paektu'.

Kim Jong-Pil

The great political survivor in the Republic of Korea (ROK), active since the 1960s.

Popularly known as JP, Kim was born in Kongju, South Chungchong Province, in 1926. After graduating from **Seoul** National University in 1947, he enrolled at the Korean Military Academy, graduating in 1949. He served in the Army Headquarters G-2 Intelligence Section as a lieutenant-colonel and married a niece of Maj.-Gen. **Park Chung-Hee**. In December 1960 Kim and other army officers, who had been contemplating a military coup for some time, advocated a purge of the army. As a result, he had to retire from active military service for insubordination. This led him to undertake even more active plotting for a coup, which eventually took place on 16 May 1961.

After the coup Kim established the Korean Central Intelligence Agency (now the National Intelligence Service), becoming its first director. In 1963 he was one of the key leaders of the **Democratic Republican Party (DRP)** that was established to support the presidency of Park Chung-Hee. Kim entered the **ROK National Assembly** in that year as DRP chairman. He served as Park's Premier from June 1971 until December 1975, and in October 1979 he became the president of the DRP following Park's assassination.

Purged in May 1980, Kim was often placed under house arrest in the following years. Following the restoration of his political rights in 1987, he reconstructed the defunct DRP, fashioning it into the New Democratic Republican Party, and was its unsuccessful presidential candidate in the December 1987 election. When the Party merged with the **Democratic Justice Party** and the Reunification Democratic Party, forming the **Democratic Liberal Party** in February 1990, Kim became one of its three supreme leaders, a position he held until early 1995. When he lost the position of party chairman in January 1995, however, he proceeded to form a new political party, the **United Liberal Democrats (ULD)**. This enjoyed some success in the 1996 National Assembly elections, when 50 of its members were elected.

In a surprise move, the ULD joined with **Kim Dae-Jung's National Congress for New Politics** in 1997, in order to contest the presidential election. Despite their long years in opposition to each other, the two Kims agreed that Kim Dae-Jung would be the presidential candidate. After his narrow victory in 1997 Kim Dae-Jung appointed Kim Jong-Pil as Prime Minister, though not without a great deal of opposition from within his party. As Prime Minister, Kim Jong-Pil advocated a cabinet system of government to replace the executive president system. Early in 2000 the coalition broke up. Kim resigned as Prime Minister, to contest the April 2000 general election as ULD leader. However, his Party performed badly in the election, and by May 2000 he was once again in a coalition with Kim Dae-Jung.

The election of **Roh Moo-Hyun** as President in 2002 and the passing from the political scene of Kim Dae-Jung in 2003 left only Kim Jong-Pil from the era of the 'three Kims', as the period since the early 1970s is known. He eventually announced his retirement from politics in May 2004. In the following month he was indicted for illegal receipt of funds, and in June 2004 received a suspended sentence of two years' imprisonment. This may finally mark the end of his long career.

Kim Sun-Il

A citizen of the Republic of Korea (ROK), Kim Sun-Il (1970–2004) was kidnapped and murdered by a group in Iraq on 22 June 2004.

Kim was born in **Pusan** and at the time of his death worked as a translator for an ROK company in Iraq. His murder was apparently committed in protest against the ROK Government's decision to send troops to Iraq in support of the US-led coalition there. Kim graduated from Hankuk University of Foreign Studies with a degree in Arabic, and was a devout Christian. His brutal death caused much outrage at home and abroad, but the ROK government adhered to its decision to send troops to Iraq.

Kim Yong Nam

Kim Yong Nam became chairman of the presidium of the **Supreme People's Assembly (SPA)** of the Democratic People's Republic of Korea (DPRK) at its 10th session in 1998. Under the present constitutional arrangements, this makes him the DPRK's nominal head of state for certain purposes. He appoints and receives ambassadors, and performs the ceremonial duties of a head of state. Real power lies with **Kim Jong Il**, however, and, officially, the late **Kim Il Sung** is still head of state. Kim Yong Nam is believed to be related by marriage to Kim Il Sung.

Kim Yong Nam was born in 1928 and was educated at **Kim Il Sung University** and Moscow State University. He has held a variety of party and government posts, including membership of the Politburo from 1978, and Minister of Foreign Affairs and Vice-Premier from 1983 until he took up his present post. As foreign minister, he played a part in the early negotiations on the **DPRK nuclear programme**. In addition to his other posts, Kim has been a member of the SPA since 1982.

Kim Young-Sam

In 1993 Kim Young-Sam, a veteran opposition figure, became the first democratically elected civilian president of the Republic of Korea (ROK) since **Syngman Rhee** left the country in April 1961.

Born in **Pusan**, South Kyongsang Province, in 1927, Kim graduated from **Seoul** National University in 1951. He joined the Liberal Party, and served as secretary to the Prime Minister in 1951. Kim then joined the **Democratic Party** and was elected to the **ROK National Assembly** in 1954 and 1960. He was re-elected in 1963 and in 1967. During the 1970s he was a fierce opponent of President **Park Chung-Hee**. Purged after **Chun Doo-Hwan** came to power in 1980, Kim was again politically active by 1984.

Kim served with **Kim Dae-Jung** as co-chairman of the Council for Promotion of Democracy in 1984. Following the establishment of the **New Korea Democratic Party** in 1986, he became its adviser. In 1987 he founded the Reunification Democratic Party, becoming its candidate in the 1987 presidential election. He lost the election, but was elected to the National Assembly in 1988. In February 1990, when his party merged with the Democratic Justice and the New Democratic Republican parties, forming the **Democratic Liberal Party (DLP)**, he became one of the three leaders of the new party, and later the executive chairman. In May 1992 the DLP nominated him as its candidate for the December 1992 presidential election.

His presidency, which ended the military dominance that had prevailed since **Park Chung-Hee**'s 1961 coup, aroused high hopes. He began well, implementing a series of reforming measures. However, when faced with the issue of the **Democratic People's Republic of Korea nuclear programme** and domestic pressure to reexamine the issue of the **Kwangju uprising**, his performance declined. His policy towards the Democratic People's Republic of Korea was inconsistent. While he authorized the trials of Chun Doo-Hwan and **Roh Tae-Woo**, he gained little credit, since he only did so under growing popular pressure. His final months in office were marred by his son's alleged corruption and tax evasion, by attempts to prevent **Kim Dae-Jung** from succeeding him as President and, eventually, by his failure to respond to the **Asian financial crisis** that struck the ROK in the autumn of 1997. In retirement Kim has made occasional references to returning to politics, but this seems increasingly unlikely.

Kobe

Japan's second largest port, after **Yokohama**.

Kobe, situated in the centre of Japan's main island of Honshu, is the capital of Hyogo Prefecture. A port developed at this site in the 8th century, but modern Kobe dates from the opening of the Port of Hyogo to foreign trade and residence in 1868. Although treaties named Hyogo as its location, the **foreign settlement** developed at Kobe. Incorporated as a city in 1889, Kobe by then already outranked Hyogo. By

1939 its population was 1m., but the city was heavily bombed in the **Pacific War**, and by 1945 the population had dwindled to 380,000. It again reached the 1m. mark in 1956; by March 2003 there were 1.5m. people living in an area of 550.69 sq km, much of which is reclaimed land. In 1995 the massive **Hanshin earthquake** struck Kobe, destroying much property and killing more than 5,000 people. Predictions that it would take many years for the city to recover were defied by its swift reconstruction.

It is an important manufacturing centre, producing ships, steel, foodstuffs and rubber shoes. 'Kobe beef' is world famous, and the city plays an important role in the Japanese fashion industry.

Koizumi Junichiro

Prime Minister of Japan since 2001, Koizumi Junichiro, who sports a mane of hair that has given him the nickname 'Lionheart', has been a far more flamboyant holder of that office than is usual in Japan. He has enjoyed periods of great popularity.

Koizumi was born in 1942 in Yokosuka City, Kanagawa Prefecture. He attended the local high school and took a degree in economics at one of the country's most prestigious private universities, Keio University, in 1967. After a spell as secretary to a political giant of the 1970s and later Prime Minister, Fukuda Takeo, Koizumi was elected to the **Diet** in 1972 on a **Liberal Democratic Party (LDP)** ticket for the Kanagawa No. 11 constituency (Yokosuka and Miura cities), which he has continued to represent ever since. He assumed an official position for the first time in 1979, as parliamentary Vice-Minister of Finance, and rose rapidly through the LDP ranks during the 1980s. In 1988 he became Minister of Health. He was associated with the Fukuda faction in the LDP, and was thus regarded as right-of-centre in political terms. However, he also established a reputation as a media personality.

He made his first bids for the LDP leadership, and therefore the premiership, in 1995 and 1998, but did not perform well. In 2001 he ran again. Faced with the prospect of losing power, the LDP turned to the relatively charismatic Koizumi in the hope of avoiding electoral defeat. Koizumi duly became LDP president and Prime Minister, and achieved an electoral victory. There was more to him, however, than his image, and he promised radical reforms in a system that had ceased to deliver by 2001.

It proved difficult to carry out the promised reforms, however. Despite the Prime Minister's rhetoric, the economy refused to revive and the powerful groups that had long dominated politics continued to do so. Koizumi found himself forced to dismiss popular ministers. One success was the journey he made to the Democratic People's Republic of Korea (DPRK) in 2002, when he made some progress on the issue of **abductees**. Although the DPRK's admission that it had abducted Japanese citizens, and its refusal or inability to account for a number of those concerned, led to an outcry in Japan, Koizumi still gained credit for his efforts. A second journey to the DPRK in 2004, which led to the release of family members of those abducted, also proved popular. His insistence on visiting the **Yasukuni Shrine** caused some international difficulties, but helped maintain his credentials as a patriotic politician.

In the July 2004 elections for the upper house, Koizumi's party failed to achieve its modest target of a simple majority, but he remained in office, promising to introduce further social reforms.

Address: Prime Minister's Office
Cabinet Secretariat
1-6-1-Nagata-cho
Chiyoda-ku
Tokyo 100-8968
Japan
Tel: 81-3-3581-2361
Fax: 81-3-3581-1910
E-mail: koizumi-e@mmz.kantei.go.jp
Internet: www.kantei.go.jp

Korea, Democratic People's Republic of (DPRK)

Choson minjujuui inmin konghwaguk

Independent republic, often referred to as North Korea, established in the northern half of the **Korean peninsula** on 9 September 1948 from the division of the peninsula into two separate states. It is bounded to the north by the **People's Republic of China (PRC)** and the Russian Federation and to the south by the **Republic of Korea (ROK)**, from which it is separated by the **Demilitarized Zone**. Its neighbour to the east, across the East Sea (or Sea of Japan), is Japan. To the west, the Yellow Sea separates it from the PRC. The country is divided administratively into nine provinces and three special cities under direct central administration.

Area: 122,000 sq km; *capital:* **Pyongyang**; *population:* 21.2m. (1993 census); current estimates of 23m. rising to 26m.–27m., almost 100% **Korean**; *official language:* Korean; *religion:* officially atheist, but small **Buddhist**, **Protestant**, **Catholic** and **Chondo-gyo** congregations permitted.

The 1992 Constitution of the DPRK (the second revision of the original 1948 Constitution, the first having been in 1972) defines the **Supreme People's Assembly (SPA)** as the state's highest organ of power and its legislative body. It is a unicameral institution with a term of office of five years. The 10th SPA, composed of 687 representatives, was elected in 1998. The presidium of the SPA is empowered to act for the SPA while it is in recess. The chairman of the presidium represents the DPRK in its dealings with foreign countries and thus takes one of the roles customarily assigned to a head of state. The Constitution incorporates the position of a President as head of state, but in 1998 the former President, **Kim Il Sung**, who died in 1994, was elevated to the rank of 'Eternal President'. When the SPA was first designated as the legislative organ, the Central People's Committee (CPC) was empowered to act as its executive body. The Constitution spells out the CPC's duties and status and names its head as the President of the DPRK. The ambiguity surrounding the position of President seems to have resulted in a diminution of the CPC's role. At provincial, district, county and city level, including the directly administered cities, a system of directly elected local People's Assemblies and local administrative and economic committees operates, with a term of office of four years. Voting is for a single list of candidates and turn-out is claimed to be virtually 100%. Responsibility for national administration lies with the Administrative Council of the SPA, which is composed of the Premier and a Cabinet of ministers. However, the whole apparatus of legislative and administrative organs is subordinate to the leadership of the **Korean Workers' Party (KWP)**, as stipulated in Article 11 of the Constitution.

History: A North Korean state began to emerge following the decision by the Soviet Union and the USA to divide the Korean peninsula in 1945 to allow each to take the Japanese surrender in its respective sector. The Soviet Union may not have intended to establish a state in the peninsula, but the administration it put in place in its zone of occupation soon began to take on the characteristics of a separate entity. A Provisional People's Committee was established in 1946 with Kim Il Sung as chairman and enacted legislation on land reform and nationalization of industry, banks and transport. It was replaced in 1947 by the North Korean People's Assembly, which similarly carried out legislative functions until 1948. The inability of the **United Nations (UN)** Temporary Commission on Korea in 1948 to obtain Soviet agreement that it might enter the northern half of the country to supervise elections there, in the hope of creating a unified government for the peninsula, meant that the Commission could only oversee elections in the southern half. Separate elections were held in the northern sector and led in September 1948 to the formation of the first SPA, the establishment of the DPRK and the creation of the first government of the DPRK, with Kim Il Sung as Premier.

Having failed to reunify the peninsula during the 1950–53 **Korean War**, Kim Il Sung concentrated thereafter on building up the DPRK, his own position and that of his family. These closely intertwined preoccupations dominated the DPRK's domestic and foreign policy until Kim's death in 1994 and, in a sense, formed the bulk of political activity in the country. Kim Il Sung soon faced the competing claims of other left-wing Korean groups that had been active in the years before 1945: a domestic group of Communists that had their roots as much in the southern half of the country as in the north; those who had exiled themselves in the Soviet Union; and a group who had fought alongside the Chinese Communists in their struggle. Through ruthless manoeuvring, Kim had managed by 1958 to eliminate or marginalize all of these rivals. Only his 'Kapsan' band of fellow partisans, who from their retreat in the north-east of **China** had engaged the Japanese colonial forces in guerrilla warfare, survived. Kim gave ideological substance to his vision for the DPRK through the launching of campaigns aimed at stimulating production (the *chollima* campaign in 1959) and at ensuring a party presence in agricultural and factory management (1960 and 1961). In 1977 he launched the 'Three Great

Revolutions' in ideology, technology and culture. Already in 1955 he had first expounded the principle of *juche*, the policy of self-reliance and man's mastery of his own destiny that has marked North Korean politics ever since.

In 1972 Kim Il Sung was named as President. From the mid-1970s onwards he appears to have taken the first steps towards passing the succession to his son, **Kim Jong Il**. The process lasted at least five years and was marked by disagreement and even reported disturbances within the country and by expressions of disapproval from the DPRK's main allies, the PRC and the then Soviet Union. By 1980, however, he appeared to have prevailed, and at the Sixth Congress of the KWP in October of that year it was clear that Kim Jong Il was to be his successor. At the Eighth SPA in 1986 Kim Il Sung was re-elected as President. In 1991 Kim Jong Il was moved into the post of supreme commander of the **Korean People's Army** and one year later was named a marshal and chairman of the National Defence Commission of the SPA. The three years following Kim Il Sung's death in 1994, although officially explained as a period of mourning, were a time of political uncertainty over the roles that Kim Jong Il might assume. Eventually, in 1997, he was acclaimed as general secretary of the Central Committee of the KWP, a position that secured him a base in the party structure in addition to the dominant place he occupied in the military hierarchy. He did not take over the role of head of state. Political confusion was exacerbated during the second half of the 1990s by a series of natural disasters that led to widespread hunger, even starvation, and distress, and which weakened an economy that was already underperforming.

Recent developments: The country, and Kim Jong Il, survived these difficulties and by June 2000, when he met the then President of the ROK, **Kim Dae-Jung**, in Pyongyang, he appeared fully in control. He regards the military as his natural ally and since mid-1999 has developed the **'Army First' policy** that esteems the military as the first line of defence against aggression and accords them priority in resources. In July 2002 a series of price and wage reforms attempted to address some of the country's economic problems. None the less, in the decade since Kim Il Sung's death the equation between national well-being and the leader's political fortunes has not seemed so clear as it once did.

International relations and defence: The guiding principle for the DPRK in its international relations is independence—an expression of *juche* philosophy. Independence has not meant isolation, rather a continual manoeuvring with other players to gain maximum advantage of the particular stage in any given relationship. This pragmatic approach may be combined with at times virulent expressions of hostility towards the same country with which negotiations may be in hand. The USA and Japan fall into this category, the ROK now less so as **Korean North-South relations** take on a more complex nature.

The DPRK's longest-standing relations have been with its two large neighbours, the PRC and the former Soviet Union, now the Russian Federation. Both countries were early backers of the new state and gave it considerable economic and technological aid in its first decades of existence. The PRC sent the Chinese People's

Volunteers to fight alongside Korean troops in the Korean War. The DPRK aligned itself with the Soviet Union and its allies, but still kept some distance and, for instance, refused to join **COMECON**, the Council for Mutual Economic Assistance. During the years of the **Sino–Soviet dispute** (which was partly provoked by Khrushchev's criticisms of Stalin from 1956), the DPRK oscillated between the two. The Soviet Union's decision to establish diplomatic relations with the ROK in 1990 and then the collapse of the Soviet Union in 1991, followed by the withdrawal of its formerly favourable terms of trade and aid, caused deep shock to the DPRK, and relations with the new Russian Federation slumped. A decade later, however, in 2000, a new treaty of friendship between the DPRK and the Federation was signed. The PRC itself established diplomatic relations with the ROK in 1992, but continued to extend aid to the DPRK through the difficult years of the late 1990s and beyond, and participated in the inconclusive four-way talks held in 1997–98 between the USA, the PRC, the ROK and the DPRK. China has more recently put pressure on the DPRK to join the **six-party talks** initiated in 2003 between the USA, the Russian Federation, the PRC, Japan and the two Koreas to discuss regional issues, in particular the **DPRK nuclear programme**. Since 2000 Kim Jong Il has made several visits to both the Russian Federation and the PRC and has received Russian and Chinese leaders in Pyongyang. The DPRK is continuing its two-handed policy with these two neighbours.

For many years the DPRK's official dealings with Japan remained frozen in recrimination over the Japanese colonial period, for which the DPRK sought large sums in compensation. Around 100,000 Japanese Koreans had come to the DPRK after 1959 through Red Cross auspices, and contacts between pro-DPRK Korean residents remaining in Japan and the DPRK have continued for years. Only in 1991–92 and again in 1997–98 and 2000 did the two governments come together for talks aimed at the normalization of relations. Among their points for discussion the Japanese raised claims that DPRK agents had abducted a number of Japanese nationals from Japan in the 1970s. In the earlier sessions, the DPRK refused to accept claims about **abductees**. It required two visits from the Japanese Prime Minister, **Koizumi Junichiro**, to the DPRK in 2002 and 2004 respectively to resolve some of the issues surrounding the abductees and their family members in the DPRK. The DPRK admitted during Koizumi's first visit that its agents had indeed carried out some 15 kidnappings from Japanese soil during the 1970s and 1980s, with the intention of training its spies in Japanese ways, and that all but five of those abducted had since died. As a result of Koizumi's visits, abductees and their children have been able to go to Japan. The DPRK clearly hoped for both food aid and a financial settlement of their request for compensation for the colonial era, but it is not clear what undertakings Koizumi may have made to the DPRK on either issue. The DPRK and Japan had further discussions on the abductees during Koizumi's second visit in May 2004. The DPRK's possible nuclear intentions are a further source of anxiety to Japan, already unsettled by the testing of two DPRK medium-range missiles eastwards over the East Sea and Japanese territory in 1993 and 1998.

Nuclear and missile issues now form the substance of US concerns over the DPRK. As with Japan, relations have not yet been normalized between the two countries. The DPRK has made it clear that it wishes to move to a peace treaty with the USA, which it has always regarded as its true enemy in the Korean War. The ROK is explicitly excluded from such a treaty (and the UN's part in the war is downplayed). The USA rejects such proposals and insists that before any understanding of any kind can be reached with the DPRK, the country must proceed to an irreversible dismantling of what it claims are nuclear installations. The US commitment to the ROK meant that for many years it shunned contact with the DPRK. The capture of a US spy ship, the *USS Pueblo*, by DPRK forces in 1968 and the detention of the crew for almost one year heightened tension. Anxiety over the possibility of a DPRK terrorist attack on the ROK during the approach to the **Seoul 1988 Summer Olympic Games** prompted the USA to seek discussions with the DPRK. The country's willingness to co-operate with the USA in the location and repatriation of the remains of US soldiers **missing in action** from the Korean War, together with growing concerns over the DPRK's possible nuclear intentions and the country's sales of arms and missiles to a number of other states, spurred the USA into further contact. A possible crisis in 1994 over the DPRK's threat to withdraw from the **Nuclear Non-Proliferation Treaty** was averted (for the time being) when former US President **James (Jimmy) Earl Carter** visited Pyongyang and secured the DPRK's participation in an **Agreed Framework** that would lead to the building of two nuclear reactors dedicated to peaceful ends. A former US Secretary of Defence, William Perry, visited the DPRK in May 1999 as part of a review of US policy towards the country. His trip was succeeded in 2000 first by a visit to the USA by Vice-Marshal **Jo Myong Rok**, the most senior military figure in the DPRK, then by a visit by the then US Secretary of State, Madeleine Albright, to the DPRK. It was hoped to proceed with some agreement on missile limitation, but this did not materialize. A change of presidency in the USA led to different, more hostile policies towards the DPRK, and, in 2002, to President George W. Bush's denunciation of the DPRK as part of the 'axis of evil'. Contact has never been broken off between the two states, and the DPRK permanent delegation at the UN headquarters in New York acts as a conduit for messages and discussions. The USA, disassociating its political objections from its humanitarian impulses, continues to be the major donor to the World Food Programme's food-aid projects in the DPRK. The issue of the Japanese abductees has also involved the USA. It was revealed in June 2004 that a US army deserter in the DPRK, **Charles Jenkins**, had married one of the Japanese women abducted from Japan.

The DPRK's relations with other parts of the world have followed more conventional paths. It has been a member of the **Non-Aligned Movement** since 1975. During the 1960s and early 1970s it widened its range of trading partners in Asia, Africa, the Middle East and Europe, but plans to boost the production of exports through the prior import of new technology encountered repayment difficulties and bad debts. Diplomatic relations were established with the four

Nordic countries in the mid-1970s, though only those with Sweden appear to have had any lasting substance. Informal contacts with European countries were maintained, but did not harden into formal relations until 2000–2001, by which time the majority of EU member states and the EU itself had established diplomatic relations. The number of foreigners, many of them Westerners, living and working inside the DPRK rose as the government found itself obliged to accept foreign aid workers as part of the assistance it sought from the outside world during the second half of the 1990s, when the country was struggling to cope with natural disasters, food shortages and the effects of economic downturn.

The armed forces of the DPRK—the **Korean People's Army (KPA)**— are estimated at 1,106,000 men and women, divided between the army (around 950,000), the navy (estimated at 46,000, with bases on both the east and west coasts) and the air force (around 110,000). The air force can deploy several thousand air-to-air and surface-to-air missiles. A medium-range ballistic missile was tested in 1998. A Special Purpose Forces Command, 88,000 strong, forms part of the KPA. Military service is compulsory for almost all young people, university students spend much time in militia drill, and some 3.5m. older people are drafted into the paramilitary Worker/Peasant Red Guard. Security forces to the strength of 189,000 operate under the direction of the Ministry of Public Security as border guards and in public security.

Korea, Democratic People's Republic of, Economy

A failing economy dependent in part on international assistance to feed its people. With a promising start, helped by the provision of aid from its then allies, the Soviet Union, the **People's Republic of China (PRC)** and East European countries, the Democratic People's Republic of Korea (DPRK) outpaced its rival, the Republic of Korea (ROK), in output and standard of living until the early 1970s. This position began to deteriorate during that decade, when an ambitious programme to modernize industry through foreign imports collapsed, leaving a string of bad debts. At the same time, fearful of what it felt was the threat from the USA, the DPRK began to augment military expenditure and has maintained the military budget at a high level ever since. Labour shortages, over-reliance on ideological exhortation rather than incentives, and obsolescent equipment contributed to a decline in output that has weakened the economy. Since the 1980s it has been first slowly, then rapidly, contracting.

The mechanisms of the DPRK's economy are not easy to discern. The ability of the military, for instance, to engage in its own economic activities, such as arms sales, and the existence of a **DPRK nuclear programme** have led to references to a 'second economy'. Only rarely has the country published economic data since the mid-1960s, and then often in the form of percentage changes in output, and it has announced only fragmentary budgetary data since 1994. Statistics are not always available, a factor that has impeded the DPRK's dealings with international bodies such as the **World Bank**. Economic indicators, therefore, are generally estimates.

GNP: US $22,000m. (2003, estimate); *GNP per caput:* US $973 (2003, estimate); *exports:* US $650.2m. (2001, estimate); *imports:* US $1,620.3m. (2001, estimate); *currency:* won (plural: won; US $1 = 140 won in spring 2004).

In 2000 the agricultural sector (including forestry and fisheries) was estimated to account for 30.4% of national production, mining and manufacturing for 25.4%, and the service sector for 32.5%. After a nine-year period of negative growth and contraction in production from 1990, small upturns in productivity were recorded from 2000, especially in agriculture, as the government directed more funds, fuel, energy and equipment into that sector. The government has also carried forward land realignment in arable regions to increase the area of cultivable land and has completed a large-scale waterway system to improve irrigation. Double cropping is practised wherever the length of growing season permits. International assistance has been another contributory factor in increased agricultural output. Even with such initiatives and support, however, the DPRK still cannot produce sufficient to meet the annual need of around 5m. metric tons of cereals and from the mid-1990s has suffered a yearly shortfall of more than 1m. tons. Commercial imports of around 100,000 tons of grains per year, mainly from Thailand, go some way to meet the gap, but the needs of weaker or unproductive sections of society—the very young, the elderly and pregnant and nursing mothers—are largely met by donations of food aid from international organs.

The current relative strength of the agricultural, fishing and forestry sector represents a considerable reversal of the pattern of earlier years. In 1987, for instance, mining and manufacturing were estimated to contribute 60% of production, and agriculture 20%. From 1993, after the failure of the third Seven-Year Plan (1987–93), the emphasis was shifted from heavy industry to agriculture, light industry and tourism. Heavy industry by that time was being affected by the withdrawal of aid and favourable trade terms for such items as fuel oil that accompanied the collapse of the Soviet Union in 1991 and the political changes in Eastern Europe (up until 1990 the Soviet Union had been responsible for 57% of the DPRK's foreign trade). Already existing inefficiencies and obstructions in supply and distribution added to difficulties, which from 1994 until 1998 were compounded by a series of natural disasters that destroyed agricultural land and crops, flooded mines, damaged hydroelectric schemes and disrupted the infrastructure. The consequent drop in energy production, coupled with the failure to replace worn-out or obsolescent equipment, have contributed to shortfalls in the extractive industries and to many factories running at well below capacity. The mining and manufacturing sector is still productive—the country continues to export non-ferrous metals, gold, iron and steel, chemical products, cement and military hardware—but light industry is being modernized and is taking an expanding share of exports with products such as textiles, garments, electronic and electric goods, computer software and assembled television sets. Many of these items are produced as processed or semi-processed goods for the ROK market. In 1984 the DPRK introduced a Joint Venture Law, which encouraged a number of joint ventures from 1985, and in 1991 created the Rajin-Sonbong **Special Economic Zone** in the northeast of the country. The zone is still in existence, but it has not prospered. Since 1988 trade and then joint ventures have been initiated with ROK firms. The two-way volume of trade between the two Koreas had grown to US $441m. by 2002. A special tourist zone in the Mount Kumgang area just north of the **Demilitarized Zone**, operated with the ROK **Hyundai Corporation**, has generated revenue since it opened in 1998, and a special industrial zone with ROK participation is planned for the **Kaesong** area. The DPRK's principal trading partners in descending order are now the PRC, the ROK and Japan.

In July 2002 the DPRK announced wage increases for selected categories of workers and rises in the prices of commodities and basic services. Other changes preceding the July 2002 announcement called for decentralization in production to local authorities, improvements in management, with less party participation, and an extension of responsibility to enterprises for pricing and selling their output. The network of informal markets that had long existed was formally recognized in June 2003 as a channel of distribution. The won, which had long stood at US $1 = 2.16, was devalued first in 2002 to around US $1 = 230 won, appeared to float during the summer of 2003 and in the spring of 2004 stood at US $1 = 140. The prime effect of the wage and price increases seems so far to have been inflationary and to have led to a fall in the disposable income of many families, who now spend more on food. The ultimate purpose of the changes, beyond achieving a reduction in state subsidies and stimulating competition and a sense of responsibility in enterprise managers, is not clear. On present showing it cannot be assumed that more structural economic changes are intended. The official goal remains that of a planned socialist economy that will support the development of a communist society and reflect its superiority. So far, the DPRK has refused to engage in any economic reforms that would orient it irrevocably towards a market economy.

Korea, Democratic People's Republic of, nuclear programme

A programme the exact nature and extent of which has not yet been determined, but which is an increasing obstacle in the Democratic People's Republic of Korea's (DPRK) relations with the outside world. The DPRK has reserves of graphite and uranium, both used in the development of nuclear energy. In the 1950s it embarked on a civilian nuclear energy programme with assistance from the then Soviet Union in order to supplement other energy resources. The Soviet Union provided training and an experimental reactor, which was built in 1965 at Yongbyon in the north-central part of the country. At Soviet insistence, this reactor was registered with the **International Atomic Energy Agency (IAEA)** in 1977 and was subject to IAEA inspection. In 1985, again at Soviet insistence, the DPRK joined the **Nuclear Non-Proliferation Treaty (NPT)**, although it did not sign the required safeguards agreement or submit a full list of its nuclear facilities to the IAEA until 1992. An IAEA inspection followed the deposition of the DPRK list. At the end of 1991 both the DPRK and the Republic of Korea (ROK) had signed a declaration on the denuclearization of the **Korean peninsula**.

By 1991, however, there was growing international concern that the DPRK might be developing a nuclear weapons programme. Satellite photographs showed that the Yongbyon facilities went beyond the Soviet reactor, a development confirmed by the list that the DPRK supplied to the IAEA. What the DPRK described as a radiochemical laboratory appeared to be a spent nuclear fuel reprocessing plant that would allow the extraction of plutonium, necessary for nuclear weapons. IAEA attempts to inspect these facilities led the DPRK to announce in March 1993 that it was withdrawing from the NPT. It was dissuaded from doing so under great international pressure that included the threat of **United Nations** sanctions. (It emerged later that the US Government under President Bill Clinton had even considered military action.)

In June 1994 the DPRK stated that it was relinquishing membership of the IAEA. In response, former US President **James (Jimmy) Earl Carter** visited the DPRK in that month and secured its agreement to negotiations between the DPRK and the USA. These led to the signing of an **Agreed Framework** at Geneva, Switzerland, in October 1994. Under this agreement, the DPRK would freeze all of its activities at Yongbyon, while an international consortium, the **Korean Peninsula Energy Development Organization**, would supply two light-water reactors (LWRs) to the DPRK to meet its energy needs and, in addition, would provide heavy fuel oil until the LWRs became operational. The USA meanwhile undertook to lift sanctions and to move towards diplomatic relations with the DPRK. Only when the new LWRs were about to become operational would the IAEA verify the accuracy and completeness of the DPRK's initial report.

In May 1999 a US team of inspectors visited a site in Taegwan County north-west from Yongbyon which had been suspected of being a nuclear facility, but determined that it was not so. Delays in implementing work on the LWR site began to cause friction between the DPRK and the USA. The beginning of the US presidency of George W. Bush in 2001 initiated the pursuit of a much harsher set of policies towards the DPRK. Deteriorating relations between the two countries now threaten the whole edifice of agreements. US concerns have centred on whether or not the DPRK would fulfil its part of the 1994 agreement to freeze its programme at Yongbyon and, since the visit of a senior US official to the DPRK in October 2002, whether the DPRK has embarked on a separate road to a nuclear weapons programme using enriched uranium. The USA claims that the DPRK has admitted to such a programme. The DPRK denies this, but claims none the less that it has the right to do so, since the USA continues to target it with nuclear weapons. In 2002 the DPRK expelled the IAEA inspectors from Yongbyon and announced it would restart its programme there of reprocessing spent fuel rods. In January 2003 the DPRK formally withdrew from the NPT, the first state ever to do so. Once again, there was much international activity, eventually leading to **six-party talks** involving the two Koreas, the **People's Republic of China**, Japan, the Russian Federation and the USA, to discuss issues of security and disarmament. The talks started in August 2003 and continued into 2004. The DPRK throughout 2003 and 2004 reported the progress of its programme to reprocess 8,000 spent fuel rods and hinted that it might use the resulting plutonium to strengthen its nuclear deterrent capacity. At the same time, it has urged acceptance of its proposal for a nuclear freeze.

The admission by the ROK government in September 2004 that ROK scientists had engaged in secret experiments in 2000 to enrich nuclear fuel through the use of lasers to a point beyond the needs of a civilian programme is likely to complicate discussions with the DPRK. The ROK is a signatory to the NPT.

Korea, Republic of (ROK)

Taehan minguk

An independent republic also known as South Korea, established on 15 August 1948 in the southern half of the **Korean peninsula**, following the division of the peninsula in 1945.

The ROK's northern boundary is formed by the **Demilitarized Zone**, which separates it from the Democratic People's Republic of Korea (DPRK—North Korea). On every other side it is bounded by water: to the east by the **East Sea** (also known as the Sea of Japan), separating it from Japan; to the west by the Yellow Sea, which divides it from the **People's Republic of China (PRC)**; and to the south by the Korea Strait running between the peninsula and Kyushu, the southernmost large island of Japan. The ROK is divided into nine provinces, including the island province of **Cheju**, and seven metropolitan cities (defined by a population of more than 1m. each).

Area: 99,000 sq km; *capital:* **Seoul**; *population:* 45,985,289 (2000 census), almost entirely Korean; *official language:* Korean; *religion:* **Buddhism** 26.3%, **Protestant Christianity** 18.6%, **Catholic Christianity** 7.0%, **Confucianism** 0.7%, other 1.1%, without religion 46.3%.

The President is the head of state, chief executive and commander-in-chief of the armed forces. He or she is elected by direct vote for a single term of five years. Legislative power rests with the unicameral **ROK National Assembly**, whose 273 members serve a four-year term. Of these members, 227 are elected from single-member electoral districts and 46 are shared by their parties in proportional representation. Executive authority lies with the State Council or Cabinet, consisting of 15–30 members, headed by the President and assisted by the Prime Minister; the President appoints the Prime Minister. This form of election and government has been in force since 1987, when the Constitution was amended to restore direct popular election of the President for a single term. Provincial and municipal governments are now also elected by direct vote for a term of four years. For a

34-year period, until 1995, local government functioned as an offshoot of central government, with local officials appointed by the central authority.

History: The period from liberation from Japan in August 1945 to the establishment of two separate states three years later was a time of considerable confusion in the Korean peninsula. Immediately after liberation, preparatory committees for national reconstruction appeared in both north and south. A short-lived Korean People's Republic even existed for six weeks in the autumn of 1945 with popular support from local People's Committees in both halves of the country. These Committees drew their membership from both right and left of the political spectrum. In the north they came under pressure from the Soviet occupation to admit equal numbers of Communist and moderate members, and eventually found themselves submerged in the increasingly Communist orientation of the new political and administrative institutions encouraged by the Soviet army. In the southern part of the country the People's Committees met with distrust from the US military government after it was installed in September 1945 for their possible Communist sympathies. For advice the US administration preferred to look to conservative Korean public figures, such as **Syngman Rhee**, who had spent many years in the USA and was well known to them. As the US military government pursued its anti-leftist line throughout 1946, it had to cope with strikes, riots and guerrilla activities, particularly in the south of the peninsula. The flow of people moving largely from north to south, but also from south to north, added to the generally unsettled conditions of the time.

The situation was complicated by the intervention, from December 1945, of the USA and the Soviet Union as members of a joint commission tasked by the wartime Allies to institute a form of trusteeship for the Korean peninsula that would guide it towards independence. The commission had to contend with general Korean protest. The problem was eventually transferred to the **United Nations (UN)**, which in late 1947 called for elections within each zone. By this time interim people's assemblies and administrative organs had been formed in each half of the country. The UN body sent to supervise elections throughout the peninsula could only do so in the south; it was denied access to the north. Many **Koreans** on both right and left were bitterly opposed to any arrangement that might threaten national unity. Elections were none the less held in the south in May 1948, which produced a National Assembly. This in turn designated the south as the Republic of Korea, promulgated a constitution and elected Syngman Rhee as its first President. The administration he formed followed the US presidential style and was recognized at the UN as the only legitimate government on the peninsula.

Rhee's period of office from 1948 until 1960 is known as the First Republic. His understanding of government was autocratic, authoritarian and centralized, an approach that marked succeeding regimes for three decades. His administration was none the less conceived of as a democracy and in theory did incorporate democratic checks and balances. Rhee did not welcome the challenge of political opposition, however, and in amendments to the Constitution sought to change the way in which the President was elected and to extend the number of times he might stand for office. The 1960 presidential elections were widely viewed as fraudulent and provoked student demonstrations. A number of students were shot on 19 April 1960 by the police; Rhee resigned and left the country. He was succeeded as President by Chang Myon, who, in the Second Republic (1960–61), made a brief attempt at a parliamentary style of government but was unable to control the unruly political scene. The army, offended by the 'disorder' of democracy, intervened in May 1961 under Gen. **Park Chung-Hee**. Martial law was imposed and the National Assembly was dissolved. Between 1961 and 1963 the ROK was administered by unelected military councils, and political activity was banned. In December 1962 a new Constitution was promulgated that promised a return to a directly elected President whose period of office would be limited to two four-year terms; and in October 1963 Park, who had resigned from the army, contested the presidency. He was narrowly elected, and ruled with a heavy hand throughout what is termed the Third Republic (1963–70). He was re-elected in 1967, and then, in 1969, as Rhee before him, forced a constitutional amendment through the National Assembly to allow him to stand for a third term. In 1971 his political opponent was **Kim Dae-Jung**, who deprived him of many votes. Park retaliated in 1972 by imposing a new constitution that permitted him to present himself indefinitely every six years for re-election by a specially formed electoral college. He was elected thus in 1972 and again in 1978. His rule during the Fourth Republic (1972–79) became increasingly repressive. In 1973 Kim Dae-Jung was kidnapped in **Tokyo**, Japan, by the Korean security services and brought back to the ROK, where he faced house arrest. Criticism of Park was forbidden and punished. An assassination attempt on Park in 1974 killed not him but his wife and he became increasingly remote. In October 1979, against a deteriorating situation of political unrest and demonstrations, Park was shot dead by the head of the ROK's security services. The positive element in Park's repeated periods in office was the economy, which started to flourish from the 1960s. His daughter, **Park Geun-Hye**, has herself entered politics.

During 1979–81 there was confusion and unrest and continued intervention by the military in national affairs. The ROK's Prime Minister, **Choe Kyu-Ha**, was named acting President in the wake of Park's assassination and martial law was imposed. Choe was elected as President in December 1979, but was soon over-shadowed by another general, **Chun Doo-Hwan**, who staged a coup within the armed forces that brought him to the fore. His colleague and fellow general, **Roh Tae-Woo**, deployed troops to secure Seoul. Unrest grew throughout the country among students and workers at the situation, which Chun moved to suppress. In mid-May 1980 political leaders were arrested and the National Assembly was closed. Rioting erupted in the south-western city of **Kwangju**, which was exacer-bated by the dispatch of special forces trained for action against the DPRK. The situation was eventually brought under control by the army, at the cost of a number of deaths. The USA had to accept Chun's use of troops that he withdrew unilaterally from the front-line defence forces (which were under combined US-ROK com-mand). In August 1980 Chun resigned his army post, Choe stepped down from the presidency and Chun was elected as interim President. His post was confirmed in February 1981 by an electoral college, which allowed him a single seven-year term as specified in yet another reworking of the Constitution. In the preceding September Kim Dae-Jung had been sentenced to death on conviction of sedition and of fomenting the **Kwangju uprising**, even though he had been in prison at the time. Domestic and international protest prevented this sentence from being carried out, and Kim Dae-Jung was allowed to leave for the USA.

Chun's Fifth Republic (1981–88) was marked by heavy-handed rule that sought to curb the press, the labour force and political opponents and to re-educate those regarded as social undesirables. Student demonstrations, industrial strikes and radical church activities inspired by liberation theology were frequent. His calm handling of the bomb assault on him and his entourage in Yangon in September 1983, attributed to DPRK commandos, won him respect. He escaped, but 17 of his colleagues died. Chun accepted that he had to stand down at the end of his term of office, but nominated Roh Tae-Woo as his successor. Chun's determination that the presidential election should again be in the hands of an electoral college sparked further popular unrest, which Roh himself defused in June 1987 by announcing that he would only proceed with his candidature if the President were elected by direct vote. Roh was returned as President in December 1987 for a single five-year term when the opposition vote was split between two candidates, **Kim Young-Sam** and Kim Dae-Jung, and he inaugurated the Sixth Republic in 1988. His term of office was marked by a measure of relaxation of social and legal restrictions, coupled with greater freedom to discuss aspects of the DPRK regime, and a livelier political scene ensued. The 1988 Summer Olympic Games were held successfully. Calls were made for an investigation into the 'Kwangju incident' of 1980.

The 1992 presidential elections were contested by Kim Young-Sam, who represented the leading **Democratic Liberal Party** and was elected, the first President since 1960 not to have a military background. He started well with an onslaught on corruption, but by the end of his term was himself facing similar accusations. In a sign of extending democracy, full local elections resumed in 1995 for the first time in 34 years (local officials had previously been appointed from the centre). Pressure mounted for the reopening of inquiries into the roles Chun Doo-Hwan and also Roh Tae-Woo had played in the 1979 coup and the 1980 events in Kwangju, and in 1995 both men were arrested and tried on charges of treason, mutiny and embezzlement while in office. In 1996 Chun was sentenced to death and Roh to a lengthy term of imprisonment. These sentences were commuted and the two men were released in 1997 at the very end of Kim Young-Sam's period of office. Kim was succeeded in the 1997 presidential elections by the long-standing opposition leader, Kim Dae-Jung, the first time power had passed to the opposition. Kim Dae-Jung was confronted on taking office with economic problems brought about by the 1997 **Asian financial crisis**. The measures he supported produced some relief; but his attempts to impose reform on the big business conglomerates (the *chaebol*) were not so successful. In general, he tried to rule by consensus rather than confrontation. The most striking example of this was his **'sunshine policy'** of engagement with the DPRK. Previous regimes had achieved contacts with the DPRK, but never as part of a sustained approach. Kim met the DPRK leader **Kim Jong Il** in **Pyongyang** in June 2000. Kim Dae-Jung's term of office was eventually weakened by the recurring flaw of corruption, which implicated two of his sons and compromised his authority at the end of his tenure. In the presidential elections of 2002 **Roh Moo-Hyun**, a lawyer before he entered politics, who had worked for Kim Dae-Jung in two of Kim's presidential campaigns, was elected as President.

Recent developments: President Roh has not had an easy period in office to date. His background as a lawyer defending student activists in the 1980s and his participation in demonstrations in 1987 have made conservative South Koreans wary of him. He is known to have called for the withdrawal of US troops and since assuming office has had public differences with US President George W. Bush on how to handle relations with the DPRK. He has maintained his predecessor's policies of engagement with the DPRK. Political and economic difficulties prompted him in October 2003 to admit that he had lost confidence in his abilities as President and to propose a referendum early in 2004 on whether or not he should remain in office. Nothing came of this suggestion, for which there was no constitutional precedent. Roh did, however, find himself in the spring of 2004 under impeachment by the opposition for alleged partisanship in expressing support for a particular political party. With the Prime Minister in charge, he stood down for 63 days before the Supreme Court found that he had no case to answer.

The ROK government is likely to face embarrassment from another quarter if it has to answer questions on how it came to engage secretly in 2000 in experiments to enrich nuclear fuel through the use of lasers. The highly enriched uranium produced is held to have uses far beyond those of a civilian programme. A team of inspectors from the **International Atomic Energy Agency** visited the ROK at the end of August 2004. In early September 2004 the government admitted the experiments following an IAEA new and more rigorous inspection regime. The ROK is a signatory to the **Nuclear Non-Proliferation Treaty**.

International relations and defence: The key international relationships for the ROK have always been in **Korean North-South relations**, in the alliance with the USA and in dealings with regional neighbours, especially the PRC and Japan.

US involvement in the Korean peninsula goes back as far as the 1880s. It was reinforced when in 1945 the USA chose the **38th parallel** as the line of division across the peninsula between its forces and those of the former Soviet Union, and subsequently installed a military government in the southern half of the country from 1945 until 1948. The USA and its allies recognized only the newly established ROK from January 1949. The new state might have yielded before the DPRK invasion of its territory in June 1950 if the USA, heading a combined UN force, had not decided to resist what it regarded as part of a world-wide Communist drive against the free world. From 1953 the USA helped liberally in the reconstruction of the ROK. It has generally refrained from intervention in ROK domestic affairs, but has on occasion put pressure on the government of the day to abandon what it viewed as repressive or extreme policies. Thus it protested at Park Chung-Hee's proposal to extend military rule in the 1960s and at Chun Doo-Hwan's death sentence in 1980 on Kim Dae-Jung. At the same time, the USA acquiesced in Chun's withdrawal of four front-line battalions from the combined US-ROK military command to secure order in 1979–80.

The two countries are bound by the 1953 Mutual Defense Treaty and since 1976 have joined most years in combined exercises. Around 35,000 US troops from all three services are still stationed in the ROK, their relationship with their host country defined in the Status of Forces Agreement of 1965, renegotiated in 2000. Both US Presidents Richard Nixon and **James (Jimmy) Earl Carter** proposed reductions in the number of troops, moves that prompted vigorous lobbying by the ROK in the USA. US servicemen have been progressively withdrawn since 1991 from front-line positions, the US army has largely vacated its base in the centre of Seoul and in 2004 the possibility was raised of withdrawing US forces even further south in the peninsula and of reallocating troops away from Korea. The ROK, in recognition of its alliance with the USA, sent Korean troops to fight in the Viet Nam War from 1965 until 1973 in support of the US action. The ROK also supplies personnel and funds to UN and other peace-keeping forces around the world.

The USA and the ROK have shared anxiety over the development of the **DPRK nuclear programme**. The DPRK's attempts to draw the USA into bilateral discussions on the issue have caused concern in the ROK, which fears being marginalized. The ROK has a stake, however, in the **Korean Peninsula Energy Development Organization**, which was set up to finance and supply two light-water reactors to the DPRK for civilian purposes; and is a party to the **six-party talks** initiated in 2003. US relations with the ROK were warm throughout the 1990s under Presidents George Bush and Bill Clinton. In 2001, however, President Kim Dae-Jung had to listen to criticism from President George W. Bush of his 'sunshine policy', and a line of disagreement has been discernible between the two countries over ways of dealing with the DPRK, sustained by President Roh Moo-Hyun's reservations over US policy.

Relations with Japan have to cope with several often sensitive issues: the residual colonial legacy from the first half of the 20th century which erupts every so often in rows over Japanese guilt and the Japanese interpretation of the history of that period; the issue of **comfort women** forced to provide sexual services to the wartime Japanese troops; the status of the **overseas Korean** community in Japan and the existence there of two associations, one pro-DPRK, the other pro-ROK; and the **Tokto/Takeshima dispute** over islands claimed by both Japan and the ROK. Relations were normalized in 1965, against ROK popular dissent, and a Basic Treaty was signed. The apparent connection between the pro-DPRK association in Japan and the would-be assassin of Park Chung-Hee in 1974 was a complicating issue. An exchange of formal visits had to wait until the mid-1980s and was used by the Japanese to express a measure of regret for their past behaviour towards Korea. In 1993 Japan acknowledged and apologized for the treatment of Korean and other Asian comfort women; Japanese statements of apology for the colonial period were made in 1995 and 1998 and were acknowledged by the ROK. Rivalry and resentment remain, however, as exemplified by the resurgence in 2001 of the **history textbooks controversy** and the dispute over which country should host the 2002 World Cup football tournament: the ROK and Japan finally acted as co-hosts.

The ROK's present fairly close relations with the PRC and with Russia are an outcome of the *Nordpolitik* or 'Northern policy' pursued by ROK leaders from the 1970s. In a fundamental shift away from its earlier refusal of any contacts with communism, the ROK announced in 1973 that it would seek better relations with the PRC and the then Soviet Union and would not break off diplomatic links with countries recognizing the DPRK. From 1988 Roh Tae-Woo elevated this approach to the key element in his foreign policy. The hope was that by extending the ROK's contacts with the DPRK's allies, they could be persuaded to exert pressure on the DPRK to be more accommodating. Benefiting from the general loosening towards the end of the 1980s in economic and political rigidities in the Soviet Union and its East European allies, the ROK hosted the 1988 Summer Olympic Games, in which the PRC, the Soviet Union and the East European bloc participated. The Soviet Union established diplomatic relations with the ROK in 1990 and the PRC did so in 1992.

The ROK's defence budget stood at US \$14,600m. in 2003, 2.8% of gross domestic product. Total armed forces number 687,700, of which an estimated 159,000 are conscripts, mostly serving in the army (army service lasts for 26 months, navy and air force service 30 months). There is a reserve civilian defence corps numbering 3,500,000. Naval vessels, as with the DPRK, include a somewhat large number of patrol and coastal combatant craft, mine-warfare and amphibious craft. The ROK also has a maritime police force of 4,500. It has air-to-surface and air-to-air missiles. By agreement between the US and ROK governments, some 35,000 US troops are stationed in the ROK.

Korea, Republic of, Economy

The economy of the Republic of Korea (ROK) has largely been a success story. From being a recipient of US and **United Nations** relief aid and funds in the years between 1945 and 1949 and again, following the **Korean War**, from 1953 until 1960 (and for even longer from the USA), the ROK was admitted in 1996 to full membership of the **Organisation for Economic Co-operation and Development**, albeit with the requirement that it undertake certain measures of reform. For many years, the average annual growth rate in the country's gross national product was around 9%. Its economy negotiated the oil crises of 1974 and 1979 and the world recession of the mid-1970s reasonably well. The 1997 **Asian financial crisis** affected the ROK severely, however, and it had to resort to a loan from the **International Monetary Fund (IMF)** of US \$57,000m. (the largest loan ever sanctioned by the IMF); but its economy has since made an impressive recovery. Per caput income in 2000 was estimated at US $9,770. By 2003 it was more than US $12,000.

GNI: US $576,400m. (2003); *GNI per caput:* US $12,020 (2003); *GDP:* US $605,300m. (2003); *GDP per caput:* US $12,635 (2003); *exports:* US $162,470m. (2002); *imports:* US $151,230m. (2002); *currency:* won (plural: won; US $1 = 1,155 won as of 2004).

The ROK economy has always had to rely on its human resources, since the division of the **Korean peninsula** in 1945 left it with a deficiency of natural resources and minerals. This has meant that as it has industrialized, the ROK has had to import, and continues to import, large quantities of mineral fuels and raw materials. The division did leave it with a larger share of the population and the best agricultural land. It has made good use of its human resources. The traditional importance accorded to education has led to a well-trained, well-educated work-force at all levels. From research and planning down to factory labour, successive ROK governments, starting with **Park Chung-Hee**'s various administrations, assumed a leading role in guiding and supervising the economy, regarding eco-nomic growth and stability as an essential element in creating a strong state. A series of five-year plans, beginning in 1962 and continuing at least until a revised plan initiated in 1993, indicated the direction of various stages in the development of the economy. Until the late 1980s government legislation on labour and trade union activism ensured a compliant workforce, which for long was obliged to accept low wages, long hours and often poor working conditions. The government used various methods to gain the co-operation of industrial leaders, principally its ability to control sources of financing, access to foreign exchange and cheap credit. It was also prepared to protect the domestic market. Manufacturing industry and parts of the service sector have long been dominated by the *chaebol*, big business con-glomerates, often run as family concerns, that have been willing to operate within official guide-lines in return for government support, particularly in funding.

Economic activity after the Korean War was confined largely to reconstruction, with some small-scale manufacturing output in textiles, light industry and proces-sing. A start was made on import substitution. It was a time of high inflation. The first Five-Year Plan, launched in 1962, aimed to turn the economy into an export-orientated one. Electrical goods and plastics were added to textiles in the range of existing manufactures and the chemical, cement, and ceramics industries were boosted. With the third Five-Year Plan (1972–76) the ROK moved into heavy industry, installing steel plants (Pohang steel works, 1973), shipyards (Ulsan, 1974) and automobile factories (Kia cars, 1974, and Hyundai Pony cars, 1976). A defence industry began. Much of the output of these heavy plants was exported. Some of the workforce was also exported during the 1970s, as several of the *chaebol* engaged in overseas construction projects, especially in the Middle East. In the 1980s the ROK, utilizing the country's research capabilities, turned towards high-technology areas, such as electronics and communications, as well as expanding its steel, refining and motor manufacturing sectors. The capital needed to finance this long and intensive programme of industrialization came in the earlier years from funds that the ROK solicited from foreign investors. By the mid-1980s, however, domestic savings were better able to finance growth.

In the 1990s the economy faced a number of problems. The higher wages that a stronger workforce was demanding eroded the ROK's competitiveness to some extent. Restrictions on recruitment of foreign labour were eased from 1991, bringing in workers who could be paid at a lower rate. Big business also started to consider overseas manufacturing ventures in a bid to reduce costs. Some of the new factories were sited within Europe, not necessarily because conditions were particularly favourable there, but because it was calculated that production inside the European Union might allow the ROK to escape the heavy duties that might be levied on imports from South Korea. The country was also beginning to come under US pressure to open its markets, including its agricultural markets, to foreign imports. The government itself was starting to move away from its special brand of 'command economy' towards encouraging greater privatization and less dependence on the former close relationship between it and big business. The closely enmeshed links between government, *chaebol* and the banks began to be a cause of weakness rather than strength as the crisis in the financial markets that affected much of Asia in 1997 exposed the insecure foundations of much *chaebol* financing. Official supervisory controls were shown to be too weak. Cross-funding between the various sectors within these big conglomerates, over-diversification and excess capacity had stretched their resources too far. Too many of their loans were non-performing. The government, while prepared to use the *chaebol*, had always tried to keep them on a rein. As part of its reorganization of the economy in the wake of the 1997 crisis and the IMF loan, it pressed the *chaebol* and banks to reform their practices, but so far has achieved only partial success in this. Some of the *chaebol* have gone bankrupt (Hanbo, 1997), defaulted on their loans (Kia, 1997) or approached bankruptcy (Daewoo, 1999); others have been obliged to divest themselves of subsidiary companies or consider mergers with foreign enterprises. President **Kim Dae-Jung**, who inherited the economic crisis on taking office in 1998, introduced measures to stimulate domestic demand and support the unemployed and thereby mitigated some of its worst effects.

The ROK economy is now predominantly an industrial and service economy. In 2001 the proportion of the economically active population engaged in agriculture stood at 10.3%, producing 5.2% of the gross domestic product (GDP); 27.1% worked in industry, accounting for 44.9% of GDP (of these, 19.7% were in manufacturing, contributing 36% of GDP); and the service sector employed 62.6%, who produced 49.9% of GDP. More than 90% of exports are manufactured goods. The agricultural sector has shrunk considerably since 1945. Two land reform acts, in 1947 and 1948 respectively, ensured an equitable redistribution of land, which did, however, result in a large number of small farms that often existed at subsistence level. The rural population has declined consistently as members of farming families, particularly the young, have migrated to the towns. In 2001 it accounted for 8.3% of the total population. The *Saemaul* movement, founded in 1971, aimed to strengthen village leadership and to give practical support to farming communities through material improvements and the introduction of new techniques; but by the late 1980s was losing its momentum. Farms have now started to increase in size as the land formerly owned by those who have abandoned farming has been taken over by those remaining. The introduction of new technology, improved rice strains and a wider range of produce is permitting farms to become more market-oriented.

The ROK's three principal trading partners are the USA, the **People's Republic of China** and Japan. In 2002 it recorded surpluses in its trade with the first two, but showed a deficit in its trade with Japan. The most significant exports in 2002 were registered as wireless communication equipment, semi-conductors, computers and vehicles, reflecting the country's continuing pre-eminence in the field of information technology. Major imports were of crude oil, steel and basic raw materials. Trade with the Democratic People's Republic of Korea has grown, albeit in a fluctuating manner, since 1989, when it was first permitted, and in 2002 its value (two-way trade) was estimated at US $441m.

Korea Advanced Institute of Science and Technology (KAIST)

In 1966 the government of the Republic of Korea (ROK) established the **Korea Institute of Science and Technology (KIST)** for the promotion of science and technology. Five years later it also established the Korea Advanced Institute of Science (KAIS). KAIS conducted research programmes and created a graduate school of physical science and engineering. In 1981 the two organizations merged to form the Korea Advanced Institute of Science and Technology (KAIST), under the control of the Ministry of Science and Technology.

The merger was not wholly successful, with the two institutions at cross-purposes. In June 1989, therefore, the former KIST became an independent research centre once again. KAIST, which was solely devoted to postgraduate and advanced research, merged with the Korea Institute of Technology, founded in 1984, where the remit was to teach science and technology to undergraduates. The main sections of KAIST, covering natural sciences, engineering, and humanities and social sciences, are located at the 'Science Town' at Taedok, near Taechon, although the Graduate School of Management remains in **Seoul**. It currently has more than 20,000 students, three-quarters of whom are studying for masters' or doctors' degrees. In July 2004 it appointed an American, Robert Loughlin, as its first ever foreign director.

Address: KAIST
373-1 Guseong-dong
Yuseong-gu
Daejeon
Republic of Korea

Tel: 82-42-869-2233
Fax: 82-42-869-2210
Internet: www.kaist.ac.kr

Korea/Corea controversy

After the establishment of Korea's Yi dynasty in 1392, **Koreans** used the name 'Choson' for their country, replacing the earlier 'Koryo'. The Yi kingdom became the 'Taehan'—Great Korean—empire in 1897, 'Han' also signifying Korean. In the Japanese colonial period (1910–45) the Japanese used 'Chosen', the Japanese reading of the ideograms for 'Choson', which Koreans continued to use. In the early colonial years, however, the Japanese often used 'Korea'. After the division of the peninsula in 1945, the Democratic People's Republic of Korea (DPRK) continued to use Choson, while the Republic of Korea (ROK) eventually revived 'Han', in the form of 'Hanguk'—the formal title of the country in Korean is 'Taehan Minguk'.

The Western name, Korea, for the peninsula derives from the Koryo dynasty (918–1392) through either Chinese *Gaoli* or Japanese *Korai*. The first known Western reference to 'Caule' is in William of Rubruck's account of his visit to Mongolia in 1253. Until the 18th century most Western mapmakers appear to have used variations of the name spelt with 'C'. Eventually, 'Corea', which first appeared in 1596, became the norm; 'Korea' appears to date from the early 18th century. During the 19th century both were common, but in the 20th century 'Korea' became the more usual form in English, though 'Corea' remained common until about 1940. Latin languages continue to use variations of 'Corea'.

In the late 1990s claims emerged in the ROK that the Japanese had deliberately fostered the use of 'Korea' rather than 'Corea', so that Japan would appear before Korea in country lists. There is no evidence that Japan actually did this, and, since Korea was not an independent country from 1910 until 1945, it rarely appeared in such lists. However, the movement gained some momentum, and in 2003 the DPRK took up the issue. This was largely in the context of opposition to Japanese colonialism, and there were no signs that the DPRK intended to change its usage. In August 2003 22 ROK **National Assembly** members introduced a bill to make the use of 'Corea' compulsory, claiming that this was the 'historically correct' way to refer to the peninsula until changed by the Japanese. Some of those involved attended a conference in **Pyongyang** in September 2003 to discuss the proposed use of 'Corea'.

Korea Foundation (KF)

Hanguk kukje koryu chedan

Established in 1991, the Korea Foundation performs for the Republic of Korea (ROK) a similar function to the **Japan Foundation** and the British Council, on which it is roughly modelled. It encourages scholarship on Korea by funding Korean studies overseas, including the work of museums and art galleries, by inviting scholars, by publishing under its own imprint and by assisting the publication of books and journals. Although separate from the ROK Ministry of Foreign Affairs and Trade, and essentially non-political, the KF works closely with the Ministry and the KF senior leadership comes from former diplomats.

Address: Korea Foundation
Seocho POB 227
Diplomatic Center Bldg
1376-Seocho-dong
Seocho-gu
Seoul 137-072
Republic of Korea
Tel: 82-2-3463-5600
Fax: 82-2-3463-6076
E-mail: info@kf.or.kr
Internet: www.kf.or.kr

Korea Institute of Science and Technology (KIST)

Originally established by an agreement signed in 1965 between the USA and Republic of Korea governments, the original Korea Institute of Science and Technology was a non-profit research organization for the promotion of science and technology. The US government provided most of its funding. In 1981 KIST merged with the **Korea Institute of Advanced Science and Technology**, but KIST maintained its separate structure and purpose and in 1989 a demerger took place, with the KIST title being revived.

KIST is a research institute, concentrating on developing technology for domestic use. It works closely with similar bodies in other countries.

Address: KIST
39-1 Hawologok-dong
Seongbok-gu
Seoul
Republic of Korea
Tel: 82-2-958-5114
Fax: 82-2-958-5478
E-mail: info@kist.re.kr
Internet: www.kist.re.kr

Koreagate

This was the name given, in ironic reference to the Watergate scandal, to a major lobbying exercise carried out by the Republic of Korea (ROK) in the USA following the decision in the early 1970s, under President Richard Nixon, to reduce the US military commitment in Asia. ROK President **Park Chung-Hee** sanctioned the exercise, which involved the Korean Central Intelligence Agency (KCIA—now the National Intelligence Service), Moon Sun-Myong and the **Unification Church**, and a businessman, Park Tong-Sun.

The introduction of President Park's authoritarian Yushin Constitution in 1972 led to widespread US criticism, which the ROK put much effort into counteracting. The main target was the US Congress, and it was claimed that a number of Congressmen took bribes. The exercise became public in 1976, and a series of Congressional hearings were held in 1977–78. Although Park Tong-Sun testified in exchange for immunity, there were no convictions. Moon left the USA when summoned for questioning, and the KCIA operatives were immune from prosecution. However, the case cast a shadow over ROK-US relations for many years.

Korean Air

Daehan hanggong

Korean Air is the **Republic of Korea**'s main airline, although it faces strong competition on both domestic and international routes from Asiana Airlines. The company began as Korean National Airlines, a government-owned company, in 1962. It became a private company and part of the transport *chaebol*, the Hanjin Corporation in 1969, when it became Korean Airlines. The company changed its name to Korean Air following the shooting down of its Flight KE007 by Soviet aircraft in 1983. It lost another aircraft in a Democratic People's Republic of Korea bomb incident in 1987.

At the end of 2003 Korean Air owned 100 passenger and 19 cargo aircraft, with Boeing 747s as the mainstay of its fleet, and it flies to 28 countries. The company also serves a variety of domestic routes.

Korean Central News Agency (KCNA)

Choson chungang tongsin

Sole news agency operating in the Democratic People's Republic of Korea (DPRK). The Korean Central News Agency (KCNA) was established in 1946 under the tutelage of the Soviet forces occupying the northern half of the **Korean peninsula** from 1945 until 1948. It was closely modelled on the Soviet news agency TASS, and on the Chinese Communist **Xinhua News Agency**. It has always worked under direct central government control and is the sole official distribution point for both domestic and foreign news to the country's mass media, producing daily bulletins that are a vital element in most newspaper and radio news coverage in the DPRK. Other news agencies' output is monitored on a regular basis by KCNA and stories favourable to the DPRK are replayed. The Agency describes itself as speaking for the **Korean Workers' Party** and the government and in that capacity is frequently used to make statements on DPRK policy, or to reply to observations about the country.

KCNA is based in **Pyongyang**, with branches in provincial capitals and in some foreign countries. Its news bulletins are issued in English, Russian, French and Spanish.

Dir-Gen.: Kim Ki Ryong
Address: 1 Potonggang-dong
    Potonggang District
    Pyongyang
    Democratic People's Republic of Korea
Internet: www.kcna.co.jp (home page provided by Korea News Service in Tokyo)

Korean North-South relations

The relationship between the two states, the Republic of Korea (ROK) and the Democratic People's Republic of Korea (DPRK), on the divided **Korean peninsula** has been fraught with emotion, rivalry and often tension ever since the mid-1940s. Since the late 1980s, however, a willingness to widen contacts has led to some relaxation in a relationship that has at times become violent, and practical co-operation and participation in multilateral discussions has to some extent replaced confrontation.

The division of the peninsula into two separate zones of occupation in 1945 and into two distinct states in 1948 was welcome neither to the **Koreans** nor to their allies. The Moscow Agreement, devised by the USA, the United Kingdom and the Soviet Union in late 1945, suggested a formula for eventually reunifying the peninsula, but was overtaken by events. **Kim Il Sung's** attempt to unify Korea by force through the **Korean War** (1950–53) was thwarted by the intervention of the **United Nations (UN)**, and the War ended with the 1953 Korean Armistice Agreement, which perpetuated the division. Despite strong unification rhetoric from each side, after 1953 each state concentrated on post-war reconstruction, and there were no official contacts between the two. The presence of US/UN forces in the ROK and of forces of the **People's Republic of China (PRC)** in the North until 1958, moreover, discouraged any escalation of the occasional clashes that occurred along the **Demilitarized Zone (DMZ)**. The DPRK resorted instead to low-level forms of terrorism. Its most audacious attack was to send a commando team across the DMZ in early 1968 with orders to assassinate the ROK President, **Park Chung-Hee**. The team got almost as far as the presidential palace in **Seoul** before being detected. In the same year 120 DPRK agents were landed on the east coast of the ROK. Such harassment reached a peak in the years 1967–70. During the 1970s the existence of three tunnels leading under the DMZ, allegedly from the DPRK side, was announced by the ROK government, and a fourth was later identified in 1990.

US-Soviet *détente* in the late 1960s, together with the US-PRC *rapprochement* of 1971, were among developments that eventually brought the two Koreas to the point of discussions. Each Korea realized that its supporters had other concerns that would be likely to take precedence over their interest in the Korean peninsula. It was in this context that the first links between the DPRK and the ROK were established in 1971 through North-South Red Cross talks, which both governments followed closely. The Red Cross channel would continue to be used from time to time thereafter, but in 1972 formal governmental-level talks led in July of that year to a statement on Korean reunification and to the formation of a North-South Political Co-ordinating Committee. This Committee met six times after its preliminary session at **Panmunjom** in August 1972 in **Seoul** and **Pyongyang** between October 1972 and July 1973. The meetings were designed to discuss and resolve various procedural steps necessary for the achievement of peaceful reunification of the country in accordance with the July statement, but petered out in mutual recrimination.

Chun Doo-Hwan made some proposals to the DPRK about resuming talks after he became President of the ROK in August 1980. The DPRK rejected them, but in October 1980 Kim Il Sung put forward a revised version of a 1960 proposal for dealing with the issue of reunification by establishing a **'Democratic Confederal Republic of Koryo'** (see below). The DPRK combined this approach with a return to violence when, in 1983, it attempted to assassinate President Chun and his party in Yangon during a state visit to Burma. Despite this assault, the Chun Government accepted a DPRK offer of flood relief in the form of rice, cement and medical supplies in 1984. The DPRK then endeavoured to destabilize preparations for the 1988 Seoul Summer Olympic Games by blowing up a South Korean civilian aircraft mid-air in 1987. The USA successfully intervened to persuade the North Koreans against any further such acts.

Chun's successor, President **Roh Tae-Woo**, drew upon already formulated policies of opening up a dialogue with the Soviet Union and the PRC to encourage the DPRK in the late 1980s to extend its own international contacts. A series of high-level talks that began in 1990 eventually led to the 1991 Agreement on Reconciliation, Non-Aggression and Exchanges and Co-operation between the South and the North, a Joint Declaration on the Denuclearization of the Korean Peninsula and other agreements. These represented the most comprehensive agreements ever reached between North and South. Although they have hardly been implemented, both sides continue to use them as a benchmark in relations.

The **DPRK nuclear programme** began to cause growing international concern and to involve the USA again. As the crisis deepened in 1994, the ROK felt increasingly marginalized by US-DPRK negotiations, but contacts continued and it was agreed to hold the first ever summit meeting between the leaders of the DPRK and the ROK in July 1994. Kim Il Sung's death on 8 July disrupted the arrangements, and the refusal of the then ROK President **Kim Young-Sam** to express condolences led to a cooling in relations. The election of the long-term opposition leader, **Kim Dae-Jung**, as President in 1998 occasioned a new policy towards the DPRK, usually described as the **'sunshine policy'**. Rather than confrontation, Kim informed the DPRK that, while any attack or intrusion would be firmly dealt with, there would be no attempt at takeover and the ROK would be ready to help the DPRK both feed its people and rebuild its economy. Despite periodic upsets, such as a renewed submarine intrusion in 1998 (an earlier intrusion had taken place in 1996), Kim Dae-Jung and the DPRK leader **Kim Jong Il** met in Pyongyang in June 2000. Other links have been forged in private initiatives, such as those of the **Hyundai Corporation**, and by a host of ROK non-governmental organizations. Kim Dae-Jung's policy of engagement has been continued by his successor, President **Roh Moo-Hyun**.

Such developments have not proved popular with all in the ROK. Many older people remain suspicious of the DPRK and its motives; others are concerned that most of the benefits from the new relationship accrue to the DPRK, which seems happy to take the ROK's money and assistance and to give little in return; and until 2005 the armed forces designated the DPRK as their principal enemy.

Proposals on reunification: Both states have put forward proposals on unification that were grounded initially in each country's contention that it alone was the legitimate government of Korea. The DPRK's first formal statement was a proposal from the 'Democratic Front for the Attainment of the Unification of the Fatherland', on 30 June 1949, two days after the Front was established in Pyongyang. The Front called for the withdrawal of foreign forces to allow the Korean people to settle their own future; simultaneous elections north and south to elect one legislature for the whole country, which should adopt a constitution based on that of the DPRK; the ending of persecution of democratic parties in the ROK and the exclusion from the election process of those who had carried out such persecution; and the merger of the armed forces of the two sides. These terms were rejected in the ROK. Reunification by force was then tried, and failed, in the three years of the Korean War.

By 1960 the DPRK was ready with a new proposal, for a North-South Confederation, that remains the basis of its position on reunification. Kim Il Sung argued that while the two Koreas should continue to function separately in domestic terms, internationally there should be one Korean state. That state would be free of all foreign links, would enter the UN and related organizations as one entity, and would be neutral and non-aligned. Only genuine 'democratic' organizations and individuals could take part. In a further refinement in 1980, the DPRK proposed that the combined state be given the title 'Democratic Confederal Republic of Koryo'. The proposal was again presented, essentially unchanged, in 1993 as Kim Il Sung's '10-Point Programme for the Great Unity of the Whole Nation for the Reunification of the Country'. It remains the official DPRK policy on reunification.

The ROK's position under its first President, **Syngman Rhee**, was that its government, established under UN auspices, after UN-supervised elections, was the only legitimate government on the Korean peninsula. Unification, therefore, was a matter of the ROK taking over the North, thereby recovering territory that was illegally occupied by what was described as an 'anti-state regime'. The pre-Korean War Rhee Government made no approaches to the DPRK, since to have done so would have implied that there was a legitimate government in the northern half of the peninsula. The outbreak of war led the ROK Government to argue too that the peninsula should be reunified by force, but neither the UN nor the ROK's main supporter, the USA, was willing to try this again once the armistice had been concluded.

Under Park Chung-Hee, Rhee's successor after a brief interlude, the ROK Government continued to view the DPRK as an illegitimate interloper. Park chose to concentrate on the economic and industrial development of the ROK, and the question of reunification was generally regarded as a less pressing issue than it had been under Rhee. The North-South contacts established in 1972–73 seemed to provide a degree of common ground, with each side appearing to accept the other's existence and agreeing that reunification was a domestic concern, but these contacts came to nothing. In the late 1980s Roh Tae-Woo encouraged some fresh thinking. By then German reunification had led to consideration of the possibility of a DPRK collapse, and the ROK began to think in terms of reunification by absorption of the North. The Government of President Kim Dae-Jung, who took office in 1997, stressed that it wished to see only a peaceful reunification of the peninsula, a line followed by Kim's successor, Roh Moo-Hyun.

Korean peninsula

The Korean peninsula extends for 1,000 km in a north-south direction from the north-east Asian landmass and covers a total area, including more than 3,000 islands that lie off its coastline, of 220,800 sq km. Save for its northern border with the **People's Republic of China (PRC)** and the Russian Federation, it is surrounded by water: to the east, the **East Sea/Sea of Japan** separates it from Japan, and to the west the Yellow Sea divides it from the PRC. The south coast faces the South China Sea. The peninsula is characterized by the mountains that cover about 70% of its surface, leaving a much reduced area for cultivation and housing.

Until 1945 Korea had for 13 centuries been a single country, with a unified history. In that year, however, when Japan's capitulation on 15 August brought the **Pacific War** to an end, the peninsula was informally divided at the **38th parallel** to facilitate the taking of the Japanese surrender by the USA to the south of it and by the Soviet forces to the north. The political polarization of the peninsula into right-wing and left-wing regimes was consolidated with the establishment in 1948 of two states within the peninsula, the Republic of Korea (ROK) south of the 38th parallel and the Democratic People's Republic of Korea (DPRK) to the north. The **Korean War** (1950–53) hardened these differences into a long period of mutual hostility. Contact resumed with talks between the Red Cross societies of both sides in 1971, in the first instance to examine the problem of divided families, and other sets of discussions and negotiations have followed. Trade and joint venture activities have become common. None the less, the history of the Korean peninsula since 1945 has been that of two separate states.

History: Archaeological evidence indicates that the peninsula was inhabited from Paleolithic times (before 10,000 BC). This early population, however, was probably replaced by a later influx of people arriving from the north during the 2nd–1st millennium BC, following an expansion of population outwards from central Asia that reached as far as the north-eastern parts of the continent. The society that emerged at that time was skilled in both metal-working techniques and rice production and was already developing forms of settled administration. Many small chiefdoms and federations of tribes existed which, especially in the north, interacted with the neighbouring Chinese. The Chinese indeed held settled areas in the northern part of the peninsula during a period of more than 300 years, but were finally expelled in AD 313 by the kingdom of Koguryo.

Koguryo was one of the four states that by the early 4th century had emerged on the Korean peninsula. The other three were Paekche and Silla and the shorter-lived Kaya. The traditional dates for the founding of these kingdoms are set much earlier, but it may be more exact to look at the first three centuries of the modern era as a time of political coalescence and formation rather than of fully-fledged states. The historiography and chronology of this early period is a subject of dispute between the ROK and the DPRK. The latter is particularly insistent that its interpretation of early history proves the antiquity and pre-eminence of a Korean civilization centred in the north and especially of the northern Koguryo dynasty.

The Three Kingdoms period is dated from around AD 300–668. By 668, Silla, with the help of **China**, had subdued Paekche and Koguryo and unified the country. A powerful, slave-owning aristocracy that could challenge the king, a bureaucratic style of government coloured by **Confucianism** (which had been introduced into the peninsula from China during the 4th century), considerable artistic achievement but at the same time a poorly developed economy, all resting on the labour of landless peasants, characterized the Korean state. During Silla and the following Koryo dynasty (935–1392), the state religion was **Buddhism**, which had been brought from China in the late 4th century. Externally, Korea had to keep on its guard against attacks from its northern neighbours, who by the late 10th century were a series of nomadic tribes that also harassed the Chinese empire. From the late 12th century to the 13th, the Koryo dynasty's authority was undermined by challenges from the army, then, from 1231, by repeated **Mongol** invasions that finally reduced the kingdom to a client state of the Yuan dynasty, the name by which the Mongol invaders of China styled themselves. The country suffered much devastation.

The Yuan were overthrown in 1368 by the Chinese Ming dynasty. Koryo gave its support to the new dynasty, but soon faced a threat of Chinese intervention. At the same time, the country had to deal with the ravages of Japanese pirates who had been raiding its coasts for more than a century. Taking advantage of Koryo's weakened state, one of its military leaders seized power and in 1392 established the Choson or Yi dynasty (both names are found), which endured until the abdication of its last ruler in 1910. The new dynasty looked for its guiding principles to a reinvigorated form of Confucianism that had emerged in China in the 12th century. Neo-Confucianist teaching was applied in Choson Korea not only to direct government and bureaucracy, but also to reorder social and family life. Buddhism was discredited and reduced to the level of personal faith. The social stratification that had marked earlier dynasties was continued and strengthened under the Choson. Korea remained in a close relationship to China, sending annual tributes to the Chinese capital and accepting its suzerainty. China's influence as a model in government, scholarship, literature and the arts was strong, but in the area of language it was challenged with the introduction, in 1443–44, of a new alphabet, *hangul*, to convey the sounds of spoken Korean. Until then, Chinese characters had been largely used as the written form of the language.

At the end of the 16th century the country was exposed to further danger when the Japanese general Toyotomi Hideyoshi invaded the peninsula as a preliminary to an invasion of Ming China. He was repulsed, but again the populace suffered terribly and had to endure a second Japanese invasion. Then, in the early decades of the 17th century, Korea was again embroiled in Chinese dynastic struggles. The nomadic **Manzhou** tribe in north-east Asia, which, after years of encroachment, finally overthrew the Ming in 1644 and established itself as the Qing dynasty, twice invaded Korea to force the king to accept its overlordship. A long period of peace then prevailed in the peninsula, to the benefit not only of the aristocracy but of other social classes as well. The boundaries of knowledge were extended in the direction of practical learning of scientific and technical issues and, through contact with China, of Western ideas as conveyed by European missionaries at the imperial court. These included the teachings of **Catholic Christianity**, known through various writings that entered the country from China. In 1784 a young Korean who had converted to Catholicism in **Beijing** brought the doctrine back into Korea and with others founded the first Catholic church.

The new religion was not well received during its first century of existence in the peninsula and was regarded as a disruptive factor. The social order was beginning to fracture, partly, in the second half of the 19th century, under pressure from foreign powers led by Japan, including the USA and several European countries, anxious that Korea should modernize and open up to trade. After some years of resistance, the country's leadership submitted and from 1876 signed treaties of 'friendship' with a number of foreign states. Foreign penetration of education and the economy and the arrival of foreign missionaries, representing both Catholic and **Protestant Christianity**, confronted **Koreans** with new situations. Some responded by experimenting themselves with new concepts; others resisted what they viewed as threats to the country's traditions and well-being. Japan's interest in Korea brought it into conflict with China, which still claimed suzerainty over Korea. Popular discontent both with foreign intervention and heavy taxation expressed itself in an uprising that started in 1894 in the south-west of the peninsula. The government called for and received Chinese armed support, but the Chinese troops found themselves confronting Japanese soldiers who had been sent to protect Japanese interests. The two forces fought out a war on Korean soil that ended in 1895 with a Japanese victory. Reforms in a number of areas—government, the administration of justice, national finances, class structure and social practices—were introduced in 1894 at Japanese insistence, to a mixed reception. Korea's position was being increasingly undermined, however, by Japan's intentions, which expressed themselves in the imposition in 1905 of a treaty that turned Korea into a Japanese protectorate. Five years later, in 1910, the last Choson king was forced to abdicate and Japan, unchecked by the Western powers, annexed the Korean peninsula.

The period of Japanese colonization of Korea, 1910–1945, had enormous consequences for the subsequent development of the peninsula. Korea was administered and policed as a colony. Japanese exploitation of the country's agricultural, natural and mineral resources led to land reclamation, a railway system, the introduction of new factories, industrial processes and styles of work, the construction of mines and hydroelectric schemes, the building of new towns, and other aspects of the systematic development of resources. Modernization was thus imposed upon Korea. Japanese aspirations were to incorporate the Koreans as citizens of the empire, albeit lowly and less well-educated citizens who would swell the workforce. By the end of the 1930s, as Japan found itself involved in war, its efforts to integrate the Koreans into the Japanese system became more rigorous and included the requirement for Koreans to speak Japanese and even take Japanese names. At the same time, Japan acted as a conduit for the introduction of Western models in painting, literature, theatre, film and music. Korea's exposure to modern Western aesthetics was through a Japanese filter. Korean students who went to Japan came into contact with Marxist thought. The Korean experimentation with new forms that had begun in the late 19th century thus continued under Japanese tutelage.

Opposition to Japanese control broadly took two forms. One was a conscious development of Korean culture and society, particularly the language, as a means of sustaining that society; this involved a measure of acquiescence and could lead to charges of collaboration. This domestic activity was supplemented by the lobbying of world opinion by Korean exiles. For another group opposition took the form of left-wing protest and activity designed to harass the Japanese. The centres for this opposition often lay outside the peninsula, in China or the Soviet Union. This distinction between moderate and left-wing reaction was later played out in a more permanent way in the tone and politics of the two Korean states that emerged after 1945. Resentment and distrust of the Japanese have persisted for a long time in both Koreas. The ROK found itself on the same side as Japan in the post-Second World War arrangement in East Asia, and the two countries normalized their relationship in 1965. The DPRK remains implacably hostile to Japan and has still not moved to the establishment of diplomatic relations.

Korean Peninsula Energy Development Organization (KEDO)

Organization established in March 1995 by the governments of the Republic of Korea (ROK), Japan and the USA to provide for the financing and supply of light-water reactors (LWRs) to the Democratic People's Republic of Korea (DPRK).

The 1994 **Agreed Framework** between the DPRK and the USA was intended to control the **DPRK nuclear programme**. KEDO was set up as the means of meeting the DPRK's demands for sources of energy. It undertook to supply two LWRs with a total generating capacity of 2,000 MW and, until these LWRs came on stream, to provide 500,000 metric tons of heavy fuel annually for heating and production of electricity. The DPRK at first resisted the ROK's participation in KEDO, but came to accept it. The ROK is a principal financier in the US $4,500m.-scheme and has supplied the reactors. The site chosen for the LWRs was Kumho, 30 km north of Sinpo in South Hamgyong Province on the east coast of the DPRK. The ground-breaking ceremony for the LWRs took place in July 1997. Construction progress has been slow: the first concrete pouring for the reactors themselves only took place in August 2002, and it was clear that the target date of 2003 for completion of the LWRs could not be met. The DPRK frequently expressed irritation with the slow pace of work. The issue of the LWRs was always tied closely to the health of the Agreed Framework, and when the DPRK came to be regarded in breach of the agreement following its supposed acknowledgement in October 2002 that it was processing enriched weapons-grade uranium, the continuing activity of the Kumho site and of KEDO was called into question. KEDO suspended further shipments of oil to the DPRK in November 2002 and one year later, in December 2003, the LWR project was itself suspended for a year. It is to remain frozen for a further year. KEDO remains in existence, however.

The three founding members, Japan, the ROK and the USA, serve on the executive board of KEDO and were joined by the European Union in 1997 as a fourth executive board member. Nine other governments subsequently also joined the organization as members: New Zealand, Australia and Canada in 1995; Indonesia, Chile and Argentina in 1996; Poland in 1997; the Czech Republic in 1999; and Uzbekistan (which has supplied labour for the construction site) in 2000. The necessity of meeting the work, administrative and living needs of the personnel engaged at the KEDO site led to the first private mail and telephone exchanges between the DPRK and the ROK since the **Korean War**, as well as to direct transport links between the two states to allow personnel to travel to and from the ROK.

Exec. Dir: Charles Kartmann
Address: 12th Floor
        600 Third Ave
        New York
        NY 10016
        USA

Tel: 1-212-455-0200
Fax: 1-212-949-8071
E-mail: hlyoon@kedo.org
Internet: www.kedo.org

Korean People's Army (KPA)

Inmingun

The armed forces of the Democratic People's Republic of Korea (DPRK), or the Korean People's Army (KPA), which embrace land, air, and naval units, totalled an estimated 1,106,000 in 2003, comprising a 950,000 strong army, a 46,000 strong navy and a 110,000 strong air force, according to the London-based International Institute of Strategic Studies. In addition to conventional military weapons, the KPA is reported to have short-, medium- and long-range missiles. There is a also a **DPRK nuclear programme**, which may include the development of nuclear weapons.

The KPA officially dates from 1932, when, it is claimed, it was personally organized by **Kim Il Sung**. The reality is that Soviet occupation forces forged the modern DPRK armed forces out of a variety of guerrilla bands after 1945. The main emphasis was on the formation of infantry units, but air and naval forces also appeared. From December 1948 a Soviet military advisory body honed these various groups into a united army. During 1949, as the Chinese civil war ended, ethnic **Koreans** from **China** joined the KPA. Some Soviet Koreans also joined the new force.

At the outbreak of the **Korean War** in June 1950, the KPA numbered some 135,000, in contrast to the Republic of Korea (ROK) forces, which numbered approximately 98,000. The KPA air force had between 110 and 180 aircraft, all Second World War vintage fighters and bombers. The naval forces were the least developed, with a small number of patrol boats suitable only for coastal operations. These armed forces were very successful in the initial stages of the war when they had the advantage both of surprise and of superior numbers. When they stopped at the **Pusan** perimeter in August 1950, however, they failed to break the ROK defences, and the DPRK forces began to suffer from extended lines and poor command. **United Nations (UN)** troops drove the KPA back from the perimeter, and the KPA position deteriorated further following the UN landing behind their lines at Inchon in September 1950. By late September the KPA's strength had been reduced to some 38,000, attempting to return to the DPRK, although large numbers remained in the ROK where they engaged in guerrilla warfare. The KPA would regroup and fight again, but it was **People's Republic of China**'s forces that carried on much of the fighting in late 1950 and 1951. By the time of the armistice in 1953 the DPRK had some 260,000 under arms.

Following the armistice, the DPRK continued to maintain large military forces. By the late 1980s ROK and US sources claimed that the DPRK had more than 1m. men under arms, and most international commentators use this figure. The DPRK disputes these numbers, claiming that its forces are no greater than those of the ROK, at about 680,000. It has also announced from time to time that it is releasing military forces for civilian work. It is not clear if these forces, which are very evident in **Pyongyang** and elsewhere, remain under military control. The likelihood is that they do. Military expenditure remains high, although again the DPRK disputes figures from outside the country. In 1992 **Kim Jong Il** became commander-in-chief of the DPRK armed forces. Under the 1998 Constitution the National Defence Commission became the most important organization in the DPRK, and its chairman, Kim Jong Il, the most important person. Kim Jong Il is particularly associated with the **'Army First' policy**, or *songun.*

While there is no doubt that the DPRK armed forces constitute a formidable threat, some claims regarding their capabilities are certainly exaggerated. The armed forces have been protected from some of the effects of the economic problems of the DPRK in recent years, but they have not escaped them entirely. Equipment stored in mountains will have deteriorated because of flooding and other damage. Lack of food seems to have affected military units as well as civilians; troops appear undernourished and ill-equipped. No doubt their families have also been affected. Military vehicles may be omnipresent on the roads, but they are as badly maintained as civilian vehicles and as often broken down. The nation may have pursued an 'Army First' policy, but it is not clear how this has in reality benefited the KPA.

Korean War

Conflict waged between the two newly emerged states on the **Korean peninsula**, the Republic of Korea (ROK) and the Democratic People's Republic of Korea (DPRK), together with their allies, from June 1950 to July 1953.

The conflict very quickly assumed an international dimension when the USA dispatched troops in support of the ROK army and mobilized the **United Nations (UN)** to call for an international armed force to assist the ROK. Faced by the threat of foreign troops arriving on its frontier, the **People's Republic of China (PRC)** in October 1950 committed forces in support of the DPRK. After 10 months of extensive movement, stalemate set in and led to calls for a cease-fire. Discussions were initiated in July 1951 and lasted more than two years, during which time hostilities continued. Finally, an armistice was signed in July 1953 between the UN Command on one side and the DPRK army and its Chinese allies on the other.

The immediate consequences of the war were manifold. Some 4m. people, of whom 3m. were **Koreans**, were killed, wounded or missing. Large numbers of refugees had moved up and down the peninsula as the line of engagement had shifted. In the confusion, numerous Korean families were split up as some members stayed and others fled or were separated during flight; many of these divided families have had no contact with each other since the War. Vast areas of the peninsula both north and south were heavily bombed or damaged by the movement of armies, and the economies of both states suffered considerably. The political consequences for the peninsula cannot be overestimated, as the division into two states became entrenched in very differing ideologies, political and economic systems, alliances and foreign policies. In the North **Kim Il Sung** had not succeeded in his attempt to unify the peninsula by force, but was none the less able to consolidate his grip on power and create a dictatorship that initially owed much to communism but increasingly to his own philosophy. In the South the War had strengthened autocratic tendencies within government and initiated nearly three decades of military dominance. Only towards the end of the 20th century was there any appreciable softening in the attitudes of the two Koreas towards each other.

The Korean War is now commonly perceived as a conflict that started as a civil war but which very rapidly took on international ramifications. In the post-Second World War atmosphere, where ideological divisions between the 'free' world and communism were sharpening, it was regarded by some as evidence of communist-inspired confrontation in which the Soviet Union and the PRC were acting as backers of a hostile DPRK. It provided an early test for the UN, which, under US pressure, deployed an international force for one side. The USA had emerged as a leading victor from the Second World War. It was the prime mover against what it viewed as communist aggression, but was prepared to seek the co-operation of a wider group of states and to mobilize support in the UN Security Council and the UN General Assembly for UN backing for military intervention in Korea. None the less, the USA was thwarted in its wish for outright victory, and the sense of defeat it suffered then has coloured its attitude towards the DPRK ever since. The armistice did not lead to a peace treaty with the ROK. The DPRK insists that its prime enemy has always been the USA, and that any treaty should be signed with that country, a position that the USA rejects.

Conduct of the war: North Korean armies launched the initial attack across the **38th parallel** on 25 June 1950 with the clear hope of seizing control of the peninsula (though the DPRK claims that it was acting in response to provocations from the ROK) and within three days had captured **Seoul**. From there they progressed down the peninsula, forcing the ROK government to flee before them. By September 1950 they held all of the country except for an area in the extreme south-east corner around the port of **Pusan**. The success of their attack prompted the USA, which in 1949 had decided that Korea lay outside its area of defence interests, to an immediate reaction. US troops were dispatched from their bases in Japan to try to stiffen the ROK response to the attack, but to little avail. The USA supplemented this response with a diplomatic offensive in the UN Security Council, where, in the absence of the Soviet Union, it secured agreement to a series of resolutions between 25 June and 7 July 1950 that called for an end to hostilities and the withdrawal of DPRK forces, recommended the assistance of UN member states to the ROK, and established a Unified Command to resist the DPRK forces. Gen. **Douglas MacArthur**, then Supreme Allied Commander in Japan, was appointed the head of this Command, while 16 nations supplied contingents to serve under him: Australia, Belgium, Canada, Colombia, Ethiopia, France, Greece, Luxembourg, the Netherlands, New Zealand, the Philippines, South Africa, Thailand, Turkey, the United Kingdom, and the USA. Denmark, India, Italy, Sweden and Norway provided medical assistance.

The DPRK position became untenable when Gen. MacArthur succeeded in a seaborne assault on the port of Inchon in early September 1950. Seoul was then soon recaptured. Meanwhile, UN troops, which had begun to arrive at Pusan, began a breakout from the Pusan perimeter that repelled the DPRK forces towards the 38th parallel and from there north, with the ROK and UN forces in pursuit. The North Korean capital, **Pyongyang**, fell on 19 October, and the UN forces drove on to the Amnok, or **Yalu**, river that forms much of the boundary between the DPRK and the PRC.

The Chinese had not opposed the DPRK plan to attack the South, perhaps accepting Kim Il Sung's assurances that his forces would easily prevail, or considering that the Soviet leader, Joseph Stalin, would ultimately guarantee the DPRK's survival. The arrival of non-Korean UN forces within reach of their borders, however, was something the Chinese were unwilling to countenance and they began to hint that, unless such troops halted their advance, they would intervene. Their warnings were discounted until the moment when large numbers of the Chinese People's Volunteers, the name by which their reinforcements were designated, confronted UN troops at the end of October 1950 and forced them into a headlong retreat south. The Chinese swept across the 38th parallel and on 4 January 1951 entered Seoul. The UN counter-attack came in February 1951, and the PRC armies were steadily forced back. Seoul was retaken on 15 March, and UN forces again crossed the 38th parallel in April. This time there was no desire to push further north, and the war settled into one of attrition.

The ensuing stalemate encouraged the belligerents to consider cease-fire talks. These began in July 1951, were suspended in August, but resumed in October 1951. The truce negotiations continued until the summer of 1953, with intermittent fighting, sometimes heavy, continuing at the same time, almost to the last minute. Sick and wounded prisoners of war were exchanged between 20 April and 3 May 1953, and diplomats and other civilian detainees held in the DPRK since 1950 were released via the Soviet Union. In an attempt to sabotage the truce negotiations, which he deplored, the ROK President, **Syngman Rhee**, released some 25,000 anti-communist prisoners of war on 18 June. Despite this, an armistice was finally signed on 27 July 1953.

Korean Workers' Party (KWP)

Choson rodongdang

The leading political party in the Democratic People's Republic of Korea (DPRK).

The Korean Workers' Party (KWP) was formed in June 1949 and **Kim Il Sung** was elected as its chairman on the amalgamation of the South Korean Workers'

Party (SKWP) with the North Korean Workers' Party (NKWP). Both the SKWP and the NKWP were themselves the outcome of earlier mergers in 1946 between the southern and northern branches of the Korean Communist Party with like-minded political groups in their respective territories. The SKWP, however, could not survive after 1950 in the hostile atmosphere of South Korean anti-left policies.

The consolidated KWP came to be dominated by Kim Il Sung, who made it his power base. From 1966 until his death in 1994 he occupied the leading post of general secretary, a position to which his son **Kim Jong Il** eventually succeeded in 1997 by a show of acclamation rather than through a process of election. The KWP is a highly hierarchical pyramid of party cells supporting local committees at provincial, county and city level upwards to the Central Committee, which is elected by the party congress. The KWP rules stipulate that a party congress should be convened every five years, but the last congress met in 1980, while the Central Committee last met in 1993. A large number of subordinate departments function under the Central Committee, dealing with organizational matters, propaganda, personnel matters, discipline (under the charge of the Control Committee), military affairs (under the charge of the Military Committee), economic and financial issues, and other matters. A party cell is organized within every army unit. The socialist youth league handles party work among young people. Real control rests with the Central Committee's Political Bureau and its presidium or standing committee, which is empowered to 'organize and direct' all party work on behalf of the Central Committee between plenary sessions.

Gen. Sec: Kim Jong Il

Koreans

People long settled in the **Korean peninsula**. The present inhabitants are thought to be the descendants of a second wave of population that entered the peninsula during the 2nd–1st millennium BC as part of an outward flow of peoples from central Asia, some of whom reached the north-eastern part of the continent. From there some moved south into the peninsula, and others into the Japanese islands. In the peninsula these incomers displaced an earlier indigenous population which was subsequently absorbed through intermarriage or driven out. Some later intermarriage took place between Koreans and Chinese. The latter are neighbours who for three centuries maintained settlements in the northern half of the peninsula. That aside, the Koreans, whether they are citizens of the Republic of Korea (ROK) or of the Democratic People's Republic of Korea (DPRK), are a remarkably homogeneous group. The country's tradition of isolation, together with a social system that insisted on an unblemished family lineage, aided such homogeneity. In the second half of the 19th century emigration from Korea into neighbouring countries commenced, and communities of **overseas Koreans** have since grown. The combined population of the two states on the Korean peninsula is around 70m.

The origins and early development of the Korean language are obscure. It is usually classed as belonging to the Altaic family and within that to the Tungusic branch. It shares some grammatical constructions with Japanese, but does not sound like that language. It has taken a large number of loan words from Chinese, but has a different grammar. It is heavily agglutinative, containing many suffixes that may be added in succession to noun and verb stems to convey conjugational, derivative and honorific forms. The Korean alphabet, *hangul*, is unique and was created specifically to meet the need for an accurate written form of the language. Korean remains the national language in both Koreas, and despite some divergence during a half-century of division, is mutually understood on both sides. In the **People's Republic of China** Korean has the status of an official language in the Korean autonomous areas.

The Koreans have embraced a number of religions over the centuries. **Buddhism** was introduced from **China** in the late 4th century, enjoyed a long period of favour until the change of dynasty in the late 14th century, and still has a large number of adherents. **Confucianism**, which is not strictly a religion, rather a system of ethical and philosophical principles, was also introduced from China in the 4th century. It flourished during the Choson dynasty (1392–1910), when it formed the basis of government, but has since lost much of its hold. Christianity, although known to a few from the 16th century through the medium of writings, first entered Korea in the late 18th century, when a Korean convert to **Catholic Christianity** brought back the doctrine from **Beijing**. **Protestant Christianity** was introduced by Western missionaries in the wake of treaties opening up the country to foreign influences in the 1880s and remains particularly strong. Indigenous beliefs and churches grew from the 19th century in response to the influx of new teachings. One of the new Korean churches most widely known outside of Korea is the **Unification Church**. **Islam** also has a following in the ROK. **Shamanism**, which is indigenous to the country, still maintains a wide base of support. The state of religious practice differs greatly between South and North Korea.

Various legends claim divine or semi-divine origins for early leaders of the Korean people, such as birth from an egg. The most persistent is the myth of Tangun, said to be the result of a union between the son of the supreme deity and a woman whom the son had transformed from a she-bear. Tangun is claimed as the founder of Choson, one of the earliest polities on the Korean peninsula, that lay in the northern half of the country. His capital is claimed to have been at **Pyongyang**. This claim was elevated in the DPRK at the instigation of **Kim Il Sung** to the status of fact. Tangun's year of birth is traditionally given as 2333 BC. A tomb to the north-east of Pyongyang, popularly associated with Tangun, was excavated in 1993 and found to contain bones. These were dated even further back than Tangun's supposed year of birth and were identified as those of Tangun and his wife. Kim subsequently ordered the construction of a new tomb to commemorate the 'national father'. Tangun has a small following in the ROK, but the DPRK has captured the myth as a means of supporting its claim to be the cradle of Korean civilization and the true upholder of Korean values and interests.

'Koryo, Democratic Confederal Republic of'

On 10 October 1980 the then leader of the Democratic People's Republic of Korea (DPRK), President **Kim Il Sung**, proposed that, in order to solve the problem of Korean unification, the two Korean states should establish a 'Democratic Confederal Republic of Koryo'. 'Koryo', from which the West derives 'Korea', was chosen because this was the name of the first Korean dynasty to fully unite the **Korean peninsula** between 935 and 1392.

The proposal, a reworking of one first put forward on 14 August 1960, has remained the basis of DPRK policy on the unification issue ever since. The proposal as now presented has 10 points but essentially provides for the continued existence of two Korean states for an undefined length of time, each preserving its social and political systems. They should, however, both be free of outside influences, and they should have a common defence and foreign policy. The Republic of Korea, while not rejecting the proposal entirely, especially since the late 1980s, has generally been sceptical of it.

Kumchang-ni

In 1998 allegations surfaced in the Republic of Korea (ROK) and the USA that, as part of the **Democratic People's Republic of Korea nuclear programme**, work was under way on a clandestine nuclear programme at the village of Kumchang-ni. Kumchang-ni is some 80 km north of the Democratic People's Republic of Korea's (DPRK) main nuclear development centre at Yongbyon. The USA challenged the DPRK on this issue, and in May 1999 a team from the US Department of State, including technical experts, visited the site. While clearly a large underground area had been excavated, the team found no evidence of nuclear-related development.

Kuomintang (KMT)

Guomindang

Political party active in **Taiwan**. Its name means 'national people's party'. From its founding in 1912 the party played a crucial role in the formation of a new order in **China**. It has had a dual existence, as a political movement and, broadly from 1928 to 2000, as a long-running party of government. Indeed, the terms 'Nationalists' and 'Nationalist China', applied to the government of China between 1928 and 1949, and then from 1949 to 2000, the government of the **'Republic of China' ('ROC')** on Taiwan, indicate the close links between party and administration.

The Kuomintang (*Guomindang* is the pinyin transliteration applied in the **People's Republic of China**) was founded in 1912 in the southern Chinese province of Guangdong by Dr Sun Yat-sen and Sung Chiao-jen from the amalgamation of several smaller groups. In elections in February 1913 for the parliament of the newly declared **Republic of China** the KMT gained a majority, but in November of the same year was dissolved by Yuan Shih-kai, the warlord who arraigned power to himself in the new situation. Sun Yat-sen fled to Japan, but after Yuan's death in 1916 returned to China to join a military government in **Guangzhou** (Canton), formed in opposition to the northern warlord government in **Beijing**, and in 1919 was able to revive the KMT as a party. Spurned by the Western nations from which he had sought support, Sun turned to the new Soviet administration. The Soviet Union was disposed at this early stage, where China's political future was fluid and uncertain, to involve itself with both the KMT and the **Chinese Communist Party (CCP)**, formed in 1921. In 1923 Soviet advisers arrived in China to help in the training of propagandists through the establishment of a political institute, and to reorganize the KMT along centralized and highly formal lines that it has retained to the present. These advisers also urged co-operation between the KMT and the CCP in the form of the first United Front and the admission of CCP members into the KMT. The KMT at that time (1922) was the larger party, with a membership of 150,000 as compared to CCP membership of 300.

In 1925 Sun Yat-sen died and was succeeded by one of his aides, **Chiang Kai-shek**. Any sense of common purpose between the two parties was destroyed when Chiang, in the course of his Northern Expedition to subdue the warlord government in Beijing (1926–28), turned against the Communist and left-wing element in the KMT. The victorious Nationalist Chinese administration that was formed by the KMT in 1928 with its seat in **Nanjing**, and which was accorded international recognition, was decidedly right-wing in its orientation. For the next nine years this administration governed China, during which time it generally maintained order and effected reforms and modernization. All the while, however, it had to deal with the continuing efforts of the CCP to establish bases for action; and from 1931 with Japanese encroachment. The start of the Sino–Japanese War in 1937 brought the KMT and the CCP together again in the second United Front, but unity did not last long and throughout the war the KMT was as much involved in pursuing the Communists as in fighting the Japanese. When the **Pacific War** ended in 1945, the Nationalists, by then plagued by corruption and inefficiency, were unable to reimpose control over China and soon faced civil conflict with the Communists. The Nationalists took the Japanese surrender in 1945 in Taiwan, which had been in Japanese hands since 1895, and established an administration there. The mainland Chinese took a harsh line with the native Taiwanese and in 1947 repressed an uprising against their rule with heavy loss of life. In 1949, as the Nationalist administration conceded defeat to the Communists, it fled to Taiwan, taking its party and government structures with it.

On Taiwan the KMT maintained a near monopoly of power for almost 40 years. In some respects it was not unlike its counterpart, the CCP. Both inherited from their former Soviet advisers a hierarchical structure of a central committee directed by a standing committee. Both were inimical to any serious form of opposition. The KMT as the party of government was able to amass considerable wealth and influence in the form of banks, businesses, and radio and television stations, and has been accused of using its assets, estimated in 2000 at US $6,500m., to buy votes. Its membership is currently estimated at about 2.5m. From the 1970s, however, the KMT was obliged to confront the implications of increasing age among its mainland constituents and began to integrate more Taiwanese into its hierarchy (a process that led to the election of **Lee Teng-hui** as the first Taiwan-born Vice-President of Taiwan in 1984 and as President in 1990). The KMT also had to face opposition from independent and 'non-party' candidates in elections. In 1986 it was opposed for the first time by another political movement, the **Democratic Progressive Party (DPP)**, support for which came from native Taiwanese and pro-independence sentiment. In response the KMT started to move away from some of its more rigid policies, such as its claim to represent the legitimate government of the whole of China. This shift towards a middle ground provoked the first open split within the KMT when, in 1993, a group of more conservative KMT members broke away to found the **New Party**. In 2000 the KMT lost its hold on Taiwan politics when it was placed third in the presidential elections, losing out to the DPP's candidate, **Chen Shui-bian**, who won the poll, and to one of its former members, **James Soong**, who ran as an independent after failing to secure the presidential nomination for the KMT and who secured second place. Lee Teng-hui broke with the KMT after the 2000 elections to give his support to Chen Shui-bian and to another new party, the **Taiwan Solidarity Union**. The KMT continued to lose ground when it came second in the 2001 elections to the **Legislative Yuan**; and it was unable, on a joint ticket with James Soong's **People First Party (PFP)**, to displace Chen Shui-bian in the 2004 presidential elections. Together with the PFP, however, it can command a majority in the Legislative Yuan. At present, the KMT must content itself with a place among a wide variety of political parties. Its line on the future of Taiwan is less sharply defined than in the past and it appears to be seeking a middle way between independence and reunification, implying that it might wish to leave the issue to be resolved by future generations.

Chair.: Lien Chan
Address: 11 Chungshan South Rd
        Taipei 100
        Taiwan
Tel: 886-2-2312-1472
Fax: 886-2-2343-4524
E-mail: internationalcenter@kmt.org.tw
Internet: www.kmt.org.tw

Kurile Islands

Chishima-retto

The Kurile Islands form an archipelago of some 56 islands that stretch 1,200 km between Russia's Kamchatka peninsula and Hokkaido, the northernmost of Japan's main islands. Many of the islands are uninhabited, but the area is rich in fishing grounds. In 1875 Russia exchanged the islands, whose resident population were mainly **Ainu**, with Japan for northern **Sakhalin**. In 1945 the Soviet Union occupied the islands, and Japan renounced its claims to them in the 1952 **San Francisco Peace Treaty**.

Japan later claimed that the four southernmost groups in the archipelago were not part of the Kurile Islands proper. This claim is the origin of the **Northern Territories dispute** between Japan and Russia.

Kwangju

Capital of South Cholla Province in the Republic of Korea (ROK), Kwangju is a special city with a population (2003) of 1.36m.

Kwangju has been a major market town and communications centre since the beginning of the 20th century. Early industry included textile production and breweries. In the 1960s it became a centre for automobile production. Its main claim to fame, however, is a long revolutionary tradition. It was the scene of a serious anti-Japanese outbreak in 1929, which spread nation-wide. During the **Korean War** it was an important military training centre. Kwangju is also closely associated with the former ROK President, **Kim Dae-Jung**. His arrest in May 1980 sparked off the **Kwangju uprising** in the same month. During **Roh Tae-Woo**'s presidency the city authorities erected a monument to the dead of 1980, and a new cemetery honouring those who died in 1980 opened in 1997.

Kwangju uprising

The Kwangju uprising of May 1980 ranks with **Tiananmen** in 1989 in terms of the use of state violence, but, perhaps because there were no foreign television crews in **Kwangju** at the time it took place, it is less well known.

The crisis in Kwangju followed violent student demonstrations in **Seoul** on 14 May 1980 against the growing power of Gen. **Chun Doo-Hwan**. The government of the Republic of Korea (ROK) extended martial law to the entire country on 17 May 1980, banned all political activities, and arrested prominent political leaders, including **Kim Dae-Jung**. Violence broke out in Kwangju, Kim's home town, with protesters clashing with the police. The situation was soon out of control, and anti-government demonstrations spread to nearby cities and towns. When police failed to restore order, the government deployed military units, claiming that the demonstrations amounted to a rebellion. This only provoked people in Kwangju the more. A violent protest movement became an open uprising as the demonstrators attacked police stations, other government buildings, and some military units, from which they seized weapons. A protest had become a bloody conflict. The government then deployed special paratroop forces, trained to deal with possible attacks from the Democratic People's Republic of Korea rather than a civil uprising. The result was an unknown number of deaths, both in the fighting and among those detained. Although the official estimate of the number of people killed was around 200, local people claimed that more than 2,000 died. The uprising ended on 27 May 1980.

In April 1988, following the end of President Chun's Fifth Republic, the government of the Sixth Republic under President **Roh Tae-Woo** designated the 1980 Kwangju uprising as a 'part of the democratization efforts of the students and citizens in Kwangju', and apologized for the resort to violence in handling the events of May 1980. In June 1988 the **ROK National Assembly** instituted a 'Special Committee for the Investigation of the Kwangju Incident'. Eventually the government agreed to provide monetary compensation to the families of the victims and to erect a proper monument in honour of the dead. However, the issue has not been finally resolved. There are regular calls for further investigations into the role of the government forces. There are also demands for an investigation into the role of the USA, as it is claimed that US commanders could have stopped the suppression, since ROK forces were under a joint US-ROK command, but failed to do so.

Kyoto

Kyoto City and the surrounding prefecture of the same name lie at the centre of Japan. The prefecture dates from 1868 and the city from 1889. Today Kyoto is a modern city, with a highly developed service industry, but the area is also a manufacturing centre and educational centre. There are six national universities in the area, as well as the Kansai (Western Japan) Science City and the Kyoto Industrial Park. Kyoto's real importance, however, is that it was the residence of the **Japanese Emperor** and the formal capital of Japan from the end of the 8th century AD until the court and its attendant councils moved to **Tokyo** in 1869. Because of this long association with the Imperial Court, Kyoto still has many historical temples, shrines and other buildings. In 1994 17 of the city's buildings were designated as a World Heritage Site. Traditional arts and crafts also flourish here. The population of the city is around 600,000, in an area of 610.22 sq km; the prefecture's population is 2,634,000, and its area 4,612 sq km.

Kyoto Protocol

Under the **United Nations** Framework Convention on Climate Change adopted in 1992, developed countries agreed to reduce their emissions of greenhouse gases. Periodic conferences have sought to implement these provisions. The conference held in **Kyoto**, the former capital of Japan, between 1–10 December 1997, adopted the Kyoto Protocol, which included a timescale for such reductions. This protocol was opened for signature from 16 March 1998 until 15 March 1999. Of the East Asian countries, the **People's Republic of China**, Japan and the Republic of Korea signed and ratified the protocol at that time, while Mongolia ratified it in December 1999.

L

Lau, Emily

Emily Lau is a major opposition figure in **Hong Kong**, where she was born in 1952.

Educated in Hong Kong, the USA, where she took a BA in Broadcast Journalism at the University of Southern California, and at the London School of Economics in Great Britain, Emily Lau joined the *South China Morning Post,* Hong Kong's leading English-language newspaper, as a reporter in 1976. During the 1980s she established a reputation as a pugnacious television and print journalist, especially when working for the *Far Eastern Economic Review* in 1984–91. In 1991 Lau became the first woman to be elected to the colonial-era **Legislative Council**, and she has been regularly re-elected ever since, winning large majorities. She was critical of British policy towards Hong Kong under **Christopher Patten**, and has continued to be a strong defender of Hong Kong's rights and a critic of the **People's Republic of China** since the handover of Hong Kong in 1997. In 1998 she received the Bruno Kreiskey Human Rights Award for her campaigning on behalf of Hong Kong.

Lee Hai-Chan

Lee Hai-Chan, a member of the Republic of Korea's (ROK) ruling **Uri Party**, was appointed Prime Minister on 29 June 2004. **Goh Kun**, his predecessor, resigned at the end of May 2004, having run the country during the impeachment of President **Roh Moo-Hyun**.

Lee, born in 1952, is the youngest Prime Minister since **Kim Jong-Pil** in 1971. He represents a new generation of ROK politicians who became political activists in the **Park Chung-Hee** era. Although he enrolled at Seoul National University in 1972, he did not graduate until 1982, since he had been engaged in student protests and was twice jailed, in 1974 and 1980. He served a total of four years in jail as a political activist. On the second occasion, the prosecution linked him with **Kim Dae-Jung**'s alleged conspiracy against the state. He continued his political activities on graduation, working with Kim Dae-Jung's Party for Peace and Democracy and its successors, and successfully standing for the **ROK National Assembly** in 1988. He was vice-mayor of **Seoul** in 1995, and Minister of Education in 1998–99. He was one of the main organizers of Roh Moo-Hyun's successful campaign for the presidency in 2002. Not surprisingly given his background, he is widely regarded as a reformer, although in fact much of his political experience has been as an organizer rather than a policy-maker.

Lee Hu-Rak

Born in **Pusan** in 1924, Lee was private secretary to President **Park Chung-Hee** in 1963–70. He was briefly ambassador to Japan in 1970, but in the same year he became director-general of the Korean Central Intelligence Agency (KCIA—now the National Intelligence Service). In this role he visited the Democratic People's Republic of Korea (DPRK) twice in 1972, initiating Park's attempt to open a dialogue with the DPRK. However, in 1973 Lee took the blame for the attempted kidnap of the opposition leader, **Kim Dae-Jung**, in **Tokyo**, Japan, and resigned as KCIA director-general. He then disappeared from view, resurfacing in 1978 as an independent member of the **Republic of Korea National Assembly**. When **Chun Doo-Hwan** came to power in 1979, Lee was one of those purged from politics, accused of embezzlement. Since then he has occasionally appeared in public, offering some insights into his past involvement with the DPRK.

Lee Teng-hui

A leading politician on **Taiwan**. In 1988 he became the first Taiwan-born leader of the **Kuomintang (KMT)** and President of the **'Republic of China' ('ROC')**. Over the years Lee has increasingly adopted a position of supporting ultimate independence for Taiwan. He was born in 1923 into a **Hakka** family. Brought up under the Japanese colonial administration, Lee apparently speaks Japanese better than Chinese or English. He attended the then Imperial University in **Kyoto** in Japan, but after the **Pacific War** he graduated in natural sciences from Taiwan National University. Later, in the USA, he took a master's degree at Iowa State University (1953) and a Ph.D. at Cornell (1968), both in agricultural economics.

By his own admission, he was a member of the **Chinese Communist Party** in 1946–48, and it was not until 1971, when he became a Cabinet minister responsible for agriculture, that he joined the KMT. He then rose rapidly, with successful periods as mayor of **Taipei** from 1978 and governor of Taiwan Province from 1981. In 1984 **Chiang Ching-kuo**, who had begun to advance native Taiwanese, selected Lee as his Vice-President. When Chiang died in 1988, Lee succeeded him as President, continuing Chiang's policy of Taiwanization. In 1991 he carried out a series of reform by which the old KMT representatives, who had dominated the **Legislative Yuan** since 1949, were ousted and replaced by native Taiwanese. These moves worried the **People's Republic of China (PRC)**, which feared that they represented a move towards Taiwan's independence. When Lee visited the USA in June 1995, ostensibly to attend an alumni meeting at Cornell, the PRC reacted with a display of missile tests in the waters around Taiwan, evoking the memories of the **offshore islands** crises of the 1950s. However, this behaviour boosted rather than reduced Lee's popularity, and in March 1996, in the first ever direct presidential elections held under the 'ROC' political structure, he won by a clear majority with 54% of the vote. From then until 2000 Lee pursued an agenda of Taiwanization but tried to avoid provoking hostile PRC reactions.

At the 2000 presidential elections Lee supported **Lien Chan**, who was his Vice-President from 1996 until 2000, as the KMT candidate, rather than the more popular **James Soong**. When the election was won by **Chen Shui-bian** of the opposition **Democratic Progressive Party**, many KMT followers charged Lee with deliberately splitting the KMT vote so that a known advocate of Taiwan's independence could succeed. Demonstrations by party activists forced him to resign as KMT chairman in March 2000, and in December he was expelled from the party. Since then Lee has actively campaigned against the KMT, encouraging moves towards a declaration of Taiwan's independence from the PRC. In the 2004 presidential elections he campaigned with Chen Shui-bian on a platform that called for a new constitution after a referendum. After the election in March 2004, however, Chen distanced himself somewhat from Lee's position.

Lee, Martin

Lee Chu Ming

Martin Lee is a veteran **Hong Kong** politician. He was born in Hong Kong in 1938, after his family moved there during the civil wars of the 1930s. Lee studied law and was called to the Bar in Britain. He returned to Hong Kong where he became a Queen's Counsel in 1979. He was first elected to the **Legislative Council** in 1985, and has served on it ever since. In 1985–89 he was a member of the **Hong Kong Basic Law** drafting committee appointed by the **People's Republic of China**. However, his outspoken comments following **Tiananmen** in 1989 and his concerns over the lack of democracy in the proposed Basic Law led to his expulsion from the committee. He was one of the organizers of Hong Kong's first political party, the United Democrats, in 1991, and later helped found the **Democratic Party**, of which he was chairman in 1994–2002. He remains a member of the party and continues to fight for more democratic rights for Hong Kong.

Internet: www.martinlee.org.hk

Legislative Assembly (Macao)

Alternatively known as the Legislative Council, the Macao Legislative Assembly is the successor to a colonial-era body with the former name. Permanent residents of **Macao** of at least seven years' standing and aged 18 years and over are permitted to vote. It is normally to have a four-year term, but the term of the first assembly after the reversion of Macao to the **People's Republic of China (PRC)** in 1999 ended in October 2001. There are no political parties in the assembly, but there are distinct interest groups.

In the 2001 elections 10 seats were directly elected, 10 indirectly, and appointments were made to seven. Of the directly elected representatives, three represented entertainment industry interests, four were pro-PRC, two pro-democracy and one pro-business. The 2005 and subsequent assemblies will have 29 members, of whom 12 will be directly elected, 10 indirectly, and seven appointed.

Pres.: Susana Chou
Address: Areros de Baia da Praia Grande
         Praça da Assembléia
         Legislativa Edif. de AL
         Macao
Tel: 853-728377/379
Fax: 853-727857
E-mail: info@al.gov.mo
Internet: www.al.gov.mo

Legislative Council (LegCo)

The Legislative Council (LegCo) is, under the terms of the **Hong Kong Basic Law**, the legislature of the Hong Kong **Special Administrative Region (SAR)** of the **People's Republic of China (PRC)**. LegCo enacts laws, examines and approves budgets, taxation and public expenditure, and monitors the work of the Hong Kong government. It also has the power to endorse the appointment and removal of judges of the Hong Kong Court of Final Appeal and the chief justice, and can impeach the chief executive.

The origins of LegCo lie in Hong Kong's colonial past. A council was established in 1843, soon after Britain acquired the colony of Hong Kong. In 1850 the first unofficial members were appointed, but the first elections to LegCo did not take place until 1985. There were then 11 official members, and 46 unofficial members. Of these, 12 were elected from functional constituencies. The first direct elections took place in 1991. In 1993 the governor ceased to be a member, and in 1995 LegCo became a fully elected body. However, in 1996 a Provisional Legislative Council was established under PRC auspices, whose members were elected by a PRC-appointed select committee in December 1996. This first met in **Shenzhen** in January 1997, transferring to Hong Kong after the SAR reverted to PRC control in July 1997. In 1998 elections for the first term of the Hong Kong SAR returned 20 members by direct election, 10 members by an election committee, and 30 members by functional constituencies. The president was elected from among the members, and the first term of this new LegCo was for two years. In September 2000 elections were held for the second term of the post-1997 LegCo. LegCo now comprised 60 members: 24 elected through direct elections in geographical constituencies; 30 members from functional constituencies; and six chosen by an election committee. At the elections held in September 2004 30 members were directly elected, and 30 were returned from functional constituencies. The pro-PRC group won 34 seats, of which 12 were directly elected, while the pro-democracy group won 25 seats, of which 18 were directly elected. Some 1.7m. people voted, 56% of those eligible, a slight increase compared with the previous election. There has been no clear indication as to how the future elections will be conducted although the Hong Kong Basic Law states that, ultimately, there will be universal suffrage.

Address: Legislative Council Secretariat
        8 Jackson Rd
        Central
        Hong Kong
Tel: 852-2869-9200
Fax: 852-2537-1851
E-mail: pi@legco.gov.hk
Internet: www.legco.gov.hk

Legislative Yuan

Li-fa yuan

The highest legislative organ of the **'Republic of China' ('ROC')** on **Taiwan**, sometimes referred to as the 'ROC' parliament. It comprises 225 members elected for a term of three years through a combination of direct voting (168 members representing the two special municipalities of **Taipei** and **Kaohsiung** and other cities and counties) and proportional representation (41 members elected from a nation-wide constituency). Eight members are elected from and by each of two other groups: aborigines and **overseas Chinese**. Members are eligible for re-election. The Legislative Yuan receives the administrative reports of the **Executive Yuan** and is empowered to hold a binding 'no confidence' vote in the latter body. It also has authority to change government policy.

In elections to the Legislative Yuan held in December 2001 the **Democratic Progressive Party (DPP)** secured 36.6% of the vote, ahead of the **Kuomintang (KMT)**, which thereby lost office after more than 50 years in power. The KMT and its fellow party, the **People First Party**, however, had a combined majority of 114 seats against the 111 seats of the DPP and its allies. Elections to the Legislative Yuan in early December 2004 confirmed opposition control.

Internet: www.ly.gov.tw

Leung, Elsie

Leung Oi-sie

Elsie Leung became the first secretary of justice in the **Special Administrative Region (SAR)** of **Hong Kong** of the **People's Republic of China (PRC)** following the British handover in July 1997.

Leung qualified as a solicitor, and began practising in 1968. As a lawyer, she acquired a reputation for taking on cases involving the weak and poor. However, she was also regarded as close to the PRC. She was a delegate to the Guangdong People's Congress in 1989–93, and then to the Eighth **National People's Congress** in 1993–98. During the approach to the establishment of the SAR, she was legal adviser to the PRC's chief executive designate, **Tung Chee Hwa**. Since 1997 she has continued to express views, and to give legal opinions, that seem to favour the PRC. She received the Grand Bahinia Medal for services to Hong Kong in 2002.

Lhasa

Lhasa is the capital of the **Tibet** Autonomous Region (TAR) of the **People's Republic of China (PRC)**. It stands some 3,760 m above sea level, on the Kyichi or Lhasa river. The name means 'City of the Gods' or 'Holy City' in Tibetan.

The city dates from the formation of the Tibetan state in the 7th century AD. There has long been rivalry between Lhasa and Xigaze (Shigatese), Tibet's other main city, with the **Dalai Lama** based at the former and the **Panchen Lama** at the latter. Before the PRC takeover of Tibet in 1951 Lhasa was remote and generally off-limits to foreigners. Even today, access is difficult, although a planned new railway will improve this. Trade has traditionally been in wool, grain, furs, tea and salt, and there is some local craft making. Heavy industry been developed come in recent years.

The city is the centre of Tibetan **Buddhism** and has a number of important religious and government buildings, including the Potola Palace where the Dalai Lama lived and governed until the present one fled to India in 1959. The Potola, widely regarded as one of the world's great buildings, divides into the Red Palace for religious purposes, and the White Palace, which was both the seat of government and the residence of the Dalai Lama and senior officials. Other prominent buildings are the Jokhang temple, the Sera monastery and the Norbulinka Summer Palace. Like other religious centres, Lhasa suffered badly during the **Cultural Revolution**, when many ancient buildings and religious artefacts were destroyed.

Conditions improved somewhat in the 1980s, when the central government provided funds for restoration. Much of old Lhasa had disappeared, however. Another threat to the traditional city has been a steady influx of **Han Chinese**. Between 1951 and 1980 the city grew in size from less than three sq km to 25 sq km, while the number of inhabitants in the Lhasa municipal area rose from some 20,000–30,000 to 110,000. By 2000 it was reported that the Lhasa municipal area covered 53 sq km and that the population of greater Lhasa had reached 470,000. PRC officials claim that **Tibetans** constitute a majority in the city, but Tibetan exiles deny this, arguing that PRC officials, troops, and some other categories are excluded from the official figures. According to these sources, the inner city has a population of about 200,000, one-half of whom are Han Chinese. Current plans would lead to a further expansion of the city by 2015, when the greater urban area would total 272 sq km.

Han Chinese are a major component in the commercial life of Lhasa, which has been promoted as a tourist destination for Chinese and foreign tourists—the latter still need special permits to visit Tibet, which are sometimes refused. Critics claim that new tourist facilities are destroying what was left of the traditional city, and that Chinese signs and shops predominate over Tibetan. A new tower hotel, with a revolving restaurant, opened in 2002, and there has been a steady increase in such facilities. In order to open up Lhasa and Tibet, a railway is under construction to link Lhasa with Xining in Qinghai Province. This will be Tibet's first railway, and the new facilities to be constructed for freight and passenger services will add to the transformation of the city when they are completed in 2007.

Li Lu

Li Lu, a student from **Nanjing**, was the 'deputy commander in chief' working with **Chai Ling** when the **People's Republic of China** crushed the student demonstrations in **Tiananmen** in **Beijing** in June 1989. Like other high-profile leaders, he escaped, travelling first to France and then to the USA. There he quickly made a name for himself with the publication of his supposed autobiography, *Moving the Mountain: My Life in China*, published in 1990, which was made into a film, *Moving the Mountain*, in 1994. Some of his former colleagues have indicated that they do not accept Li's story as presented. Li Lu, meanwhile, acquired a BA, MBA and a JD from Columbia University and established his own hedge fund, Himalaya Capital. Other former student leaders and dissidents accuse him of having abandoned his principles.

Li Peng

Premier of the **State Council** of the **People's Republic of China (PRC)** at the time of the 1989 **Tiananmen** incident. Although deeply unpopular in the PRC thereafter, it was only in 2003 that he finally left office.

Li was born in 1928 in Sichuan Province. The Chinese Nationalists executed his father, the writer Li Shouxun, in 1930, and according to some accounts **Zhou Enlai** adopted the orphan. (A slogan on the gates of the leaders' compound, **Zhongnanhai**, in 1989 read: 'Li Peng is a test-tube baby', an apparent reference to this uncertain background.) Li joined the **Chinese Communist Party (CCP)** in 1945. He trained as an electrical engineer and studied at the Moscow Power Institute in 1948–54. On his return he worked in the power industry until 1980, when he became Vice-Minister and later Minister of Power. From 1983 he was concurrently a Vice-Premier and in charge of the State Education Commission. He was also rising in the CCP hierarchy, joining the Politburo in 1985 and the Standing Committee in 1987. He became acting Premier in 1987.

Li was a target of the student criticisms in 1989, and adopted an increasingly hard line towards the demonstrations. In particular, he was associated with the decision to introduce martial law. However, with **Deng Xiaoping**'s support, he survived and remained Premier until 1998, despite suffering a heart attack in 1993. He seems to have been a strong advocate of the **Three Gorges Dam Project**, but in general he was conservative in his economic and social outlook. He moved from the premiership to head the PRC parliament, the **National People's Congress (NPC)**, in 1998. He retired from the CCP Politburo in 2002 and from the NPC in 2003. He is reportedly working on his memoirs.

Li Zhaoxing

Li Zhaoxing, a career diplomat, became foreign minister of the **People's Republic of China** in 2003, succeeding **Tang Jiaxuan**.

Li is reported to speak English, some French and a little Swahili. He was born in Shandong Province in 1940, and graduated from Beijing University in 1964. In 1964–68 he worked as a language student and then as a researcher in foreign affairs. In 1968–70 he was in the countryside for re-education during the **Cultural Revolution**. In 1970 he reappeared on his appointment as a member of the Chinese embassy in Kenya. Spells in the Ministry of Foreign Affairs information department followed, as did a posting to Lesotho in 1983–85. He became an Assistant Minister of Foreign Affairs in 1990, and was Chinese representative to the **United Nations** in 1993–95, returning to **Beijing** as Vice-Minister of Foreign Affairs in 1995–98. In 1998–2001 he was PRC ambassador to the USA. On his return he was again a Vice-Minister of Foreign Affairs in 2001–03 before taking up his present appointment.

Li represents the increasingly professional side of the Chinese foreign policy machine, which has long since emerged from the doldrums of the Cultural Revolution period. At the same time, he is probably less influential than his predecessors, since he lacks any real wider experience.

Liberal Democratic Party (LDP)

Jiyu Minshuto or *Jiminto*

The Liberal Democratic Party (LDP) of Japan was formed in 1955 by the merger of two conservative parties, the Liberal Party and the Democratic Party. The LDP ruled Japan on its own from 1955 until 1983, when it formed a coalition with the small New Liberal Club—itself a breakaway group from the LDP—and then again from 1986 until 1993. Since August 1994 it has been the major party in the coalition governments that have ruled Japan. It won all of the lower house general elections for the **National Diet** until 1993, although in some cases it only achieved its majority by persuading independent candidates to join it after the election. It also won every upper house election until 1989, when it lost its majority; this has been an important factor in creating the conditions for coalition government.

The Party has always represented various interest groups. It has had close links with the government bureaucracy, many of whose members join it on retirement. It has equally close links with big business. At the same time, it has a strong rural following. Given its long period in power, it is perhaps not surprising that it has increasingly became a party of professional politicians, nor that seats are handed down to family or staff members. It has also proved adept at modifying its position as required. Thus, while formally committed to reform of the Constitution, the LDP has in reality done little about it. The Party is made up of various factions, or interest groups, centred on a particular leader. It is customary for the factions to share out office, including the presidency of the Party and the position of Premier. From time to time there have been attempts to curb the factions. They were formally abolished in 1994, but soon re-emerged.

The LDP has been revitalized under **Koizumi Junichiro**, who was elected as President and Prime Minister in 2001 on a reform ticket. However, while Koizumi has had some successes, for example in negotiating with the Democratic People's Republic of Korea (DPRK) on the issue of **abductees**, he has not been able to carry out his stated aim of normalizing relations with the DPRK. In other ways, too, his reforms have not gone as far as promised.

Pres.: Koizumi Junichiro
Address: Liberal Democratic Party
        1-11-23 Nagatacho
        Chiyoda-ku
        Tokyo 100 8910
        Japan
Tel: 81-3-3581-6211
E-mail: koho@ldp.jimin.or.jp
Internet: www.jimin.jp

Liberal Party (Hong Kong)

Jiyutang

A pro-**Beijing**, pro-business party in **Hong Kong** that dates from 1993.

The Liberal Party developed among a group calling itself the Co-operative Resources Centre in 1993. The Party dates its official formation from 18 July 1993. It has performed moderately well in elections, and holds 10 seats in the **Legislative Council**.

Chair.: Tien Pei-chuan, James, GBS, JP
Address: Liberal Party HQ
        4th Floor
        Henley Bldg 5
        Queen's Rd Central
        Hong Kong
Tel: 852-2869-6833

Fax: 852-2533-4239
E-mail: liberal@liberal.org.hk
Internet: www.liberal.org.hk

Lien Chan

Academic, administrator and politician; Premier of the **'Republic of China'** (**'ROC'**) on **Taiwan** in 1993–97, Vice-President of the 'ROC' in 1996–2000, chairman of the **Kuomintang (KMT)** since 2000.

Lien Chan was born in 1936 in Xi'an in Shaanxi Province of **China**. He completed his studies at Taiwan National University in 1961, then went to the USA for further study and taught political science at various US universities before returning to Taiwan in 1968, again to an academic post. His career as an official began in 1975 and included one ambassadorial posting, ministerial posts and the office of governor of Taiwan Province (1990–93). In 1993 he was appointed as Premier and in 1996 he was named Vice-President. During the 1990s he worked closely with President **Lee Teng-hui**, but quarrelled with him after the presidential elections held in 2000. Lien had presented himself as the KMT candidate, but took third place after **Chen Shui-bian** of the **Democratic Progressive Party**, who was elected President, and **James Soong**, who ran as an independent after failing to be selected as the KMT choice. Lee was ousted from the KMT on suspicion of having engineered the party's failure by endorsing Lien's candidacy, and Lien assumed chairmanship of the KMT. In 2004 he joined with James Soong, who had formed his own **People First Party (PFP)** in 2000, to present a combined KMT-PFP ticket against Chen Shui-bian's re-election. Chen won by a narrow margin. Lien Chan refused to concede defeat, however, and called for a recount.

Address: c/o Kuomintang
11 Chungshan South Rd
Taipei 100
Taiwan
Tel: 886-2-2312-1472
Fax: 886-2-2343-4524
Internet: www.kmt.org.tw

Lin Biao

Lin Biao, who was born in 1907, came to prominence as a military commander first with the **Kuomintang** forces under **Chiang Kai-shek** in the 1926 Northern Expedition. However, when Chiang turned on the **Chinese Communist Party** in 1927, Lin joined **Mao Zedong** and the Red Army. He fought all through the civil wars and the war against Japan, acquiring a formidable reputation. After the founding of the **People's Republic of China**, he became Deputy Prime Minister in 1954 and a marshal in the **People's Liberation Army** in 1955. In 1959 he replaced Peng Dehuai as Minister of Defence. He was a prominent figure in the **Cultural Revolution**, building up the cult of personality around Mao using what became known as the 'Little Red Book' of *Quotations from Chairman Mao*. However, he quarrelled with Mao, and apparently tried to stage a *coup d'état* against him. When this was discovered, he fled with his wife and son. All three were killed when the aircraft in which they were travelling crashed in the Mongolian People's Republic (now Mongolia) on 13 September 1971.

Loh, Christine

Loh Kung-wai

Politician, active in **Hong Kong** politics since the 1980s.

Loh was born in Hong Kong in 1956, and was educated there and in Britain, where she took a degree in law. Returning to Hong Kong in 1979, she worked in the private sector, but became involved in political matters following the 1984 Sino-British Joint Declaration. In 1992 she joined the **Legislative Council (LegCo)** at the invitation of the Hong Kong government. Although a firm defender of Hong Kong's right to democracy, she was less virulent in her criticism of the **People's Republic of China** than many other Hong Kong political figures. In May 1997, on the eve of the handover of Hong Kong, she founded the **Citizens' Party**, and she was its only successful candidate in the 1998 LegCo elections. She decided not to stand in the 2000 elections, and formally left politics to found Civic Exchange, an independent, non-profit-making public policy think-tank. In this role she continues to campaign on educational, equal opportunity and democracy issues.

Long March

Changzheng

In October 1934 the **Kuomintang** forces drove the **Chinese Communist Party (CCP)** and its supporters out of the area known as the Jiangxi Soviet. Over 100,000 set out from Jiangxi on 15 October of that year, with no clear destination in mind. The largest group travelled west and reached Zunyi in Guizhou Province in January 1935. There, at what became known as the Zunyi Conference, **Mao Zedong** emerged as the main leader of the CCP, a position he would hold until his death in 1976. Mao led the remaining forces north to **Yanan** in Shaanxi Province, where some 28,000 arrived after enduring much hardship in October 1935. There the CCP rebuilt its base camp, which it would hold until 1947. The Long March has become a major component of the history of the CCP, and the subject of many books, including novels, and films. It is also a popular brand name in the **People's Republic of China**.

Lu, Annette

Lu Hsiu-lien

Vice-President of the **'Republic of China' ('ROC')** on **Taiwan**.

Annette Lu has been the Vice-President of the 'ROC' since March 2000. She was born near **Taipei** in 1944, and was educated in Taiwan and in the USA. When it became clear in 1978 that the USA was about to withdraw diplomatic recognition from the 'ROC' in favour of the **People's Republic of China (PRC)**, she abandoned her studies and returned to Taiwan. She at once began to campaign on human rights and Taiwan independence. This led to a term of imprisonment, but on her release in 1985 she again became active in politics. When political parties began to emerge in the late 1980s, she joined the **Democratic Progressive Party (DPP)** and entered the **Legislative Yuan** in 1993 on a DPP ticket. She was far more advanced than most of the DPP, calling for Taiwan independence and demanding a seat at the **United Nations** for Taiwan. She also campaigned on feminist issues. Her statements on Taiwan led the PRC to attack her by name.

When **Chen Shui-bian** contested the presidency in 2000, he selected her as his running mate, but it was soon rumoured that the two had quarrelled. Whatever the truth, and Chen denied the rumours, he selected her again in 2004. Both she and Chen were allegedly injured when shots were fired at them on 19 March 2004, but they suffered no lasting harm and were both re-elected. Lu continues to be controversial and outspoken. Claims that she made in the summer of 2004, that a race of 'extinct black pygmies', and not the aborigine peoples or Chinese, were the original inhabitants of Taiwan provoked aborigine protests. The PRC remains wary of her.

M

Macao

Macao is a small enclave on the south-east coast of **China**, west of the Pearl river, some 60 km from **Hong Kong** and 145 km from **Guangzhou**. Since 1999 it has been a **Special Administrative Region (SAR)** of the **People's Republic of China (PRC)**, with the **Macao Basic Law** providing a mini-constitution.

The enclave consists of the Macao peninsula on the mainland, and the islands of Taipa and Coloane; a 2.2 km road joins the islands to the mainland. Macao has steadily increased in size because of land reclamation. Before reclamation began its area was 10.28 sq km, but today it occupies 26.8 sq km. At the end of 2003 its population was 444,000. Most are of Chinese origin, and Cantonese is the most common language. Of these, 45% were born in Macao and an equal number in the PRC.

Macao has a warm and humid climate, with temperatures ranging from 10 °C in November–February to more than 30 °C in the summer. Tropical cyclones may affect the weather during the typhoon season.

Macao came under Portuguese control in the 16th century, but was only formally ceded to Portugal in 1887. From then until 1999 it was a Portuguese colony. From the mid-17th century until the early 19th century it was the only place in China where Western traders could live, and companies such as Jardine Matheson had offices there. With the opening of China's ports and the creation of the **foreign settlements** after 1842, it lost its earlier importance and became something of a backwater. During the **Pacific War** it had some importance as a neutral enclave in a war-torn area, but with the end of the war in 1945 it reverted to its earlier somnolence. For many in Hong Kong its main attraction was gambling, which became a major industry in the 1960s.

Portugal effectively lost control of Macao during the **Cultural Revolution**, and after the Portuguese revolution of 1974 tried to return the colony to the PRC. The latter was not interested, however, fearing that any premature return of Macao would affect Hong Kong. In 1979 the PRC and Portuguese ambassadors in Paris, France, reached an agreement that there should be negotiations on a suitable date for the return of Macao to PRC sovereignty. Following the conclusion of the Sino-UK negotiations on the return of Hong Kong in 1984, negotiations on the return of

Macao concluded in 1987. On 20 December 1997 the formal handover took place and the Macao SAR replaced the former colony. The PRC is now responsible for Macao's security.

Macao has a thriving textile industry, and gambling remains an important factor in the economy. It also enjoys an active tourist trade, helped by the development of the **Macao International Airport.**

Macao Basic Law

The Macao Basic Law provides a constitution for the **Special Administrative Region** of **Macao** of the **People's Republic of China (PRC).** The Basic Law has its origins in the Sino-Portuguese Joint Declaration of 13 April 1987. It was adopted at the PRC's 8th **National People's Congress** on 31 March 1993. Like its counterpart, the **Hong Kong Basic Law,** the Macao Basic Law embodies the concept of 'one country, two systems'. Macao will continue to enjoy a high degree of autonomy from the PRC for 50 years after the former Portuguese colony's reversion to the PRC on 20 December 1999, and will be able to act internationally in certain areas, including trade and aviation matters. There have been far fewer challenges to the Macao Basic Law compared with its Hong Kong counterpart.

Details of the Macao Basic Law and related matters are available at: www.imprensa.macau.gov.mo/bo/i/1999/leibasica

Macao Economy

Macao's small size and population have limited its economic development. Long before the territory became a **Special Administrative Region (SAR)** of the **People's Republic of China (PRC)** in 1999, its main economic activity was gambling. This has continued under the new regime, and has ensured that the SAR Government has a healthy revenue from gambling taxes. The rest of the economy also benefits through providing services for the millions who visit Macao each year to gamble. The SAR suffered an economic downturn from the mid-1990s, but began to recover from this in 2001, and the economy has continued to grow ever since. Even the **Severe Acute Respiratory Syndrome** epidemic of 2003 did not have much affect on Macao.

GNP: US $6,740m. (2003 estimate); *GNP per caput:* US $15,045 (2003 estimate); *GDP at PPP:* US $9,100m. (2003 estimate); *GDP per caput at PPP:* US $19,400; *exports:* US $2.356m. (2002); *imports:* US $2.539m.; *currency:* pataca US $1 = 8.2 patacas (31 December 2002).

In economic terms Macao has always been in the shadow of its larger neighbour, **Hong Kong.** Although in the early 19th century the enclave enjoyed some economic prosperity as part of the **Guangzhou** trade system, the opening of the **foreign settlements** along the **China** coast and the British acquisition of Hong Kong in 1842 turned Macao into a backwater. The Portuguese colonial authorities did little to develop Macao until the 1970s. By then gambling had already become a major feature of the local economy. Gambling and related service industries now account for some 87% of Macao's gross domestic product (GDP). In 2003 direct taxes on gambling accounted for some 40% of government revenue. Tourist numbers, especially from the PRC, have steadily increased, from 8.1m. in 1996 to 11.9m. in 2003. As the PRC becomes richer, so these visitors spend more. There are other aspects to Macao's economy, however. It is a free port. The SAR also produces textiles, together with toys and fireworks. Macao is an important fishing port, and there is an active food processing industry. The building of the **Macao International Airport** has increased the SAR's economic potential, although the airport faces much regional competition. The budget in 2002 forecast revenue of US $1,900m., and expenditure of $1,680m. The USA takes the largest share of Macao's exports—48.5% in 2002. The PRC accounted for 15.5% of exports in that year, but this figure may increase as a consequence of the Closer Economic Partnership Agreement signed by Macao and the PRC in September 2003.

Macao International Airport

For many years **Macao** relied on **Hong Kong** for international air connections, with passengers making the onward connection by sea. However, in 1995 Macao International Airport opened. Facing competition from established airports such as **Chek Lap Kok—Hong Kong International Airport** and **Guangzhou**, as well as from new ones such as **Shenzhen**, Macao International Airport has never been used to full capacity. However, it serves as a home airport for Air Macau and receives flights from more exotic airlines such as **Air Koryo**.

MacArthur, Douglas

Douglas MacArthur (1880–1964), General of the Army from 1944, was commander-in-chief of the US forces in the Pacific theatre at the end of the Second World War.

Following Japan's surrender he became Supreme Commander for the Allied Powers (SCAP) in Japan. In this role he was the driving force behind the programmes of the **Allied Occupation of Japan**. Following the outbreak of the **Korean War** in June 1950, US President Harry S. Truman appointed him additionally as commander of the **United Nations** Command (UNC). On 14 July 1950 the Republic of Korea (ROK) President, **Syngman Rhee**, also placed the ROK armed forces under MacArthur's command.

In September 1950 MacArthur planned and executed 'Operation Chromite', which led to the capture of the port city of Inchon. This opened the way to **Seoul**, and for the crossing of the **38th parallel** into the Democratic People's Republic of Korea (DPRK). The UNC met little opposition from the remaining DPRK forces, and MacArthur discounted reports that the **People's Republic of China (PRC)** would intervene if the UN forces approached the **Yalu river**. When PRC forces attacked in November 1950, MacArthur panicked and demanded that the war be extended to PRC territory. Truman refused, and after initial PRC successes had faltered because of extended supply lines, the line of battle stabilized around the 38th parallel in mid-1951.

Truman had by then dismissed MacArthur for insubordination, following a public letter in April 1951 in which he had called for the use of **'Republic of China'** forces from **Taiwan** against the Chinese mainland. MacArthur was relieved of his command on 11 April 1951, and Gen. Matthew Ridgeway took over both as SCAP in Japan and UN Commander in Korea.

For a time it appeared as though MacArthur might stand as the Republican Party candidate in the 1952 US presidential election, but the moment passed. Gen. Eisenhower won the Republican nomination, and MacArthur quickly faded from the political scene. In retirement he continued to blame those who he believed had prevented him from winning the war in Korea. In Japan he is remembered for the relatively beneficial role of the occupation authorities. The ROK remembers him as the saviour of the country, while the DPRK still condemns him as an invader.

Machimura Nobutaka

A politician whose career has followed one of the classic paths to power in Japan, Machimura Nobutaka became foreign minister when Prime Minister **Koizumi Junichiro** reshuffled his Cabinet in September 2004.

Machimura was born in 1944, and graduated from the Faculty of Economics at **Tokyo** University. He entered the Ministry for International Trade and Investment (MITI) in 1969, and worked there until he retired in 1982, when he first entered the **National Diet** as a **Liberal Democratic Party (LDP)** member of the lower house. He has been re-elected seven times. During a brief period as Minister of Education in 2001 he became embroiled in the **history textbooks controversy**, when he approved a new textbook that was criticized by a number of neighbouring governments. He is generally believed to be on the right wing of the LDP.

Manchuria

Term used in the West to describe the homeland of the **Manzhou** people of the **People's Republic of China**, but not one used by the Chinese themselves; they call the area *dongbei* or north-east.

The area now comprises part of **Inner Mongolia** (Inner Mongolia Autonomous Region), and the provinces of Heilungjiang, Liaoning and Jilin. It lies north of the **Korean peninsula**, at the head of the Yellow (Liao) river. It has long been an important agricultural area for both herd and crop farming, and it also has extensive mineral resources. In the early 20th century Russia and Japan contended for control of the region, which ultimately led the Japanese to establish the puppet state of **Manzhouguo** in 1932. After 1949 major industrial development took place in the region, but today much of the industry is in poor condition and the agricultural land has suffered badly from pollution.

Manzhou

A minority nationality of the **People's Republic of China (PRC)** who have become almost totally absorbed into the **Han Chinese** majority.

The Manzhou were a nomadic people who originally came from the area north of the Liaodong peninsula, where they emerged as vassals of the Chinese Ming Empire (1368–1644). By the late 16th century, although still fiercely independent, they were heavily influenced by Chinese culture through trade and through the importation of Chinese craftsmen. From *c*. 1582 onwards, under Nurchai (1559–1626), the Manzhou were organized into groupings, known as 'banners', which helped in raising taxes and organizing military units. Nurchai established his capital at Shenyang, renamed Mukden in 1626, and began the process of conquering **China**. This was completed in 1644 under his grandson, who became the first of the Qing emperors who were to rule China until 1910.

After conquering China the Manzhou remained a distinct group until the 19th century, when many of the barriers that had previously existed between them and the majority Han people began to break down. Han settlement began in the Manzhou homeland, and most Manzhou spoke standard Chinese. Their political influence waned with the end of the empire in 1910. In the 1990 population census they numbered about 10m., living mostly in north-east China but virtually indistinguishable from the Han.

Manzhouguo

Wade-Giles *Manchukuo*; Japanese *Manshukoku*.

Japanese puppet state established in **Manchuria** in 1932. This followed the complete takeover of the area by Japan's Kwantung Army from 1931 onwards. Rehe Province was added in 1933. Nominally independent under **Henry Puyi**, the last emperor of **China**, Manzhouguo's capital was at Changchun. The country was run entirely for the benefit of Japan. From 1937 onwards, with the spread of war in China following the **Marco Polo Bridge incident**, the Japanese faced growing guerrilla opposition within Manzhouguo, and the Soviet Union thwarted attempts to expand westwards. In 1945 Soviet troops quickly occupied the area after the Soviet declaration of war on Japan, and returned the area to Chinese control.

A number of people later prominent in the Republic of Korea (ROK), including President **Park Chung-Hee**, trained or studied in Manzhouguo. Many features of Japan's economic and political programmes in Manzhouguo later surfaced in both the ROK and the Democratic People's Republic of Korea.

Mao Zedong (1893–1976)

As leader of the **Chinese Communist Party (CCP)**, Mao Zedong transformed **China** during his years in power.

Mao was born in 1893, the son of a small landowner in Henan Province. He went to **Beijing** and worked for a time as assistant librarian at Beijing University. There he first read Marx and Lenin, and met some of their early Chinese followers. His belief that the Chinese peasantry would be the key to revolution, however, would make him a less than orthodox Marxist-Leninist. Mao was one of the founders of the CCP in 1921, and its leader from the **Long March** until his death in 1976. After fighting against Japan in the **Pacific War**, Mao and the CCP renewed their earlier war with the **Kuomintang** in 1946. Despite US support for the Nationalists, the CCP was victorious in 1949, and established the **People's Republic of China (PRC)**.

Mao became the first head of state, while retaining his party role. In 1950, urged on by the Soviet leader, Josef Stalin, and in response to pleas from **Kim Il Sung**, he ordered military intervention in the **Korean War**, thus saving the Democratic People's Republic of Korea from destruction. At home, the war allowed Mao to launch a campaign to eradicate those deemed to be enemies of the new state. Impatient with the slow progress of the revolution and what he believed was bureaucratic obstruction, Mao launched a series of campaigns to accelerate change. These included the 'Great Leap Forward' in 1959, by which the PRC was to rapidly overtake Britain in economic development, but which left millions dead of famine, and the even more disastrous **Cultural Revolution**, which Mao initiated in 1966. During the Cultural Revolution a huge cult of personality developed around Mao, while the PRC plunged into a chaotic period in which the state and party ceased to function effectively, and many of Mao's comrades suffered banishment, imprisonment or death. Mao's third wife, Jiang Qing, a former actress, played a major role in these events, and in the widespread destruction of much of China's traditional culture. Those who suffered included Mao's successor as the PRC's head of state, Liu Shaoqi, and the man who would ultimately inherit his power, if not his titles, **Deng Xiaoping**. **Zhou Enlai**, the PRC Premier, protected some, and eventually restored order with the aid of the **People's Liberation Army**.

In foreign affairs Mao quarrelled with the Soviet Union over de-Stalinization and other matters in the late 1950s. Although the PRC had fought the USA in the Korean War, and endured US hostility thereafter, in 1970 Mao signalled that the PRC favoured contact. He received Henry Kissinger in 1971, and President Richard Nixon in 1972.

Mao died in 1976, still head of the CCP. His successor, **Hua Guofeng**, turned on Jiang Jing and her supporters, but otherwise favoured the continuation of Mao's policies. However, Deng Xiaoping rapidly ousted Hua, and, while not abandoning all of Mao's legacy, soon began to move away from it. Today, Mao's cult of personality has largely faded, though some Chinese have a nostalgic attachment to those days. The CCP has judged Mao's legacy to be 70% good and 30% bad.

Marco Polo Bridge Incident
Luguoqiao shijian

The beginning of the Sino–Japanese War (1937–45), which led to the wider **Pacific War**, dates from a clash on 7 July 1937 between **Kuomintang** forces and the Japanese Kwantung Army at the town of Wanping, a railway junction near **Beijing**. Chinese resistance led to a full-scale Japanese invasion of northern China. The Marco Polo Bridge, so named because the Venetian traveller described it, is just outside the town.

Meiji Restoration
Meiji ishin

Term to describe the transfer of power in 1868 from the Tokugawa clan to the **Japanese Emperor**, thus ending several hundred years of imperial isolation from power.

The emperor, who had taken the name 'Meiji' or 'bright government', moved his capital from **Kyoto** to **Tokyo**, thus beginning the Meiji period. This development is always associated with the beginning of the modern Japanese state. When the Republic of Korea's **Park Chung-Hee**, a former Japanese military officer, staged his internal coup in 1972, he named his new Constitution the '*Yushin*' Constitution, using the same Chinese characters as the Meiji leaders had used for 'Restoration'.

Miao

Ethnic group, the fifth largest in the country, based in the central and south-west regions of the **People's Republic of China**.

The 1990 population census reported a figure of 7,383,600 for this group. Around one-half of the Miao live in Guizhou Province, a poor and mountainous area largely dependent on agriculture. Another 1.5m. live in Hunan Province, where the Xiangxi Miao and **Tujia** Autonomous Prefecture occupies about one-tenth of the provincial land area. Other Miao autonomous prefectures and counties are in Yunnan, Sichuan and Hubei provinces, in Guangxi Zhuang Autonomous Region and in Hainan island. In general, they are settled in hilly or mountainous regions, though some have moved into the large cities

The Miao have an ancient history, in the course of which they appear to have been gradually driven southwards as the **Han Chinese** themselves migrated south over the centuries from their heartlands in the **Yellow river** valley. Relations between the Miao and succeeding Chinese dynasties were marked by periods of Miao independence, but also by continuing Chinese attempts to subdue them, the last of which occurred in the mid-19th century. In the 18th century Miao migrations took place into what are now Viet Nam, Laos and Thailand. Outside of **China** the Miao are known as the Hmong. Their language, which encompasses 30–40 mutually unintelligible dialects, belongs to the Miao branch of the Miao-Yao group of languages in the Sino-Tibetan family. A similar diversity exists among the different groups of Miao, who distinguish themselves principally by the main colour of their clothing; thus, Red, Black, Flowery, White and Green Miao. They are skilled silversmiths, who produce fine silver jewellery and headdresses worn by Miao women.

MIAT

Mongol irgeniey agaaryu teever

MIAT is the Mongolian acronym for Mongolian Civil Air Transport, Mongolia's airline. It began as part of the air defence section of the then Mongolian People's Army (now the **Mongolian Armed Forces**) in 1925. From then until after the **Pacific War**, when it acquired a DC 3, all of its aircraft were supplied by the Soviet Union. In 1971 the Air Communications Directorate under the Ministry of the Army and Public Security was renamed the Main Directorate for Civil Air Transport. In the 1990s MIAT began to acquire non-Soviet aircraft; the government of the Republic of Korea (ROK) supplied it with a Boeing 727. MIAT leased other aircraft, but fuel shortages hindered its operations. In 2001 a privatization programme was initiated. Most MIAT flights have always been internal, or to the Soviet Union/Russia, but it has extended its routes to include the **People's Republic of China**, Japan, Germany and the ROK.

Millennium Democratic Party (MDP)

Minjudang, or *Saechonyonminjudang*

Following the presidential election in the Republic of Korea (ROK) in 1997, which brought the veteran opposition leader, **Kim Dae-Jung** to power, the party that he had formed in 1996, the **National Congress for New Politics**, in 1999 renamed itself the Millennium Democratic Party (MDP). Although its Korean name included 'Millennium' in the title, in fact most Koreans referred to it as the *Minjudang* or **Democratic Party**, emphasizing the continuation of the opposition tradition. For the 2002 presidential election the Party selected as its candidate **Roh Moo-Hyun**, who defeated Lee Hoi-Chang. In the autumn of 2003, however, the MDP split, with those supporting Roh forming the **Uri Party**. The MDP thus ceased to be the official ruling party, and rapidly declined in importance. It supported the **Grand National Party**'s moves in the spring of 2004 to impeach President Roh. As a result, it suffered badly in the April 2004 **ROK National Assembly** elections, with its representation reduced to nine seats. The Party's website continues to link it with the ROK's traditional opposition groups.

Chair.: Hahn Hwa-Gap
Address: Millennium Democratic Party
        Chungan Bldg, 17–13
        Yoido-dong
        Yongdongpo-ku
        150-874 Seoul
        Republic of Korea
Tel: 82-2-784-7007
Fax: 82-2-784-4077
E-mail: webmaster@minjoo.or.kr
Internet: www.minjoo.or.kr

Minority nationalities (People's Republic of China)

The 55 nationalities that together with the majority **Han Chinese** comprise the population of the **People's Republic of China (PRC)**. The national census carried out in 2000 showed that, of the total population of 1,265.83m., 91.59% (that is, 1,159.40m. people) were Han; the remaining 8.41%, or 106.43m. people, were identified as belonging to a minority nationality. Comparison with the 1990 population census showed that the Han population had increased by 11.22% (116.92m. people) over the decade and the minorities' population by 16.70% (15.23m. people).

Eighteen of the 55 minority nationalities number more than 1m. each. The largest group is the **Zhuang** (around 15.5m., on the basis of the 1990 census), living in southern China. The next biggest minorities, again on the basis of the 1990 census, are the **Manzhou** (Manchu) in northern China (9.8m.), the **Hui**, a religious group—Muslim—who are none the less treated as if they were a national minority (8.6m.), the **Miao** (or Hmong) in southern China (7.3m.), the **Uygur** in north-west China (7.2m.), the **Yi** in south and south-west China (6.6m.), the **Tujia** in central-south China (5.7m.), the **Mongols** in northern China (4.8m.) and the **Tibetans**, living in **Tibet** and north-west China (4.5m.). The remaining nine in the category of those numbering more than 1m. range in number from 2.5m. down to 1m. Beyond them is a group of 37 increasingly lesser minorities, the smallest of which numbers about 2,300.

The definition of a minority nationality is by no means settled; a certain amount of self-categorization and self-referral went on in the past as ethnic groups came forward to register in response to the state's call for information; names for minorities were imposed; and the criteria that now prevail may in some cases be arbitrary. The Manzhou, for instance, speak standard Chinese and are virtually indistinguishable from the Han. The Hui are also Chinese speakers. In the 1950s, when the Chinese government was developing its policies, Soviet prescriptions for deciding how to classify a minority nationality influenced its decisions. Religion does not seem to have been allowed as a factor (although that is the only point by which the Hui distinguish themselves). Language and custom, together with a recognized territory of origin, style of life and ethnic concentration, have been the important considerations. The situation can be considerably complicated. The Hui are scattered thoughout China. **Xinjiang**, though officially a Uygur region, contains a number of other nationalities; and the south-west province of Yunnan, although not an autonomous region, has 22 different nationalities. Patterns of settlement can vary within an area, with different nationality communities occupying different geographical sectors (plains, mountains); or split between towns and countryside. The economy of many minority areas was backward and poorly managed when the Chinese state started to implement its policies. Helping such regions to advance economically and socially through, in some instances, the location of heavy industry in them, allocating subsidies and allowing the autonomous regions to retain tax revenues, became one of the aims, even though it may have led to standardization, influxes of Han Chinese settlers and advisers and, in the view of some critics of the PRC's practice, to exploitation of resources. The growing divide between the affluent coastal provinces of east China and the general stagnation of inland areas has affected the considerable number of minority nationalities living in inhospitable western regions in recent years.

One of the freedoms accorded to minority nationalities is that of using their own language alongside standard Chinese, in particular in education up to at least primary school level and in criminal proceedings. Fifty-two minority languages are recognized, most of them falling into two main families, Sino-Tibetan and Altaic. Some have long histories as spoken and written languages and these tend to predominate at a national level. Thus China National Radio offers a domestic service in Uygur, Mongolian, Tibetan, **Korean** and **Kazak** in addition to standard Chinese, **Hakka** and Amoy. The Nationalities Publishing House publishes books and periodicals in Uygur, Mongolian, Tibetan, Korean and Kazak. These five languages together with **Dai** have the standing of official languages in their respective autonomous areas, to be used by Party and government organizations, and they may be used for middle school as well as primary school teaching. Twenty-one ethnic minorities have their own writing systems. Other minority languages such as Zhuang had an oral tradition alone and were transcribed into written form only in the 20th century. Following the example of Vietnamese, the written language may use Roman script rather than Chinese characters.

From the outset, the Chinese government was prepared to grant a limited degree of autonomy to the minority nationalities. The first autonomous region, **Inner Mongolia**, was established as early as 1947. Four more autonomous regions (Xinjiang Uygur, Ningxia Hui, Tibet and Guangxi Zhuang), giving five in all, 30 autonomous prefectures, 120 autonomous counties and more than 1,300 ethnic townships are designated as areas in which the nationalities may practise cultural freedom and a measure of self-government, including decisions on education, marriage and family planning. Minority nationalities numbering less than 10m. are not bound by the one-child family directive. The autonomous areas may furthermore scrutinize central government laws and adapt, or not implement, those that do not suit their needs. The national minorities now have some flexibility in selecting their own names in preference to those earlier imposed on them. These relaxations on national policies may be intended in part to retain the support of the minorities. Many of them inhabit large border regions that the PRC is unwilling to see slip out of its control. In all, two-thirds of the land area of the PRC has a population dominated by minority people. To that end, the 1982 Constitution, while safeguarding the rights and status of the minority nationalities, does not tolerate any encouragement of secession and describes the autonomous areas as 'inalienable parts' of the PRC. Matters relating to nationalities are handled at the highest levels of government, with the State Nationalities Affairs Commission placed under the State Council and headed by a minister. The state's official policies on the minorities are a combination of co-option at all levels of government, support for their economic development, tolerance for their languages and cultures and a reining in of 'Han chauvinism', checked by the requirement that they implement most state policies and do not attempt to break away from central control. Clashes between minorities or between the Han majority and the minorities are hardly ever reported, so it is not known how often they occur; but in October 2004 fighting between Han Chinese and local Hui was reported from Henan Province in central China. Several deaths occurred.

Missing in action (MIA)

In all wars a certain number of combatants have remained unaccounted for at the end of fighting. High explosives can destroy all remains, and in wars of movement or in remote regions, bodies are buried where they fall, and records of graves are sometimes lost. When prisoners of war move frequently, as happened in the **Korean War**, details of deaths may be lost. In East Asia there are missing in action (MIA) from every war since 1937, when the **Pacific War** began, until the end of the Cold War in the early 1990s.

Some East Asian countries have occasionally raised the issue of MIA. These have included the Republic of Korea, which did so in 2002 after Japan's Prime Minister, **Koizumi Junichiro**, persuaded the Democratic People's Republic of Korea (DPRK) to admit to the existence of a group of Japanese **abductees**. However, of all the countries involved in these various conflicts, only the USA has pursued a determined and vigorous programme to track down the remains of its MIA. The USA has developed an elaborate set of mechanisms to assist its MIA programme. Since the early 1970s the focus of this effort has been the US Army Central Identification Laboratory in Hawaii, which from 1992 was joined by a group called Joint Task Force-Full Accounting. In October 2003 these two organizations combined to form the Joint POW/MIA Accounting Command.

The USA has enjoyed good co-operation with the **People's Republic of China (PRC)** on the issue of MIA from all wars from the Pacific War onwards since the mid-1970s. This began in 1975 when the Chinese authorities handed over to the

USA two sets of remains from the Viet Nam War, and has continued ever since. In January 1997 the PRC invited a US team to investigate the site of a Pacific War bomber crash. An even bigger breakthrough came in 2002, when the USA was allowed to investigate a site connected with a Cold War Central Intelligence Agency operation. In March 2003 the PRC and the USA agreed on a programme of enhanced co-operation to investigate all those missing since 1941. Combined PRC-US investigations continued in 2004, and have included both the Viet Nam and the Korean War.

The other main concentration of US efforts has been on the DPRK. At the end of the Korean War more than 8,000 US servicemen were unaccounted for, together with a number of foreign civilians who disappeared in the early days of the war and have not been heard of since. Soon after the end of the Korean War the DPRK returned the remains of some 4,000 US military personnel, but subsequently, although the **United Nations** Command regularly raised the issue at **Panmunjom**, the DPRK/PRC side always denied any knowledge of those missing. In 1987 direct discussions began on the issue between the USA and the DPRK, and this led in 1990 to the return of what were said to be the remains of five US soldiers.

In the following four years the DPRK returned some 200 sets of what it claimed were the remains of US soldiers. However, the remains were not easy to identify, and the USA constantly sought a more scientific basis for searching. In 1991 the two sides agreed to establish a joint committee to conduct searches. A further agreement in 1993 involved US payment, and in 1995 formal talks on the issue took place in Hawaii. These talks led to an agreement in May 1996 on future operations, involving joint evacuation teams. In May 1997 the 1996 agreement was reaffirmed.

Despite the change in US administrations in 2001, and constant DPRK attempts to change the nature of the exchanges into a state-to-state relationship, the agreements remain in force. The number of US teams deployed in the DPRK increased from one in 1996 to six in 1997. They have fallen back in recent years, but continue to function and, since 1996, have recovered some 200 sets of remains. The most recent discovery of a body was on 25 May 2004, and it was repatriated on 1 July 2004. The programme provides one of the few direct contacts between the DPRK and the US military, and therefore can be viewed as a rare confidence-building measure between the two sides.

Mongolia

An independent republic, situated between Russia and the **People's Republic of China (PRC)**.

The country is completely land-locked. The border with Russia is some 3,441 km in length; that with the PRC 4,673 km. About 30% of the population live in the state capital. The majority of those outside the urban areas are herdsmen, although the old nomadic way of life is changing rapidly. The climate is extreme, with temperatures ranging between 10 °C–20 °C in the summer, and from –21 °C to –31 °C in winter.

Most precipitation falls in the summer. Mongolia is a plateau from 900 m–1,500 m above sea level. In the south-west the Altay Mountains rise to more than 4,000 m.

Area: 1,564,116 sq km; *capital:* **Ulaan Baatar**; *population:* 2,751,314 (2004 estimate), **Mongols** 94.9%, Turkic 5%, other (including Russian and Chinese) 0.1%; *official language:* Mongolian; *religion:* Buddhist 50%, no religion 40%, Christian, Shamanist 6%, Muslim 4%. For administrative purposes Mongolia has 21 provinces and one municipality.

Mongolia's present political structure dates only from the early 1990s. It is based on universal suffrage for all those aged 18 years and over. Following developments in Eastern Europe and the Soviet Union, Mongolia, then the Mongolian People's Republic, began a move towards democracy. References to the 'leading role' of the **Mongolian People's Revolutionary Party (MPRP)**, the Soviet-style ruling party, were removed from the Constitution. Opposition parties became legal. In addition to the **State Great Hural (SGH**—the parliament), a Standing Little Hural (SLH), a standing legislature, came into existence. The MPRP continued to dominate the SGH, but in the SLH the opposition won 19 out of 50 seats at the first elections in September 1991. In 1992 a new constitution came into force, with the Great or State Hural as the national parliament. The Hural has a term of four years, as does the President. At the first elections held under this Constitution, the MPRP won 70 out of 76 seats, the others going to opposition parties, most of which eventually came together as the Mongolian National Democratic Party (MNDP).

In the 1996 elections the MNDP allied itself with the Mongolian Social Democratic Party (MSDP), which had won one seat in 1992, to form the Democratic Alliance (DA). The DA swept the MPRP from office, winning 50 seats compared with the latter's 25; the remaining seat went to a conservative candidate. However, in elections held in 2000 the positions were reversed, the MPRP winning 72 out of 76 seats. At the most recent elections, held in June 2004, the MPRP won 36 seats, and a slightly differently configured DA 34.

History: The Mongols swept into world history in the 13th century when, under Genghis Khan, they came out of their small enclave in what is now Mongolia to create a vast Eurasian empire. This broke up in the following century, and the Mongols never again achieved anything like the same importance. Lamaistic **Buddhism** spread into Mongolia in the 16th century. When the **Manzhou** conquered **China** in the 17th century and established the Qing Empire, they brought both **Inner Mongolia** and then Mongolia, known as Outer Mongolia, under their control. Manzhou civil and military officials took up residence in Mongolia, the better to control the area, and contacts with Russia were forbidden.

The Chinese revolution of 1911 allowed the Mongols to evade Chinese control. Outer Mongolia declared its independence under the Bogd Khan, or head of state. In 1912 Outer Mongolia signed a treaty with Russia, but as with Britain and **Tibet**, the Russians were only prepared to recognize Outer Mongolia as autonomous under Chinese suzerainty, not as an independent state. The new government of the **Republic of China (1912–49)** made some effort to regain the position formally held by the Manzhou. In 1921, however, Mongolian revolutionaries, assisted by the Soviet Union, declared Mongolia independent, and in November 1924, after various struggles within the Mongolian People's Party (MPP) led to the triumph of the leftist groups, it became the Mongolian People's Republic (MPR). The MPP renamed itself the Mongolian People's Revolutionary Party (MPRP). Until the late 1980s the MPR boasted that it was the second country in the world to become communist.

For the next 70 years MPR politics followed those of the Soviet Union. The planned economy was introduced, and Mongolia's economic fortunes were linked first to the Soviet Union, and eventually to **COMECON**. The same type of purges took place, with the Buddhist monasteries in particular targeted for attack. Some industry was introduced, and there was heavy exploitation of the country's mineral resources. On the positive side, modern health and education facilities spread throughout the country. Mongolia was effectively run for the Soviet Union's benefit, but the latter also heavily subsidized it.

When the Soviet Union began to introduce reforms in the 1990s, the MPR followed suit, and in 1990 it became a multi-party democracy. The tradition of a one-party state is still powerful, however, and the MPRP has continued to exert a strong influence. The move away from dependence has not been easy, and Mongolians have complained that they have not received much international support in their transit to democracy. The economy has suffered from the end of the COMECON system, and Mongolia's land-locked position has always been a difficulty. The political process has not yet stabilized, as evidenced by the big variations in allegiance that have occurred between elections. The Mongolians have been disappointed that the **Tumen River Area Development Programme** has not been more successful, since they regarded it as a way of breaking out of their land-locked isolation. However, they have developed links with the Republic of Korea, partly based on a supposed common ancestry, which have produced some economic benefits, while also maintaining ties with the Democratic People's Republic of Korea. Suspicions of the PRC, which was thought to hold irredentist views despite having accepted the MPR's independence in 1950, surfaced from time to time before 1990, but now seem to have abated. Mongolia joined the **United Nations** in 1961.

Mongolia, Economy

An economy that has faced severe difficulties in moving away from the Soviet-style economic system imposed from 1924 until the early 1990s. As a land-locked country, Mongolia remains heavily dependent on its neighbours, Russia and the **People's Republic of China (PRC)**.

GNP: US $1,100m. (2002 estimate); *GNP per caput:* US $480 (2002 estimate); *GDP at PPP:* US $4,882,000m. (2004 estimate); *GDP per caput at PPP:* US $1,800 (2004 estimate); *exports:* US $524m. (2002 estimate); *imports:* US $691m. (2002 estimate); *currency:* tugrik; plural tugriks; 1 tugrik = 100 mongos (US $1 = 1,171 tugriks (2003)).

Mongolia is well endowed with minerals and other natural resources, though they are largely underdeveloped. The resources include copper, nickel, zinc, tungsten, zinc, gold, lead and petroleum, which have been found in recent years. However, much of the country's economy is tied up in the herd—the generic term for the large numbers of sheep, goats, cattle, horses and other animals collectively owned in Mongolia.

Before 1990 the economy of the then Mongolian People's Republic (MPR) had extensive links with those of the Soviet Union and the **COMECON** countries. The MPR received both aid and subsidies from the Soviet Union. The result may have distorted the economy, but it was all that the Mongolians had known. All of this disappeared almost overnight, taking with it about one-third of the country's gross domestic product (GDP). Not only was the new state struggling with democracy, but its relatively inexperienced leaders had also to face major decisions on economic matters. Since, initially, the same people who administered Mongolia before the political upheavals of 1990 remained in charge, there was reluctance at first to engage in sweeping economic changes. The principle of the market economy was accepted, however, and the state collective farms, and with them the herd, were privatized. Before long shortages of foodstuffs arose as the new private farms proved unable to meet the demands of the population. Per caput income fell drastically, perhaps by as much as 50% between the late 1980s and 2002.

Some changes were unavoidable. From 1991 the Soviet Union demanded that all payments should be made in US dollars, a move which depleted the country's foreign exchange reserves. Speculation on the foreign exchanges further depleted the reserves. There was also a debate between the two countries about the repayment of past debts. Eventually, in February 2004, Russia wrote off all but US $300m. of Mongolia's debt, although that still represented a large sum for a poor country. An attempt to encourage privatization and the redistribution of wealth by issuing vouchers failed to achieve either goal. Mongolia suffered from a world-wide collapse in cashmere prices in the mid-1990s. Dissatisfaction with these developments led to a change of government in 1996, but the economic problems continued. In addition to all of the other difficulties, the winter of 2000–2001 proved to be the worst for 50 years. Unemployment soared and the herd sustained heavy losses. So bad was the situation that in February 2001 the **United Nations** appealed for $8.7m. to support the herdsmen. Later in that year the **International Monetary Fund** approved low-interest loans totalling $40m. for Mongolia. According to the US Central Intelligence Agency, per caput GDP declined from some $2,300 in 1999 to a low of $1,770 in 2001, and then gradually recovered to $1,800. During 2000–2001 the rate of unemployment surged to more than 20%, before falling to about 4.5% in 2002.

The Mongolian economy is still in a precarious position, even if it is has recovered somewhat since the mid-1990s and real GDP is on the rise. The rate of growth of GDP has risen from –1% in 2000 to about 5%—though, in real terms, it is estimated at only about 1.1%. Per caput income has still not recovered to its pre-1990 level. The issue of outstanding debt remains problematic. In 2001 Mongolia's foreign debt was estimated at $887m. Agriculture provides about 20.6% of GDP, industry 21.5% and services 58%. The country's main trading partners are Russia (33.1%), the PRC (21.5%), the Republic of Korea, which has rediscovered its links to the **Mongols** (8.5%), Japan (7.9%) and Germany (4.7%). Mongolia received some $332m. in international aid in 2003.

Mongolian Academy Of Sciences

Sinjleh Uhaany Akademi

The Mongolian Academy of Sciences is the principal centre of research in the humanities, science and technology in Mongolia. It traces its origins to the Institute of Scriptures and Manuscripts (sometimes known as the Committee of History or the Committee of Letters) founded in 1921, which was concerned with the collection of material relating to Mongolia's history. In 1931 this became the Committee of Sciences, and added botany, agriculture, geography, geology and map-making to its historical functions. This Committee had close links to the Soviet Union's Academy of Sciences. In 1959 the Committee of Sciences and the **Mongolian State University** came together as the Committee of Science and Higher Education. However, they demerged in 1961, and the Committee of Sciences then became the Academy of Sciences. The Central Public Library and a number of research institutions also came under the control of the Academy of Sciences. It currently has seven departments: agriculture, chemistry and biology, geology and geography, medicine, physics and mathematics, social sciences, and technology. Numerous specialized institutions are also part of the academy. Since the early 1990s many new academies have appeared in Mongolia, but none belong to the Academy of Sciences.

Pres.: B. Chadraa
Address: Mongolian Academy of Sciences
　　　　　Sukhbator Sq. 3
　　　　　2010620 Ulaan Baatar
　　　　　Mongolia
Tel: 976-11-32-22-48
Fax: 976-11-32-19-93
E-mail: mas@mas.ac.mn
Internet: www.mas.ac.mn

Mongolian armed forces

Mongol zevseg huchin

The Mongolian armed forces have their origins in partisan forces that eventually became the People's Revolutionary Army in 1921. After the establishment of the Mongolian People's Republic in 1924, the Soviet Union provided technical assistance and equipment. Mongol forces were engaged in action against Japan in 1939 and, together with Soviet forces, at the end of the **Pacific War** in 1945. The army underwent many changes of title and command structure after 1945, but continued to receive modern weapons and training from the Soviet Union. Uniforms and badges of rank resembled those of Soviet forces. During this period, the armed forces also operated **MIAT**, the civil airline.

Great changes have taken place following the democratic movement that has transformed Mongolia since 1990. The armed forces, which include ground and air forces as well as border guards and a construction corps, have been much reduced. In 2004 there were 8,600 active members of the armed forces. The vast majority are in the ground forces, whose strength is 7,500; about 50% are conscripts who serve for one year. The air force, which has no combat aircraft, has 13 armed helicopters and 800 men. In addition, there are some 6,000 border guards (4,700 are conscripts) and 1,200 internal security troops (800 conscripts). Some 130 Mongolian troops are deployed in Iraq as peace support troops.

Mongolian Nuclear Weapons-Free Zone (MNWFZ)

After the collapse of the Soviet Union allowed Mongolia to pursue an independent foreign policy for the first time in its existence, one of the first moves of the new government was to seek support for the concept of the country as a nuclear weapons-free zone (NWFZ). During the Cold War, Soviet forces in Mongolia were equipped with nuclear weapons, and Mongolia had felt that it was threatened because of its links with the Soviet Union by both the West and by the **People's Republic of China (PRC)**. Even with the end of the Cold War, Mongolia still found itself positioned between two nuclear powers, Russia and the PRC.

Against this background, the then Mongolian President, **Punsalmaagiyn Ochir-bat**, in an address to the **United Nations (UN)** General Assembly in September 1992, declared his country's territory nuclear weapons-free, and stated that Mongolia would work to have this status internationally guaranteed. In the following year Mongolia received support for its position first from Russia, then from the PRC and, by the end of the year, from the other declared nuclear powers, and the other permanent members of the UN Security Council, the USA, Britain and France (P5). The **Non-Aligned Movement** also declared its support for the concept. However, while expressing general support, the P5 states were not prepared to go beyond this at first. The main concern expressed was that recognition of a single state as an NWFZ would somehow undermine the concept of regional NWFZs. Eventually, recognizing that Mongolia occupied a special geographical and political position, with no formal links to its neighbours or to military groupings, the P5 did not oppose a 1998 UN General Assembly resolution that noted 'Mongolia's international security and nuclear weapons-free status' (Resolution 53/77/D). Although Mongolia has taken further measures under domestic law to define its status, it has still not been able to persuade the P5 to accept it as an NWFZ and provide security guarantees beyond those contained in the **Nuclear Non-Proliferation Treaty**.

Mongolian People's Revolutionary Party (MPRP)

Mongol Ardyn Huvsgult Nam

Mongolia's oldest political party, which dates from the early 1920s.

The Mongolian People's Revolutionary Party (MPRP) began as the Mongolian People's Party in 1921. It had adopted its present name by 1925. For most of its existence, the MPRP has been a Marxist-Leninist party closely modelled on the Communist Party of the Soviet Union. From its early days until his death in 1952, the chairman of the Council of Ministers, Horlougiyn Choybalsan (1895–1952), dominated the party. Under Choybalsan, the MPRP introduced a one-party state, with a Soviet-style economic system. **Buddhism**, the traditional belief of Mongolians, was suppressed and monasteries were destroyed. Choybalsan's successor, Yumjaagiyn Tsendbal (1916–91), who led the MPRP until 1984, followed the post-Stalin line as carefully as his predecessor had followed **Stalinism**. He was ousted in 1984 and Jambyn Batmonh (1926–97), who had been Premier from 1974, took his place. It fell to Batmonh to handle the upheavals of 1990, but without Soviet backing he could not resist the democratic pressures and quickly abandoned his party and state posts. Gombojavyn Ochirbat (1929–) then became MPRP leader.

The MPRP now set about recreating itself as a democratic party; it even sought to revive its original name but was thwarted because another group had already registered it. Some left but many remained members of the Party, which enjoyed a comeback in the 1992 elections for the **State Great Hural (SGH)**, with its candidates sweeping all before them. However, this victory was reversed in the 1996 elections, when the MPRP once again found itself out of office. In 1997 **Natsagyn Bagabandi** became MPRP chairman, but following his election as state President in June 1997 he was succeeded by Nambaryn Enhbayar (1958–). In 2000 Enhbayar led the MPRP to victory in elections to the SGH and became Prime Minister. Enhbayar, who was partly educated in Britain and claims to admire Tony Blair, the British Prime Minister, attempted to modernize the MPRP. Despite these efforts, the Party fared badly in elections held in June 2004, losing 35 seats to a coalition of opposition democratic parties. Eventually the MPRP entered into a coalition government, but Enhbayar was no longer Prime Minister, although he did become speaker of the Hural.

Chair.: Nambaryn Enhbayar
Address: MPRP
         Baga Toiru 37/1
         Ulaan Baatar 11
         Mongolia

Tel: 976-11-321626
Fax: 976-11-32164
E-mail: admin@mprp.mn
Internet: www.mprp.mn

Mongolian Stock Exchange

The Mongolian Stock Exchange is defined as a profit-making, state-owned share-holding company.

Established in **Ulaan Baatar** in January 1991 as part of the first wave of economic reform in Mongolia, the Stock Exchange has steadily grown in importance with increasing privatization. In 1992 it began primary market trading. Two years later a Securities Law and the Mongolian Securities Commission, founded in November 1994, were introduced. A Security Dealers and Brokers Association followed in July 1995, and security market trading started in August 1995. In 1998 the Mongolian Stock Exchange joined the Federation of Euro-Asian Stock Exchanges as a full member. A major reorganization in March 2003 led to the emergence of two independent bodies, the Mongolian Stock Exchange and the Securities Clearing House and Central Depository.

Address: Mongolian Stock Exchange
Sukhbaatar Sq. 2
Ulaan Baatar
Mongolia
Tel: 976-11-321315
Fax: 976-11-325170
E-mail: mse@mongol.net
Internet: www.mse.mon

Mongol(s)

The people of Mongolia, and members of minority nationalities in the **People's Republic of China (PRC)** and in several republics of the Russian Federation. The population of Mongolia at the 2000 census was 2,365,269, excluding 8,128 foreign citizens. Of that population, 81.5%—1,934,700—belonged to the majority Mongol ethnic group, the Halh or Khalkha. Other ethnic groups are the Oirat or West Mongols living in the western regions of the country (9.5% of the total population); the **Kazak**, a Turkic people settled in the far west of Mongolia (4.3%); and the Buryat (1.4%), who live along the northern border. The Mongol population in the PRC numbered 4,802,400 in the 1990 population census, living mostly in the **Inner Mongolia** Autonomous Region but also in **Xinjiang** and Gansu and Qinghai Provinces to the west of Inner Mongolia, in **Tibet**, in Liaoning, Jilin and Heilongjiang Provinces to the east of Inner Mongolia, and in Hebei and Henan Provinces to the south. There is even a small community of 6,000 in the south-western province of Yunnan, who claim to be the descendants of Mongol armies that invaded the area in 1253. The large territory over which the Mongols were scattered in **China** has led to distinctions between Mongol groups and variations in their language. Several much smaller ethnic groups are also of Mongol origin.

The Mongolian language belongs to the Altaic family and has remote links with the Turkic languages. Forms of Mongolian are spoken by around 6m. people inside and outside Mongolia. Halh Mongolian is the country's national literary language. Dialects of it are spoken in the various parts of the country. A number of scripts, some ancient, some quite recent, were devised over time for the written language, including a Latin script used experimentally in Mongolia in the 1930s alongside the older Mongolian script. The Mongolian script is said to have derived from **Uygur** script, introduced in the 12th century, which underwent subsequent modifications. It was ousted in 1941 in Mongolia, when Cyrillic script was made the official medium for the written language. Mongolian script is still used by Mongols in China; attempts have been made since 1990 to reintroduce it in Mongolia, but so far with little success, and Cyrillic script remains in use there.

In the past the Mongols practised **shamanism**, but in the 13th century accepted Lama **Buddhism**. The Kazak minority in Mongolia is Muslim.

The origins of the Mongols have not been precisely determined, though it is clear that they belonged to the nomadic herding tribes that roamed over the grasslands of what are now Mongolia and Siberia. They themselves claim descent from the Huns, whose raids penetrated as far as Europe in the 4th and 5th centuries AD. United under Ghenghis Khan in 1206, the Mongols subdued the Southern Song dynasty in China in 1276 and ruled over that country as the Yuan dynasty until 1368. They also mounted successive invasions throughout the 13th century that allowed them to conquer great stretches of Asia as far west as the present-day Caucasus and Middle East and took them into the **Korean peninsula** and into south-east Asia. They were driven back north by the Ming dynasty from the late 14th century; but in the course of the 17th century submitted first to the neighbouring **Manzhou** tribe, then to the Qing emperor, under which name the Manzhou ruled China until 1911. Under Qing control, Mongol territory was divided into Inner Mongolia, south of the Gobi desert, and Outer Mongolia, which followed a separate path after 1911, evolving eventually into the modern state of Mongolia.

Within the Russian Federation, two republics, the Kalmyk Republic north-west of the Caspian Sea, and the Altay Republic on the north-western border of Mongolia, have sizeable populations of Oirat Mongols. The Kalmyk are descended from Oirat who moved west in the 17th century to escape Manzhou domination and settled on the lower reaches of the Volga river. Some returned to Mongolia, but those who remained found themselves eventually absorbed into the Soviet Union with the status of an Autonomous Soviet Socialist Republic. During the Second World War they lost their autonomy and were scattered to other parts of the Soviet Union as punishment for allegedly having collaborated with the occupying German forces;

but in 1957 regained their autonomous status. Following the collapse of the Soviet Union in 1991 the Kalmyk took the title of republic. Around 45%—174,000—of the republic's population are Kalmyk, of whom 10% still speak Mongolian. The population still adheres to Lama Buddhism. The Oirat Mongols in the Altay Republic form around one-third of the population. They are Turkic-speaking herdsmen, but their way of life is still Mongolian.

The Tuva Republic on the northern border of Mongolia originally formed part of Outer Mongolia, but passed under Russian control in 1914 and was finally taken into the Soviet Union in 1944 and made an Autonomous Socialist Soviet Republic in 1961. It became the Tuva Republic in the early 1990s. The Tuvan are a Turkic people found also in northern Mongolia. They follow the Mongols in their religion, Lama Buddhism, and in their lifestyle and occupation as herdsmen. The Buryat minority within Mongolia is related to the Buryat element—around one-third—of the population of the Buryat Republic also on the northern border of the country. With the fall of the Soviet Union in 1991 the Buryat-Mongol People's Party within the Buryat Republic started to press for union with Mongolia, but appears to have made no progress towards this aim. In 1992 Mongolia concluded bilateral agreements with the Altay, Buryat, Kalmyk and Tuva republics to promote economic and cultural agreements.

MONTSAME

The official Mongolian News Agency.

Owned by the government, the Agency dates from 1921. In the Soviet period it maintained close links with the Novosti and TASS agencies, and later worked closely with Mongolian State Radio and Television. Since 1990, however, it has operated as a wholly independent agency. It currently has 120 staff in all fields, and maintains overseas correspondents in eight capitals, including **Beijing**, Berlin, Moscow and Washington, DC. It also has an extensive network of links to other news agencies. Foreign news bulletins appear daily in Russian and English, and the agency publishes a number of magazines, in English, Russian and Chinese. MONTSAME is a member of the Organization of Asia-Pacific News Agencies and of the Non-Aligned News Agency Organizations. Since 1997 MONTSAME has been accessible online.

Address: MONTSAME News Agency
  Jigjid St, 8
  Ulaan Baatar
  POB 1541
  Mongolia
Fax: 976-11 327857
E-mail: montame@magicnet.mn
Internet: www.montsame.mn

Mount Paektu

Paektu-san

Mount Paektu (sometimes also spelled Paekdu) is, at 2,750 m, the highest mountain on the **Korean peninsula**, part of the Changbaek range. It is volcanic in origin, and last erupted in the first half of the 11th century. Lake Chon occupies the former crater. The **Yalu river** (Amnok) flows westward from Paektu, and the **Tumen river** flows eastwards. Traditionally, the mountain is associated with Tangun, the mythical founder of the Korean nation, and with other myths. Since 1712 the border between **China** and Korea has run along the summit. Maps produced today in the Democratic People's Republic of Korea and in the Republic of Korea show the whole of the mountain as Korean. Maps produced in the **People's Republic of China (PRC)** show the traditional border, but the dispute is not thought to be active. Access is generally easier from the PRC side. Mount Paektu is associated with the anti-Japanese guerrilla activities of **Kim Il Sung**, and it is also claimed to be the birthplace of his son and successor, **Kim Jong Il**.

Murayama Tomiichi

In June 1994 Murayama Tomiichi became Japan's first Socialist Prime Minister since 1947.

Murayama was born in 1924. He was active in local politics until he entered the House of Representatives of the **National Diet** in 1972 as a member of the Japan Socialist Party (JSP—now the **Social Democratic Party of Japan**). In 1993 he became chairman of the JSP following its failure at the July 1993 elections. In the following year the collapse of **Hosokawa Morihiro**'s coalition led the **Liberal Democratic Party (LDP)** to seek a deal with the JSP, whereby Murayama would become Prime Minister in a coalition government. Although in theory at opposite ends of the political spectrum, both parties were anxious to defend their respective interests, and the agreement was successful.

Murayama was Prime Minister from June 1994 until January 1996, when he stepped down in favour of the LDP's Hashimoto. Murayama had some successes as Prime Minister. He managed the difficult 50th anniversary of the end of the **Pacific War** well, issuing a clearer apology than his predecessors had done. He also abandoned the JSP's long-standing opposition to the **Self-Defence Forces** and to the US-Japan Security Treaty, although in the process he damaged the JSP irreversibly. Murayama remained active in politics after his resignation, finally retiring from the Diet in 2000.

N

Nagasaki

City in western Japan and the capital of the prefecture of the same name.

Nagasaki, a city with a population of some 421,000 and an area of 241 sq km, is an important shipbuilding, fishing, and tourist centre. It first began to develop as a port after the arrival of the Portuguese in 1571, and until the introduction of the **closed country policy** in the early 17th century it was an important centre of **Catholic Christianity**. From 1636 the city became the only place in Japan where foreigners could reside, with a substantial Chinese community, some of whose members had a distinct influence on Japanese traditional arts such as calligraphy and ink drawing. There was also a Dutch minority, who were confined to the artificial island of Deshima created in the harbour.

In the 1850s Nagasaki was one of the Japanese ports opened to foreign trade, which led to the establishment of a **foreign settlement**. Two other foreign settlements, **Yokohama** and, later, **Kobe**, both overshadowed Nagasaki, which remained small, though nearby coal mines and the establishment of Japan's first modern shipyards in 1865 gave the city some importance in the mid-19th century. The discovery in 1872 of a small Christian community that had survived the persecutions of the 17th century revived foreign interest in Nagasaki for a time, but by the early 20th century it had become a backwater. The Urakami Catholic Church, built in the 1870s, survives from that period.

Nagasaki once more came to the world's attention on 9 August 1945, when the second atomic bomb was dropped over the city. This was more powerful than that used at **Hiroshima**, but the damage was not so great because of the local terrain. Nevertheless, some 60,000–70,000 of the city's total population of 200,000 were killed, and the devastation was enormous. Nagasaki eventually recovered, but the city's Peace Park, located near the epicentre of the bomb, remains an important place of pilgrimage.

Naha

The capital of **Okinawa** prefecture in Japan, Naha is a city of some 311,000 people. It was formerly the capital of the Ryukyu kingdom, and the centre of the US administration from 1945 until 1972. Little of historic Naha remained after a bombing raid on 10 October 1944. Today it is the chief industrial city of Okinawa.

Nakasone Yasuhiro

Prime Minister of Japan in 1982–87, and an important figure in Japanese politics since the end of the **Pacific War**.

Nakasone Yasuhiro was born in Gunma Prefecture in 1918. He attended Tokyo Imperial University, and on graduation joined the Home Ministry. During the Pacific War he served in the Imperial Japanese Navy. He made a brief return to the bureaucracy after Japan's defeat, but in 1947 he entered the **National Diet** for a Gunma constituency that he would represent until 2003. Early in his career he began to argue for reform of the Japanese Constitution in defence matters. From 1959 onwards he held a series of ministerial posts, in which he established a reputation as a radical. With the backing of former Prime Minister **Tanaka Kakuei**, he became Prime Minister in 1982.

Nakasone initiated a radical programme that included privatization of Japan National Railways, changes in the post and telecommunications system, and modifications in Japan's defence position. He established a higher international profile than had been usual with Japanese Prime Ministers, especially with US President Ronald Reagan and British Prime Minister Margaret Thatcher. Domestically, however, he suffered a set-back over his refusal to accept that the **Ainu** and other groups constituted genuine minorities. He resigned from the premiership in 1987 as his popularity steadily declined after it was revealed that his government intended to introduce a value added tax. He then handed over the premiership to Takeshita Noboru; three years later, after the Recruit scandal, his faction passed to Watanabe Michio.

Nampo

Formerly known as Chinnampo, Nampo is the principal port on the west coast of the Democratic People's Republic of Korea (DPRK). It is also the port for the country's capital, **Pyongyang**.

Nampo's population currently numbers around 700,000, and there are road and rail links to the capital. Developed during the Japanese colonial period, the city and the port suffered heavy damage during the **Korean War**. Since the economic difficulties of the 1990s, Nampo has been one of the main centres for the arrival of supplies for the World Food Programme's assistance to the DPRK. Nampo has regular connections with Chinese ports, and, although not widely publicized, a weekly container service to and from the port of Inchon in the Republic of Korea. There are currently plans to expand its capacity to take containers. Some 20 km from Nampo city is the **West Sea Barrage**.

Nanjing

Capital of Jiangsu Province in the **People's Republic of China**. The city has also been the capital of **China** on a number of occasions, most recently under the **Republic of China (1912–1949)** between 1928 and 1949. It is the burial place of Dr Sun Yat-sen, founder of the **'Republic of China'**, and his mausoleum is one of the many tourist sites in the city. It was the capital of the 19th century Taiping Rebellion, and the scene of a massacre by Japanese troops in 1937 at the outbreak of the Sino–Japanese War. Nanjing is an important transportation hub and an industrial centre, producing electronics, automobiles and chemicals. In the past it was famous for a special type of yellow cloth, which became known as *nankeen* after the city. It is also an important educational centre. Today the city has some 5.2m. inhabitants and covers an area of 6,516 sq km.

National Assembly (Republic of Korea)

Daehanminkuk Kukhui

The National Assembly of the Republic of Korea (ROK) is now a single-chamber legislature. It came into existence as a Constituent Assembly in June 1948, following the general elections held in May of that year under the supervision and sponsorship of the **United Nations** Temporary Commission on Korea. Of the 300-member assembly, 198 were from mainland South Korea, each representing 100,000 constituents. Elections could not be held on **Cheju Island**, which was in a state of rebellion, until May 1949; then two members were elected there. One hundred seats, allocated for North Korea, remained vacant. The Constituent Assembly had a two-year term of office that commenced on 31 May 1949. It elected Dr **Syngman Rhee** as its chairman, and on 12 July it adopted a constitution for the ROK. The Constituent Assembly acted as an electoral college as well as a legislative assembly. In accordance with the Constitution, the Assembly elected Rhee as President and Yi Si-Yong as Vice-President for four-year terms of office.

In May 1950 a second general election was held, a new legislative National Assembly of 210 members was established, and the term of office of each assemblyman was extended to four years. It remained a single-house legislature until July 1960, when a bicameral legislature was briefly established. This lasted only until 16 May 1961, when, following a military coup, it was dissolved.

In November 1963 the Assembly re-emerged as a unicameral legislative assembly. The seventh constitutional amendment in 1972 introduced a new system. A 'National Conference for Unification', upon the nomination of the President, appointed 73 of the Assembly's 219 members. Thus, one-third of the total number of seats of the ninth, 10th and 11th National Assemblies were occupied by members of the *Yujonghoe* ('Political Fraternal Society for Revitalizing Reform'), a political group closely associated with the ruling **Democratic Republican Party**. With the fall of the Fourth Republic in 1979, this system was abolished.

In October 1980 the 'Legislative Council for National Security', appointed by the President, replaced the National Assembly. In the following year a new Assembly replaced this Council. The selection of candidates continued to be through a mixture of direct elections and proportional representation.

Today the National Assembly has a speaker, two vice-speakers, 16 standing committees, and a secretariat. It holds one regular session per year (up to 100 days), extraordinary sessions (up to 30 days), and occasional special sessions requested by the President. The 17th National Assembly elections were held in April 2004.

Address: National Assembly
Yeouido-dong
Yeoungdeungpo-gu
Seoul
Republic of Korea
Tel: 82-2-788-3804
Fax: 82-2-788-3375
E-mail: info@assembly.go.kr
Internet: www.assembly.go.kr

National Congress for New Politics (NCNP)

Sae jungchi kukmin hoiee

The National Congress (sometimes Council) for New Politics (NCNP) was a short-lived political party founded by veteran Republic of Korea opposition leader, **Kim Dae-Jung,** on his return from self-imposed exile in Great Britain in 1993, and which brought Kim to the presidency in 1997. In 2000 the party changed its name to the **Millennium Democratic Party**.

National Diet (Japan)

Kokkai

Japan's first modern constitution provided for an Imperial Diet (*Teikoku gikai*), which met for the first time in December 1890. The Imperial Diet had a House of Representatives of 300 members elected by a limited suffrage at first, and then by universal male suffrage from 1925; and a House of Peers, the number of whose members eventually rose to more than 400, comprising members of the imperial family, nobles and representatives of high tax payers. The authority of the Imperial Diet was very limited, even at the height of its power in the 1920s, and disappeared almost entirely as Japan prepared for war in the 1930s. The National Diet never-theless enacted legislation during the **Allied Occupation of Japan** in 1945–47.

Under the 1947 Constitution the Diet became the National Assembly, or *Kokkai*, deriving its authority from the people and not the **Japanese Emperor**. It is the highest organ of state and the sole legislative authority. The Cabinet is responsible to the Diet.

There are two houses, both elected by all citizens over 20 years of age. The House of Representatives (*shugiin*), the lower house, whose term is four years, has had 480 members since 2000 and is the more powerful of the two. Since 1994 members have been elected under a system of part direct election and part proportionate representation. Members of the House of Councillors (*sangiin*), the upper house, total 252—one-half of them are elected every three years— and serve six-year terms. A mixed direct election and proportionate representation system is also in operation for the House of Councillors.

The National Diet Building (*Kokkai gijido*), construction of which began in 1920 and was completed in 1936, is a Western-style building. As well as the National Diet, the complex also includes the National Diet Library, the national depository, created in 1948 after the model of the US Library of Congress.

Address: House of Representatives
       1-7-1 Nagato-cho
       Chiyoda-ku
       Tokyo 100-8961
       Japan
Tel: 81-3-3581-5111
E-mail: webmaster@shugiin.go.jp
Internet: www.shugiin.go.jp

       House of Councillors
       1-7-1 Nagato-cho
       Chiyoda-ku
       Tokyo 100-8961
       Japan
Tel: 81-3-3581-3111
E-mail: webmaster@sangiin.go.jp
Internet: www.sangiin.go.jp

National People's Congress (NPC)

Quanguo renmin daibiao dahui

The parliament of the **People's Republic of China**.

The National People's Congress (NPC) dates from 1954. It has a five-year term, but during the **Cultural Revolution** (1966–76) the NPC did not meet from January 1965 until January 1975. The first NPC had 1,226 delegates; the highest number of delegates was 3,497 for the fifth meeting, held in March 1978. The current, 10th NPC has 2,985 delegates, elected indirectly by local People's Congresses throughout the country. The last NPC elections took place between December 2002 and February 2003; elections are next due towards the end of 2007–early 2008. The

NPC meets for a short period each year. Between meetings a Standing Committee performs the functions of the NPC. The NPC in theory chooses the President, Vice-President, chairman of the **Central Military Commission**, the president of the Supreme Court, and the head of the Supreme People's Procurate. In practice, the NPC follows the guidance of the **Chinese Communist Party (CCP)**. In voting for the President in March 2003, for example, 2,937 voted for **Hu Jintao**, four voted against, four abstained, and 38 did not vote. The NPC is also the legislative body, but here too it follows CCP guidance. The NPC joined the **Inter-Parliamentary Union** in 1984.

> *Chair. of the Standing Committee:* Wu Bangguo
> *Address:* National People's Congress
> Great Hall of the People
> Tiananmen Sq.
> Beijing 100805
> People's Republic of China
> *Tel:* 86-10-6309-9519
> *Fax:* 86-10-6309-7914
> *E-mail:* fab@npc.gov.cn
> *Internet:* www.npc.gov.cn

New Community Movement

Saemaul undong

Republic of Korea President **Park Chung-Hee** launched the New Community Movement in 1972, as a means of modernizing rural society.

The aim was not only to improve the living environment of rural dwellers, but also to improve educational standards, and to increase rural incomes so as to prevent rural jealousy of urban development. To do this, rural communities were encouraged to work together to transform their villages. At first, the main emphasis was on environmental improvement, through projects such as the cleaning of villages, sanitation works, housing renovation, and reconstruction of roads and waterways. Between 1972 and 1984 24m. people from 36,000 villages took part in some 18,600 projects. After 1973 the emphasis shifted in the rural areas to the promotion of income-generating enterprises. At the same time, the Movement spread to include the urban sector and schools in a comprehensive national regeneration reform movement.

The Movement was always a means of building support for the government, and under President **Chun Doo-Hwan** (President 1981–87) this aspect became more prominent, especially when he appointed his younger brother, Chun Kyong-Hwan, as the Movement's secretary-general. The Movement also suffered because the younger Chun was widely regarded as corrupt. Under Chun, it also became an instrument of foreign aid, with the launch in 1984 of a training scheme, 'Saemaul for foreigners'. With the steady decline of the rural population, and many other outlets for **Koreans**, the international training aspect has grown in importance.

Although it is far less important in rural areas than in the past, the Movement still exists, a second phase having been formally launched in December 1998. Its aims were then redefined as revitalizing the country, constructing a sound society, providing a good environment, preparing for reunification, and working for international co-operation.

New Korea Democratic Party (NKDP)
Shin Hanguk minjudang

In November 1984 the government removed from a political blacklist all but 19 former political leaders in the Republic of Korea. In January 1985 politicians who had regained their civil rights launched the New Korea Democratic Party (NKDP). Yi Min-Woo became the NKDP's president, and **Kim Young-Sam** was one of its key leaders. **Kim Dae-Jung**, who returned from exile in the USA in February 1985, agreed to serve as adviser to the party's president. The NKDP became the main opposition party to the **Democratic Justice Party** and the Government of President **Chun Doo-Hwan.** In 1986 it launched a nation-wide movement for constitutional revision. However, the NKDP suffered badly when, in May 1987, Kim Young-Sam broke away to form his own Reunification Democratic Party (RDP), which Kim Dae-Jung joined in August. The NKDP then steadily dissolved as members left it to join either the RDP or the new Party for Peace and Democracy that Kim Dae-Jung formed in November 1987.

New Party
Hsintang/Xindang

Political party formed in 1993 in **Taiwan**. The party first named itself the 'Chinese New Party' and was the result of a split within the **Kuomintang (KMT)** between the main body and the New Kuomintang Alliance faction. The Alliance broke with the KMT out of fear that, under its chairman **Lee Teng-Hui**, the party was abandoning its commitment to reunification with mainland China. Later in 1993 the New Party merged with another small group, the China Social Democratic Party. In the mid-1990s it gained support from sections of the KMT and even from some government ministers. Its programme, as currently presented, suggests that it is following a middle way in which it both advocates co-operation with the KMT and the **Democratic Progressive Party** in negotiations with the **People's Republic of China**; and calls for maintenance of security in the Taiwan Straits and modernization of the island's defence systems. The Party's initial attraction does not seem to have endured, especially as it came to be associated too closely with the mainland Chinese settled in Taiwan. It has also lost supporters since 2000 to the **People First Party** and to the KMT. It contested the presidential elections held in 2000 and secured a single seat in elections held in 2001 for the **Legislative Yuan**. In municipal elections held in 2002 the New Party won five seats on the **Taipei** city council. It is usually placed in the **Pan-Blue coalition**.

Chair.: Hao Long-bin
Address: 4th Floor
          65 Guangfuh South Rd
          Taipei
          Taiwan
Tel: 886 2 2756 2222
Fax: 886 2 2756 5750
E-mail: npncs@ms2.hinet.net
Internet: www.np.org.tw

New religions

A wide range of religious organizations often termed syncretic, since they draw their beliefs from a variety of sources, generally established religions but also folk religion, spiritualism and the occult, onto which new beliefs may be grafted. They function outside of traditional religious structures such as temples, shrines and churches. Both Japan and the **Korean peninsula** have produced a number of new religions over the past two centuries, and some have also emanated from **China**. The largest vie with older established religious communities in terms of numbers and organization, while others may be no more than a large congregation grouped around a preacher. In these three East Asian countries the principal sources for the new religions have been **Buddhism**, **Daoism**, **Shinto** (in Japan), **Confucianism**, Christianity, **shamanism** and ancestor worship.

Despite enormous variations in inspiration, style and functioning, which make generalization difficult, observers have suggested a few common elements among the new religions: a concern with spiritual self-cultivation and accumulation of spiritual merit that will allow one to achieve harmonious relations with the rest of society and cope with an uncertain world; a preoccupation with the healing of sickness; and, sometimes, the promise of acquisition of supernatural abilities. These new groups often draw the support of sections of society that may feel debarred from access to worldly or material power, such as women or the economically disadvantaged. Some cults are apocalyptic, predicting cataclysms that only the members of the sect can avoid or survive. The founders or leaders of new religions are often charismatic men or women. Some have experienced a form of mental or 'spiritual' sickness involving a divine vision that has prompted them to their mission. The majority of new religions have, politically and socially, been conservative and even nationalistic, but in the past, as in Japan and Korea, some of them have collided with prescriptive state religions and policies. The separation of state and religion in post-war East Asian societies has made it easier for new religions to flourish unless they engage in socially harmful activities, as **Aum Shinrikyo** did in Japan in 1994–95.

In Japan more than 3,000 new religions, with combined membership of 30m.–40m., were identified in the early 1990s, of which about 15 were estimated to have more than 3m. members each. Some were older churches or movements established in the first half of the 19th century; others began in the first half of the 20th century, such as the influential Buddhist-inspired lay movement Soka Gakkai (1930), which in 1964 created the **Clean Government Party** (*Komeito*). In the period since 1945 and the defeat of Japan new religions have burgeoned, encouraged in part by the move from the land and the rural base of Buddhism and Shinto to urban life. Some of the new religions have turned from the communal pattern of older new religions, which sought to provide a supportive structure for their members, to a more individualistic approach. These groups proselytize vigorously both within Japan and abroad.

The Republic of Korea (ROK) has inherited the older Korean tradition of new religions. The only syncretic religion to have survived in the Democratic People's Republic of Korea (DPRK) is **Chondo-gyo**, formed in 1905 with a nationalistic element from the earlier Donghak or 'eastern learning', itself founded to resist the 'western learning' of **Catholic Christianity**. In the north Chondo-gyo functions as a political party as well as a religion. The Chondo-gyo church has about 15,000 adherents in the DPRK and around 845,000 in the ROK. After the **Korean War** several charismatic religions arose in the ROK, often placing an emphasis on healing and salvation. Among those to have survived are the Yoido Full Gospel Church, founded in 1958, and the **Unification Church**, established in 1954. Many more exist, and Korean missionaries from these churches are active abroad. As many as 1,000 new missionaries are reportedly sent overseas each year. Their presence has been noted in the **People's Republic of China (PRC)**, in south-east Asia and in the Gulf and Middle East in recent conflicts there. They are reported to be targeting Muslim countries, despite intense hostility and bans on attempting the conversion of Muslims.

The generally orderly diversity that prevails in Japan and the ROK might well obtain in the PRC if the Chinese state adopted a less restrictive position on religious groups. Churches and temples are required to register, but this measure appears to be matched by the growth of what is termed 'illegal religious activity'. There has been a profusion of Christian churches, both registered and unauthorized, and a similar rise in the number of irregular groups. Their beliefs are often syncretic, combining folk religion, evangelical Christianity and faith-healing (the latter popular at a time when the state's health provision no longer covers sections of the population), and their practices can be unorthodox, even violent. Other groups have turned to indigenous religious practices and to traditional *qigong*, a combination of mental and physical exercises. A relative relaxation in political controls since 1977, together with the dislocating effects of economic restructuring and social change, may account in part for this resort to religion. There is a long history in

China both of heterodox sects and of state attempts to control them for fear of social disruption. The PRC government's harsh approach is not new. Its great fear is of possible foreign influences and of people acting outside of its control, as it claims members of the **Falungong** movement have done in recent years. Meanwhile, a situation exists in which a few large religions are permitted to function against the background of a multiplicity of smaller unauthorized groups of which the state may have little knowledge.

New Tokyo International Airport

Shin Tokyo kokusai kuko

This airport, now generally known as Narita airport, has long been the subject of controversy, even before it became **Tokyo**'s main international airport after it opened in May 1978.

Narita, which replaced the former Tokyo International Airport at Haneda, is 66 km east of Tokyo's centre and the airport has been controversial from the planning stage. Passengers complain that it is too far from the city centre, even though there are good train and bus services from the airport to the centre. In addition, there has been a long-running dispute between the airport authorities and local farmers, who have maintained a constant barrage of protest over the loss of their land and inadequate consultation. Radical groups have also joined in the dispute, in support of the farmers. Even before the attacks that took place in New York on 11 September 2001 the airport was noted for the strictness of its security procedures. Since then these have become even more obtrusive.

Nikkei Index

This is Japan's leading Stock Exchange Index, and like the **Hang Seng Index** in **Hong Kong** it is known and quoted world-wide. Produced by Japan's leading economic journal, *Nihon Keizei Shinmun*, it was initiated in September 1950. It is currently based on 225 leading stocks traded on the Tokyo Stock Exchange. Its peak, of 38,915.87 points, was reached on 29 December 1989.

Nogun-ri massacre

Site of a massacre perpetrated during the **Korean War**.

In October 1999 newly declassified documents from US archives, released after enquiries by investigative journalists, appeared to confirm long-standing reports that, in late July 1950, during the early stages of the Korean War, US forces had carried out a massacre at the village of Nogun-ri in the Republic of Korea's (ROK) South Kyongsang Province. Former US soldiers who came forward to testify provided further evidence, though some of this testimony was later shown to be inaccurate. The Nogun-ri material led to many similar allegations about the conduct of both the ROK and the US forces, and both launched inquiries, which have generally proved inconclusive. In January 2001 the then US President Bill Clinton expressed regret over the incident, while not admitting any blame. The allegations have added to anti-US feeling in the ROK.

Non-Aligned Movement (NAM)

International grouping of states and liberation movements.

The Non-Aligned Movement (NAM), a reaction to the Cold War between the West and the Communist bloc, traces its origins to the regional Asia-Africa Conference held in Bandung, Indonesia, in 1955. This gathering of the leaders of 29 countries examined ways of retaining their independence in the face of pressure from the great powers. Moving from a regional to an international scope, based on the acceptance of shared principles, the first NAM conference of 25 states was held in 1961 in Belgrade, the capital of former Yugoslavia, itself committed to independence from Soviet control. The Movement thereafter met regularly. The NAM was popular with developing countries and with countries newly achieving independence from colonial rule. By 1992, however, when the NAM met in Jakarta, Indonesia, it was clear that the end of the Cold War had weakened former alliances and entrenched positions. The Movement now concentrates much of its effort on the restructuring of the global economic order and maintains links with **United Nations (UN)** agencies and other international and regional groups and organizations. Its activities are largely administered through the foreign ministry and the permanent mission to the UN at New York of the state currently holding the rotating chairmanship of the Movement.

The membership of the NAM now comprises 115 countries. Within East Asia the Democratic People's Republic of Korea and Mongolia are members.

Address: Department of Foreign Affairs
Republic of South Africa
Internet: www.nam.gov.za

Northern Territories dispute

'Northern Territories' is the term that the Japanese use in English to describe the southernmost islands of the **Kurile Islands** chain. According to the Japanese, these islands, Etorofu, Kunashiri, Shikotan and Habomai, were not part of the Kurile Islands proper, but had always been Japanese territory.

Under the terms of the **San Francisco Peace Treaty**, Japan renounced its claim to the Kurile Islands, which the Soviet Union had occupied since 1945, but the islands were not formally assigned to the Soviet Union because it was not a party to the Peace Treaty. When Japan and the Soviet Union began negotiations on a possible peace treaty in 1955, the Japanese raised the issue of the return of the islands. The Soviet Union offered to return Shikotan and Habomai, but when the Japanese insisted on the return of all four islands, the offer was withdrawn. Therefore, although Japan and the Soviet Union reached agreement on the establishment of diplomatic relations, there was no peace treaty between the two sides.

The dispute has never been resolved. Although the Soviet Union maintained that the islands were not Japanese, in 1964 a group of Japanese were able to visit graves on the islands. Because of a dispute over procedures for visiting, this arrangement was halted almost immediately and did not resume until 1986. Since then such visits have continued without interruption. After the then Soviet President Mikhail Gorbachev visited Japan in 1991, further people-to-people exchanges took place.

The Northern Territories issue remains on the political agenda in Japan, and various right-wing groups have used it to attack successive Japanese governments. However, the number of former residents of the islands, who once formed a strong pressure group, is now diminishing with age. In November 2004 the Russian foreign minister offered to reopen discussions with Japan on the issue in advance of a planned visit by Russian President Putin to Japan.

Nuclear Non-Proliferation Treaty (NPT)

The Nuclear Non-Proliferation Treaty (NPT) dates from 1968, and has been signed and ratified by the majority of the world's states. It entered into force in 1970.

The NPT makes a distinction between declared nuclear weapons states and non-nuclear weapons states; the latter may have nuclear power for peaceful purposes but undertake not to develop nuclear weapons. To this end, they are required to sign an agreement with the **International Atomic Energy Agency (IAEA)** under which they agree to accept IAEA safeguards on all nuclear material at all of their nuclear establishments. This is to verify that there is no diversion of such material for weapons use. The nuclear weapons states, the **People's Republic of China (PRC)**, France, Russia, the United Kingdom and the USA, have safeguards agreements with the IAEA that cover their civilian nuclear programmes only. Apart from the PRC, in East Asia only the **'Republic of China'** on **Taiwan** has not ratified and acceded to the NPT, but the Democratic People's Republic of Korea, which signed the NPT in 1985 and concluded a safeguards agreement in 1992, announced its withdrawal from the treaty in January 2003.

O

Ochirbat, Punsalmaagiyn (P. Ochirbat)

P. Ochirbat was the last communist and the first post-communist President of the Republic of Mongolia.

Born in 1942, Ochirbat was a member of the **Mongolian People's Revolutionary Party**, the ruling party before 1990. After Mongolia asserted its independence from the Soviet Union and became a multi-party democracy, the **State Great Hural (SGH**—National Assembly) elected Ochirbat as President after the July 1990 elections. In the country's first direct presidential election, held in 1993, Ochirbat stood again, but this time as the candidate of the Mongolian National Democratic Party, and won with a 58% majority. However, Mongolia's growing economic and social problems, and the government's austerity programme, led to dissatisfaction with the post-1990 politicians. In 1997 Ochirbat lost the presidential election to **Natsagin Bagabandi**, the former chairman of the SGH, and retired from politics.

Offshore islands

When the **Kuomintang (KMT)** fled from the Chinese mainland to **Taiwan** in 1949, they held on to various groups of small islands along the coast. These included Quemoy (Jinmen in *pinyin*; Kinmen and Chinmen are also found), a group of islands in Xiamen (Amoy) Bay, and Matsu (Mazu), both off the coast of Fujian Province, and the Tachen (Dazhen) Islands further north, off the Zhejiang coast. The argument for keeping these various sets of islands was that they would provide bases from which to recapture the Chinese mainland. During the **Korean War** the **People's Republic of China (PRC)** could not take the islands because the US Seventh Fleet, which patrolled the Taiwan Straits to prevent either a PRC attack on Taiwan or a KMT attack on the PRC, protected them.

However, in February 1953 US President Eisenhower ended this arrangement, and the KMT began reinforcing the islands, with a view to launching an attack on the PRC. In August 1954 several thousand troops were moved to the islands, which appears to have provoked **Zhou Enlai**, the PRC Premier and foreign minister, into announcing that Taiwan must be liberated. PRC artillery then began to fire on Quemoy, and in November PRC aircraft bombed the Tachen Islands. The USA, which still recognized the **'Republic of China'** as the legitimate government of **China**, then concluded a Mutual Defence Treaty with it in December 1954. This was followed by the 'Formosa resolution' of January 1955, which pledged US support for the defence not only of Taiwan but also of the offshore islands. The Chinese responded in February 1955 with increased pressure on the Tachen Islands, leading to the complete evacuation of the group's military and civil population with US naval assistance, and their takeover by the PRC on 14 February 1955. The Chinese bombardments of the other islands continued; the USA responded with threats of a nuclear attack. This may have led to Soviet pressure on the PRC to end the crisis, for the shelling stopped in May 1955, and some months later the PRC released a number of captured US airmen.

In the following years the KMT steadily reinforced their garrisons on Quemoy and Matsu, deploying newly acquired US weapons on the islands. This seems to have been one factor behind a Chinese decision to renew attacks on the islands in 1958. Another was a generally harder stance on many issues after the **Sino–Soviet dispute** and the (domestic) Great Leap Forward had begun. The islands were subjected to heavy shelling in August–October 1958, in an apparent attempt to cut them off from Taiwan. The USA threatened to intervene, which prompted the Soviet Union to announced in turn that it would view any attack on the PRC as an act of war. The PRC, having realized that it could not prevent the KMT from supplying the islands, and perhaps under Soviet pressure, then ended the artillery attack.

Tension over the islands did not end then, however. Until 1969 the KMT launched small attacks on the mainland from the islands, and until 1979 both sides fired shells filled with propaganda leaflets at each other on alternate days. The PRC then stopped, and the KMT followed soon after. Until the 1990s the islands remained heavily fortified military outposts, and were off limits to ordinary visitors from Taiwan. Matsu, which is further off the mainland, still has some military presence, but Quemoy is now fully civilianized. Both have become popular tourist destinations, with links to the mainland.

Ogasawara Islands

A group of volcanic islands located some 1,000 km south of Japan's capital, **Tokyo**, currently administered by the Tokyo city government. They are generally known in the West as the Bonin Islands. In the 19th century a motley group of Westerners and Japanese lived on the islands, and in 1876 the Japanese government annexed them. After the **Pacific War** the USA administered them until they reverted to Japanese administration in 1968.

Okada Katsuya

President of the **Democratic Party of Japan (DPJ)**.

Okada followed the classic **Liberal Democratic Party (LDP)** pattern of political life until the brief eclipse of the Party in the early 1990s. He was born in Mie

Prefecture in 1953, and graduated in law from **Tokyo** University in 1976. He then joined the Ministry of International Trade and Industry (MITI), where he served until 1988. His time at MITI included a spell at Harvard University in the USA. Elected from a Mie constituency on the LDP ticket in 1990, he has served in the **National Diet** for the same constituency ever since. He left the LDP in 1993, and eventually joined the DPJ in 1998. He served as deputy secretary-general and then secretary-general of the Party before becoming its president in May 2004.

Okinawa

Okinawa is the name of both the largest island in the Ryukyu Island group, and of the Japanese prefecture that covers part of the islands.

Until 1879 the Ryukyu kingdom enjoyed quasi-independence, although it paid tribute to, and traded with, both **China** and Japan. The people of the islands were very similar to the Japanese in language, customs and culture. In the 1850s, as Western pressure for the opening of Japan intensified, the Ryukyu kingdom even concluded treaties with the USA, France and the Netherlands. However, Japan gradually asserted control over the islands, and in 1879 the former kingdom became Okinawa Prefecture, while the last king became a member of the Japanese peerage. Although in theory full citizens of Japan, Okinawans were often looked down upon as poor and backward by the rest of the country.

Okinawa was the scene of some of the fiercest battles of the **Pacific War**, with heavy military and civilian losses. After the war the USA retained control of the prefecture and established numerous bases there. These played a major role during the **Korean War**, and became an important part of the US presence in the Pacific. The islands remained under direct US administration until 1972. While in theory Japan enjoyed 'residual sovereignty' over Okinawa, in practice, the USA did as it liked. The threat of removing even 'residual sovereignty' was also used to force Japan to follow US wishes from time to time.

During the 1960s the Japanese government made determined efforts to obtain the return of the islands. In order to do this, it agreed to the continued US use of the bases, and promised greater co-operation with the USA in securing the peace of East Asia. However, the Japanese government publicly stood out against the presence of nuclear weapons on the islands, and the final agreement for the return of the islands to Japanese sovereignty in 1972 accepted that the USA would remove all nuclear weapons. It emerged in the 1990s, however, that a secret protocol allowed for the return of nuclear weapons in an emergency.

The continued presence of the bases, which occupy a large amount of the available land, and complaints about the behaviour of the large number of US troops on the islands, have led to demands for either their withdrawal or a reduction in their strength. In 1995, following the rape of three schoolgirls, the then governor of Okinawa refused to sanction the renewal of the leases on a number of the bases, but was overruled by the central government. Some relocation of bases away from population centres has taken place, however, and the issue has subsided. One problem is that the bases bring employment and economic benefits to what is still a poor and backward part of Japan. Nevertheless, much resentment against the US presence remains.

Organisation for Economic Co-operation and Development (OECD)

Global forum for discussion of economic and social policies.

The Organisation for Economic Co-operation and Development (OECD) does not dispense funds. One of its main tasks is the collection of comparable statistical, economic and social data among its member states. It also set down formal agreements on issues of common concern, as well as non-binding agreements. Membership is open to countries committed to the market economy and pluralistic democracy.

The OECD has its origins in the Organisation for European Economic Co-operation (OEEC), which was set up to administer aid from the USA and Canada dispensed under the post-Second World War Marshall Plan. In 1961 the OEEC was reconstituted as the OECD. OECD is funded by its members, which contribute to an annual budget in accordance with a formula related to the size of each member's economy. The USA is the largest contributor, accounting for one-quarter of the budget, followed by Japan.

Asian states among the 30 member countries are Japan, which joined in 1964, and the Republic of Korea, which joined in 1996. The OECD is also in dialogue with 70 non-member organizations that include countries, regions, non-governmental and civil organizations. These include the **People's Republic of China**, **Hong Kong**, **Macao**, **Taiwan** and Mongolia. The OECD, in working with economies in transition and emerging market economies, seeks to promote adherence to OECD standards and instruments.

Sec.-Gen.: Donald J. Johnston
Address: 2 rue André Pascal
           F-75775 Paris Cedex 16
           France
Tel: 33-1-45-24-82-00
E-mail: webmaster@oecd.org
Internet: www.oecd.org

Orthodox Christianity

One of the principal branches of the Christian church, along with **Catholic** and **Protestant Christianity**.

Orthodox Christianity was based on the four eastern churches of the early Christian church: Alexandria, Jerusalem, Antioch and Constantinople, all sited around the eastern end of the Mediterranean. After 1,000 years of slowly diverging development, the western and eastern traditions of Christianity separated in 1054. The western church, based on Rome, went forward as the Catholic church; the eastern church did not devise a similar hierarchical unity, but allowed local forms to emerge, such as the Russian, Greek and Serbian Orthodox churches. Other autocephalous churches have been added subsequently. All share the same tradition of the divine liturgy and all use the priest as a mediator between the people and God.

In East Asia the most common form of Orthodox Christianity is the Russian church, which followed expansion into the **Russian Far East** and the spread of Russian influence in **China** and the **Korean peninsula**. Russian Orthodox churches primarily served Russian communities in those countries, but also received converts. A Russian ecclesiastical mission was established in **Beijing** in 1727 for political and scholarly rather than religious reasons, but was none the less staffed by priests. In the later part of the 19th century it extended its missionary activities; but the advent of Communist, anti-religious regimes in both the Soviet Union and the **People's Republic of China** during the first half of the 20th century brought such missionary work to an end. Beijing now has a sizeable Russian community of traders, so it is likely that Russian Orthodox services have been restored for this new population, following the general resurgence of the Orthodox faith in Russia since 1991.

Russian Orthodoxy also established a presence in the Korean peninsula at the very end of the 19th century, at a moment when Russia's political and diplomatic influence was at a high point. Korean immigrants to the Russian Far East returned to Korea, bringing the faith with them. A mission dates from 1900 and a church was dedicated in 1903. A small congregation was active in **Pyongyang** from 1929 until 1939. From 1947 management of the Orthodox church in **Seoul** passed into Korean hands; and after the **Korean War** (1950–53) the church came under the jurisdiction of the Greek Orthodox Church of North America. In the Democratic People's Republic of Korea (DPRK) construction of an Orthodox church is under way following the announcement, in 2002, of plans for it by the DPRK leader **Kim Jong Il**. The new church is intended for a Korean congregation.

A Russian Orthodox church opened in Mongolia in 1870, again for a Russian congregation. It closed in 1930 but reopened in 1997 for the Russian community. In Japan the Orthodox religion first entered the country as an adjunct to the Russian consulate in Hokkaido in northern Japan in 1861, but attracted Japanese converts and moved its base to **Tokyo**, where a cathedral was constructed towards the end of the 19th century. After the Second World War the Orthodox church, as in Korea, came under the charge of the Orthodox church in the USA, but returned to the Russian branch in 1970. The present Orthodox community in Japan numbers around 24,800.

Osaka

Japan's second largest city, and an economic centre to rival **Tokyo**.

Osaka is the capital of the Kinki region, some 514 km to the west of Tokyo, and it has its own distinctive dialect, which differs from standard Japanese. Under the name Naniwa, it was the first known capital of Japan in the 7th century AD. It began to develop as a major commercial centre when the warlord Hideyoshi Tokutomi built a castle there in the late 16th century; the castle survives, although it was rebuilt in ferrous concrete in 1931. Osaka opened to foreign trade in 1868, but the **foreign settlement** there never prospered; nearby **Kobe** always overshadowed it. However, the city, incorporated in 1889, became an important centre for the Japanese textile industry, known to foreigners as the 'Manchester of Japan'. It suffered badly in the **Pacific War**, but recovered in the 1950s. It hosted the first Asian trade exhibition, Expo 70, in 1970.

Today many important companies, including Matsushita, Sharp and Daimaru, maintain their headquarters in Osaka rather than Tokyo. The city has had an international airport since before the Second World War, but has assumed a new importance as a transport centre with the opening of Kansai International Airport in 1994. In 2003 its population was about 2.6m.; it occupies an area of 221.3 sq km. The surrounding Osaka Prefecture has a population of just under 9m., and an area of 1,893.18 sq km.

Overseas Chinese

Term applied in its loosest sense to those of Chinese birth or ancestry who are settled in countries outside of the **People's Republic of China (PRC)**.

In its narrowest sense, it applies to those with PRC citizenship who are temporarily living abroad. Some commentators include the **'Republic of China' ('ROC')** on **Taiwan** and **Hong Kong** in a concept of 'greater **China**' and only describe those living outside of this entity as overseas Chinese. The PRC's use of the term *tongbao*, rendered as 'compatriot', for residents of Taiwan, Hong Kong and **Macao** reinforced the concept of an augmented Chinese nation; but since the reversion of Hong Kong to the PRC in 1997 and Macao in 1999, the word *tongbao* can apply only to Taiwan. Other observers exclude Taiwan and Hong Kong from the calculation and instead list them among the overseas Chinese. Such varying definitions make it difficult to estimate world-wide numbers. Figures relating to the early 1990s range between 23.5m. and 30.7m., drawing the line from outside 'greater China'.

Communities of Chinese descent are found in most parts of the world, though they appear to be less numerous in Africa, the Middle East and South Asia. The largest groups, often with a history of many centuries' settlement, still live in the countries of south-east Asia. The proportion occupied by those of Chinese descent in the populations of these countries varies greatly, from the 77% Chinese majority in Singapore to around 30% in Malaysia (representing 4.25m. people), down to 10% in Thailand (4.5m.–6m.) and around 3% in Indonesia (5m.–6m.). Such divergences reflect the differing histories of the Chinese communities in these countries, as well as large variations in the total size of the national populations.

Among Western destinations, the USA is the most popular, with more than 2m. claiming Chinese ethnic descent in the USA's population census in 2000.

Emigration from China has been predominantly from the provinces of Guangdong and Guangxi on the south coast of the mainland and of Fujian and southern Zhejiang on the south-eastern coast, all areas that had an outward-looking maritime tradition. Emigrants were in the main **Han Chinese** and **Hakka**. From an early point after its settlement by the British in 1842, Hong Kong was an important transit city for Chinese emigration from Guangdong and Fujian and an intermediate post for the remittance of funds to China from overseas workers. In addition, it sent a considerable number of emigrants in the 1950s and 1960s from its New Territories to the United Kingdom. The reversion of Hong Kong to the PRC in 1997 prompted many Hong Kong Chinese to secure residency rights in Canada, Australasia and the USA, even if they retain a foothold in Hong Kong.

The great majority of overseas Chinese are now citizens by birth or naturalization of the country where they reside. 'Chineseness' for them is more a matter of ethnicity, language or culture. Until 1957 the government of the PRC regarded all Chinese, whether they were living abroad temporarily or were permanent settlers, as Chinese citizens and under its protection, and described them as *huaqiao*, those staying outside of China. In this it was following earlier legislation, such as the 1909 and 1929 Nationality Laws of the Qing dynasty and of the **Republic of China (1912–49)**, which took ancestry—*ius sanguinis*—as the basis of nationality, rather than place of birth—*ius soli*. Ancestry is the principle that still obtains in the 'ROC', which continues to offer its protection to all Chinese; and friction, first between the **Chinese Communist Party (CCP)** and the Nationalist **Kuomintang (KMT)** party, and later between the PRC and the 'ROC', has been a feature of many overseas Chinese communities. From the mid-1950s, however, the PRC began to urge the overseas Chinese communities, first of all in south-east Asia, to accept the laws and customs of their countries of residence and to consider naturalization. This position was reiterated in legislation of 1957 and 1980. Since 1980 citizenship of the PRC has been confined to those born there and can be relinquished.

Relations between China and those who have left to work and settle elsewhere have often been uneasy. Trading contacts with the regions to the south of China were recorded from the 13th–14th centuries onwards. Such visits were often temporary, and where traders settled they intermarried with local women. Trading activities, however, became a vehicle for political defiance and piracy from the mid-15th century, and first the Ming dynasty (1368–1644), then the succeeding Qing (1644–1911), banned overseas trade for varying periods and the Qing, in 1662, even had the south-east coastal provinces depopulated so as to discourage piracy. From 1717 emigration and return to China were forbidden. Those residing overseas were rejected as bad subjects, unworthy of protection. The restrictions on emigration were increasingly evaded, but the ban was not lifted until 1860 and was officially rescinded only in 1893. The 19th and early 20th centuries became the great period of Chinese emigration, to south-east Asia and beyond. Western settlement in Asia, the Americas, Australasia and the Pacific region attracted large numbers of Chinese, generally unaccompanied men employed as indentured labourers in plantations and industrial exploitations, often working in harsh conditions. Foreign requirements, however, helped to relieve the pressures of a growing population and the wish to escape social and political unrest in China. Eventually these men were permitted to bring wives and families and, as a consequence, settled Chinese communities appeared, supporting themselves often by commerce, educating their children in Chinese schools and, in effect, 'resinicizing' older Chinese groups that had started to merge with the wider society around them.

Further migration took place in the late 1930s under the threat of Japanese invasion, and again in 1949, when a number of wealthy Chinese fled the incoming communist regime to Hong Kong and Taiwan. From the 1950s until the late 1970s emigration from the PRC almost ceased as the country, preoccupied with its own redevelopment as a communist state and suspicious of foreign contacts, monitored its citizens' movements. Since the decision in 1978 to open up the PRC to trade and modernization, few obstacles have been placed in the way of emigration, which as a consequence has risen considerably, whether it be temporary or permanent. Those leaving are no longer confined to the coastal residents of Guangdong and Fujian, but come from many parts of the country, are often well-off and may travel for business or study, particularly to North America, Australasia and Europe.

The inconstancies of Chinese official views on emigration have been paralleled by the varying degrees of tolerance shown by host countries towards the Chinese communities in their midst. Attitudes have swung from acceptance and willingness to make use of the particular skills these communities have brought with them, to discrimination in employment and education, bars on further immigration, bans on the remittance of funds from the country, refusal of citizenship, outbursts of violence and even expulsion. Chinese settlers, engaged in trade, generally fared well under the colonial administrations that governed much of south-east Asia between the 16th and 20th centuries.

Nationalist movements in colonies pressing in the 1920s and 1930s for independence clashed with similar nationalistic sentiments among their Chinese communities. Once independence was achieved, nationalism might be directed against outsiders—often the Chinese. In riots in protest against other grievances the Chinese, who were regarded as enjoying greater prosperity, were frequently targeted. Such has been the case in Indonesia, Burma and Malaysia. In some instances, notably in Malaysia but also in Thailand, Burma and Indonesia, the communist affiliations of sections of the Chinese community sometimes posed big problems between the late 1940s and the 1970s. The presence of remnants of the KMT armies in Burma and Thailand until the 1960s was a further complication. Chinese emigration into neighbouring territory, such as Japan, the **Korean peninsula** and Viet Nam, has always been under tight control. Further afield, the USA began to admit large numbers of Chinese labourers in the 19th century to work in the goldmines, on infrastructral projects, in industry, farming and fishing; but in

1882 further Chinese immigration into the USA was stopped. In 1943 restricted immigration was permitted and the ban was lifted altogether in 1965. From that time onwards the Chinese have moved upwards in the USA in terms of employment and aspirations.

Since the end in 1893 of the ban on returning to the Chinese mainland, Chinese governments have reacted in varying ways to the needs of returning overseas Chinese. Those sections of the Qing government that were anxious to promote the country's modernization welcomed the funds and knowledge of Western ways that overseas Chinese could bring. Indeed, the movement to overthrow the Qing dynasty and establish a republic (achieved in 1911–12) owed much to the activities of groups of Chinese students in such places as Japan and Hong Kong. The Nationalist Chinese government set up succeeding offices to handle overseas Chinese affairs and ensure the welfare of those returning to the mainland. After 1949 the Communists took up the practice in the form of the Overseas Chinese Affairs Commission, and those returning came under the umbrella of the CCP's United Front Department. Places were, and still are, reserved for overseas Chinese delegates in the **National People's Congress** in recognition of their links with the mainland. (The **Legislative Yuan** of the 'ROC' likewise reserves seats for such delegates.) Many overseas Chinese were resettled in specially designated farms and accommodation. However, campaigns against those viewed as privileged or having foreign connections intensified during the 1950s and 1960s, culminating in the **Cultural Revolution** (1966–76), and harmed the returned overseas Chinese severely. Their situation improved post-1978. Their interests are now handled by the Office of Overseas Chinese Affairs under the **State Council** and their position is protected by legislation.

Overseas Chinese have always been expected to contribute through remittances to the welfare of families, clans and villages on the mainland. Nowadays, it is more likely that they will be urged to involve themselves in the PRC's economic development through investment and the funding of joint ventures.

Overseas Japanese

In the Tokugawa period (1600–1867) strict rules forbade Japanese from travelling overseas. In the Meiji period (1867–1912), however, the Japanese government encouraged emigration as a way of reducing pressure on Japan's rural areas. Although the Japanese government was well aware of the problems associated with the 'coolie' or indentured workers' trade to Hawaii and South America, it nevertheless permitted emigration to such areas from the 1880s. In due course this emigration led to the creation of large Japanese communities in Hawaii, in the mainland USA, and in Brazil and Peru in South America. Many only stayed for a short period, but others remained, and they and their families became the basis of sizeable permanent Japanese communities. Japanese also emigrated to Australia. All of these groups suffered much discrimination, both formal and informal. In the

1920s, in particular, discrimination was increasingly legally sanctioned, as were formal restrictions on further immigration.

During the **Pacific War** groups of Japanese were detained in the USA, Canada and Australia, even though in some cases they were third-generation settlers. Conditions were especially hard in Canada. Much later some of these groups were able to claim compensation for the way in which they had been treated. In certain cases active discrimination continued well after the war. Only in the late 1980s were measures taken to redress the injustices done during the war years.

In South America the large Japanese communities in Peru and Brazil have become involved with Japan in somewhat unexpected ways in recent years. In the case of Brazil, some 230,000 Brazilian Japanese have returned to Japan, where they form the third largest minority, after Chinese and **Koreans**. A revision of the immigration laws in 1989 allowed such people to go to Japan on renewable visas. However, since most perform menial tasks, and their command of the Japanese language is limited, most native Japanese do not regard them as Japanese and they suffer much discrimination.

Peru too has a large Japanese community. In 1990 Albert Fujimori, who is of Japanese descent, became that country's President. During the next 10 years he made frequent visits to Japan. In 2000, however, against a background of increasing criticism of his presidency, he fled to Japan where he has remained ever since, despite attempts to extradite him.

Overseas Koreans

Settled communities of ethnic **Koreans** living in a number of countries, principally the **People's Republic of China (PRC)**, the Commonwealth of Independent States (CIS), Japan, the USA, including Hawaii, South America and Europe. Recent estimates for the size of some of these overseas Korean communities are: PRC, 1.923m.; Japan, 660,214; the CIS, 486,857; the USA, 1.076m.; South America, 100,000. The total figure for overseas Koreans is between 4m.–4.5m.

Emigration from Korea was prohibited for much of the country's history, but even before the ban on movement into **China** was rescinded in 1881, impoverished Korean farmers were crossing into north-east China and the **Russian Far East** in pursuit of a livelihood. The period of Japanese colonization of Korea (1910–45) led to increasingly high rates of emigration, some of it forced, as Koreans moved or were taken to Japan to work there. Emigration to North and South America was voluntary, in the hope of a better life, but did not really grow until 1965, when changes in US immigration laws relaxed the former small quotas on Asian applicants. Those coming to Europe have usually been temporary residents studying or working for some years.

Numbering 1,923,400 in the 1990 population census of the PRC, Koreans rank 14th in size among China's 55 ethnic minorities. They are clustered in the three provinces of north-east China bordering on Korea, with the strongest concentration in Yanbian Korean Autonomous Prefecture in Jilin Province, just north of the **Tumen river**. Others live in other northerly parts of China and in the largest Chinese cities. Within Yanbian and the smaller Changbei Korean Autonomous County, Korean has the status of an official language; the Korean community enjoys a measure of self-administration, runs its own schools and university and has its own Korean-language radio and press. Those settled in the north-east region of the PRC are recognized as Chinese citizens; those living elsewhere in China had the choice between citizenship of the PRC or of the Democratic People's Republic of Korea (DPRK). Over the past 10 years the Republic of Korea's (ROK) interest in Yanbian has increased greatly as contacts and investment have been permitted. The border with the DPRK has always been porous, and during the years of hunger and distress in the DPRK in the second half of the 1990s numbers of North Koreans entered China, in particular Yanbian, to seek food and employment. Their needs were ministered to by Buddhist and Christian missionaries from the ROK. Since 2002 some of those fleeing from the DPRK have travelled to **Beijing** and Shenyang, where, aided by foreign Non-Governmental Organizations, they have forcibly entered foreign diplomatic missions in search of protection and a passage out of China.

From their original settlements in the late 19th century in the then Maritime Province of the Russian empire, later the Soviet Far East (now the Russian Far East), Korean migrants were compulsorily removed to central Asia in 1937. Soviet policy had been to encourage naturalization, and most of the Korean settlers in the region had become Soviet citizens by the time of the 1926 census. The Japanese occupation of north-east China, however, persuaded Stalin that the Korean population in this area of the Soviet Union might act as a cover for Japanese espionage. He accordingly ordered the relocation of this group away from the Korean border. Koreans thus found themselves resettled in what are now the republics of Kazakhstan and Uzbekistan, where they were welcomed for their skill in cultivating rice. They have kept some of their traditions, but their language has not received official status and is being displaced by Russian. With the collapse of Soviet control and the establishment of independent states in central Asia, a sense of cohesion is emerging among the various Korean communities in the region. Together with the much smaller groups of Koreans (thought to number now between 40,000 and 60,000) who were taken by the Japanese to the southern half of **Sakhalin** Island during the **Pacific War** and who then came under Soviet authority, the Central Asian Koreans are now starting to claim the identity of 'Koryo saram'—people of Koryo, i.e. Koreans. In a reflection of these links, the ROK has become an important foreign investor in Uzbekistan.

The Korean community in Japan, estimated at around 70,000, is imperfectly integrated into Japanese society. Despite having been regarded as citizens of the Japanese empire in colonial times, those who remained in post-war Japan were classed as aliens. A small number who, after the normalization of relations between Japan and the ROK in 1965, were able to prove that they were overseas nationals of the ROK, were able to acquire permanent resident status. In 1992 all Korean residents, including the 75% born and brought up in Japan, were accorded 'special permanent resident' status. The ambiguity surrounding the community is doubtless a legacy of the earlier pattern of Korean emigration to Japan. In the first half of the 20th century emigration was largely a function of Korea's status as a Japanese colony. A small number of Korean students had gone to Japan from the 1880s onwards, attracted by the modernizing and more liberal atmosphere in that country, and they continued to go there to study even after 1910 (the date of Japan's annexation of the **Korean peninsula**). Other Koreans migrated to Japan after 1910, first as agricultural labourers left landless by colonial policies of land ownership, then, increasingly, as industrial production in Japan grew to meet the needs of the First World War, as industrial workers. They were confined to less skilled, arduous employment and were paid much less than Japanese workers. From the 1930s an expanded Korean workforce in Japan, Korea and north-east China was directed into Japanese war industries. At Japan's capitulation in 1945 more than 2m. Koreans found themselves in Japan and north-east China. Many were repatriated, but about 545,000 remained in Japan. Their situation there has been complicated by the competing claims of the two states that emerged in the Korean peninsula. Many of those remaining took a strong pro-DPRK orientation, forming themselves in 1955 into the **Chosen Soren** (Korean: *Chongnyon*) association, organizing their own educational institutions and directing money and investment back to North Korea. Some chose to go to the DPRK, and from 1959 about 100,000 Japanese Koreans were repatriated there through Red Cross auspices. For long the Japanese government used *Chosen Soren* as an unofficial channel of contact with the DPRK. The association's effectiveness and its ability to channel funds to the DPRK may now be waning, but it has had a greater impact than the rival pro-ROK organization, *Mindan*.

The Korean community in the USA (only a small number of Koreans go to Canada), though not as large as the Chinese and Vietnamese communities as enumerated in the US census of 2000, is still a big group and outnumbers the Japanese. Nearly all immigrants have their origins in the ROK. Some of them arrive as the wives of US servicemen stationed in the ROK; others were adopted as babies by US families. Most of those who have settled in America have taken US citizenship. Around half of them are thought to live in the western states of the union, with California and the city of Los Angeles particularly favoured for settlement. Other centres for the Korean population are New York and Chicago. Clubs, churches, and a Korean-language press and radio stations cater to their interests and needs. Many are self-employed in the service and retail sector. Their presence as small shopkeepers in the Afro-American and Hispanic areas of New York and Los Angeles contributed to uneasy relations with these other sections of American society and made them targets of boycotts and looting in 1991 and 1992.

The first Korean emigrants, around 7,200 in number, were those permitted to go in the early 1900s to Hawaii to work in the sugar plantations there. Many of them turned to shopkeeping, and about 2,000 moved on to the US mainland, generally to

California, thus starting two long-lasting trends. The volume of Korean immigration into the USA, in line with the pattern of Chinese and other Asian immigration, was held in check between 1924 and 1965 by discriminatory US legislation and the application of quotas. Japanese resistance to the emigration of its colonial subjects also contributed to the low numbers. After 1965 the Korean outflow rose rapidly, aided by the ROK government's decision in 1962 to ease emigration for its own nationals. Many Koreans, eager to take advantage of the good educational and work opportunities in the USA, at any one time have members of their family studying or settled there.

P

Pacific War

The conventional dates for the outbreak of the Second World War are either 1 September 1939 (German invasion of Poland) or 7 December 1941 (Japan's attack on Britain and the USA). In East Asia, however, the more usual date is 7 July 1937, when fighting broke out between Chinese and Japanese forces in the **Marco Polo Bridge Incident** outside **Beijing**. This conflict continued for the next four years, eventually merging into the wider world war in 1941.

The Pacific War—and the Second World War—ended with the Japanese surrender on 15 August 1945, but its legacies live on. It was a war of great brutality, with heavy loss of life and much disruption of people. Issues such as **comfort women**, **prisoners of war of the Japanese**, the division of the **Korean peninsula**, and many others, have their origins in this period. The Japanese occupation of large parts of **China** and south-east Asia, even if it assisted the movement towards eventual independence, has left suspicions of Japan and Japanese power that are hard to eradicate.

Paik Nam Sun

Foreign minister of the Democratic People's Republic of Korea (DPRK) since 1998, Paik was born in 1929, and educated at **Kim Il Sung University**. He has been active in foreign affairs and inter-Korean relations since the early 1970s. In 1973–79 he was the DPRK's ambassador to Poland, his only known overseas appointment. He is polite and courteous in his dealings with foreign officials, but overshadowed by his nominal deputy, vice-minister **Kang Sok Ju**. There are also persistent reports that he is not well and needs regular hospital treatment for kidney failure.

Pak Gil Yon

Pak Gil Yon is an experienced diplomat from the Democratic People's Republic of Korea (DPRK), who is particularly associated with his country's relations with the **United Nations (UN)**. He was born in 1943, and first appeared as the DPRK consul-general in Singapore in 1973. In 1986 he was a delegate to the **Supreme People's Assembly**, and in the following year headed the DPRK's observer mission to the UN. When the DPRK entered the UN in 1991 he became the permanent representative for a short period before becoming DPRK ambassador to Colombia. From 1996 until 2001 he was a Vice-Minister of Foreign Affairs, before again becoming head of the DPRK mission to the UN in 2001. In the absence of US-DPRK diplomatic relations Pak has played an important part in links between the two countries.

Pak Pong Ju

Little is known about Pak Pong Ju, who became Prime Minister of the Democratic People's Republic of Korea in September 2003, replacing **Hong Song Nam**. Some reports indicate that he may have been born in 1939. He first came to notice in the early 1980s as an alternate member of the Central Committee of the **Korean Workers' Party**. In 1998 he was a delegate to the **Supreme People's Assembly**, and became Minister for the Chemical Industry in the same year. This appointment may point to a technical background.

Pan-Blue coalition

Fan lan chun

Political coalition formed in **Taiwan** in the early 2000s between elements of the **Kuomintang (KMT)**, currently led by **Lien Chan**, the **People First Party (PFP)**, under **James Soong**, and the **New Party**. The coalition has no formal force and the parties maintain their separate identities and structures, but they work closely together. In the presidential elections of 2000 Lien Chan was nominated as the KMT candidate in preference to James Soong. Soong presented himself as an independent candidate, but in so doing helped to divide the vote and thereby contributed to victory for **Chen Shui-bian**, the leader of the **Democratic Progressive Party**. Learning from this experience, the three parties of the Pan-Blue coalition now co-ordinate their electoral strategies to avoid splitting the vote to the benefit of their opponents. In the presidential elections of 2004 the KMT and PFP jointly presented Lien Chan as candidate for the presidency, with James Soong running for vice-president. However, the combination did not succeed in dislodging Chen Shui-bian.

The Pan-Blue coalition on the whole favours a Chinese nationalist identity and policies supporting reunification and increased economic links with the **People's Republic of China**. The KMT and PFP appear to draw support from those who came from the mainland in 1949 and their descendants, and this ethnic link, although not made explicit, may be an element in the coalition. Its views on reunification do not, however, constitute the whole of its programme, and it enjoys a measure of support among a cross-section of society. It takes its name from the blue party colours of the KMT.

Panchen Lama

Title given to the second most highly placed official in the Tibetan Buddhist hierarchy, after the **Dalai Lama**. The name, signifying 'great scholar', was first conferred by the fifth Dalai Lama in 1642 on his teacher, the abbot of Tashilumpo, with the intention of reinforcing the authority of the Gelugpa or 'yellow hat' order.

The Panchen Lama's traditional role has been to assist in the search for and recognition of the new reincarnation of the Dalai Lama and to act as his teacher; though in the case of the current Dalai Lama and the 10th Panchen Lama such a relationship was hardly possible. A dispute between the 13th Dalai Lama and the ninth Panchen Lama caused the latter to remove to **China**. He died in 1937 while returning to **Tibet**. In the wartime conditions of the 1940s a long interval ensued before his successor, Choekyi Gyaltsen, born in 1935, was recognized and finally, in June 1949, approved by the Chinese Nationalist government of the **Republic of China (1912–49)**. The Nationalists, however, were shortly afterwards ousted by the Communist Chinese, who took the education of the 10th Panchen Lama in hand, constantly reminding him of the need for loyalty to the new **People's Republic of China (PRC)**. The flight of the 14th Dalai Lama to India in 1959 removed any opportunity for a personal relationship to develop between the Dalai Lama and the Panchen Lama. PRC hopes that the Panchen Lama could be used as a point of contact between the Tibetan people and the PRC authorities seem to have been disappointed in face of the Panchen Lama's doubts over the pace and direction of Chinese control of Tibet. The Panchen Lama was imprisoned during the period of the **Cultural Revolution** (1966–76), and was released in 1978. He broke with tradition by marrying and having a daughter. He spent much of his life outside of Tibet, but died there on a visit in early 1989, reportedly of a heart attack.

His death raised again the problem of succession. The Dalai Lama's recognition is one of the requirements for a new choice of Panchen Lama, together with other processes. In May 1995 the Dalai Lama announced that the reincarnation of the 11th Panchen Lama had been found in a boy named Gedhun Choekyi Nyima, born in April 1989 inside Tibet. This child was immediately removed by the Chinese, who in turn produced their own choice for Panchen Lama, a boy of similar age named Gyaltsen Norbu, whose selection was shown on television in November 1996. He is the son of Communist Party officials. In mid-August 2004 he made his third visit to **Lhasa**, where his activities were again recorded on Chinese television, and is now reported to be living in Zhaxi Lhunbo lamasery in Xigaze, the residence of previous Panchen Lamas. The Chinese admitted in 1996 that they had taken the first child away. They confirmed on the occasion of Gyaltsen Norbu's August 2004 visit to Lhasa that the first boy was in good health but was not permitted to meet outside groups. He is probably living in Gansu Province.

Tibetans fear that on the death of the present Dalai Lama, the Chinese will use their choice of Panchen Lama to confirm the recognition of the reincarnation of the next Dalai Lama, in circumstances under their control.

'Panda diplomacy'

During the 1950s, when the Soviet Union and the **People's Republic of China (PRC)** enjoyed close links, the PRC sent a pair of pandas to Moscow Zoo. However, 'panda diplomacy' really came into its own in the 1970s, as the PRC began to rebuild its links to the outside world after the **Cultural Revolution**. Beginning with Ling Ling and Hsing Hsing, presented to US President Richard M. Nixon in 1972, Chinese leaders regularly presented giant pandas to international visitors, including the Japanese Prime Minister, **Tanaka Kakuei**, and the British politician Edward Heath. Between 1953 and 1982 some 23 pandas went abroad. The practice was stopped for a time because of concerns about the dwindling stocks of pandas. It was revived in the 1990s, but now the Chinese only allow pandas to go on loan for 10 years, after which they are returned to **China**. In 2004 Meimei and Yongming, a pair of pandas at Japan's Wakayama Zoo, produced a cub, which was returned to China for breeding purposes.

The success of this 'panda diplomacy' may be one reason why the term 'panda-hugger' is used in the USA with reference to those who are thought to be too friendly towards the PRC.

Pan-Green coalition

Fan lü chun

Political coalition formed in **Taiwan** between the **Democratic Progressive Party (DPP)**, the **Taiwan Solidarity Union (TSU)** and the Taiwan Independence Party in the wake of the presidential elections held in 2000. Within the coalition the DPP is the larger and more moderate element and is the party of the current President of Taiwan, **Chen Shui-bian**.

The Pan-Green coalition does not generally co-ordinate election strategies, and inter-party competition can be strong within it. The common element in the parties that make up the coalition is their preference for a Taiwan identity and, in greater or smaller measure, Taiwan independence rather than reunification with the **People's Republic of China**. The TSU takes a pro-independence line and can put pressure on the larger DPP. The coalition has moreover benefited from a perception that its constituent parties are less corrupt than the long-entrenched **Kuomintang (KMT)**.

The Pan-Green coalition emerged when the KMT expelled former President **Lee Teng-hui**, on the grounds that he had weakened the KMT's chances of securing victory in the 2000 presidential elections by nominating **Lien Chan** as the party's candidate rather than the more popular **James Soong**. Lee supported the formation of a new, pro-independence party, the TSU, which attracted members from both the DPP and the KMT. Both of these parties gain much of their support from native Taiwanese.

The coalition's title comes from the colours of the DPP, which originally adopted green. The coalition is quite distinct from the Green Party of Taiwan.

Panmunjom

Site of the signing, on 27 July 1953, of the armistice that ended the **Korean War**, and the location of the Military Armistice Commission (MAC) that administers that agreement.

Panmunjom, situated towards the western end of the **Demilitarized Zone** that bisects the **Korean peninsula**, is about 168 km south of **Pyongyang**, the capital of the Democratic People's Republic of Korea (DPRK), and 40 km north of **Seoul**, the capital of the Republic of Korea (ROK). In late 1951 the site was selected as the second meeting place for the armistice talks between the **United Nations** Command and the DPRK/Chinese command that sought to resolve hostilities. Discussions were held intermittently at Panmunjom from October 1951 until the armistice was signed there in July 1953. The armistice document designated Panmunjom as the site for the MAC and for other temporary bodies. Prisoners of war were exchanged through Panmunjom on various occasions in 1953

Thereafter, Panmunjom was for decades the only regular point of contact between the DPRK and the ROK. It hosted the meetings initiated in 1971 between the Red Cross organizations of both sides on family reunions that led on to parallel political discussions from 1971 until 1973, and again, in 1984, initial meetings on economic issues and between parliamentarians. It is the customary exchange point for bodies of those **missing in action** in the Korean War that have since been unearthed, as well as, increasingly, the crossing point for important visitors to the DPRK. President **James (Jimmy) Earl Carter** of the USA entered the DPRK through Panmunjom in June 1994 on his way to visit **Kim Il Sung**. Since the 1990s, however, Panmunjom has no longer had the same unique role as a point of contact, and delegates of the two Koreas now have a wider choice of venues for their discussions.

The area is strictly known as the Joint Security Area (JSA), covers a roughly circular terrain some 800 m across, and is divided by the Military Demarcation Line, which runs straight through the building constructed for direct talks. Since September 1976, following a violent confrontation between US and DPRK soldiers that resulted in the death of two US army officers, the movement of soldiers and police inside the JSA has been restricted to the section controlled by each side and the demarcation between the two zones has been made clearer. A small number of defections have none the less been made across the JSA.

Park Chung-Hee

President of the Republic of Korea (ROK) from 1961 until his assassination in 1979. Although an authoritarian dictator, he succeeded in building the ROK into a modern, economically powerful state, well able to stand up to the Democratic People's Republic of Korea (DPRK).

Park was born in 1917, the youngest of seven children in a poor farming family. In 1937 he became a primary school teacher, but later went to the Japanese puppet state of **Manzhouguo**, and in 1942 enrolled at the Manzhouguo Military Academy, moving to the Japanese Military Academy in 1944. On graduation he joined the Imperial Army as a second lieutenant. Park returned to South Korea in 1945, becoming a captain in the Korean Constabulary, later transferring to the newly formed ROK army. In 1948 he was implicated in a rebellion and sentenced to death, but was reprieved. During the **Korean War** he rose to the rank of brigadier-general, becoming a major-general in 1958.

In May 1961 Park and a group of fellow officers overthrew the Second Republic. Park at first headed the Military Revolutionary Committee, then served as chairman of the Supreme Council for National Reconstruction from July 1961. He became acting President upon the resignation of President Yun Po-Son in March 1962. He retired from the army as lieutenant-general in 1963.

Elected in October 1963 as President of the Third Republic, he was re-elected in 1967, 1971, 1972 and 1978. He carried out a series of five-year national development plans, launched the **New Community Movement**, and contributed to the modernization and industrialization of South Korea. However, he grew more authoritarian as the years passed, especially after the death of his wife in an assassination attempt of which he was the intended target in 1974. By 1978 there was widespread opposition to his rule. Following disagreement among Park and his advisers on the handling of this opposition, the then director of the Korean Central Intelligence Agency (now the National Intelligence Service) shot him at dinner on 26 October 1979.

Park's political legacy endured under President **Chun Doo-Hwan** until 1987, and to a lesser extent under Chun's successor **Roh Tae-Woo**. Today, various ROK politicians and groups trace their line back to Park, while the DPRK's **Kim Jong Il** is reported to admire his methods and his results. Park's daughter, **Park Geun-Hye**, has inherited his political mantle.

Park Geun-Hye

Park Geun-Hye was born in 1952, the only daughter of **Park Chung-Hee**, President of the Republic of Korea (ROK) in 1961–79. She graduated in electronic engineering from Sogang University in 1974. After her father's assassination in 1979, she avoided politics and publicity, involving herself with various educational organizations.

In 1995, however, she became an adviser to the then ruling **Grand National Party (GNP)**, and entered the **ROK National Assembly** in 1998 on the GNP ticket. She became a GNP vice-president during the 16th National Assembly session (2000 onwards), but left the party in 2002 after a dispute with its president, Lee Hoi-Chang. She founded her own party, the Korea Coalition for the Future, which she represented in the National Assembly, and received the party's nomination for the presidential election of 2002. However, she rejoined the GNP before the election and acted as campaign manager for Lee Hoi-Chang in his second bid for the presidency. When Lee resigned, Park became president of the GNP in March 2004.

She visited the Democratic People's Republic of Korea in March 2002, and met **Kim Jong Il**, who reportedly expressed respect for her father.

Patten, Christopher Francis (Chris Patten)

British politician and last governor and commander-in-chief of the British colony of **Hong Kong**.

Chris Patten was born in 1944. After a period as a Conservative Party official, he became member of parliament for Bath in 1979, and held a variety of ministerial appointments. As chairman of the Conservative Party in 1990–92 he was widely credited with creating the organization that won the 1992 British general election for the Conservatives, but lost his own seat at Bath. The then Prime Minister appointed him as governor of Hong Kong, in succession to Sir David Wilson (now Lord Wilson of Tillyorn), a career diplomat.

Patten made it clear that he would not follow what he regarded as the over–conciliatory policies of his predecessor towards the **People's Republic of China (PRC)** during the approach to the handover of Hong Kong to the PRC in 1997. In particular, he sought a greater measure of democracy in Hong Kong, and the international acceptance of Hong Kong travel documents. The PRC objected to the proposals for more representative government, making it clear that it would dismantle any system in place which it had not approved. Patten's relations with the PRC steadily deteriorated during his governorship; the PRC media famously described him as a 'whore' and a 'tango dancer'.

After leaving Hong Kong, Patten became the European Commission's senior official dealing with external relations. This allowed him eventually to rebuild links with the PRC. In May 2001 Patten accompanied the Swedish Prime Minister, Goran Persson, and the European Union's foreign policy adviser, Javier Solana, on a visit to the Democratic People's Republic of Korea (DPRK). During the visit, the European Union and the DPRK established diplomatic relations.

People First Party (PFP)

Qinmindang

Taiwan political party founded in 2000 by **James Soong** and his supporters in a breakaway from the **Kuomintang (KMT)**. It takes a conservative stance in favour of reunification with the **People's Republic of China**.

Soong left the KMT after being passed over as the official party candidate for the 2000 presidential elections in favour of **Lien Chan**. He ran as an independent, but came second to **Chen Shui-bian** of the **Democratic Progressive Party (DPP)** and formed his party thereafter. The PFP secured 46 seats in the present **Legislative Yuan**. The KMT and the PFP are in competition for a similar set of voters, but none the less co-operate within the framework of the **Pan-Blue coalition** to oppose the ruling DPP and together command a majority in the legislature. Mindful of the effects of the 2000 presidential elections, when the KMT vote was split, the two parties campaigned jointly in the 2004 presidential elections, but failed to unseat Chen Shui-bian.

Chair.: James C. Y. Soong
Internet: www.pfp.org.tw

People's Bank of China (PBC—People's Republic of China)

The central bank of the **People's Republic of China (PRC)**.

The People's Bank of China (PBC) was established in December 1948, even before the founding of the PRC in 1949, out of the amalgamation of three other banks. From 1949 until 1983 the PBC functioned as the PRC's only bank, but in 1983 the **State Council** authorized it to operate as a central bank and in 1995 this status was confirmed by law. The PBC's principal functions include the formulation and implementation of monetary policy, the issue of currency, licensing and supervision of financial institutions, regulation of financial markets, management of official foreign exchange and gold reserves and of the payment and settlement system, and collection and analysis of financial statistical data. Since 1984 its commercial functions have been carried out by four other banks, including the **Bank of China**.

The PBC's head office has 13 functional departments supported by five other specialized departments. The Bank has nine regional branches, 326 district sub-branches and 1,827 county-level sub-branches. It oversees the State Administration of Foreign Exchange, and is also involved in the printing of banknotes, a clearing centre and foreign exchange trading centre, and is represented in major international financial centres.

Gov.: Zhou Xiaochuan
Address: 32 Chengfang St
Xicheng District
Beijing 100800
People's Republic of China
Tel: 86-010-6619-4114
Fax: 86-010-6842-4493
E-mail: master@pbc.gov.cn
Internet: www.abocn.com

People's Daily

Renmin Ribao

Leading daily newspaper of the **People's Republic of China (PRC)**. *People's Daily* was established in 1948 as the organ of the **Chinese Communist Party (CCP)**, one year before the founding of the PRC.

Its role is to record CCP and government policies and decisions as well as releasing domestic and international news. It claims a current circulation of 3m. and publishes a further 10 newspapers, several of which cover financial affairs, and six monthly magazines. Since 1997 *People's Daily* has been available online in Chinese and, since 1998, in English. It publishes an overseas edition for Chinese communities outside China.

Leadership: Xu Zhongtian (Dir); Wang Chen (Editor-in-Chief)
Address: 2 Jintaixi Rd
          Chaoyang District
          Beijing 1000733
          People's Republic of China
Tel: 86-010-6536-8971 (Foreign Affairs Department, General Office)
      96-010-6536-8676 (International Department)
Fax: 86-010-6536-8974/8984
E-mail: rmrb@peopledaily.com.cn

People's Daily Online

Address: 2 Jintaixi Rd
          Chaoyang District
          Beijing 100733
          People's Republic of China
Tel: 86-010-6536-8330 (Chinese version)
      86-010-6536-8361 (English version)
Fax: 86-010-6536-8393 (Chinese version)
      86-010-6536-8360 (English version)
Internet: www.peopledaily.com.cn

People's Liberation Army (PLA)

Remnin jiefangjun

The People's Liberation Army (PLA) is the title used for the armed forces of the **People's Republic of China (PRC)**. The PLA encompasses naval and air forces as well as ground troops.

Its original title on its foundation in 1927 was the Workers' and Peasants' Red Army. During the war against Japan that began in 1937, it had a variety of titles, including the Eighth Route Army, but it became the PLA on 1 May 1946. The PLA has always been closely associated with the **Chinese Communist Party (CCP)**, with an interlocking leadership at all levels. Senior military figures hold party positions, but in theory overall control of the PLA lies with the CCP's **Central Military Commission**; this is in line with **Mao Zedong**'s argument that the party controls the gun but the gun must not control the party.

Since the foundation of the PRC, there has always been some tension between the role of the PLA as a 'People's Army' and the desire of many senior PLA officers to make it a more professional army. Under Mao, the trend was towards the former, and in the early years of the PRC, the PLA performed many of the functions of government while a civilian organization developed. Since Mao's death in 1976, the broad trend has been towards a professional army. The brief war with Viet Nam in 1979 reinforced the case for a more professional military body, since it showed how out of date the PLA had become. The modernization and professionalization of the PLA suffered a brief set-back after the **Tiananmen** incident in 1989, but resumed in the mid-1990s, with troop reductions and increased specialization. The PLA, though large with some 2.2m. under arms, has a very dated inventory. Both the naval and air forces, whose strengths are small at about 250,000 and 420,000 respectively, are heavily dependent on obsolete equipment. The PLA, while important in the Asia-Pacific region, does not pose a significant challenge to either Japan or the USA in the Pacific, even though it has a nuclear capability. It is not even clear how much of a challenge it poses to the **'Republic of China'** on **Taiwan**, even though much of its military build-up appears to be for a possible attack on Taiwan.

Perry Review

Review carried out in 1999 by former US Secretary for Defense William Perry of US policy towards the Democratic People's Republic of Korea (DPRK).

Following the 1994 **Agreed Framework** and the inauguration of the **Korean Peninsula Energy Development Organization**, the USA, under President Bill Clinton, remained concerned about the threat from the DPRK and about its commitment to the Agreed Framework. Clinton therefore asked William Perry to conduct a review of US policy and options. Perry visited the DPRK, although he did not meet the DPRK leader **Kim Jong Il**, and consulted widely. He concluded that while the USA was capable of handling any military threat from the DPRK, this could not be done except at great cost, and that a continued engagement policy was more likely to achieve results. The US Administration's acceptance of the Perry proposals led to the visit to **Pyongyang** in 2000 by Secretary of State Albright, and to the possibility of a presidential visit. The new Administration of President George W. Bush abandoned the Perry approach on coming into office in January 2001.

Policy for Peace and Prosperity

Following his election as President of the Republic of Korea (ROK) in 2002, **Roh Moo-Hyun** endorsed the so-called **'sunshine policy'** of his predecessor, **Kim Dae-Jung**, towards the Democratic People's Republic of Korea, but restyled it as the Policy for Peace and Prosperity. This policy aimed to continue the slow but steady improvement in relations between the two Koreas following the June 2000 summit meeting in **Pyongyang**, with the ultimate objective of replacing the 1953 Korean armistice agreement with a peace treaty. At the same time, Roh hoped to use the ROK's wealth as a means of improving the prosperity of the north-east Asian region as a whole. He also pledged that he would pursue these policies with more openness and more widespread involvement of the ROK public than had been the case under Kim Dae-Jung.

Potsdam Conference

In July 1945, after the defeat of Germany, leaders of the Soviet Union, Britain and the USA met at the Berlin suburb of Potsdam to discuss policies towards Germany and the war against Japan. Josef Stalin led the Soviet delegation. US President Roosevelt had died in April 1945, and his successor, President Harry S. Truman, was the US leader. Wartime Prime Minister Winston Churchill headed the British delegation, but, having lost a general election, was replaced by Clement Attlee before the end of the conference.

Most of the proceedings related to Germany, but on 26 July 1945 Britain and the USA issued the Potsdam Declaration, with which they associated the **Republic of China (1912–1949)**. This stated that, as far as Japan was concerned, they would carry out the terms of the 1943 **Cairo Declaration**. The Declaration repeated the call for Japan's unconditional surrender. It is unclear how far the Republic of China was consulted on this declaration since, contrary to some accounts, its leader, **Chiang Kai-shek**, was not present at Potsdam. This conference was the last wartime meeting of the so-called 'Big Three'.

Prisoners of war of the Japanese

The question of compensation for both military and civilian prisoners of war (POWs) captured and maltreated by Japanese forces during the **Pacific War** has affected Japan's relations with many Western countries since the country regained its independence in 1952. As in the related matter of compensation for **comfort women**, successive Japanese governments argued that the issue had been resolved by the **San Francisco Peace Treaty**, and that Japan was under no obligation to do anything more.

The speed of Japan's advance against Western forces in south-east Asia in 1941 meant that large numbers of Allied forces became POWs, and the Japanese also detained civilians. In **China** the further extension of the war meant that many Western civilians fell into Japanese hands. In all more than 35,000 military personnel and many thousands of civilians were captured. These developments took the Japanese by surprise. They had made few preparations for handling large numbers of detainees and throughout the war worked on improvised systems. Civilians were largely left to their own devices, but suffered from lack of appropriate food, lack of medical supplies, poor housing and casual brutality from guards. Military POWs suffered from similar deprivations; in addition, many had to work in severe conditions and with insufficient food for the heavy labour demanded. There was also more systematic brutality directed at POWs, and some were the subject of chemical and biological experiments. As a result, death rates were high. Western (but not Soviet) POW deaths in German hands during the Second World War were about 4% of the total held. In the Japanese case, the figure was 27%.

Article 16 of the Japanese Peace Treaty provided for modest compensation for those detained. The amount available depended on Japanese assets in a particular country and the number of POWs to be compensated. Since Japan's pre-war assets in Switzerland were large and the number of Swiss detained small, Swiss detainees received a comparatively large sum. The USA did not make any claims under Article 16, but paid POWs one dollar a day for their time in captivity; POWs in other countries, where relatively small sums available were distributed during the late 1950s, took note of this generosity.

The sums concerned were not large when distributed, and as the years passed inflation made them seem even smaller. The ascent of the Japanese economy in the 1960s also affected attitudes. If Japan could not pay in the 1950s, this was no longer the case by the mid-1960s. In addition, as POWs grew older the effects of their incarceration began to tell on their health. From the 1970s onwards, therefore, there were campaigns in a number of countries for more compensation from Japan and for a proper Japanese apology for the treatment of POWs during the war. Overseas visits by the **Japanese Emperor** often provided a focus for such campaigns, as did the death of the Japanese Emperor (the Showa Emperor, or Hirohito), the wartime leader of Japan, in 1989.

Successive Japanese governments after 1952 were willing to offer apologies for the treatment of POWs. This was controversial within Japan and the terms of such apologies failed to meet POW expectations. All Japanese governments refused to offer compensation, however, arguing that Japan had met its international obligations in the Peace Treaty. POW attempts to raise the issue in the Japanese courts were unsuccessful. The **Murayama Tomiichi** coalition Government, in power during the 1995 anniversary of the end of the Pacific War, went further than most. Murayama offered the fullest apology ever by a Japanese Prime Minister, and the government provided funds for schemes to bring about reconciliation. There was also an attempt to establish a private fund for compensation, to be financed by Japanese companies. Few Japanese companies showed any interest in this, and it did not develop. In any case, POW organizations rejected these proposals.

By the late 1990s it was clear that Japan would not offer the compensation demanded. A number of Western governments then decided to offer compensation to the dwindling number of former POWs and civilian detainees, and the campaigns declined in intensity. The issue has not, however, disappeared entirely, since in a number of countries the children and grandchildren of former POWs continue to campaign.

One reason for Japan's reluctance to engage with this issue has been concern that if Japan paid compensation to Western POWs, this might raise the broader issue of compensation to Chinese and other Asians who suffered during the Pacific War. The formal position is that the **People's Republic of China (PRC)** waived all claims against Japan for compensation when the two countries signed a peace treaty in 1978. The PRC government has not raised the issue subsequently, but in recent years a number of individual Chinese citizens have tried to pursue legal claims for compensation for wartime treatment, so far without success.

Protestant Christianity

One of the three main branches of the Christian church, alongside **Catholic** and **Orthodox Christianity**.

Protestantism traces its origins to a movement of reform initiated in 1517 by a German monk, Martin Luther, within and eventually against the Catholic church. This movement, known as the Reformation, repudiated papal authority and formulated new doctrines. It took hold largely in northern Europe and led to an era of religious antagonism and warfare as the two sections of the Western Christian church struggled for ascendancy. Diversity of belief has encouraged the formation of many different Protestant denominations; though all accept the direct revelation contained in the Bible in seeking divine guidance and the need for personal salvation. From Europe the varying denominations spread to North America and other parts of the world. Over the past century the pentecostal movement, with its emphasis on the power of the Holy Spirit, has permeated some of formal Protestant practice.

Protestant Christianity was brought to East Asia in the 19th century almost entirely by missionary activity, which itself was made possible through the securing of diplomatic and political agreements between various Western powers and the governments of **China**, Japan and Korea. The Conventions of **Beijing** (1860) opened up the capital and inland areas of China to foreign penetration (the coastal areas had already received some missionaries, some based in **Macao**), and missionary and Bible societies from Europe, North America and Australasia, both Protestant and Catholic, proliferated. Conditions for missions operating inland, far from consular protection, could be dangerous as missionaries and their converts met with hostility from local populations. Some of the more enduring effects of missionary activity have been the hospitals, schools and universities they set up and the training these provided. In the 1920s and 1930s Chinese Protestant converts began to exert leadership of their churches through the 'three-self' movement of responsibility for administration, financing and proselytization, thereby reinforcing an indigenous element. Among prominent Protestant converts was the Nationalist leader, **Chiang Kai-shek** (1887–1971), who became a Methodist in the 1920s. Independent sects sprang up, and by 1949 there were 700,000 Chinese Protestants in the country. The government of the **People's Republic of China (PRC)** installed in that year imposed a single structure on all Protestant churches, gathering them in 1951 into a unified church that overrode former missionary-led denominations. In an echo of the Chinese Protestant churches' own earlier practice, a Three-Self

Patriotic Movement was instituted to provide a channel of administration. Foreign missionaries could no longer operate and their missions had to sever contact with the Chinese church. In 1980, as church activity resumed after the **Cultural Revolution** (1966–76), the China Christian Council (CCC) was formed as an internal co-ordinating organization (Christian here having the meaning of Protestant). Some churches are affiliated to the CCC, but some of the indigenous groups dating from the 1920s–1930s have chosen to remain apart. Such churches are particularly strong in the coastal and central regions of China. Yet further churches have emerged since the Cultural Revolution, mostly evangelical in nature, which refuse to affiliate even to the Three-Self Patriotic Movement. Others are gathered around a single charismatic preacher. Some heterodox sects are not recognized by either the CCC or by the government. In such a fluid situation it is difficult to distinguish the status of individual churches, and the PRC government's desire to control Christian activity through imposing a system of registered churches seems to be leading to a plethora of 'underground' and potentially unlawful groups. The contrast between official estimates of 25m. Protestants and unofficial estimates of more than 60m. confirms the state of confusion.

Following the persecution of the Catholic missionaries in the 17th century in Japan, religious activity was only tolerated again in the country after 1873. The Meiji Constitution of 1889 lifted all religious bans. Missionary propagation, whether Catholic or Protestant, won few converts, but the missionaries' early work in medicine and education, particularly women's education, had a longer-reaching effect. Japanese converts were leaders in introducing socialist ideas and concepts of labour relations into Japan in the early part of the 20th century. Like their counterparts in China, Japanese Protestant Christians worked to minimize the foreign element in their churches and to achieve independence from missionary control in administration, financing and evangelizing. Foreign missionaries had left Japan by 1941 and the declaration of war with the Allies. Today, Japanese Protestantism is largely associated with the middle classes. Some of its more superficial aspects, such as Christmas celebrations and white weddings, have become popular in many sections of Japanese society; Christmas is widely celebrated, for example, though largely in secular fashion. The total number of Christians of all denominations in Japan is around 1m., of whom about one-half are Catholics. The United Church of Christ in Japan, a union of 34 Protestant denominations, represents about 200,000 members. Anglicans, Baptists and Lutherans are further smaller groups.

The first Protestant church in the **Korean peninsula** would appear to have been started in around 1880 by a Korean convert of a Scottish missionary and translator of the Bible. Following treaties with the USA in 1882 and with several European countries from 1883, Western Protestant missionaries began to arrive from 1884, introducing their various denominations into the country. Again, many of them established hospitals, schools and universities, some of which survive to this day, and were responsible for extending education to women. Propagation included extensive translations of the Bible, hymns, revival missions and a generally evangelical approach to religion. Protestants were among those signing the 1919 Declaration of Independence from Japanese colonial rule (members of the **Chondogyo** church being also prominent), but under the Republic of Korea (ROK) the Protestant churches have often taken a politically conservative line. The first President of the ROK, **Syngman Rhee**, was a Methodist. Protestant denominations in the ROK are said to number more than 160, embracing some 10m. adherents. Korean missionaries are active in foreign countries.

The northern half of the Korean peninsula was particularly fertile ground for Protestant missions and **Pyongyang** was a centre for their activity. This earlier intensity may account for the preponderance of Protestant adherents, around 12,000, in the small Christian community in the Democratic People's Republic of Korea. Another reason for the group's survival may be the fact that the mother of the late President **Kim Il Sung** was a Protestant Christian. The Protestants, administered through the Korean Christian Federation since 1946, have two churches in Pyongyang and a number of 'house churches'.

Protestants in **Taiwan** form a small percentage of the population (around 3.6%); **Hong Kong** has around 527,000 Christians, of whom more than 371,000 are Catholics; and **Macao** about 2,500 Protestants. An association of Mongolian Protestants has been in existence in Mongolia since 1990.

Pusan

The Republic of Korea's (ROK) major port, and an industrial city in the south-east of the **Korean peninsula**. Its population (2003) was about 4m. Former President **Kim Young-Sam** was born in the city.

Pusan developed in the Yi dynasty (1392–1910) as the harbour for nearby Tonghae, an important point of contact with Japan, and the only place where Japanese merchants were allowed to reside. After the 1876 Kangwha Treaty between the two countries, the Japanese presence increased rapidly. A railway from **Seoul** to Pusan opened in 1904; this was later extended to the border with **China** and connected to the **Trans-Siberian Railway**. The city developed as the main port for Korean-Japanese trade in the Japanese colonial period, and was the centre of anti-Japanese strikes in 1921. Following the outbreak of the **Korean War** in 1950, retreating ROK and **United Nations (UN)** forces, and eventually the ROK government, arrived in the city in August 1950. The military forces established the Pusan perimeter around the city, thus preventing the Democratic People's Republic of Korea from overrunning the whole peninsula. Pusan remained the seat of government until 1954.

As well as its role as a port and industrial centre, Pusan is the site of the major Korean War cemetery, established in 1951, and named the UN Memorial Cemetery in 1955. In 2002 Pusan hosted the Asian Games, the second ROK city to do so.

Puyi

Aisin Gioro Puyi/Henry Pu Yi

Last Emperor of the Qing dynasty of **China**.

Born in 1906, Puyi became the Emperor on the death of his uncle in 1908. In 1912 the new **Republic of China (1912–1949)** forced him to abdicate, but allowed him to continue living in the Imperial Palace, in something like the former imperial style. In 1924 he moved to **Tianjin** where he lived in the Japanese concession. After the establishment of **Manzhouguo** in 1932, he became President and later Emperor of what had been his ancestral homeland. Captured by Soviet forces at the end of the **Pacific War** in 1945, he was held a prisoner in the Soviet Union, but after the founding of the **People's Republic of China (PRC)** in 1949, the Soviet Union surrendered him for trial as a war criminal. He was pardoned in 1949.

Until his death in 1967, he worked in the **Beijing** botanical garden. His autobiography, *From Emperor to Citizen,* appeared in two volumes in 1964–65. In the 1980s a film about his life, *The Last Emperor*, made by the Italian director, Bernardo Bertolucci with the co-operation of the PRC, enjoyed great success.

Pyongyang

Capital of the Democratic People's Republic of Korea (DPRK) and the country's principal city, with a population of around 2.7m. (a new estimate at the end of 2003 put it at 3.8m.).

Pyongyang is situated in the central western section of the country on the lower stretches of the Taedong river, about 55 km from the coast. In keeping with a historical tradition of the central role of the capital wherever situated, Pyongyang is the seat of government and administration of the DPRK, headquarters of the **Korean Workers' Party**, the cultural and educational centre for the nation, and home to the country's leading banks and trading houses. As such, it vies with **Seoul**, the capital of the Republic of Korea to the south. The right to live in Pyongyang is restricted and much sought after, and to have one's residency reassigned away from the city is a form of punishment.

The city has a long history that in official DPRK accounts stretches back to the mythical origins of the Korean people around 5,000 years ago. In these accounts Pyongyang's association with the birth of the Korean nation underlines its antiquity and pre-eminence. From 427 to 668 AD it was the capital of the Koguryo kingdom, the most northerly of the three kingdoms within the **Korean peninsula**, which in 668 was subdued by the southern kingdom of Silla. Thereafter, in a unified state, it languished until the Choson or Yi period (1392–1910), when it was designated the western capital, subordinate to the central capital in Seoul.

One of the country's first encounters with Western intervention was in Pyongyang in 1866, when an American merchant ship, the *General Sherman*, sailed up the Taedong river in an attempt to impose contact but was trapped and set alight by

Koreans and the crew and passengers all killed. In the period (1910–45) of Japan's colonial annexation of Korea, the city was a focus of opposition to Japanese rule and a centre for Christianity, which by that time had become established in Korea.

In 1945, on liberation from Japan, Pyongyang became the 'temporary capital' of North Korea during the years (1945–48) of Soviet occupation of the north and, on the founding of the DPRK in 1948, the capital. It suffered badly in the **Korean War**. It was seized by **United Nations** forces on their advance north in September 1950 and experienced their retreat south three months later. It was heavily bombed throughout the war, so that little was left standing in 1953. This gave **Kim Il Sung** the opportunity to rebuild his capital in monumental style with tall buildings, wide boulevards and many open spaces, to equip it with a good transport system, including a metro, and to develop industry in and around the city. Population density is low. The centre of the city is laid out attractively on both banks of the Taedong, but is somewhat overshadowed by the many monuments to the revolutionary exploits of Kim Il Sung that extend throughout the capital and its suburbs. In line with the DPRK's general economic decline, Pyongyang's heavy industry has fallen sharply since the late 1990s, though it has to some extent been replaced by light industry and service activities.

R

Rhee In-Je

Born in 1948, Rhee graduated in law from **Seoul** National University in 1972. In 1987 he entered the **Republic of Korea National Assembly** as a member of **Kim Young-Sam**'s Reunification Democratic Party. When the Party merged to form the **Democratic Liberal Party**, Rhee too switched. Following Kim Young-Sam's election as President, Rhee was Minister of Labour in 1993–94, and then governor of Kyonggi Province in 1995–97. In 1997 he left what had by then become the New Korea Party to stand as presidential candidate for the newly formed New Korea Party for the People. He lost the election, but split the vote, allowing **Kim Dae-Jung** to become President. Following this, Rhee eventually became a senior member of Kim Dae-Jung's **Millennium Democratic Party (MDP)**. However, Rhee failed to win the Party's nomination for the presidential elections held in December 2002, and he left the MDP to join the **United Liberal Democrats**. In September 2003 he published a book in which he alleged that he had failed to win the MDP nomination because he knew too much about how the June 2000 North-South summit had come about. In May 2004 Rhee was arrested and charged with taking bribes from the **Grand National Party**.

Rhee Syngman (1875–1965)

First President of the Republic of Korea (ROK) in 1948, Rhee ruled in an increasingly authoritarian fashion until ousted in 1960.

Rhee was from an aristocratic background, but received part of his education at a mission school in **Seoul**. This led him to political activism, and he was imprisoned in 1898 for an alleged plot to establish a republic. On his release in 1904 Rhee went to the USA to study, earning a Ph.D. degree in political science in 1910 from Princeton University. He returned to Korea, now annexed by Japan, but in 1912 the Japanese forced him to leave. He returned to the USA and resumed his political activities. In 1919 he became Premier, and later President, of the Shanghai Provisional Government, established by Korean nationalists. Rhee sought recognition of the Provisional Government without success.

Returning to Korea in October 1945 following the end of the **Pacific War**, Rhee became leader of the South Korean right wing. Although he did not get on with Gen. Hodge, the US military commander, Hodge allowed him to become chairman of the Representative Democratic Council established in 1946. In 1948 the Constituent Assembly elected him as the first President of the ROK. Re-elected in 1952, 1956, and 1960, he became more autocratic at each stage. During the **Korean War** Rhee argued against any compromise with the Democratic People's Republic of Korea (DPRK) or with the **People's Republic of China**. He opposed the Korean armistice agreement, which he tried to jeopardize, even though he eventually agreed to abide by its terms. After the war Rhee pursued increasingly authoritarian and anti-left policies at home, and refused all dealings with the DPRK or other communist countries.

In April 1960 his supporters' heavy-handed rigging of the presidential election led to nation-wide student demonstrations. Forced to resign on 26 April 1960, Rhee left for Hawaii, where he died in 1965. His body was brought back to the ROK and buried at the National Cemetery. His role in fighting for an independent Korea led to the decision in 2000 to erect a statue to his memory in the **ROK National Assembly**. His other legacy has been an authoritarian presidency, with power heavily concentrated around the President and his advisers.

Ri Kwang Gun

Ri Kwang Gun became Minister of Foreign Trade of the Democratic People's Republic of Korea (DPRK) in December 2000. He is also the chairman of the DPRK Football Association. Born in **Pyongyang** in 1954, he was educated at **Kim Il Sung University**, and, possibly, in the former German Democratic Republic. In 1996 he was attached to the DPRK trade office in Germany, a post he held until he became a minister. He is polite and easy to talk to, and appears to favour economic change. He speaks German and understands some English.

Rodong Sinmun

Labour Daily

Organ of the Central Committee of the **Korean Workers' Party**.

Rodong Sinmun was founded in 1946 and is thus one of the longest-established institutions of the Democratic People's Republic of Korea. It provides the editorial lead to all other news publications in the country. It claims a circulation of 1.5m.

Editor-in-Chief: Choe Chil Nam
Address: Haebangsan St
        Central District
        Pyongyang
        Democratic People's Republic of Korea

Roh Moo-Hyun

Sixteenth President of the Republic of Korea (ROK), in office since 2003.

Roh was born in a farming village in South Kyongsang Province. He attended **Pusan** Commercial School, graduating in 1966. After military service he studied for the Bar, becoming a lawyer in 1975. In the following year he became a district court judge in **Taejon**, but opened his own law office in 1978. In the 1980s, during the protests against President **Chun Doo-Hwan**, he defended a number of student activists. This led him to an active role in the June 1987 demonstrations that followed Chun's nomination of **Roh Tae-Woo** as his successor. As a result, Roh Moo-Hyun was sentenced to a short term of imprisonment for helping striking workers.

He entered the **ROK National Assembly** in 1988 as a member of the opposition Reunification Democratic Party (RDP), serving in a variety of roles. In 1990 he broke with the RDP over its decision to amalgamate with the ruling party, and helped to form a new **Democratic Party**. In that year he resigned his National Assembly seat in protest at the forced passing of a broadcasting bill. In 1992 he managed the unsuccessful presidential campaign for the opposition candidate, **Kim Dae-Jung**, and failed to be re-elected to the National Assembly. He campaigned unsuccessfully to become mayor of Pusan in 1995, and for the Chongno (central **Seoul**) National Assembly seat in 1996. In 1997 Roh managed Kim Dae-Jung's successful campaign for the presidency as the candidate of the **National Congress for New Politics (NCNP)**, and in 1998 he won the Chongno seat for the NCNP in a by-election. He gave up this seat in 2000, but failed to be elected for Pusan.

In 2000–2001 he was the Minister for Maritime Affairs and Fisheries, and served as an adviser and senior member of the Central Committee of the ruling **Millennium Democratic Party (MDP)**. In 2002 the MDP chose him as its presidential candidate. In the elections Roh, campaigning for the continuation of Kim Dae-Jung's policies towards the Democratic People's Republic of Korea (DPRK), achieved an unexpected victory over the opposition **Grand National Party**'s **Lee Hoi-Chang**, to become President of the ROK. His election was widely viewed as representing the end of the political era of the 'three Kims'—**Kim Jong-Pil, Kim Young-Sam** and Kim Dae-Jung.

Roh has not had an easy time as President. Conservatives view his radical background with suspicion. He is regarded as anti-US, and there have been public differences between him and the Administration of US President George W. Bush on how to handle the DPRK. He seemed unable to cope with the economic and political problems that beset the country, and by the summer of 2003 his popularity had plunged. The MDP split, leaving him with only a small group of supporters in the National Assembly. This eventually became the **Uri Party**, which reorganized itself as the ruling party. Roh, however, quit the Uri Party, casting doubts on its future viability. Faced by mounting problems, Roh announced in October 2003 that he had lost confidence in his own ability as President, and suggested that there should be a referendum early in 2004 on whether or not he should continue. There was no constitutional precedent for such a move, and Roh did not attempt to pursue it.

In the spring of 2004 he was beset by a major problem, when the opposition, alleging that he was being partisan in expressing support for the Uri Party, impeached him. Roh stepped down, temporarily, leaving Prime Minister **Goh Kun** in charge. However, after some 63 days of uncertainty, the Supreme Court ruled that Roh had no case to answer, and he returned to office. In the mean time the Uri Party had performed well in elections to the National Assembly held in April 2004, thus bolstering Roh's position. Roh subsequently announced that he had joined the Uri Party.

Roh Tae-Woo

Born into a middle-class farming family in Talsong, North Kyongsang Province in 1932, Roh became President of the Republic of Korea (ROK) in 1988. He is best known for his pursuit of a *Nordpolitik* which eventually led to diplomatic relations with the Soviet Union and the **People's Republic of China (PRC)**.

After graduating from Kyongbok Middle School in 1950, Roh joined the army. In 1951 he entered the Korean Military Academy. He graduated in 1955 and then served in various positions in the army. In 1959 he attended the Special Warfare School in the USA and later the Korean Army War College. In 1979, as commander of the Capital Security Command, he took part in the December coup engineered by **Chun Doo-Hwan**. In August 1980 he became commander of the Defense Security Command.

Roh joined the **Democratic Justice Party (DJP)** on its inauguration, and after retiring from the army in July 1981 he served in a number of ministerial positions before becoming president of the **Seoul** Olympic Games Organizing Committee in July 1983. In the following year he became president of the Korean Olympic Committee. Elected as a member of the **ROK National Assembly** in 1985, Roh became chairman of the DJP, which nominated him as its presidential candidate for the 1987 presidential election, but following anti-government demonstrations Roh demanded that Chun introduce reforms and address political grievances. Chun accepted the demand, which defused the political crisis, and on 5 August 1987 Roh replaced President Chun as president of the ruling DJP.

Roh was victorious in the presidential election held in December 1987, winning 36.6% of the popular vote and defeating four other candidates. On 25 February 1988 Roh became the 13th President. His presidency was notable for the successful Seoul Olympic Games in 1988, and for his *Nordpolitik*. The same policy led to a series of agreements with the Democratic People's Republic of Korea (DPRK) in 1991–92, but these remained largely unimplemented. The beginning of the DPRK nuclear crisis overshadowed the end of his presidency. In 1990 he concluded a political alliance with the veteran opposition leader **Kim Young-Sam**, who succeeded him as President in 1993.

After he left office Roh, like Chun, came under constant attack for his role in the 1979 coup and the 1980 **Kwangju uprising**. Eventually, in 1995, both Roh and Chun were arrested on charges of bribery and corruption, to which charges of treason and mutiny were later added. Roh was sentenced to 22 years' imprisonment and a fine in 1996, but both he and Chun were released in 1997 when **Kim Dae-Jung** became President, although in theory the fine was not cancelled. Since then Roh has kept a low profile, though he appears in public from time to time in the capacity of an elder-statesman.

Russian Far East

Dal'nii Vostok

The area of the Russian Federation bordering the Pacific coast.

The Russian Far East extends north from the frontier with the **People's Republic of China (PRC)** and the Democratic People's Republic of Korea (DPRK) up to the East Siberian Sea within the Arctic Circle and includes the island of **Sakhalin**. To the west is the Siberian Federal District. (The Russian Far East was separated from Siberia in 1884.) The area forms the Far Eastern Federal District and comprises seven separate territories and the autonomous Sakha Republic (also known as Yakutia). Among its important cities are Vladivostok and Khabarovsk. The eastern Russian section of the **Trans-Siberian Railway** runs through the area to terminate at Vladivostok. The region is rich in natural resources, such as timber and petroleum, but has suffered economically and socially since the collapse of the Soviet Union in 1991, when it lost its status as the eastern bulwark against the USA in the Cold War. The Soviet Union had extended the settlement of the area and had maintained its Pacific fleet at Vladivostok.

The far eastern regions of Russia were first explored from the west of the country in the 17th century. Traders and settlers pushing into the area came into conflict with the Chinese Qing empire. Among the earliest treaties negotiated between **China** and what might be termed a Western power were those signed in 1689 and 1727 between Russia and China to regulate relations between the two countries and to establish a border. This was fixed along the middle course of the **Amur river**. As Russia sought to extend its empire eastwards from the mid-19th century and to establish settlements in the Pacific region, it again found itself in dispute with China. Joining in the general pressure being exerted on China by Western powers to open up to diplomatic relations and trade, Russia succeeded in 1860 in securing from China the land east of the **Ussuri river** (a tributary of the Amur) across to the Pacific coast. (Part of this area now forms the Primorskiy region of the Russian Far East.) The border between Russia and China was thus largely fixed along the two rivers. Against the background of the **Sino–Soviet dispute**, armed clashes broke out in 1969 between the PRC and the Soviet Union over the exact line of the frontier, leading to some loss of life. In 1997 the PRC and the Russian Federation decided to resolve this source of friction. Agreement on this issue formed part of the deliberations of the 'Shanghai Five', which in 2001 reconstituted themselves in the **Shanghai Co-operation Organization**.

The same 19th-century Russian presence on the Pacific coast brought Russia up against Japan, then also expanding beyond its basic territory, and is the source of the long-running dispute between the two countries over the status of the southernmost of the **Kurile Islands**. This chain of islands runs from the southern tip of the Kamchatka peninsula southwards to the northern end of Hokkaido. In a treaty of 1875 Russia acknowledged Japanese control over the entire chain, while Japan recognized Russian sovereignty over the whole of the island of Sakhalin. The status of Sakhalin had until then been undetermined. (Japan was later ceded the southern half of Sakhalin after the Russo–Japanese War of 1904–05.) The rights of each country to trade in each other's ports in the coastal Pacific area and for the Japanese to fish in Russian waters were also agreed. Subsequent hostility between Russia (and the successor Soviet Union) and Japan was largely played out in the Russian Far East. At the very end of the Second World War Stalin broke the Neutrality Pact of 1941 between the two countries, declared war on Japan and let Soviet troops occupy territories that Japan had held as part of its empire. These included the southern half of Sakhalin and the southernmost islands in or attached to the Kuriles, which had also passsed into Japanese hands. Failure to resolve the competing claims to the southern Kuriles has prevented the signing of a peace treaty between the two states, even though diplomatic relations were restored in 1956. In the 1970s Japan expressed interest in participating in the development westwards of an oil pipeline from the Russian Far East, but this came to nothing.

From the 1860s impoverished Korean farmers had been moving north from the **Korean peninsula** into the north-east region of China and the southern part of Primorskiy district of the Russian Far East in search of land. A number of **Koreans** settled in the area around Vladivostok, which eventually acquired a Korean suburb. In 1937 these **overseas Koreans** were transported to central Asia on Stalin's orders, on suspicion of providing a cover for Japanese espionage. China and the Soviet Union continued to give shelter to Korean guerrillas fighting the Japanese, who by the late 1930s had moved into north-east China from Korea. The guerrillas, who included the Korean leader **Kim Il Sung**, were pushed back into the Soviet Far East. It is thought that Kim's son, **Kim Jong Il**, may have been born in that part of the Soviet Union, possibly at Khabarovsk (whatever the claims made for a birthplace in the DPRK). As another consequence of the disruption of war, a small community of Koreans exists on Sakhalin, having been taken to the southern half of the island by their Japanese colonial masters to exploit the island's reserves of coal. After the end of the war they were prevented from leaving by the Soviet authorities. The Korean population of Sakhalin is now ageing as younger members go elsewhere. Economic links are maintained between the Russian Far East and the DPRK, which since the late 1960s has supplied labour against payment to first Soviet, then Russian logging camps in the Khabarovsk region. Other workers have been recruited through DPRK official channels for labour in mines and on construction sites in the area. The small stretch of border between the DPRK and the Russian Far East forms part of the **Tumen River Area Development Programme**.

S

Sakhalin

Karafuto

The island of Sakhalin (*Karafuto* in Japanese) lies north of the Japanese mainland. Japanese seem to have begun to move there in the 18th century, although some **Ainu** may have been there before. From 1807 the Bakufu, the then central government of Japan, ruled the island directly, but the growing Russian presence in the area increasingly challenged Japanese rule. In 1855 a Russo-Japanese Treaty provided for the joint administration of the island. Twenty years later, however, under the May 1875 Treaty of St Petersburg, the Japanese gave up their claim to Sakhalin in return for the **Kurile Islands**.

The position of the island changed again in 1905, following Russia's defeat in the Russo–Japanese War. Under the terms of the 1905 Treaty of Portsmouth, Japan took over Sakhalin south of the 50th parallel. From then until 1945 the Hokkaido authorities administered this area at first, followed by a local administration based at the capital, Toyohara. Japan's main interest was in the timber resources of the island. In 1920–23, following the Japanese intervention in Siberia, Japan occupied the north of the island as well, exploiting coal and other mineral resources. Although the northern half of the island returned to Soviet control in 1923, Japan retained some exploitation rights in the north until 1945. By 1945 there were 415,000 Japanese citizens (Japanese and **Koreans**) in Southern Sakhalin. Japanese efforts concentrated on the development of the timber, coal and fishing industries.

The **Yalta Conference** of 1945 agreed that Southern Sakhalin should be restored to the Soviet Union, and when the latter declared war on Japan in August 1945 it quickly occupied the area, renaming the capital Yuzhno-Sakalinsk. The Japanese population was repatriated between 1946–48, leaving several thousand **overseas Koreans**, mostly from South Korea. The Soviet Union, which had no relations with South Korea (later the Republic of Korea—ROK), refused to repatriate the Koreans.

At the 1951 San Francisco Peace Conference the Soviet Union demanded the formal return of Southern Sakhalin and the Kurile Islands to Soviet sovereignty, but although Japan renounced its rights to these territories they were not formally assigned to any other state in the **San Francisco Peace Treaty**.

In February 2000 the first group of 120 South Koreans out of some 43,000 from Sakhalin were able to return to the ROK, under a deal arranged by the ROK and Russian Red Cross Societies. This group was resettled in the **Seoul** area, in accommodation provided by Japan. Most of the others were dead, and although some 36,000 Koreans still live in Sakhalin the Russian authorities have so far refused to allow descendants of the original settlers to return to the ROK.

San Francisco Peace Treaty

As early as 1947 the USA began pressing for a peace treaty to end the **Allied Occupation of Japan**. However, some Allied countries, including Australia, objected to what were viewed as excessively generous terms, and it was not until 1950 that substantive negotiations began, led by John Foster Dulles as the US special envoy. The Soviet Union, which had been excluded from any role in the Occupation, disagreed with the US approach, and so Dulles conducted a series of bilateral negotiations rather than organizing a conference of the wartime Allies. In September 1951 Britain and the USA presented an agreed text to those countries willing to attend a conference in San Francisco, USA. The Soviet Union refused to attend and there was no Chinese representation. On 8 September 1951 Japan and 48 other countries signed the Treaty, which came into force on ratification.

The Treaty ended the **Pacific War** and restored Japan's sovereignty, but this was confined to the four main islands plus some small island groups. Japan abandoned all territorial gains made since 1875. The USA controlled the **Ogasawara Islands** and **Okinawa** under a **United Nations'** trusteeship. The Soviet Union refused to recognize the Treaty, and remained technically at war with Japan until 1956, when the two countries established diplomatic relations. They have never signed a peace treaty. Japan and the **'Republic of China'** concluded a peace treaty in 1952. A number of Eastern European countries did not sign the San Francisco Peace Treaty, but subsequently concluded normalization treaties with Japan. Japan and the **People's Republic of China (PRC)** established diplomatic relations in 1972, and signed a Treaty of Peace and Friendship in 1978. In this, the PRC waived all rights to compensation for Japan's wartime activities.

Sangiin

The upper house, or House of Councillors, of Japan's **National Diet**.

Sapporo

Capital city of Japan's Hokkaido region.

The city dates from 1869, when Hokkaido became integrated into Japan and the Hokkaido Development Agency, the *Kaitakushi*, was established. Today it is the third largest city by area in Japan, and has a population of 1.87m. Sapporo is unlike other Japanese cities, and has an open and spacious feel about it. It is noted for its winter sports and snow festival, and was the host city for the Winter Olympic Games in 1972. In 1986 it hosted the first Winter Asian Games. In addition to its attractions as a tourist city, its local economic activity includes agriculture, mining, construction and manufacturing. Sapporo beer has acquired a world-wide reputation.

Self-Defence Forces

Nihon jietai

Under the terms of Article 9 of its post-war Constitution, Japan renounced the maintenance of military forces and war as a means of settling international disputes. However, while still under occupation, during the **Korean War** in 1950, the Japanese government organized a National Police Reserve. This became the Public Security Force in 1952. In 1954, after Japan had regained its independence, this became the Ground, Air and Maritime Self-Defence Forces (SDF).

The SDF are under the control of the Prime Minister, through the director-general of the Defense Agency, who is a member of the Cabinet. The SDF took responsibility for defence procurement in 1958 and for liaison with the US forces in Japan in 1962. There has been constant pressure from right-wing politicians to remove civilian control from the armed forces, so far without success The SDF's role has increased since September 2001, and this may lead to further pressure for a modification in the control structure.

Despite the euphemism, the SDF are effectively the same as the armed forces of other countries. There have been numerous challenges to the legality of the SDF, but although lower courts have ruled that they are unconstitutional, the Supreme Court has not declared a position on the matter. Since 1976 the official target for defence spending has been 1% of the gross national product. This was exceeded for a time in the 1980s, but current spending is slightly under this figure. Nevertheless, because of the strength of the Japanese economy, Japan's defence expenditure had become the third largest in the world by the late 1980s. In 2004 the SDF had 239,000 personnel. Defence expenditure in 2000 was US $42.9m. Most military equipment, including aircraft, is manufactured in Japan, some under licence. Japanese military forces served overseas for the first time since 1945 in 1991, when the Maritime SDF took part in minesweeping operations in the Persian (Arabian) Gulf. Since 1992 SDF forces have been permitted to take part in **United Nations** peace-keeping operations. Such activities still cause some concern among Japan's neighbours, who claim to fear a possible revival of Japanese militarism.

E-mail: info@jda.go.jp
Internet: www.jda.go.jp

Seoul

Capital of the Republic of Korea (ROK) since 1948 and former capital of unified Korea from 1392 until the end of the **Pacific War**. In the course of those centuries, it became the political, cultural and social heart of the country.

Seoul is situated at the mid-point of the western side of the **Korean peninsula** (which places it in the extreme north-west corner of the ROK) and lies on the Han river, some 32 km from the port of Inchon. With a population of more than 10m. (representing between one-fifth and one-quarter of the national population) and an area of 602.5 sq km, the municipality is densely occupied. As well as housing parliamentary and government offices, the capital has a large number of universities, colleges and research institutes and many cultural institutions and is the financial and business centre of the country. It is served by an extensive subway system, but, with ever-increasing car and vehicle use, traffic congestion has risen inexorably. In 1986 Seoul hosted the Asian Games, in 1988 the Summer Olympic Games and in 2002 (jointly with Japan) the World Cup football championship.

Under Japanese colonial rule in the first half of the 20th century, Seoul was transformed into a modern city and a major economic and transport centre. So important had it become that the decision to draw the line for the Japanese surrender in 1945 at the **38th parallel** was partly based on the wish to have the capital in the US zone. Seoul suffered great damage during the **Korean War** and lost much of its population, when it was fought over four times. The ROK government withdrew and spent much of the war in the southern port city of **Pusan**. On the outbreak of fighting in June 1950 Seoul was a prime target for the forces of the Democratic People's Republic of Korea (DPRK), which captured the city within three days. They held it for three months and introduced political and social reforms similar to those already in place in the DPRK; but by the end of September 1950 had been driven out by **United Nations (UN)** forces, which by that time had started to advance north. Chinese intervention in the war on the DPRK side in October 1950 pushed the UN forces back down the peninsula. Seoul fell to the Chinese in early January 1951, after being fired by UN troops. It was recaptured by UN forces in March 1951, and remained in UN hands for the rest of the war. The ROK government moved back to Seoul only at the end of 1953.

It was not until President **Park Chung-Hee** introduced economic reforms in the 1960s that major changes began to take place in the capital, which started to suck in new residents, particularly from rural areas. Its vulnerability to attack from the DPRK for many years inhibited growth to the north of the city, and urban development took place largely to the south of the Han river; but since the late 1980s Seoul has spread continuously both north and south and is now surrounded by many satellite towns. In June 2004 President **Roh Moo-Hyun** announced plans to construct a new administrative capital for the ROK in an area south of Seoul. The site eventually chosen was in South Chungchong Province. Work was to begin in 2007 and was scheduled for completion by 2014. Roh's stated intentions are to break up the concentration of power and wealth in the present metropolitan area, relieve the capital's overcrowding and promote balanced regional development. The proposal formed part of his presidential campaign in 2002 and received parliamentary approval when it was presented to the **National Assembly** in December 2003. **Park Geun-Hye**, the leader of the main opposition **Grand National Party**, which constituted the majority party in the Assembly at the time that the relocation bill was presented, has since apologized for letting it through without sufficient scrutiny. In October 2004 the Constitutional Court of the ROK, announcing its verdict on a petition presented by a group of Seoul residents, declared that the 2003 law violated the country's Constitution. Seoul is not cited in the Constitution as the capital, but the Constitutional Court argued that the city's centuries-long designation as capital had the weight of an unwritten constitutional provision. As such, the proposal to relocate the capital should have been presented as a constitutional amendment and have then been put to a national referendum for approval. Instead, it was passed as a general law. The Court claims its verdict is final and cannot be appealed against.

Severe Acute Respiratory Syndrome (SARS)

An atypical form of pneumonia of which the causes are as yet unknown. It is now described as SARS coronavirus (SARS-CoV).

Symptoms include a high fever (above 38°C), muscular pain, a dry cough, shortness of breath or breathing difficulties. The disease is contagious, although the mode of transmission has not yet been determined; airborne transmission through droplets or transmission from body fluids may both be possible. Healthcare workers who have come into contact with cases and medical research workers who may have been exposed to the virus have been particularly affected. Treatment has so far taken the form of isolation, barrier nursing and supportive care. In some instances, ventilator support has become necessary. A number of deaths have occurred

SARS was first recognized in February 2003 in a case reported in Hanoi, Viet Nam. The first cases of the illness, however, were identified earlier, in November 2002, in Guangdong Province of the **People's Republic of China (PRC)**, and World Health Organization data for the period 1 November 2002–31 July 2003 indicate that the greatest number of probable cases occurred in the PRC: 5,327 out of a total of 8,096 world-wide. Of the 774 deaths world-wide attributed to SARS for the same period, the PRC recorded 349, somewhat fewer than one-half of the total. After China, **Hong Kong** suffered most severely, with 1,755 probable cases and 299 deaths. From the PRC and Hong Kong the virus was carried by travellers to a number of points world-wide, in particular **Taiwan** and Singapore. The relatively high number of probable cases in Canada—251 cases and 43 deaths—may be explained by the introduction of the illness through travellers from Hong Kong. Of other countries in East Asia, both Mongolia and the Republic of Korea reported a small number of cases—nine and three respectively; while **Macao** recorded only one case. Japan does not appear to have been affected. The Democratic People's Republic of Korea did not report any cases and practised stringent quarantine measures. Health checks were introduced elsewhere at airports to screen incoming and departing passengers. The effects of the epidemic on tourism and travel into the region were damaging.

By mid-June 2003 the epidemic appeared to have abated, but not before criticism of the way in which the authorities in **Beijing** had sought to cover up the extent of the illness in the Chinese capital. Late in December 2003 two separate cases were again identified in Guangdong, where the first cases had occurred. Nine cases reported by the PRC Ministry of Health in April 2004 involved researchers at the National Institute of Virology Laboratory in Beijing and those who had had close contact with them. As of 19 May 2004 no further cases of SARS had been reported anywhere in the world.

An official report issued in Hong Kong in early July 2004 on the handling of the SARS epidemic in Hong Kong between March and June 2003 criticized the health secretary for confusing and misleading statements on the course of the illness, which gave the impression that the Hong Kong government was attempting to minimize the severity of the epidemic. In response, the health secretary resigned.

Shamanism

Belief in, and the practice of, communication through a shaman with both good and evil spirits, generally for the purposes of soliciting good fortune, healing sickness or appeasing the spirits of the deceased.

A shaman may be male or female. The term comes from the Tungusic languages of Siberia, where the practice had deep roots. Shamanism is indigenous to Mongolia and the **Korean peninsula**. In both areas **Buddhism** sought to marginalize it. In Mongolia it survived the general Communist persecution of religion after 1924 and was reinstated in 1993 as one of the country's three native religions. The Buryat minority has practised shamanism. A few active shamans, mainly men, remain and are free to perform. They have their own professional association, and the country has a centre for shamanist studies. The Asian Shamanism Association moreover is based in the Mongolian capital, **Ulaan Baatar**. In Korea shamanism was held in much scorn by the **Confucianism** of the Choson or Yi dynasty (1392–1910) as superstition and the preserve of women and was banned from contact with the court. None the less, shamans continued to be consulted by the royal queens. Shamanism persists to this day in the Republic of Korea (ROK) and has its main centre in **Seoul**. Attitudes in the ROK towards shamanism remain ambivalent, but shamans, who in Korea are usually women, are still consulted on family matters and illness and asked to officiate at public ceremonies to invite good fortune or cleanse a site of bad influences.

There are no uniform stages in the formation of a shaman. For some, the position is hereditary. Others experience an illness, which they interpret as the descent of the spirits and a sign that they must take up activity as a shaman. Training from other shamans and guidance by a master spirit seem essential. Many shamans, but not all, communicate with the spirits through an ecstatic trance, aided by drumming, singing and dancing. Mongolian shamans, in the course of this trance, claim their soul flies into the spirit world to seek assistance, and they may disguise themselves in a costume representing a magic animal body. Korean shamans often dress in a variety of robes to represent different spirits. Korean shamanist rituals may take place indoors or in the open.

Such elaborate systems do not appear to exist in other parts of East Asia. References in the press from time to time to the need to combat witchcraft and superstitious practices in rural areas of the **People's Republic of China** suggest the persistence of rituals to ward off ill fortune and influence events. Until at least the 19th century, shamans were consulted in Japan over such problems as illness, but it is difficult to know if they still exist. The many **new religions** that have established themselves in Japan since the early 19th century have sometimes incorporated shamanist practices, thereby offering a continuing outlet for this particular approach to the spirit world.

Shanghai

Shanghai, often described as the largest city in the **People's Republic of China (PRC)**, is in fact now smaller than **Chongqing** in terms of population. Greater Chongqing's population at the end of 2003 was more than 30m., while Shanghai's permanent population totalled about 13.5m. at that time. In addition, a large influx of immigrant workers pushes Shanghai's regular population to more than 20m. However, if Shanghai has lost its population lead, in every other sense it is the PRC's chief city.

Although Shanghai was an important local port long before it opened as a centre for foreign trade, the 1842 Treaty of **Nanjing** began the city's modern development. From this came the modest **foreign settlement** of the 1840s that expanded after 1853 as the government lost control of central **China** during the Taiping Rebellion. Shanghai's position at the centre of China's long coastline made it the port for the whole of the vast central area of the country. From the 1890s onwards Shanghai also began to develop as an industrial centre, with Chinese enterprises soon joining Japanese and Western factories. Western banks and financial institutions also made the city their headquarters. By the outbreak of the **Pacific War** Shanghai was the main commercial and industrial city in China, accounting for about one-half of the country's total industrial production. It was also a major educational and political centre; the **Chinese Communist Party** held its first Congress there in 1921.

Although occupied by the Japanese during the war, Shanghai made a quick recovery after 1945, and by 1949 it had recaptured much of its pre-war eminence. Its population was then about 5m. However, the PRC viewed Shanghai with suspicion, despite its industrial role. It was too cosmopolitan in outlook and too tainted by its hedonistic past. Many of its leading industrialists fled before the advancing Communists. Yet, there was no choice but to exploit its productivity, but the centre kept Shanghai on a tight rein, spending little on its development and the modernization of its industries. The centre needed the revenue that Shanghai generated, but Shanghai got little in return, even after **Deng Xiaoping** began the period of reform and opening after 1978. The lack of investment in the city showed in rundown buildings, poor roads and a general decline in the quality of life. At the same time, the economic experiments that were transforming cities such as **Guangzhou** were not extended to Shanghai for fear that there would be a loss of revenue.

The position began to change in the 1990s, when Shanghai was allowed to implement new economic policies, including the development of the Pudong region, on the other side of the Huangpu river from the traditional centre of the city. This process speeded up after Deng's trip to the south in 1992, when he decided that Shanghai had been held back, and that this policy should be reversed. Shanghai's subsequent economic development put it back into the leading position it had previously occupied. It also marked a change of direction, away from the city's traditional industrial base towards modern hi-tech industries, and the development of banking and other financial services. There are now numerous development zones attached to the city, which, at the same time, remains an important agricultural production and processing centre.

By 1997 Shanghai's gross domestic product (GDP) had reached US \$40.5m., and per caput GDP stood at US \$3,000. The city now occupies 6,340 sq km. Its infrastructure has undergone major changes, with new hotels, road systems and a subway network. Skyscrapers have returned. Housing is a priority, and there has been a reform of housing policy so that house purchase is easier. Shanghai is now, again, one of the world's major trading cities. It has also recovered its former role as a major educational centre, with some 39 institutions of higher education. It has think-tanks and study groups that can match those of **Beijing**.

Shanghai Co-operation Organization (SCO)

Multilateral organization grouping the **People's Republic of China (PRC)**, the Russian Federation and four Central Asian republics, Kazakhstan, Kyrgyzstan, Tajikistan and Uzbekistan.

From less formal gatherings that began in April 1996 with a meeting in **Shanghai** of the first five members of the group and developed into annual meetings of the 'Shanghai Five', a group of six members (Uzbekistan joined in 2001) had emerged by 2001 as the Shanghai Co-operation Organization (SCO). In January 2004 it announced the installation of a permanent secretariat and secretary-general in **Beijing** (Zhang Deguang, a PRC career diplomat whose last posting was as ambassador to the Russian Federation, was chosen as the first secretary-general), and of a permanent anti-terrorist structure based in Tashkent, the capital of Uzbekistan. This structure was officially inaugurated at the June 2004 summit, held in Tashkent. In September 2004, at a meeting in the capital of Kyrgyzstan, Bishkek, the SCO further approved an agreement on co-operation in the areas of trade, science, technology, humanitarian projects and terrorism. Annual meetings of the six heads of state are envisaged under a rotating presidency, and the Organization has its own budget, emblem and flag.

The Shanghai Convention that accompanied the formation of the SCO in 2001 called for a struggle against 'terrorism, separatism and extremism'. These issues sum up the principal concerns that the six members share in varying degrees. The PRC has always been vigilant against the danger of separatist movements in its western region of **Xinjiang**, where the local population is substantially Muslim and shares a common background with ethnically similar peoples in Central Asia. One of the most important elements in the SCO's operation has been the formation of a regional anti-terrorism body that would facilitate co-operation between the border control, law enforcement and secret service agencies of the six member states and allow mutual assistance in emergencies. Priorities have changed during the eight years of the SCO's existence. The Shanghai Five met first in the context of the PRC's and Russia's desire to resolve old border disputes left over from the Soviet era and to demilitarize their long common border. Afghanistan, from being an object of suspicion to Russia and the Central Asian republics as a source of fundamentalist-generated unrest, was invited to send the head of its interim government to the June 2004 summit as a guest. A delegation from Mongolia also attended as guests.

Sec.-Gen.: Zhang Deguang

Shenzhen

City in Guangdong Province of the **People's Republic of China (PRC)**, symbol of the PRC's post-1978 development.

Before 1980 Shenzhen was a small village on the border between the PRC and the then British colony of **Hong Kong**. However, in that year the PRC party and government designated it the first of the country's **Special Economic Zones (SEZs)** and Shenzhen began to develop rapidly. The total area of Shenzhen is 2,200 sq km, with a population of 4.67m. in 2002; that of the SEZ is 391.7 sq km with a population of 2.5m. More than 90% of the population are immigrants from other parts of the PRC. Shenzhen has close links with Hong Kong, and is a popular destination for Hong Kong tourists. It is also a manufacturing centre, producing electronic goods, pharmaceuticals, chemicals, textiles, building materials, and processed foods. Wages and the standard of living in both the SEZ and the surrounding area are higher than the norm.

Shin Ki-Nam

Shin Ki-Nam, born in 1952, is a lawyer turned politician, who became chairman of the government **Uri Party** in the Republic of Korea (ROK) in May 2004. However, in August 2004 he resigned after it was revealed that his father had been a military policeman in the Japanese colonial period (1910–45).

Shin was educated at **Seoul** National University and the University of London, and spent some time as a naval officer. In 1996 he entered the **ROK National Assembly** as a member of **Kim Dae-Jung**'s **National Congress for New Politics (NCNP)**. He was special assistant to Kim Dae-Jung during the latter's successful bid for the presidency in 1997, and then became spokesman for the NCNP. He later transferred to the **Millennium Democratic Party**, and then to the Uri Party. Until his resignation, he worked closely with the current ROK President, **Roh Moo-Hyun.**

Shinkansen

In Japan, what are called in the West 'Bullet Trains' are known as the *Shinkansen*, or new trunk line. The system dates from 1964, when the first of these new trains ran from **Tokyo** to **Osaka**. Since then, the original line has been extended and many new lines using the fast trains have been added to the network, but it is still centred on Tokyo. The maximum speed is 270kph. The introduction of these fast trains transformed the Japanese railway system.

Shinto

Shinto, which means 'the way of the gods', is a hard-to-define set of religious beliefs found only in Japan or among **overseas Japanese**. It appears to be a survival from the animistic beliefs that prevailed before **Buddhism** reached Japan in the late 6th century AD. It has no founder, no formal body of beliefs, no scriptures, and only the loosest form of priesthood. Places are sacred, and Shinto followers are very aware of the natural world of trees, streams and silent places.

After the **Meiji Restoration** in 1868, the government promoted Shinto as a means of bolstering the status of the **Japanese Emperor**. This form of 'state Shinto' reached its peak just before and during the **Pacific War**, and extended to Japan's colonial possessions such as **Taiwan** and the **Korean peninsula**. In this period Shinto came to resemble a more orthodox religion and, as a result, tensions arose between several Christian denominations and the Japanese authorities over the insistence that all schools, for example, should follow Shinto rites.

The **Allied Occupation of Japan** abolished state Shinto, and it has never revived. However, the emperor still performs some Shinto-related rites, and right-wing political groups often profess a belief in Shinto. For many Japanese, Shinto is a comforting set of rituals associated with everyday life, rather than a grand set of doctrines, and most find no difficulty in combining Shinto and other beliefs. This may explain why it is difficult to find accurate figures for Shinto followers. Figures vary from 2.8m. to 107m., or 86% of the total Japanese population. Outside Japan, a small number of people of Japanese descent claim to be Shinto followers.

Shugiin

The lower house, or House of Representatives, of Japan's **National Diet**.

Sino–Soviet dispute

Name given to the long period of friction between the **People's Republic of China (PRC)** and the former Soviet Union that appears to have begun in 1956.

Even before the establishment of the PRC in 1949, there had been strains in the **Chinese Communist Party's (CCP)** relations with the Soviet Union. Both the CCP leader **Mao Zedong** and Josef Stalin, the Soviet leader, seem to have been suspicious of each other, and the CCP was aware of past Soviet-**Kuomintang** links. In 1949, however, given Western hostility, the CCP had little choice but to 'lean to the East' for support. Mutual suspicions seem to have increased during the **Korean War**, when the PRC found the Soviet Union less than generous. Tensions increased further after Stalin's death, however, as the new Soviet programme of de-Stalinization cast doubts on Mao's cult of personality. Economic developments also caused tensions, as the Soviet Union refused to support the PRC's Great Leap Forward. The Soviet refusal to help the PRC develop a nuclear weapons capability was a further cause of friction.

In 1960 the Moscow Conference of Communist parties brought the dispute into the open, and PRC students and technical staff were withdrawn from the Soviet Union. For another 20 years the two sides exchanged polemics. In 1969, with the PRC in the middle of the **Cultural Revolution**, the verbal attacks led to military conflict on the Sino-Soviet borders. Each side drew back, but the tensions remained, exacerbated by developments such as the Soviet invasion of Afghanistan in 1979. In the 1990s, however, there was a gradual easing of tensions, culminating in the visit of Mikhail Gorbachev to the PRC in May 1989. Talks resumed on border issues, which were mostly resolved after the collapse of the Soviet Union in 1991. A further sign that the tensions of the past were over was the development of the **Shanghai Co-operation Organization** from the late 1980s onwards.

One unexpected side effect of the dispute was that it allowed the Democratic People's Republic of Korea (DPRK) some room for manoeuvre between the two big Communist powers. **Kim Il Sung**, the DPRK leader, who had fought with both the CCP guerrilla forces and the Soviet Red Army, was able and happy to exploit this.

Sinuiju

Capital of the Democratic People's Republic of Korea (DPRK) province of North Pyongan.

Sinuiju lies near the mouth of the **Yalu river**, opposite the city of Dandong in the **People's Republic of China (PRC)**. In 2002 the city's population was an estimated 377,000. Sinuiju began to develop as a commercial and industrial centre after the construction of the first bridge across the Yalu in 1910. Thereafter, it became an important transportation system for river and rail traffic, a role it still fulfils today. Because of its strategic position, **United Nations** forces heavily bombed Sinuiju during the **Korean War**.

Sinuiju is a major industrial city, producing paper, alcohol and chemicals. Some reports claim that it is also a military industrial centre. However, like most DPRK industrial cities, there have been few signs of activity since the mid-1990s, and it seems far less busy than Dandong across the river.

In September 2002 the DPRK government announced that Sinuiju was to become a **Special Administrative Region (SAR)**. Like the PRC's **Hong Kong** SAR, on which it appeared to have been modelled, the Sinuiju SAR would have its own flag, laws and visa-free entry facilities. To administer it, they appointed Yang Bin, a former PRC national, now a Dutch citizen, and a successful businessman with extensive interests in north-east China. Yang Bin announced an ambitious programme, which included the removal of most of the city's existing population and their replacement by young, technically-minded people from elsewhere in the country. Nothing was said about the possible fate of those displaced. However, in October 2002 the authorities in the PRC city of Shenyang arrested Yang Bin on tax-evasion and related charges. In July 2003 he was sentenced to 18 years' imprisonment. Although the DPRK has said that the development of the Sinuiju SAR will continue, there seems to be little evidence that any work is being done to implement the original proposal.

Six-Party talks

Set of multilateral talks, which began in **Beijing** in August 2003, as a means of resolving the issue of the **Democratic People's Republic of Korea nuclear programme**.

Following the breakdown of the **Agreed Framework** in the latter part of 2002, and the unwillingness of the USA to engage in bilateral discussions with the Democratic People's Republic of Korea (DPRK), the Administration of US President George W. Bush eventually devised the idea of a multilateral forum in which to handle the issue of the DPRK nuclear programme. The other participants in such a forum, apart from the DPRK and the USA, would be the Republic of Korea, Japan, the **People's Republic of China**, and Russia. These were all neighbours of the DPRK and, the USA argued, had an interest in restricting its alleged development of nuclear weapons.

Three rounds of talks took place, in August 2003, February 2004 and June 2004. A fourth round, scheduled for the autumn of 2004, did not take place, apparently because the DPRK preferred to wait until the US presidential election had concluded. The talks did not make much progress, but all parties seemed willing to continue them, in the absence of any alternative. In November 2004 the DPRK rejected claims that it wished to abandon the process, and indicated that it would be willing to participate in further talks in 2005.

Snow, Edgar (1905–72)

A journalist who played an important role in relations between the **Chinese Communist Party (CCP)** and the USA from 1928 until the 1970s.

Snow, born in 1905, studied journalism at the University of Columbia. In 1928 he went to **Shanghai**, where he worked on the *China Weekly Review*. His first book on **China**, *Far Eastern Front*, appeared in 1933, and dealt with Japan's aggression in **Manchuria**. In that year he moved to **Beijing**. There he taught at Yenjing University and was also foreign correspondent for the *Saturday Evening Post*. In 1936 Snow's interviews with the CCP leader, **Mao Zedong**, led to *Red Star over China*, a book that introduced the CCP to the world. Snow reported on East Asia during the **Pacific War** and after, but in the 1950s he was attacked by US Senator Joseph McCarthy as being pro-communist. Snow left the USA and settled in Switzerland. He continued to write about China, and revisited the country in 1960 and 1965.

In 1970 the **People's Republic of China (PRC)** invited him to visit once more. His interviews with Mao and a photograph of Snow and the chairman on **Tiananmen** on National Day (1 October) 1970 were a signal to the USA of the PRC's wish to improve relations. Snow died in Switzerland in 1972 just as those relations were beginning to improve. His ashes are interred on the campus of Beijing University, where he taught in the days when it was Yenjing University.

Social Democratic Party of Japan (SDPJ)

Nihon shakaito/Nihon minshushakaito

Once the main opposition party in Japan, but now in decline.

Known as the Japan Socialist Party (JSP) for most of its existence, the Social Democratic Party of Japan (SDPJ) dates from the end of the **Pacific War** in 1945. In the autumn of 1945 various left-wing but non-communist groups came together to form the JSP. The Party was briefly in office in 1947, but it suffered badly in the 1949 elections, and remained in opposition until the early 1990s. During these years the Party suffered many splits and disagreements. It had a strong Marxist-Leninist wing and opposed the emergence of the **Self-Defence Forces** and Japan's security links with the USA, positions that did not always find favour with the electorate. Its fortunes improved in the mid-1980s, when **Doi Takako** became the first female head of a Japanese political party.

Under Doi the Party enjoyed some electoral successes, but she departed in 1991. In the 1993 lower house elections the JSP lost ground, but it benefited from the break up of the **Liberal Democratic Party (LDP)**, and was the largest party in the coalition put together by **Hosokawa Morihiro**. Following Hosokawa's resignation in April 1994, the SDPJ, as the Party now called itself, negotiated an alliance with the LDP—hitherto its staunchest opponent—and its leader, **Murayama Tomiichi**, became the first Socialist Prime Minister since 1947.

Murayama survived until 1996. While he introduced some Socialist policies, he was increasingly forced to compromise on issues such as defence that had long been dear to the Party. The strain proved too much, and when he resigned, to be replaced by Doi Takako, the old JSP/SDP effectively disappeared. The name remains, but Doi now leads a small group, mainly of women, who campaign on a narrow range of feminist and peace issues.

Chair.: Doi Takako
Address: Social Democratic Party
        1-8-1 Nagata-cho
        Chiyoda-ku
        Tokyo 100-8909
        Japan
Tel: 81-3-3551-1171
Fax: 81-3-3580-0691
E-mail: kokusai@sdp.or.jp
Internet: www.sdp.or.jp

Song Du-Yul

In March 2004 Song Du-Yul, a German national who was originally from the Republic of Korea (ROK), was sentenced to seven years' imprisonment under the ROK's anti-communist laws for allegedly working for the Democratic People's Republic of Korea (DPRK). Song had been under investigation by the National Intelligence Service (NIS) for such links since his return to **Seoul** in September 2003.

Song was born in 1944 and studied at Seoul National University before moving to West Germany, where he continued his studies at Heidelberg and Frankfurt am Main. He became a German citizen and was appointed Professor of Sociology at the University of Münster in 1982. He has published on a wide range of subjects, including the question of relations between the ROK and the DPRK. It has repeatedly been alleged in the ROK that he is a DPRK supporter, especially after he visited the North in 1991. In 1999 the DPRK defector, **Hwang Jang-Yop**, claimed that Song was a member of the DPRK **Korean Workers' Party**'s Political Bureau, using the name of Kim Chul-Su. Song denied the charge, and successfully sued Hwang for defamation in 2001.

In 2002 the Korean Democracy League invited him to return, but withdrew its invitation when the NIS announced that it wished to interview him about alleged links with the DPRK. The invitation was reissued in 2003. However, when Song returned to Seoul in September 2003, the NIS promptly began its investigation, leading to his eventual arrest despite a number of international protests.

Song appealed against his conviction, and in July 2004 the Seoul High Court ruled that there was not sufficient evidence to prove that he was a member of the DPRK Politburo, but that he had entered the DPRK illegally. His sentence was reduced from seven to three years' imprisonment, suspended. The prosecution announced that it would appeal, but in August 2004 Song returned to Germany.

Song has been the subject of a film, *Border City*, made in the ROK, which was shown at the 53rd Berlin Film Festival and the 2002 **Pusan** Film Festival.

Soong, James Chu-yu

Soong Chu-yu

'Republic of China' ('ROC') politician, former secretary-general of the **Kuomintang (KMT)**, 1989–93, former governor of **Taiwan** Province, 1993–98, founder and chairman of the **People First Party (PFP)**, 2000. James is his adopted Western name.

Soong was born in 1942 in Hunan Province of **China**, the son of a career soldier and supporter of **Chiang Kai-shek** who fled with his family to Taiwan in 1949. Soong studied at Taiwan and US universities in 1967–74, and in 1974–81 and 1984–89 served **Chiang Ching-guo** as secretary during the latter's terms as, first, Premier, and subsequently President. From 1979 until 1984 Soong was director-general of the Government Information Office. He was criticized for his use of censorship and his harsh handling of the **Kaohsiung incident** in 1979. Upon Chiang's death in 1988, Soong helped to secure **Lee Teng-hui**'s position as successor to Chiang in the presidency and in 1989 was appointed secretary-general of the KMT by Lee and, in 1993, as governor of Taiwan Province. He held this position until the post of governor was abolished in 1998 under a restructuring of the administration of the 'ROC' and the ending of the island's provincial status under the Nationalist government. Lee's failure to appoint Soong as Premier in 1996 when that position became vacant led Soong to turn away from Lee.

The split between the two men was confirmed when Lee, then still chairman of the KMT, promoted Vice-President **Lien Chan** as the KMT candidate for the presidential elections in 2000, in preference to Soong. Soong broke with the party and ran as an independent. He came second after **Chen Shui-bian**, chairman of the opposition **Democratic Progressive Party**. The KMT expelled Soong amid allegations that as secretary-general of the party he had diverted funds intended for the KMT for his own use. After the 2000 elections, Soong and his supporters set up the PFP. Its direction has openly been towards reconciliation with the **People's Republic of China** through not challenging the mainland's one-China policy. Soong has proposed a cross-straits union modelled on the European Union. This has led to charges that he is betraying Taiwan, and his mainland origins have counted against him. In the 2004 presidential elections he and Lien campaigned together, since their parties appeal to basically the same set of voters. They nevertheless failed to oust Chen Shui-bian, despite modifying their cross-straits policy, such that unification was no longer their ultimate stated goal.

Internet: www.pfp.org.tw

Special Administrative Regions (SARs)

Since 1997 the **People's Republic of China (PRC)** has created two Special Administrative Regions (SARs—not to be confused with the disease **Severe Acute Respiratory Syndrome**, which is abbreviated to SARS), one based on the former British colony of **Hong Kong**, the other, since 1999, on the former Portuguese colony of **Macao**. The Chinese leader **Deng Xiaoping** originally devised the concept of the SAR in the late 1970s, with the **'Republic of China'** on **Taiwan** in mind. However, the 'ROC' has rejected the idea.

The present SARs derive their existence from Article 31 of the PRC Constitution, which authorizes the **National People's Congress (NPC)** to create such areas. Each SAR has its own Basic Law, which serves as a local constitution, but which is subject to revision by the NPC. Under the Basic Law, each SAR has a high degree of local autonomy, with local people forming the administration under a separate political system. Non-Chinese residents of Hong Kong and Macao can also hold certain offices in the SAR. The Chinese SARs also maintain a capitalist economic system. In addition, they conduct their own economic policies, and form their own customs areas. This allows them to participate independently in international economic activities.

In 2002 the Democratic People's Republic of Korea (DPRK) announced that it would establish a similar SAR at **Sinuiju** on the **Yalu river** border with China, and that a Chinese-born Dutch national, Yang Bin, would administer it. There is no evidence that the DPRK authorities consulted or informed the PRC government in advance of their intentions. In the event, the Shenyang city authorities arrested Yang Bin on charges of tax evasion, and the Shinuiju project seems to have been suspended.

Special Economic Zones (SEZs)

In both the **People's Republic of China (PRC)** and the Democratic People's Republic of Korea (DPRK) certain areas have been designated as Special Economic Zones (SEZs). These zones are similar to export processing zones found elsewhere in the world.

The practice began in the PRC when such zones were created, under **Deng Xiaoping**'s auspices, at **Shenzhen**, Zhuhai and Shantou in Guandong Province in 1979. These regions were allowed to receive foreign investment and were also subject to special tax and customs regimes, designed to encourage the development of manufacturing and foreign trade. The original group were selected because of their proximity to **Hong Kong**, as well as their distance from the traditional manufacturing areas of the PRC in the north-east. In the mid-1980s another 14 areas and the whole of Hainan Island were added, and others have been created since then. Although some SEZs, such as Shenzhen, have had spectacular success, in general the benefits have been mixed. The special privileges accorded to the zones have caused problems with other regions of **China**, but the experiment has continued.

The DPRK established its first SEZ at Rajin-Sonbong in the far north-east of the country in 1991. The decision to open such a zone so far from the capital or other centres may have been partly to avoid political contamination from such a development, but it was also linked to expectations that the planned **United Nations**-sponsored **Tumen River Area Development Programme** would bring prosperity to the area. The Tumen River project has not been successful, however, and while Rajin-Sonbong has had some modest investment, it has not flourished as was hoped. A planned SEZ at **Kaesong**, involving **Hyundai Corporation** of the Republic of Korea, may have more chance of success, but it is still at a very early stage. An even more ambitious development for **Sinuiju** on the **Yalu river**, announced in 2002, seems to be moribund.

Stalinism

Term used to describe the communist policies associated with Josef Stalin (1879–1953), who ruled the Union of Soviet Socialist Republics from the death of Vladimir Lenin in 1924 until his own death in 1953.

The term is associated with the most hard line, centralist and undemocratic forms of communism and is now regularly applied to the Democratic People's Republic of Korea (DPRK), whose leaders are considered to be pursuing the same heavy-handed methods as Stalin, with no tolerance of debate or dissent. Many also claim to detect echoes of Stalin's policies in the DPRK's economic and social policies. In practice, the term is now used too imprecisely to have much real meaning.

Standard Chartered Bank

Standard Chartered is a major international bank, closely associated with East Asia and especially **Hong Kong**. It is quoted on both the London and Hong Kong Stock Exchanges.

The merger of two existing banks created the current bank in 1969. The two original banks were the Chartered Bank of India, Australia and China, founded in 1853, and the Standard Bank of British South Africa, which dates from 1862. The former, as the name implies, was closely connected with East Asia. It opened a branch in **Shanghai** in 1859, and has maintained operations in **China** ever since, with the exception of the **Pacific War** years. In 1860 a branch opened in Hong Kong, and in 1862 the Chartered Bank began to issue banknotes there. Standard Chartered, together with the Hong Kong and Shanghai Bank of **HSBC Holdings**, and the **Bank of China**, is still one of Hong Kong's three note-issuing banks. Although the Bank is now a world-wide organization, employing some 30,000 people in more than 50 countries, it still maintains a strong presence not just in Hong Kong but elsewhere in the East Asian region as well.

In 2000 Standard Chartered acquired Chase Consumer Banking operations in Hong Kong, thus increasing its role there. In November 2004 it signed an agreement to take a stake in a new national bank to be established in the **People's Republic of China**, the Bohai Bank based in **Tianjin**. In January 2005 Standard Chartered acquired the South Korea first Bank.

State Council

Guowu yuan

The State Council is the highest administrative body in the **People's Republic of China**. It dates from the 1954 Constitution, and its role has been preserved in all subsequent constitutions. It brings together the Premier, Vice-Premiers, state councillors, and ministers. Its numbers have varied from 30 to more than 100, although a smaller group meets at least once a week. Its term of office corresponds to that of the **National People's Congress**, to which it is formally responsible.

State Great Hural

Ulsyn Ikh Khural

The State Great Hural—*hural* means assembly or gathering—is the national parliament of Mongolia.

It dates from 1924, and although its exact title has varied over the years, it was generally known as the People's Great Hural until 1990. In its current form, it dates from the constitutional reforms of 1992. It has a four-year term, and has 76 members. In 1992–96 these were returned from multi-seat constituencies; since 1996 candidates have been elected from single-seat constituencies. The **Mongolian People's Revolutionary Party (MPRP)** dominated the first post-1992 assembly, but was defeated by an opposition coalition in 1996. In 2000 the MPRP was victorious, winning 72 out of 76 seats. In the June 2004 elections the MPRP, while it remained the single largest party with 36 seats, faced an opposition alliance of 34, three independents and one representative of the Republican Party. The State Great Hural is a member of the **Inter-Parliamentary Union**, which it joined in 1962.

Address: State Great Hural
　　　　　State Palace
　　　　　Ulaan Bataar 12
　　　　　Mongolia
Tel: 976-1-322-150/1-329-210
Fax: 976-1-322-866
E-mail: choidong@mail.parl.gov.mn
Internet: www.parl.gov.mn

'Sunshine policy'

When **Kim Dae-Jung** became President of the Republic of Korea (ROK) in 1998, he announced that his government would follow a 'sunshine policy' towards the Democratic People's Republic of Korea (DPRK). The origins of the term lie in a folk tale, in which the wind and the sun contend in trying to persuade a traveller to take off his overcoat. The wind blows and buffets as hard as possible without success, but the sun, by shining steadily, succeeds.

In essence, the policy was one of engagement with, and assistance to, the DPRK, with certain clear rules to be applied if the DPRK behaved in hostile fashion towards the South. The idea of such a policy of engagement was not new; ever since **Park Chung-Hee**'s decision in 1972 to talk to the DPRK, ROK presidents had at some stage tried such a policy. Unlike his predecessors, Kim persisted with it even when the DPRK's actions appeared provocative. The policy appeared to have worked when Kim and the DPRK leader, **Kim Jong Il**, met in **Pyongyang**, at the June 2000 North-South summit, but there were always critics who claimed that the ROK was giving away too much for too little in return. When, towards the end of Kim Dae-Jung's term in office, it began to emerge that large sums of money had passed to the DPRK to facilitate the summit meeting, the criticism increased. The decline of US support for the policy after George W. Bush became President in 2001 also fostered criticism. However, Kim's successor, President **Roh Moo-Hyun**, announced in 2003 that he would continue the policy, albeit with a somewhat different title. By mid-2004, with growing economic co-operation between the two Koreas, and the first positive military contacts since 1953, the 'sunshine policy' seemed to be succeeding, despite vocal criticism from the opposition.

Supreme People's Assembly (SPA)

Chego Inmin Hoeui

The Supreme People's Assembly (SPA) of the Democratic People's Republic of Korea (DPRK) is a unicameral legislature, with 687 delegates elected by popular suffrage. It first met in August 1948, when there were 572 delegates. In the last election, for the 11th Assembly, held on 3 August 2003, 99.9% of the electorate participated, according to official sources. There is a single list of candidates, approved by the **Korean Workers' Party**.

Although in theory the term for the SPA is five years, in practice there have been long intervals between elections. The SPA only meets for one or two days annually. Between the regular meetings the SPA presidium conducts business. In addition, since 1994, the president of the presidium, currently **Kim Yong Nam**, has acted as head of state for certain functions, such as receiving ambassadors.

Address: Supreme People's Assembly
      Pyongyang
      Democratic People's Republic of Korea

T

Taipei

Since 1949 the leading city of the **'Republic of China'**, which has gradually acquired the attributes of a capital city.

In 1949, when the **Kuomintang** retreated from the Chinese mainland to **Taiwan**, the island's capital, Taipei, was a small, provincial city, though it had undergone some redevelopment in the Japanese colonial period. In 1967 it became a special municipality. Today it is the commercial and industrial capital of Taiwan in addition to its administrative role. Major industries include metals, engineering and chemicals, as well as more modern industries, such as electronics. The city covers some 271.8 sq km and has a population of 2,627,000.

Taiwan

An island some 160 km off the coast of the **People's Republic of China (PRC)**, opposite the coast of Fujian Province. In older Western books and maps, it often appears as 'Formosa', meaning 'beautiful', a name given by the Portuguese who discovered it in the 16th century. In 1949 the remnants of the defeated **Kuomintang (KMT)** government fled to Taiwan, and it has been the seat of the **'Republic of China' ('ROC')** ever since.

Taiwan and the nearby Penghu (Pescadores) Islands total 36,000 sq km in area. The main island is very mountainous. About one-quarter of the land is cultivable. Most of the island is sub-tropical, except for the tropical extreme southern tip. The monsoon cycle affects the islands, which have very heavy rainfall, especially in October–March. Summer temperatures reach 33 °C, and the climate is very humid. Taiwan receives an average of 3.6 typhoons a year.

The current population of the islands is about 22m. At the first census, conducted in 1905, it was just over 3m., and at the end of the **Pacific War**, 6m. The majority are **Han Chinese**. There is a small group of aboriginal people, who account for less than 2% of the population; in 2002 their number totalled 433,689 who belonged to 11 distinct groups. The aboriginal peoples have lived on the islands since at least 1500 BC. Chinese began to settle on Taiwan in the 12th century AD, but the real influx only began in the 17th century, when many loyal to the Ming court fled to the islands to escape the new Qing (Manchu) government of **China**. The island also served as a base for Chinese and Japanese pirates from the 13th century onwards. The Spanish and Dutch competed for control of the island in the 17th century, with the Dutch driving out the Spaniards in 1642. However, Ming loyalists in turn drove out the Dutch in 1662.

In 1683 the Qing conquered Taiwan, and from then until 1886 administered it as part of Fujian Province. In 1886 it became a province in its own right. In 1895, however, China ceded Taiwan and the Pescadores to Japan, following the Sino–Japanese War of 1894–95, and Taiwan became a Japanese colony. Although the Japanese faced resistance in the early years, in general the colonial period did not create in Taiwan the bitterness that it did in the **Korean peninsula**.

At the **Cairo Conference** in 1943 the Allies decided that Japan should relinquish all territories acquired since 1875, and that Taiwan should therefore be restored to China. Following the defeat of Japan in 1945, Chinese forces took the surrender of Japanese forces on the islands, which in October 1945 came under formal KMT control. Legally, the islands remained Japanese territory until a peace treaty could effect a formal transfer.

The KMT administration was harsh and exploitive, and created much resentment. In February 1947 this resentment turned to open rebellion, which was suppressed with a heavy loss of life. Then, in December 1949, the defeated government of **Chiang Kai-shek** fled to Taiwan, together with some 2m. supporters. In addition to Taiwan and the Pescadores, the KMT also held various groups of **offshore islands** off the Chinese coast that had no geographic or historical connection with Taiwan. The KMT continued to claim to be the legitimate government of China, and set up a national administration on Taiwan, which continued to call itself the government of the 'ROC'. This situation persisted with little change until the 1980s.

In the mean time, in the **San Francisco Peace Treaty** signed in 1951 and in force from April 1952, Japan had formally renounced its claims to Taiwan and the Pescadores. However, neither the PRC nor the 'ROC' were represented at the Treaty conference, and the Treaty made no reference to the transfer of the islands to either of them. Technically, therefore, although the original intention of the Allies was to transfer sovereignty to 'China', no such transfer has taken place. In the view of many international lawyers and governments, the islands' status remains legally undetermined.

The PRC and the 'ROC' contest this, however, and both have maintained that Taiwan is 'a province of China'. The PRC has insisted that its claim is acknowledged by states wishing to have diplomatic relations, and opposes any moves towards an independent Taiwan. The PRC also opposes any move that would accord the regime on Taiwan international recognition as a government. The 'ROC', for its part, has now abandoned the claim to be the government of China, but its leaders stop short of declaring themselves an independent 'Republic of Taiwan'. Instead, they argue that the 'Republic of China' dates from 1912, and that there are two separate states, the PRC and the 'Republic of China' existing in what was once a unified China.

The PRC has not ruled out the use of force to settle what it claims is an internal matter, but at present probably lacks the means to invade Taiwan. It must also take into account continued US support for the authorities on Taiwan, and the possibility of intervention to prevent an invasion.

Taiwan Relations Act (TRA)

Enacted by the 96th Congress of the USA to come into effect on 1 January 1979. The Taiwan Relations Act (TRA) followed the US decision to withdraw diplomatic recognition from the **'Republic of China' ('ROC')** on **Taiwan** in December 1978 and to accord it to the **People's Republic of China (PRC)**, and offered an immediate definition of the relationship it envisaged with the 'ROC' in the interests of maintaining stability in the region. The Act makes it clear that the continuation of 'commercial, cultural and other relations' with Taiwan forms part of US foreign policy.

The Act further spells out the USA expectation that the future of the 'ROC' will be determined by 'peaceful means', states that the use of anything other than peaceful means would be a cause of concern to the USA, and expresses the US decision to provide the 'ROC' with 'arms of a defensive character' and to maintain US capacity to 'resist any resort to force or other forms of coercion that would jeopardize the security, or the social or economic system, of the people on Taiwan'. In undertaking to provide defence equipment and services, the Act indicates that the USA will determine what is necessary for the 'ROC' to maintain an adequate self-defence capability. Existing or future export licences for nuclear exports to the 'ROC' will remain unaffected by the withdrawal of diplomatic recognition. Investments in Taiwan are to receive the same level of US support as before.

To handle future transactions with the 'ROC' within the country and to provide consular services to US citizens, the Act provided for the establishment of a non-profit-making corporation to be known as the American Institute in Taiwan. US government personnel seconded to the Institute would lose their government affiliation for the duration of their posting and would not function as employees of the USA. None the less, Congress is still required to monitor the implementation of the Act and all aspects of the US-Taiwan relationship.

In 1996 President Clinton, invoking the TRA, sent an aircraft carrier into the waters off the south coast of Taiwan in response to the PRC's action in conducting missile tests in the Taiwan Straits. The tests marked the PRC's displeasure at the first direct presidential elections on the island.

Taiwan Solidarity Union (TSU)

Taiwan tuanjie lianmeng

Taiwan political party founded in July 2001 by followers of former President **Lee Teng-hui**. It takes a pro-independence stance.

Lee supports the Taiwan Solidarity Union (TSU) and, since his expulsion in late 2000 from the **Kuomintang**, has spoken strongly in favour of Taiwan independence. The TSU's aim is, through its presence and activities in the **Legislative Yuan**, to prevent the ruling **Democratic Progressive Party** from moving too far from a pro-independence programme. On domestic issues it takes a centrist position. It secured 12 seats in the 2004 elections to the legislature, largely displacing the Taiwan Independence Party. It did less well in municipal elections in 2002 in **Taipei** and **Kaohsiung**, winning only two seats on Kaohsiung city council. The party forms part of the **Pan-Green coalition**.

Chair.: Huang Chu-wen
Address: 5th Floor
          180 Hoping East Rd
          Taipei
          Taiwan
Tel: 886-2-2367-8990
Fax: 886-2-2367-8408
Internet: www.tsu.org.tw

Tanaka Kakuei (1918–93)

An important political figure in Japan from the early 1960s, when he first attained ministerial office, until scandal drove him out of the **National Diet** in 1976.

Tanaka was born in Niigata in 1918. Unlike most Japanese politicians, he did not attend university. He spent some time in the army during the **Pacific War**, and later worked in the construction industry. He entered the Diet in 1947 as a member of the Liberal Party. In 1972, at the unusually young age of 55, he became Prime Minister.

He set himself three tasks. The first was normalization of relations with the **People's Republic of China**, which he achieved very quickly. The second was to reduce the chronic overcrowding in Japanese cities, which proved more difficult. It and the third policy, to introduce a welfare system, caused an inflationary spiral that damaged the Japanese economy. By that stage Tanaka had become embroiled in a major scandal involving payments from the Lockheed Corporation. He resigned and left the Diet but continued to run his faction of supporters from outside. In 1983 he received a suspended prison sentence for his role in the Lockheed affair, but continued to play a political role until he suffered a severe stroke in 1985. After his death his daughter, **Tanaka Makiko**, also entered politics, and she too became something of a maverick.

Tanaka Makiko

In January 2001 Tanaka Makiko became the first female foreign minister in Japan, in **Koizumi Junichiro**'s first Cabinet.

She was born in 1944, the daughter of **Tanaka Kakuei**, Prime Minister in 1972–76. After attending Waseda University, she worked for a bus company for a time, and helped nurse her father after he suffered a stroke in 1985. On his death in 1993 she entered politics, and was elected in her father's former constituency in Niigata as an independent. She then joined the **Liberal Democratic Party (LDP)** and became director of the Science and Technology Agency in the first **Murayama Tomiichi** coalition government. She performed well, but tended to quarrel with her officials. However, she was increasingly popular nationally, increasing her majorities in the 1996 and 2000 elections, and making frequent media appearances. Her time as foreign minister was marked by further quarrels with her officials and other LDP politicians, and by critical comments about the USA under the George W. Bush Administration. This led Koizumi to dismiss her in January 2002. She remained in the **National Diet** for a time, but her alleged involvement in a scandal over staff salaries led her to resign her seat in August 2002, while the LDP banned her from party activities for two years. She has continued to be critical of the USA and of Koizumi, and may well return to politics in due course.

Tang, Henry

Tang Ying-yen

Henry Tang, a former **Hong Kong** businessman, became financial secretary in the Hong Kong government in August 2003. He succeeded Anthony Leung, who resigned over claims that he had misused his position to avoid paying car tax.

Tang was born in Hong Kong in 1953. He studied at the University of Michigan in the USA. He is from a family with close ties to the **People's Republic of China (PRC)**; his father was a member of the PRC's **Chinese People's Political Consultative Conference**. Tang was a successful textile tycoon, who received international recognition for his work. In 1993 the World Economic Forum named him as a future 'Global Leader'. In Hong Kong he was active in social and charitable work, but also acquired a reputation as a free-market capitalist who favoured minimal government involvement in the economy. He served on the **Legislative Council** in the colonial period, and has been a member of the **Executive Council** since 1997. In 2002–03 he was secretary for commerce, industry and technology, before moving to his present position. He received the Gold Bahinia Star, a Hong Kong decoration, in 2000.

Team Spirit

A joint US-Republic of Korea (ROK) military exercise that was first staged in 1976.

Team Spirit's main purpose was the co-ordination of the two armed forces in time of war, and the putative enemy was the Democratic People's Republic of Korea (DPRK). Team Spirit was not the first such exercise, but it was more comprehensive than anything that had gone before. It normally lasted several weeks, tested all aspects of army, navy, marine and air force co-operation, and involved troops airlifted from the mainland USA in addition to those already in the ROK. During the exercise the DPRK always went onto an enhanced state of military preparedness, claiming that Team Spirit could be used as cover for a real attack. Team Spirit was held annually until 1991 despite DPRK protests.

Following the 1991 North-South Agreement on Reconciliation, Non-aggression and Co-operation, the exercise did not take place in 1992, but was reinstated in 1993. Despite tension because of the **DPRK nuclear programme** in 1994, Team Spirit was not held then or in subsequent years.

A number of other joint exercises, such as 'Ulchi Lens' and 'Foal Eagle', have continued and seem to cover much of the same ground as Team Spirit, although much is now done by computer. The DPRK continues to object to all such exercises.

38th parallel

Latitude 38 degrees north, dividing the **Korean peninsula** at roughly mid-point. It does not constitute a natural frontier and is an arbitrary division, chosen in some haste in August 1945 to permit the taking of the Japanese surrender by Soviet forces to the north of it and by US troops to the south. Soviet troops had already entered the peninsula by the time of the Japanese surrender on 15 August 1945. Stalin was prepared to accept the US proposal that Soviet and US forces should both take the Japanese surrender in Korea and agreed on the line of division put forward by the USA. The 38th parallel was chosen, it appears, largely on the grounds that the Korean capital, **Seoul**, lying south of it, would be in the US zone of occupation. Since 1945 the parallel has been a symbol of the division of Korea, even though the Military Demarcation Line, which constitutes the 'boundary' between the two states, runs a little north of it for much of its length.

Three Gorges Dam Project

Project to dam the **Yangzi river** (the Changjiang) at Yichang, Hubei Province, in the **People's Republic of China (PRC)**. Work on the project began in 1993 with the preliminary diversion of the Yangzi. Construction on the dam wall started in 1997, the resulting reservoir was filled in mid-2003 to a length of 560 km and a depth of 135 m, and the entire project is due to be completed by 2009, when the reservoir is expected to extend upstream as far the city of **Chongqing** and to attain a depth of 175 m. A permanent ship-lock is part of the installations. The containing wall is 181 m high and 1.93 km wide. On completion, sufficient energy should be produced to supply 26 700-MW turbine generators, which in turn are expected to yield 18,200 MW of electricity. The first generator was connected to the power grid in July 2003. Funding for the project comes from a variety of sources: from the China Yangtse Three Gorges Project Development Corporation, constituted in 1984 as the owner and manager of the project and the consequent power station; from revenue produced by an existing power plant at the Gezhouba dam further downstream; and from loans from the China Development Bank and domestic and foreign commercial banks, and from corporate bonds. The **World Bank** has not participated.

The Yangzi river, **China**'s longest river, flows for a length of 6,300 km from its headwaters in the Kunlun mountains in Qinghai Province to its mouth in the East China Sea north of **Shanghai**. It is presently navigable by steamer as far as Yichang, 1,600 km from the sea, located at the point where the river flows out of the gorges, and the site of the dam. The river has a drainage area of 1.8m. sq km. The Yangzi deposits large amounts of silt annually in its lower reaches, which contribute to the fertility of neighbouring provinces, but it has also been the cause of recurring floods in these areas. As early as 1919 Sun Yat-sen (1867–1925), first President of the Republic of China (1912–49), had proposed controlling and exploiting the waters of the Yangzi by means of a dam in the Three Gorges. Surveys conducted with foreign participation in the early 1930s were abandoned amid the increasingly unsettled conditions prevailing in China. Further surveys and feasibility studies, carried out in 1944–46 with US participation, were again not followed up as China became engulfed in civil war. The Communist government returned to the problem in the early 1950s with schemes to construct reservoirs and flood areas, and to strengthen banks in the regions most likely to be affected. In 1958 **Zhou Enlai**, Premier of the PRC, was put in charge of plans for a hydro project and flood protection schemes, but the disasters that followed the Great Leap Forward (1958–60), a period of intense economic experimentation, and then the upheaval of the **Cultural Revolution** (1966–76), yet again delayed implementation of any plans for the Three Gorges dam. Not until 1984, by which time economic reform was under way in the PRC, was the decision finally taken to construct a dam at the Three Gorges and feasibility studies were renewed.

Although the scheme has received official sanction, it has engendered doubts and disquiet both within and without the PRC on many grounds: the dam's structural safety, its likely impact on the local environment and ecology, the loss of natural habitats and of cultural sites and the human cost of resettling those displaced from a considerable number of towns and villages. Around 700,000 people may have already been moved and the figure may rise further to more than 1m. Cracks were reported to have appeared in the dam wall in 2003 after the reservoir was filled and it was feared that the bed of the reservoir itself may not have been sufficiently decontaminated from the residue of human settlements before being flooded. Criticism has been persistent, if largely muted, and has generally been unreported by the government and at times suppressed. The government prefers to point to the benefits that will accrue from the completion of the dam: extensive hydroelectric power and a reduced risk of flooding in downstream areas.

Tiananmen

The Gate of Heavenly Peace in central **Beijing**.

The term refers in the first instance to the massive structure, surmounted by a pavilion, that serves as the southern and principal entrance to the former imperial city. The vast open area stretching to the south of the gate is, properly, Tiananmen Square. The name 'Tiananmen' has been used loosely in recent decades as a shorthand reference to the rallies and demonstrations held in the square. In particular, Western observers have spoken and written of 'Tiananmen' to discuss the incidents of early June 1989.

The Ming dynasty (1368–1644) of **China** restored Beijing as the capital of their empire, and Tiananmen was first raised in 1420 in the course of the construction of the imperial palace. The present structure dates from 1651. It was the focus of a number of imperial rituals, including the delivery of proclamations. The Chinese Communist leader **Mao Zedong** spoke from the upper pavilion on 1 October 1949 to announce the establishment of the **People's Republic of China (PRC)**. His portrait now hangs above the main arched entrance of the gate, facing the square.

The square itself is of post-1949 design and construction. In dynastic times a T-shaped area stretched south from Tiananmen, with the wider horizontal section running in front of the main gate and enclosed at each end with a further gate. The lower tapering end was quite narrow and was flanked by government offices and barred by yet another gate. Access to this space was denied to ordinary people, since it was the route taken by the emperor when he left the palace to perform various rites. The fall of the Qing dynasty in 1911 ended such practices and made the area accessible, as when students gathered in front of it on 4 May 1919 to protest against the signing of the Versailles Peace Treaty by the Chinese representatives. The Communist government installed in 1949, however, wished to open up the space to all and to create its own set of memorials. The reconstruction of Tiananmen Square in its present dimensions (40–50 ha) was completed by the 10th anniversary of the PRC, in 1959. To the west stands the Great Hall of the People, home of the **National People's Congress**; to the east the Museum of the Chinese Revolution and the Museum of Chinese History. The Monument to the People's Heroes occupies a central place in the square. It was built of granite and marble between 1952 and 1958 and stands more than 37 m high. It carries inscriptions by Mao Zedong and **Zhou Enlai**. The bas-reliefs that adorn the lower plinth depict scenes from the revolutionary struggle of 1839–1949 against foreign and domestic—Nationalist—enemies. To the south of this monument and on the same north-south axis is the Mao Memorial Hall, constructed in 1976–77, where Mao's embalmed body may be viewed.

The enormous capacity of Tiananmen Square was demonstrated during the **Cultural Revolution** (1966–76) when thousands of young Red Guards filled it on several occasions to greet Mao. The Monument to the People's Heroes became a focus of popular, if unsanctioned, sentiment in April 1976 around the time of the traditional Qingming commemoration of the dead. Memorial verses and wreaths were deposited at the monument for Zhou Enlai, who had died in January of that year. These peaceful demonstrations were dispersed on 4 and 5 April by police and troops. The pattern repeated itself in April 1989, when similar mourning took place for **Hu Yaobang**, the former secretary-general of the **Chinese Communist Party** Central Committee, dismissed in 1987, who had died on 15 April. This time the official reaction was initially milder, and demonstrations gathered pace as students marched on Tiananmen Square in April and May, occupied the square and set up a headquarters around the base of the Monument to the People's Heroes. Their demands were for democracy, an end to nepotism and corruption, and a dialogue with the authorities. Some discussion between students and government leaders did take place, notably with **Zhao Ziyang**, but in the end the hardline decision was taken to deploy tanks and troops to disperse the six-week-long occupation of the square on the night of 3–4 June.

Access to Tiananmen Square is free, but the area is more closely supervised and the presence of soldiers and police more noticeable than before. Any attempts at private demonstrations, such as by members of the **Falungong** movement, are immediately broken up. The government is clearly determined not to allow any challenge to its authority or to its interpretation of the significance of this symbolic space.

Tianjin

Tianjin (the form Tientsin is the Wade-Giles romanization of the city's name) lies 113 km south-east of **Beijing**, on the coast of the Gulf of Bohai of the **People's Republic of China (PRC)**. It serves as the capital's port and is linked by rail and expressway with Beijing. The city's population at the 2000 census was 10.01m. It covers an area of 11,919 sq km and has the status of a special municipality coming directly under the government. Its educational establishments include Nankai and Tianjin Universities.

Tianjin, in addition to its importance as a rail and road hub, is the largest trading port in the north of the PRC, handling both exports and imports, and is a leading industrial centre. Its principal areas of activity are the automotive industry, machinery and equipment, micro-electronics and telecommunications equipment, chemical industries, and steel products. As one of the open coastal cities, it attracts much foreign direct investment and has many foreign-funded enterprises.

Tianjin's comparatively long history as a city with strong foreign connections has doubtless encouraged such attention. It was obliged to open up to foreign trade and settlement following treaties imposed on **China** in 1858 by Britain, France, Russia and the USA and enforced in 1860 by the Conventions of Beijing/Peking. Chinese reluctance to implement the 1858 Treaty of Tianjin/Tientsin led to the arrival of punitive British and French forces and naval vessels. Tianjin was attacked and seized before the foreign troops advanced on the capital. (A similar route was taken in 1900 by forces of the eight allied countries sent to relieve the siege of the legation quarter in Beijing.) After 1860 Tianjin was settled as a treaty port and built up as a number of foreign concessions, whose distinctive architectural styles can still be noted. Chinese resentment expressed itself again in 1870 in an incident known as the 'Tianjin massacre' in which the French Catholic church was attacked and 10 foreigners were killed. In 1924 the last Chinese emperor, **Puyi**, took refuge in the foreign concessions in Tianjin after he was ejected from the former imperial palace in Beijing by the ruling warlord.

Tibet

(Tibetan: *Bod*; Chinese: *Xizang*)

Region in the far south-west of the **People's Republic of China (PRC)**, administered as the Tibet Autonomous Region (TAR).

It is bounded to the north and east by **Xinjiang** and by Qinghai, Sichuan and Yunnan Provinces, and to the south and west by India, Nepal, Sikkim, Bhutan and Myanmar. The TAR covers an area of 1,228,400 sq km but has a population of only 2.62m. (2000 census), giving a population density of two persons per sq km. The majority of the region's inhabitants—95.46% at the 1990 population census—are **Tibetan**, with around 7,500 Mongba and 2,300 Loba ethnic minorities. Since the late 1980s the PRC has encouraged **Han Chinese** settlement in the TAR, but the exact size of the Han population is not clear since census figures do not include military personnel, of whom a number are stationed in Tibet. One recent estimate that does includes the military within the territory suggests a figure of 338,000 Chinese. Tibet is the only autonomous region where the indigenous population outnumbers the Han element.

The TAR is sited in the world's highest region. It lies on the western section of the Tibet-Qinghai plateau, which has an average elevation of 4,000 m. Vast mountain ranges hem it in to the north, where the land rises to an average 5,000 m, and to the south-west; much of the Himalayan range lies within Tibet; and Mount Everest (Qomolangma) is on the Tibet-Nepal border. The north Tibet plateau is an arid desert draining to the interior, with low temperatures, which supports little agriculture and few inhabitants. To the east the terrain is characterized by high peaks and deep gorges that carry a number of large rivers south into Yunnan Province and south-east Asia. The most fertile area is the valley of the Yarlung Zangbo river in southern Tibet (which flows into India as the Brahmaputra). It enjoys a milder climate and higher rainfall. The capital **Lhasa** is on a tributary of the Yarlung Zangbo. The TAR's economy has traditionally been agrarian and pastoral, supplemented by handicrafts and carpet-making. It has mineral deposits that are now starting to be exploited, and industry is being encouraged. Its raw materials, including timber, are exported to the Chinese interior. It has long been a recipient of Chinese subventions, including suspension of some taxes, and the PRC has borne the cost of creating and maintaining a modern infrastructure. A road-building programme into Tibet started in the 1950s and 1960s, and a railway link from the existing railhead in Golmud in Qinghai Province has been under construction since

2001. Direct investment into the TAR is now permitted from foreign countries and international aid organizations, and tourism is being developed.

Tibet's relations with **China** have generally been complicated and often uneasy. The integral part played by **Buddhism** in Tibetan life, the tradition of spiritual and temporal authority combined in the person of the **Dalai Lama**, the existence since 1959 of a government in exile (the **Central Tibetan Administration**), the strength of secessionist sentiment and the recurrence of international protest are particular problems for the government of the PRC. Its repudiation of any challenge to Chinese state sovereignty or authority, which is a constant element in its responses to domestic or international protests, has frequently caused the PRC to take a hard line in Tibet. Its occupation of central Tibet in 1951 marked its determination to reassert control over territory that it (and the Chinese Nationalist government before it) viewed as Chinese. The Seventeen-Point Agreement of 1951 obliged the Tibetans to accept the incorporation of Tibet into the Chinese state in exchange for extensive regional autonomy that included religious freedom, consensual reforms and continuing self-administration; but an uprising in 1959, sparked by rumours that the Dalai Lama was to be abducted, brought Chinese military reprisals and a heavier degree of control. The relative autonomy of the 1951 Agreement was rescinded, and reform measures that included the emancipation of serfs (of whom there were reportedly more than 700,000 in 1953) were implemented. The Dalai Lama fled in 1959 to India, accompanied by many refugees. In 1965 the TAR was created within an area covering the central province of Ü-Tsang and western Kham. The outer area composed of eastern Kham and Amdo had already been divided between neighbouring provinces. The TAR suffered severely during the **Cultural Revolution** (1966–76), when Red Guard fury, in parallel with similar excesses all over China, resulted in the destruction of temples, monasteries, religious images and artefacts and the persecution of monks and nuns. In 1980 the then general secretary of the **Chinese Communist Party (CCP)**, **Hu Yaobang**, visited the TAR. Shocked by the region's backward state and its resentment of the Chinese presence, he apologized for past policies and promised reforms leading to greater autonomy and cultural freedom and an increase in the number of Tibetan cadres in the administration. In 1984 Hu presided over plans for the economic development of the region. His removal from power in 1987, however, was followed by the reversal of reforms and intensified Chinese settlement in the region. Pro-independence agitation in 1987 was suppressed, as were demonstrations triggered by the death in early 1989 of the 10th **Panchen Lama** and the 30th anniversary of the 1959 uprising. Further anti-government demonstrations were suppressed in 1993 and 1996. More than 1,000 Tibetans were reported to be in Chinese prisons in 1998. In 1995, six years after the Panchen Lama's death, the Chinese government had a successor installed in an assertion of its right to oversee religious activity. The recurring anxiety of the central government, as in Xinjiang, is that of secession, and all calls for independence, often led by the clergy, are rejected. From 1988 until 1992 the party secretary for the TAR was **Hu Jintao**, now general secretary of the CCP.

History: The first three centuries of Tibet's known history, from the 7th to the 10th, were a time of political strength and religious formation. The Tibetan state extended its influence as far north as present-day Gansu in the 9th century and challenged Tang-dynasty China and other states. At the same time it was absorbing Buddhism, brought by Indian missionaries, and developing the concept of a fused religious and political authority that has continuously marked the Tibetan style of leadership. By the 13th century several sects were established as land-owning monastic orders that exercised civil and religious powers. From this time dates the close link between Tibetan and Mongol Buddhism. In 1207 Tibet, anxious to avoid Mongol attack, had already agreed to pay tribute to the Mongol leader Ghenghis Khan. In 1247 the leader of the Sakya sect, Sakya Pandita, renewed submission to Ghenghis Khan's successor, who had sought moral and spiritual guidance from him. In return for Sakya Pandita's religious support, the Mongol king invested him with temporal authority over central Tibet and agreed to protect the Buddhist religion, thus establishing a 'patron-priest' relationship. In 1254 Phagspa Lama, Sakya Pandita's nephew, visited the court of Khubilai Khan and was given authority over the whole of Tibet. This close relationship between Tibetan religious figures and Mongol leaders was responsible for the conferment of the title 'Dalai Lama' in 1578 on the head of the Gelugpa sect, which from then on became the dominant form of Lama Buddhism.

The Qing dynasty (1644–1911), who were of **Manzhou** nationality, were not originally Buddhists, but were prepared to use the Tibetans as intermediaries in their dealings with the **Mongols** and to involve themselves in Tibetan politics. In 1721 the Kangxi emperor imposed Chinese control over Tibet and in 1723 created the post of resident commissioner in Lhasa to represent Chinese interests. A brief period of British intervention in Tibetan affairs in the first decade of the 20th century (aimed at discouraging Russian interest in the region) achieved little other than Chinese renewal of its claim to sovereignty over Tibet. In 1910 Chinese troops entered Lhasa, but the fall of the Qing in 1911 brought in a period of confusion that allowed the Dalai Lama to re-establish his authority and, with Mongolia, to proclaim joint Tibetan-Mongolian independence from China in 1913. The close association with Mongolia fell away when Mongolia was placed under a Communist government in 1924. Despite a Chinese Nationalist attempt in 1934 to reimpose Chinese control, Tibet was largely left alone until the Chinese Communist reassertion of sovereignty in 1951. Its social structure of monastic and aristocratic landowners, a small class of craftsmen, herdsmen and a large body of serfs remained in place until even after that date.

Tibetans

Ethnic group originating in **Tibet** in the far south-west of the **People's Republic of China (PRC)**.

Tibetans are also settled in the neighbouring provinces of Sichuan (more than 1m. in the 1990 census), Yunnan, Qinghai and Gansu, over an area that reflects earlier, wider limits of Tibetan authority. As a result, there are as many Tibetans, living generally in autonomous prefectures, outside of the Tibet Autonomous Region (TAR), created in 1965 out of part of the former Tibetan territories, as inside it. In the 2000 population census the TAR had a population of 2.62m., among which Tibetans considerably outnumbered **Han Chinese**, a figure that may be set along-side that of 4,593,072 for the total Tibetan population of the PRC as recorded in the 1990 census. Tibetan cultural influence is evident in the neighbouring states of Nepal, Bhutan, Sikkim and Ladakh, and there are Tibetan communities in India, clustered around the **Dalai Lama**, and in Nepal and Bhutan. Other groups are settled in North America, Australia and Western Europe. In all, Tibetans are said to be living in more than 33 countries. Some 80,000 Tibetans fled from Tibet along with the Dalai Lama in 1959. Sources for the Tibetan movement in exile put the present number of Tibetans living outside of Tibet at between 111,200 and 120,000.

The Tibetan language belongs to the Tibeto-Burman group of the Sino-Tibetan family. It encompasses three styles of speech: the vernacular, formal speech and literary style. Tibetan is spoken throughout Tibet, in most of Qinghai and in much of Sichuan. Within Tibet the Tsang dialect serves as a common means of communica-tion and is related to the forms of Tibetan spoken in the frontier Himalayan area and in regions south of the Tibet borders. The written form of the language is a script derived from Sanskrit, created in the mid-7th century with the assistance of Indian Buddhist monks. Tibetan is one of the six minority languages that have official status in their respective autonomous areas within the PRC.

The indigenous Tibetan religion was Bön, a form of **shamanism**. In the 7th century **Buddhism** was introduced from India and, mingling with Bön, developed into the distinctive form of Lama Buddhism. Much of Tibetan architecture, sculpture, painting and craftwork is inspired by religious belief.

Tokto/Takeshima dispute

The Tok islands, known as Takeshima in Japanese, are a group of barren rocks east of the **Korean peninsula** and north-west of Japan. Older Western maps show them as the Liancourt Rocks, after a French ship that called there in 1849. The Korean name means 'Solitary island', the Japanese, 'Bamboo island'. The former is more accurate since there is very little vegetation on the islands, and no natural water. The seas around are good fishing grounds, however, which may partly explain why both sides have pursued the dispute with some intensity. Both the Republic of Korea (ROK) and Japan have claimed these islands since 1952. The Democratic People's Republic of Korea also claims them as Korean territory, but does not dispute that they are under ROK jurisdiction. No other country has taken a position on their status. The intensity of the dispute has tended to depend on the broader state of ROK-Japan relations. Since 1953 a small ROK police force has occupied the islands, which otherwise have no permanent inhabitants. All three parties have issued stamps depicting the islands, and each has stated that it will not accept correspondence bearing stamps issued by either of the other two.

Tokyo

Capital city of Japan since 1869.

Tokyo, or 'Eastern Capital', is located on the Kanto plain in the centre of Japan's main island, Honshu. It is a self-governing city, occupying more than 2,000 sq km. The city and its adjacent suburbs and dormitory towns have more than 12m. inhabitants.

Before 1869 the city was called Edo, a castle town, and the centre of power of the Tokugawa clan, who effectively ruled Japan from 1600 to 1868. Following the **Meiji Restoration**, the **Japanese Emperor** moved to the newly renamed capital in 1868, with the imperial family occupying what had been the Tokugawa castle, as they still do today. The city is the centre of the national government, and the economic, cultural and social heart of the country. It is a major international finance centre and leads the world in a number of fields, including technology.

Modern Tokyo, which was created in 1943 by the merger of the City of Tokyo and Tokyo Prefecture, has absorbed many once independent towns and villages, whose distinctive characteristics can still be found in the districts that bear their names. Much of old Tokyo was destroyed in the 1923 **Kanto earthquake**, which struck both Tokyo and the nearby port of **Yokohama**. Further extensive damage took place as a result of heavy Allied bombing in the **Pacific War**. Post-war reconstruction led to much undistinguished building, but the tide began to turn with the 1964 Olympic Games and the great affluence that developed from the late 1960s onwards. Today's Tokyo may still have areas of unprepossessing buildings but it also has many eye-catching modern developments. Its subway and rail system are highly efficient at moving large numbers of people to and from the city centre. However, because of the sprawl of the city, many of its citizens spend long hours commuting, and there is much concern about the quality of life.

Tokyo Stock Exchange

The original Tokyo Stock Exchange was established on 15 May 1878, and commenced trading on 1 June 1878. During the **Pacific War** the 11 existing stock exchanges in Japan were amalgamated into a quasi-public organization, the Japan Securities Exchange. The **Allied occupation of Japan** dissolved this in 1947, and in 1949 three new stock exchanges opened in **Tokyo**, **Osaka**, and Nagoya. Trading began on 16 May 1949, and later in the same year five additional exchanges opened, in **Kyoto** (merged with Osaka Securities Exchange in March 2001), **Kobe** (dissolved October 1967), **Hiroshima**, Niigata (both merged with the Tokyo exchange in March 2000), and Fukuoka. In addition, a securities exchange opened in **Sapporo** in April 1950. The stock trading floor closed in 1999. The Tokyo Stock Exchange was demutualized in 2001, and Tokyo Stock Exchange Incorporated opened for business on 1 November 2001. It has more than 700 employees, lists 2,235 Japanese and 30 foreign stocks, and has a capital value of 11,500m. yen.

Pres.: Takuo Tsurushima
Address: Tokyo Stock Exchange
2-1 Nihonbashi
Kabutocho, Chuo-ku
Tokyo 103-8220
Japan
Tel: 81-3-3665-1881
Fax: 81-3-3662-0547
E-mail: info@tse.org.jp
Internet: www.tse.org.jp

Trans-Siberian Railway

The Trans-Siberian Railway from Moscow to Vladivostok on the edge of the Pacific, and two spur lines, one travelling through Mongolia and one through north-east China (**Manchuria**), have linked Europe with East Asia since the early 20th century.

Work on the Railway began in 1891 and was completed in 1905. Later lines linked **Pusan** in Korea to the route through **Beijing** and, in theory, it was possible to travel by rail from Pusan to Paris, France. A few did so, but the First World War and then the Russian Revolution limited use of the railway as a link between Asia and Europe until the 1960s. Then it developed as a route to Japan, via the port of Nakhodka, the alternative to Vladivostok which, as, a major naval port, was closed to foreigners. Since the changes in the **People's Republic of China (PRC)** in the 1980s, and even more since the collapse of the Soviet Union, the Railway and its various sections have enjoyed a new burst of activity. As well as being a major freight transport facility for the PRC, the Democratic People's Republic of Korea (DPRK) and Mongolia, Chinese and Russian traders make much use of it, as do tourists who want to experience something more interesting than air travel. There are hopes in the Republic of Korea (ROK) that if the link between the DPRK and the ROK is again connected, ROK businesses can make use of the Trans-Siberian system to send goods to Europe. There are also plans for another railway, known as the New Eurasia Landbridge, to run from Lianyugang in the PRC, through Urumchi to Druzhba in Kazakhstan.

Tsang, Donald

Tsang Yam-Kuen

Donald Tsang has been chief secretary for administration in the **Special Administrative Region** of **Hong Kong** of the **People's Republic of China (PRC)** since May 2001, when he succeeded **Anson Chan**, the first holder of the post. He is ranked number two in the Hong Kong government, advising the chief executive, **Tung Chee Hwa**, and deputizing for him in his absence.

Tsang was born in Hong Kong in 1944. Educated at Hong Kong University, he joined the Hong Kong civil service in 1967 and by 1985 was the deputy general secretary for general duties, responsible, among other things, for administering the Sino-British Joint Declaration. In 1993 he became secretary of the treasury, and in 1995, financial secretary. Although regarded by many as pro-British, the new administration reappointed him after the British handover in July 1997, and he continued to be financial secretary until he took over the secretary of administration portfolio. As financial secretary, he steered Hong Kong through the **Asian financial crisis** in 1997. He became a Knight Commander of the Order of the British Empire in 1997, and received the Hong Kong Grand Bahinia Medal in 2002.

Tujia

Ethnic minority group of the **People's Republic of China (PRC)**, numbering 5,725,000 in the 1990 population census. The Tujia, who form the eighth largest minority nationality in the PRC, are concentrated in the mountainous regions of north-west Hunan and south-west Hubei Provinces in the central area of the PRC, where they share two autonomous prefectures with the **Miao**. They have an established history, but through prolonged assimilation into the majority **Han Chinese** have lost much of their language and customs. Some 20,000–30,000 speakers of Tujia, a branch of the Tibeto-Burman linguistic group, remain, the majority using the Chinese or Miao languages. They are admired for their singing, composition of songs and traditions of collective dance.

Tumen river

Tumangang

The Tumen river rises in **Mount Paektu** and forms the eastern boundary between the **People's Republic of China** and the Democratic People's Republic of Korea (DPRK). At its extreme eastern end, just before it enters the sea, it also forms the short boundary between the DPRK and Russia. Since the early 1990s there has been an ambitious plan to develop the region, the **Tumen River Area Development Programme**, but so far little progress has been made in implementing it.

Tumen River Area Development Programme (TRADP)

A regional development project sponsored by the **United Nations** Development Programme and a number of East Asian countries for the area lying on either side of the delta reaches of the Tumen river where it flows into the **East Sea/Sea of Japan** on the eastern side of the **Korean peninsula**. The Tumen River Area Development Programme (TRADP) was launched in 1991 with the intention of taking advantage of the good sea and rail links available in the area to stimulate investment in the region and facilitate the growth of intra-regional trade and transit trade. A further hope was closer integration of the regional economies and the development of an international free port. A memorandum on environmental protection and two agreements were signed in 1995, which led to the establishment of two intergovernmental bodies. The **People's Republic of China (PRC)**, the Democratic People's Republic of Korea (DPRK), the Republic of Korea and Mongolia were involved in the TRADP from the outset; the Russian Federation joined in later, but Japan, whose role would be that of investor, has not committed itself. Development costs have been projected at US \$30,000m. over 15–20 years. The TRADP region lies within the Tumen River Economic Development Area, an area of some 10,000 sq km that encompasses the Yanbian Korean Autonomous Prefecture in Jilin Province of the PRC, the part of North Hamgyong Province in the DPRK that lies north from the city of Chongjin, and the southern end of Primorskiy region in the **Russian Far East**, taking in Vladivostok and Nakhodka. The area has a population of some 4m.

Reservations over the high cost of the programme have stalled any rapid progress, as has the emergence of rival national plans. The DPRK's anxieties over excessively easy access to its territory led it to suggest development of three separate zones within the region. In 1991 the DPRK had already taken steps to set up the Rajin-Sonbong **Special Economic Zone** on its side of the Tumen. The PRC designated the area around Hunchun on its side of the river as an Economic Development Zone in 1992; and Russia hopes to develop Vladivostok and the port of Zhalubin. Some work has been done on improving land connections between the cities and border points within the area, but there is not much sign as yet of any other intra-regional co-operation.

Internet: www.tumennet.org
www.unido.org

Tung Chee Hwa

A **Hong Kong** businessman turned politician, who in 1997 became the first chief executive of the **People's Republic of China**'s **(PRC)** first **Special Administrative Region (SAR)** of Hong Kong.

Tung was born in 1937 in **Shanghai**, where his father, Tung Chao Yung, was a shipping magnate. As the Chinese civil war progressed, Tung Chao Yung decided to move to Hong Kong in 1947. Tung Chee Hwa attended school in Hong Kong, and then studied marine engineering at the University of Liverpool in the United Kingdom. After graduating in 1960, he worked in the USA for some years before returning to Hong Kong in 1969. In Hong Kong he concentrated on the family business, which was mainly focused on the Orient Overseas Container Line, one of the world's largest container, dry bulk and tanker operations. However, the group encountered difficulties in the 1980s, and the PRC government apparently provided funds to rescue it. Some have viewed this as one reason why Tung was selected to head the Hong Kong SAR in 1996.

From the early 1990s onwards Tung was involved in Hong Kong affairs, as a member of the Hong Kong **Executive Council** from 1992 until 1996, and as a member of both the Eighth **Chinese People's Political Consultative Conference** from 1993 and as the vice-chairman of the Preparatory Committee for the Hong Kong Special Administrative Region. It came as little surprise, therefore, when in December 1996 a specially selected electoral college chose him as the first chief executive of the Hong Kong SAR, a post he took up on 1 July 1997. He was elected to a second term in July 2002.

Ever since his selection Tung has been regarded as close to the PRC authorities. His period in office has not been easy. It began with the major problem of the **Asian financial crisis**, with regard to which it was felt by many in Hong Kong that he had not shown the sort of decisive leadership that was required to preserve Hong Kong's position as an international financial centre. His subsequent actions in removing civil servants who were associated with the former British administration also cast doubts on his role, as did his publicly expressed view that Hong Kong should forget the past and concentrate on the future. In general, he is considered to be eager to support Chinese interests, as distinct from those of Hong Kong.

Address: Office of the Chief Executive
Hong Kong SAR
People's Republic of China
5th Floor
Central Government Bldgs
Main Wing
Lower Albert Rd
Hong Kong
Tel: 852-2878-3300
Fax: 852-2509-0577
E-mail: ceo@ceo.gov.hk
Internet: www.info.gov.hk/ce

U

Ulaan Baatar

(alt. Ulan Bator)

Capital of Mongolia, Ulaan Baatar is the economic, cultural and educational centre of the country. It is also the location of its only international airport. It lies on the banks of the Tuul river, and is 1,310 m above sea level. Current industrial production includes textiles, building materials and articles for daily use. Livestock are also important, as is the production of vegetables.

The city's population was 282,000 in 1971, 575,000 in 1992, and is now estimated at 813,000, or nearly one-third of Mongolia's total population of 2.6m. The current name, which dates from 1924, means 'Red Hero', and may be a tribute to the revolutionary leader, Damdiny Sukhbaatar, who drove out the Chinese and established an independent Mongolia in 1921.

The city began as a monastery town in the 17th century. Until the communization of the country under Soviet influence in the 1920s it was a major centre of Lama **Buddhism**. The original Mongol name was Hurae. It was better known in the West as Urga, a name derived from the Russian pronunciation of another Mongol word, Orgo, which means 'palace of a high official'. In the mid-19th century it was an important trading post for Sino-Russian trade. Later, its importance was linked to the development of the **Trans-Siberian Railway** and related lines.

Unequal treaties

A term used in East Asia to describe the first Western-style treaties between **China**, Japan and Korea and the outside world. The unequal treaty system began with the treaty that ended the first war between Great Britain and China, the 1842 Treaty of **Nanjing**. This, and the other treaties that followed it, provided for a system of open ports and cities, at which were established **foreign settlements**. In these special enclaves foreigners could live and trade under their own legal systems, thus avoiding what were regarded as the excessive and arbitrary punishments practised in East Asia. The individual treaties concluded by each nation were linked by most-favoured-nation clauses, so that all enjoyed additional concessions gained by one. The system spread to Japan in the 1850s and to the **Korean peninsula** in 1876. Ironically, it was

Japan, itself still subject to unequal treaties, that introduced the system to Korea. The early treaties allowed for trade and the practice of professions, but the treaty ending the Sino–Japanese War of 1894–95 allowed Japan, and by extension all other treaty powers, to set up manufacturing industries in the Chinese foreign settlements.

Japan sought the revision of its unequal treaties as early as 1872, and succeeded in the 1890s. The Korean treaties ended with the establishment of the Japanese colony in 1910. In China, however, the system continued until 1943. Then, in a largely symbolic gesture to a wartime ally, since most of the foreign settlements were under Japanese control, Great Britain and the USA signed new, equal treaties with the **Republic of China (1912–49)**.

During the **Sino–Soviet dispute** the **People's Republic of China (PRC)** accused the Soviet Union of having imposed unequal treaties on China in the 1920s, and of having tried to do so again in the 1950s. The PRC also denounced the Soviet Union for its insistence that the territorial provisions of the unequal treaties between China and Russia, which form the basis of the present frontiers between the two countries, were still valid.

The issue of unequal treaties is now largely a matter of historical debate, but both Mongolia and the Democratic People's Republic of Korea have denounced modern treaties, such as the **Nuclear Non-Proliferation Treaty**, as reflecting the spirit of the older treaties.

Unification Church

A charismatic sect with the full title of the Holy Spirit Association for the Unification of World Christianity.

It was founded in **Pusan**, a port city in the south of the Republic of Korea (ROK), in 1954 by the Reverend Moon Sun-Myong. The number of adherents grew, and in 1959 he sent his first overseas missionary to the USA. Missionary activity spread further, to Japan, Europe, the Near East and Latin America. In the 1970s Moon moved the Church's headquarters to the USA, opened a seminary and launched into commercial activities that included production of ginseng, publishing interests, ownership of hotels and of newspapers, including the *Washington Times*, and of the US news agency United Press International, and for a while the manufacture of small arms. The Church also sponsors the Little Angels children's dance troupe. Both the Church and its founder have attracted hostility, in the USA and elsewhere. In 1983 US investigation of Moon's personal finances led to his imprisonment on charges of tax evasion. Another cause of concern is the Church's methods of recruiting and retaining believers.

Moon was born in 1920 into a Christian family in what is now the Democratic People's Republic of Korea (DPRK). At the age of 16, he claimed, he received a divine mission to reform the Christian church. His first proselytizing took place around **Pyongyang** on liberation from Japanese rule in 1945, but later led to his imprisonment by the newly installed Communist authorities. Released by **United**

Nations troops in 1950 as they moved north, he fled to the south. His strong anti-Communist line for a while caused him to be tolerated in the ROK, especially under **Park Chung-Hee**. The Unification Church's involvement in the 1977 **Koreagate** scandal over lobbying tactics in the US Congress arose out of its support for the ROK regime's attempts to improve the country's image in the USA. In the early 1990s he visited Pyongyang, where he met **Kim Il Sung**. His involvement with the DPRK has been of a practical nature: an ROK company with strong links with the Unification Church has set up a car-assembly plant near Pyongyang and organizes tours into the country from the South.

The Unification Church's teaching incorporates some aspects of Christian doctrine, but accords only partial significance to Christ's sacrifice, holding that he achieved only spiritual salvation for mankind. To complete man's redemption, physical salvation is also necessary through the second coming of another Lord. His marriage with a perfect woman will expunge the sin that entered the world when Eve had sexual relations with Satan and transmitted evil to succeeding generations. For long Moon did not claim to be this second Lord, although his followers identified him as such, but he is now reported to have proclaimed himself 'God's ambassador', a 'messiah' and 'returning Lord' in a ceremony held in March 2004 in Washington, DC. Moon, his wife, Hak Ja-Han, and family play a central role in the beliefs and organization of the Unification Church. Marriage is a central tenet, and Moon and his wife conduct mass weddings from time to time.

The Unification Church is only one among a number of similar charismatic Christian sects in the ROK, and its membership there is not particularly large. It has attracted greater attention outside of Korea.

Address: Unification Church World Mission Office
12th Floor,
Dohwa Bldg
292–20 Dohwa-dong
Mapo-ku
Seoul 121-040
Republic of Korea
Tel: 82-2-711-5323
Fax: 82-2-701-1804
E-mail: mission@tongil.or.kr
Internet: www.unification.net
The Unification Church also has a large number of international addresses.

United Liberal Democrats (ULD)

Jayu minju yonmaeng

A political party created in 1995 by the veteran Republic of Korea (ROK) politician **Kim Jong-Pil**, following his forced departure from the leadership of the **Democratic Liberal Party**.

The United Liberal Democrats (ULD) claimed to be the only genuine conservative party in the ROK and it gained 50 seats in the 1996 **ROK National Assembly** elections. Then, in a surprise move, the party joined with **Kim Dae-Jung**'s **National Congress for New Politics** in 1997 to contest the presidential election. Despite years of hostility, the two Kims agreed that Kim Dae-Jung would be the presidential candidate. After his narrow victory in 1997 Kim Dae-Jung appointed Kim Jong-Pil as Prime Minister. Early in 2000 the coalition collapsed, and Kim Jong-Pil contested the April 2000 general election as ULD leader. However, the ULD performed badly in the election, and by May 2000 he was again in a coalition with Kim Dae-Jung.

Roh Moo-Hyun's election as President in 2002 and the consequent departure from the political scene of Kim Dae-Jung left only Kim Jong-Pil from the era of the 'three Kims', as the period since the early 1970s is known. When the ULD's representation declined from 10 to four seats in the April 2004 National Assembly elections, Kim Jong-Pil finally resigned, to be replaced by Kim Hak-Won.

Address: ULD
         Insan Bldg
         103–4 Shinsu-dong
         Mapo-gu
         Seoul 121-110
         Republic of Korea
Tel: 82-2-701-3355
Fax: 82-2-707-1637
E-mail: info@jamin.or.kr
Internet: www.jamin.or.kr

United Nations (UN)

The world international organization, established by charter in June 1945 to provide a framework for the maintenance of world peace and security. The **Korean War** (1950–53) presented it with an early challenge, to which it responded with the formation of the United Nations (UN) Command and a full-scale military campaign against what it defined as an aggressor—the Democratic People's Republic of Korea (DPRK), supported by troops from the **People's Republic of China (PRC)**. The 1953 armistice was signed between the UN Command and the DPRK and Chinese combatants.

The UN has 191 member states. These include Japan (a member since 1956), Mongolia (since 1961), and the PRC, which took over the **'China'** seat from Nationalist China in 1971. The Republic of Korea and the DPRK, after many years of lobbying by both parties, were accorded observer status in 1973 and both joined the UN in 1991 as separate member states. The **'Republic of China'** on **Taiwan** was displaced by the PRC and no longer has a seat. The PRC represents **Hong Kong** and **Macao**.

Among the principal organs of the UN is the Security Council. Its five permanent members include the PRC.

Sec.-Gen.: Kofi Annan
Address: United Nations Plaza
New York, NY 10017
USA
Tel: 1-212-963-1234
Fax: 1-212-963-4879
E-mail: inquiries@un.org
Internet: www.un.org

United Nations Security Council and Japan

Japan joined the **United Nations (UN)** in 1956, and co-operation with the UN has been a major feature of the country's foreign policy ever since. On eight occasions Japan has served as a non-permanent member of the UN Security Council, and in the 1980s, as the country's contribution to the UN's finances steadily increased, Japan rescued the UN from a major financial crisis caused by the USA's refusal to pay its contributions. These factors, together with the size of the Japanese economy and the extent of its international development assistance, have led Japanese governments to argue since the early 1990s that Japan is entitled to a permanent seat on the Security Council.

Many countries, especially in the West, agreed that there was a case for Japanese membership, but even supporters admitted that there were difficulties. One was that the limitations on Japan's use of force, imposed by Article 9 of the country's Constitution, meant that it could not play a full part in the UN's peace-keeping operations, however much it might be funding them. The enactment of an International Peace Co-operation Law in 1992 has partly removed this objection, but the tight restrictions that still apply to Japanese forces meant that the issue was not completely resolved. Further developments since 11 September 2001 have helped, but have still not convinced all of the critics that Japan is willing or able to take a full part in UN peace-keeping operations. In August 2004 the US Secretary of State, Colin Powell, stated that Japan would need to reconsider Article 9 if it wished to be a member of the Security Council.

More difficult is that a number of other countries argue, with reference to either the size of their populations or their economic development, that they too are entitled to a Security Council seat. This, together with the reluctance of the existing permanent members of the Security Council to give up their veto power, has meant that the issue will remain effectively shelved for the present. Japanese pressure for change is likely to continue, however, and the Japanese Ministry of Foreign Affairs still places the issue high on its agenda.

A third group of countries claim to have doubts about Japan's suitability as a member of the Security Council because of what they maintain is its past record of aggression. Most vociferous in opposing Japanese membership is probably the Democratic People's Republic of Korea, but the Republic of Korea and the **People's Republic of China** have also expressed reservations.

United States of America (USA)

Although the USA has not formally been an Asian power since the independence of the Philippines in 1946, its power and influence over both south-east and East Asia is strong and must be taken into account in any assessment of Asian politics. The US economic and commercial involvement in the region is equally important. The USA has diplomatic relations with all of the East Asian countries except the Democratic People's Republic of Korea (DPRK) and the **'Republic of China' ('ROC')**, although it does have a close informal relationship with the latter through an extensive network of diplomatic, consular, trade and information offices. There are US forces in Japan, especially in **Okinawa**, and in the Republic of Korea (ROK). While recent developments in military technology and the inevitable problems associated with the presence of large numbers of foreign troops are likely to lead to a reduction in US forces in both countries in the near future, there are no plans for their complete withdrawal. Another factor in US interest in East Asia is the presence of large communities in the USA of Chinese, Japanese and Korean origin, the result of immigration since the mid-19th century.

The US presence in Asia dates back to the first years of the new republic. US ships traded at **Guangzhou** in the 1780s, and the 'Canton trade' remained important to the USA well into the 19th century. US merchants substituted for British opium traders during the periodic Chinese attempts to suppress this trade. In the 1850s it was the USA and not the European powers, preoccupied with the Crimean War, that forced Japan to open up to western trade and residence. Thirty years later the USA followed Japan by opening Korea, again in advance of the Europeans. In 1898 the USA proclaimed an 'Open Door' policy in **China**, and would maintain such a policy well into the 1920s. US missionaries were prominent in all East Asian countries from the mid-19th century onwards, which would continue to affect US policies towards these countries. While maintaining its trade links with Japan, eventually supplanting the British, the USA supported China against Japan in the 1930s. This and other issues led to war in 1941.

At the end of the **Pacific War** in 1945, the formal **Allied Occupation of Japan** notwithstanding, it was the USA that was in control of Japan and, equally, of South Korea, which, under US tutelage, became the ROK in 1948. The USA was also involved in the civil war that split China in the 1940s. Despite some wartime overtures to the **Chinese Communist Party (CCP)**, the USA ultimately threw its support behind the **Kuomintang (KMT)**. When the CCP emerged victorious in 1949 and proclaimed the **People's Republic of China (PRC)**, the USA refused to recognize the new state, preferring to maintain links with the KMT on **Taiwan**. The **Korean War** confirmed US rejection of the CCP and the PRC. At the same time, it endorsed the US role as the continued guarantor of both the 'ROC' on Taiwan and the ROK. Several countries in Asia were linked via bilateral defence arrangements with the USA. These included Japan, the ROK and the 'ROC'. These arrangements included US bases and the consequent stationing of large numbers of US forces. In the Japanese case, although the USA formally returned **Okinawa** to Japanese sovereignty in 1972, large tracts of the prefecture remained as US bases, an issue that still causes grievances to this day.

In recent years the USA has shown more interest in international groupings in East Asia. It takes an active part in **Asia-Pacific Economic Co-operation** for example, and has joined the **ASEAN Regional Forum**. It has used first 'Four-Party' and then 'Six-Party' talks to try to engage the DPRK. At the same time, the signs are that the USA prefers bilateral relationships if it can achieve them. It also moved swiftly to stop Japan pursuing the idea of an Asian Monetary Fund during the **Asian financial crisis** of the late 1990s. Again, despite membership of the **World Trade Organization**, the USA often prefers to handle trade issues on a bilateral basis.

Only under President Richard Nixon (1968–72) did the USA begin to change its position on the PRC. Nixon's overtures to the PRC began with only the minimum of consultation of US allies, even though the consequences of US actions had major implications for Japan, the ROK and, most of all, the 'ROC'. Eventually, these overtures led to diplomatic relations with the PRC in 1978, and the abandonment of formal agreements with the 'ROC'. Informal arrangements have continued, however, and many regard the USA as the only possible guarantor of the continued existence of the 'ROC' as a political entity separate from the PRC.

Since 1978, while US-PRC relations have had their difficulties, the two countries have gradually developed a *modus vivendi*. As long as the Soviet Union existed, the PRC was a useful counterbalance to it. The combination of the suppression of the 1989 **Tiananmen** student demonstrations and the collapse of the Soviet Union both had negative effects on US-PRC relations. Not only was there now no requirement for a major power to counterbalance the Soviet Union, but also the sight of **Beijing** in flames and the reports of brutality against the demonstrators produced revulsion in the USA. Although there were further set-backs during the 1990s, and some predict that at some point in the future there could be conflict between the two, for the present each side seems to accept the other's existence. The USA has sought PRC assistance over the **DPRK nuclear programme**; this has been forthcoming but the PRC remains cautious and may well seek a trade-off on the Taiwan issue for long-term support.

The US-DPRK relationship remains tense. The hopes raised by the 1994 **Agreed Framework**, which included the possibility of diplomatic relations in some form between the two, have receded under President George W. Bush. The DPRK maintains a diplomatic presence at the **United Nations** in Washington, DC, which sometimes deals with the US government, but there is no US presence in the DPRK. Memories of the Korean War still produce a very negative effect in the USA, now reinforced by reports of human-rights abuses and fears that the DPRK's nuclear capability might be used against the USA or nuclear know-how might be supplied to anti-US terrorist groups. At the same time, a number of US Non-governmental Organizations (NGOs) have operated in the DPRK since the mid-1990s.

Uri Party

Uri dang or *Yeolin uri dang*

Pro-government party in the Republic of Korea (ROK), formed in October 2003 by supporters of President **Roh Moo-Hyun** who were dissatisfied with the **Millennium Democratic Party (MDP)**.

The name, which means 'Our Own Party', is intended to indicate inclusiveness. Originally, there were 42 ex-MDP members and five from the **Grand National Party (GNP)**. Allegations that Roh favoured the Uri Party led to his impeachment in March 2004, but the Party's success in the April 2004 **ROK National Assembly** elections, when it won 152 seats and obtained a slim majority, indicated that the impeachment was unpopular. Roh formally joined it in May 2004.

One of its campaigns has sought to track down those whose families collaborated with the Japanese during the colonial period (1910–45), a move possibly aimed at the GNP, whose leader is the daughter of former President **Park Chung-Hee**, who made no secret of the fact that he had been a military officer under Japanese command. The campaign backfired somewhat in August 2004, when the chairman, **Shin Ki-Nam**, resigned following revelations, which he at first denied, that his father been a military policeman under the Japanese.

> *Address:* Uri Party
> 134 Yongdongpo-6 ga
> Yongdongpo-ku
> Seoul
> Republic of Korea
> *Tel:* 82-2-784-0114
> *E-mail:* webmaster@eparty.or.kr
> *Internet:* http://uritv.eparty.or.kr

Ussuri river

Wusuli

A major river that rises in the Southern Sikhote Alin Range in the **Russian Far East**, and flows north-north-east 870 km to join the **Amur river**. 'Ussuri' is the Russian name. It forms part of the border between the **People's Republic of China (PRC)** and the Russian Far East. It is frozen in November–April, but when open it is used for transport and to float logs for processing. In 1969 there were clashes along the river between PRC and Soviet forces that led to some fatalities.

Uygur

Ethnic minority, settled almost entirely in **Xinjiang** in the north-western region of the **People's Republic of China (PRC)**.

The Uygur form the sixth largest minority nationality in the PRC, numbering 7,207,000 in the 1990 population census. They are thought to have migrated westwards to the area in the 8th–9th centuries AD from what is now Mongolia. The Uygur are Muslim and in their customs and culture, such as dress and music, share similarities with populations of the Central Asian republics. They are the largest minority group in the Xinjiang Uygur Autonomous Region, where their language has official status and is taught in schools and at university. Uygur, described as the eastern branch of the Turkic linguistic group, itself part of the Altaic family, has links with Turkish and Uzbek. The written language adopted Arabic script after the Uygur converted to **Islam** in the 15th–16th centuries, but was recast in a modified Latin script in 1958 as part of the Chinese language reform programme. This new script lasted only until 1980, when the former Arabic script was again authorized, in a modified version, as the written form of both Uygur and **Kazak**.

The Uygur are skilled cultivators settled mainly in the oases of the Tarim basin in the southern part of Xinjiang. They are also craftsmen and traders. Their relationship with the Chinese government and with the **Han Chinese** migrants who have been entering the region since the 19th century can be uneasy—neither Uygur nor Han appear willing, for instance, to overcome the language barrier that exists—and demonstrations and disturbances have been reported intermittently since the 1960s. These may be taking on an increasingly political tone.

W

Wang Dan

Wang Dan, who was born in 1969, studied history at Beijing University. He was active in the student demonstrations that followed the death of **Hu Yaobang** in April 1989, and the authorities of the **People's Republic of China** listed him as the 'most wanted' of the student leaders after the suppression of the demonstrations in **Tiananmen**. Although at first he fled from **Beijing**, unlike others, such as **Chai Ling** or **Li Lu**, Wang did not go abroad, and he was arrested when he returned to the city on 2 July 1989. He was sentenced to four years' imprisonment. Released in 1993, he was rearrested in 1996, charged with subversion and subsequently sentenced to 11 years' imprisonment. However, in April 1998 he was exiled to the USA, in a gesture towards US President Bill Clinton. Wang has returned to his historical studies in the USA, completing a master's degree in 2001, and beginning a Ph.D. He has perhaps been less self-promoting than some of his former colleagues.

Wei Jingsheng

A leading dissident in the **People's Republic of China (PRC)**, now in exile in the USA.

Wei Jingsheng was born in **Beijing** in 1950. He came to international attention in 1979, when he was tried for having passed secret information about PRC relations with Viet Nam to a foreigner. Since he was an electrician at the Beijing Zoo, it was hard to know what secret information he could have had. His real crime, however, was that he had criticized the Chinese leadership in an essay on the 'Democracy Wall' in Beijing. For this he was sentenced to 15 years' imprisonment. Released in 1993, within six months he had been rearrested and sentenced to a further 14 years' imprisonment as a 'counter-revolutionary'. In 1997, as a gesture from the then PRC President, **Jiang Zemin**, to US President Bill Clinton, Wei was expelled to the USA. He continues to live in Washington, DC, still pursuing his campaign for democracy in the PRC. Among other activities, he founded the Overseas Chinese Democracy Coalition in 1998 as a co-ordinating body for advocates of Chinese democracy.

Wen Jiabao

A member of the Standing Committee of the Political Bureau of the Central Committee of the **Chinese Communist Party (CCP)** and, since March 2003, the Premier of the **State Council** of the **People's Republic of China (PRC)**.

Born in **Tianjin** in 1942, Wen Jiabao is another technically trained member of the current PRC political leadership. He studied geological surveying and prospecting in **Beijing** in 1960–68, during which time he also joined the CCP. There followed 14 years in Gansu Province, at the same time that **Hu Jintao**, now CCP secretary-general and President of the PRC, was also active in the province. Wen returned to Beijing in 1982 as a senior member of the Ministry of Geology and Mineral Resources, becoming vice-minister and a leading party official in the ministry in 1983–85. In 1986 he became director of the General Office of the CCP Central Committee. At this stage he was close to **Zhao Ziyang**, Premier and later party secretary, but he avoided becoming entangled with Zhao's downfall at the time of the **Tiananmen** incident in 1989, although his progress slowed for a time. He was made an alternate member of the party Political Bureau in 1993, and a full member in 1997. In the following year he also became a Vice-Premier.

West Sea Barrage

One of the Democratic People's Republic of Korea's (DPRK) major engineering works, completed at the mouth of the 450-km Taedong river in 1986. It took five years to build, and the **Korean People's Army** mainly carried out the work. The barrage has theoretically turned the formerly tidal Taedong river into a freshwater lake, making it available for irrigation purposes, while allowing the use of the lower reaches of the river for navigation. Fields in the lower reaches of the river no longer suffer from salt damage, and a system of irrigation canals allows the water to be distributed in a wide area of the Ongjin peninsula, south of the capital, **Pyongyang**. Problems with silting have been reported, but the DPRK has not confirmed these.

Whaling

Japan has a long tradition of whaling. In the Edo period (1600–1868) whalemeat formed an important part of the Japanese diet and the whaling industry grew in importance. This was partly because **Buddhists** did not classify whalemeat as meat but as fish, and therefore it did not fall under the prohibition on eating meat. After 1868 there was a further expansion of the industry, as Japanese whalers learnt new techniques from Western whalers; the northern port of Hakodate, one of Japan's **foreign settlements**, was largely established to meet the needs of Western whalers.

After the **Pacific War** whalemeat continued to play an important part in the Japanese diet. Up to the 1960s it accounted for as much as 30% of the total Japanese protein intake, and the government promoted its use in schools and other public institutions. However, from the 1970s onwards Japan came under increased pressure from the **International Whaling Commission (IWC)** and other bodies to end commercial whaling. Formally, Japan has complied with such requests, but it has also pressed for increased 'scientific whaling', which allows the capture of a limited number of whales each year. Eventually, some of these whales enter the food chain, which has led to charges that Japan cheats on the issue. The Japanese government has denied such charges. Some whalemeat is imported legally from Russia, and it is not easy to distinguish what has been caught illegitimately from that caught in accordance with the scientific quotas. Japan remains a member of the IWC, but regularly threatens to withdraw. In July 2004 it was reported that the ruling **Liberal Democratic Party** had drawn up an outline plan for a new body to replace the IWC.

There is also a less developed tradition of eating whalemeat in the Republic of Korea, especially around the East Coast port of Ulsan where an annual whale festival is held. Whalemeat is sometimes available in small quantities at this festival. The source of this is claimed to be whales caught accidentally when other species are being fished.

Wonsan

A major port on the east coast of the Democratic People's Republic of Korea (DPRK), with an estimated population of about 380,000, Wonsan is also an industrial centre, with shipyards, chemical factories, oil refineries and railway works. It is also a tourist centre, with good bathing beaches and the Kumgang or Diamond mountains lying to the south. Like most DPRK cities, its heavy industry has suffered from lack of power and resources since the early 1990s.

World Bank

Specialized agency of the **United Nations** with responsibility for long-term financing of reconstruction projects and for programmes aimed at the reduction of poverty.

It was set up at the same time as the **International Monetary Fund (IMF)**, following the conference held in July 1944 at Bretton Woods, New Hampshire, USA, to devise a framework for post-war economic reconstruction. The World Bank formally began operations in June 1946. It currently has 184 members, the same number as the IMF, and membership of the IMF is a prerequisite for adherence in the Bank. The World Bank is composed strictly of two elements, the International Bank for Reconstruction and Development (IBRD) and the International Development Association (IDA). As with the IMF, the IBRD is funded by members' subscriptions, which are calculated on the basis of economic strength. A wider grouping, the World Bank Group, incorporates the IBRD, the IDA and three other entities. In common with other international financial and trade organizations, the World Bank has been the subject of international criticism over social and environmental issues and perceived inefficiencies.

Members among East Asian countries are the **People's Republic of China** (which assumed representation of **China** in the five institutions of the World Bank Group in May 1980), Japan (acceded to all five bodies in August 1952), the Republic of Korea (acceded to all five in August 1955) and Mongolia (acceded to all five bodies in February 1991).

Pres. of the World Bank Group: James D. Wolfensohn
Address: 1818 H Street NW
        Washington, DC, 20433
        USA
Tel: 1-202-473-1000
Fax: 1-202-477-6391
E-mail: info@worldbank.org
Internet: www.worldbank.org

World Trade Organization (WTO)

International organization dealing with the rules of trade between states and regions.

The World Trade Organization (WTO) arose out the Uruguay Round negotiations conducted from 1986 until 1994 to tackle problems in global trade. From 1947 until 1995, the year in which the WTO was established, the General Agreement on Tariffs and Trade (GATT) had served as a framework for regulating the world's multilateral trading system in the interests of free trade. WTO has now replaced GATT. It is a membership-based organization that negotiates and administers agreements on a consensual basis and mediates in trade disputes. Its work, like that of GATT, is sometimes criticized as favouring the interests of powerful nations over those of developing countries and as inimical to environmental and health concerns.

WTO's membership in April 2004 stood at 147 countries and regions. Within East Asia, Japan, the Republic of Korea, **Hong Kong** and **Macao** have been members since the inception of WTO on 1 January 1995. Mongolia acceded in January 1997, the **People's Republic of China** in December 2001 and **Taiwan** in January 2002.

Dir-Gen.: Dr Supachai Panitchpakdi
Address: Centre William Rappard
        154 rue de Lausanne
        CH-1211 Geneva 21
        Switzerland
Tel: 41-22-739-5111
Fax: 41-22-731-4206
E-mail: enquiries@wto.org
Internet: www.wto.org

Wu Bangguo

In March 2003 Wu Bangguo succeeded **Li Peng** as the chairman of the Standing Committee of the **National People's Congress**, the parliament of the **People's Republic of China (PRC)**. In theory, Wu thus ranks third in the PRC's political hierarchy.

Wu was born in 1941. He joined the **Chinese Communist Party (CCP)** in 1964, when he was an electronic engineering student at Qinghua University in **Beijing**. From 1967 onwards he worked in **Shanghai**, where he also began to play an important role in the local CCP. From 1985 he was successively deputy secretary and then secretary of the CCP Shanghai Municipal Committee. In these positions he became close to **Jiang Zemin**. In 1994 he joined the CCP Politburo Central Committee, and in 1995 he became a Vice-Premier, charged with reforming state industries. He is rumoured to have quarrelled with the then Premier, **Zhu Rongji**, and, like others before him, to have failed to reform state enterprises. His present post probably indicates that he will not rise any further in the political hierarchy.

Wu, Harry

Wu Hongda

Chinese-American human rights activist, who founded the Laogai Research Foundation.

Wu Hongda, now more generally known as Harry Wu, was born in **Shanghai** in 1937. By his own account, his family were well off, and after the establishment of the **People's Republic of China (PRC)** in 1949 they suffered because of their bourgeois background. In 1956 Wu began to study geology in **Beijing**, but he claims that after criticizing the **Chinese Communist Party** he was convicted as a 'counter-revolutionary' and sent to a labour camp.

He was not released until 1979. Eventually, he went to the USA and for a time was a visiting professor of geology at the University of California. While there, he began to draw attention to human rights abuses in the PRC, and especially to the existence there of many labour camps. Before long Wu had abandoned his academic work to concentrate on human rights activities. In 1991 he and his wife returned to the PRC and secretly filmed some of the camps. He made a number of subsequent visits, examining not only the camps, but also issues such as forced abortions and the sale of human organs. During these years Wu began writing, publishing *Laogai: The Chinese Gulag* in 1991, and a memoir of his own experience in the camps, *Bitter Winds*, in 1994. He also established the Laogai Research Foundation, to investigate and publicize conditions in the camps.

In 1995 he attempted to enter the PRC for the fourth time, now with a US passport, but was detained and sentenced to 15 years' imprisonment for stealing state secrets. As a result of international pressure, however, he was expelled from the PRC. He published an account of these events, *Troublemaker*, in 1996. Since then he has continued to campaign on human rights issues.

Wu has received much international acclaim for his campaigns, and is the recipient of a number of awards. Some members of the Chinese-American community have criticized him as a publicity-seeker and troublemaker; nobody, however, has disputed his broad depiction of the extensive labour camp system that operates in the PRC.

Wu'er Kaixi

Wu'er Kaixi came to prominence in May 1989 during the student demonstrations in **Beijing**. He appeared on television, dressed in hospital clothes—he was on hunger strike—berating **Li Peng**, the Premier of the **People's Republic of China**, for his failure to listen to the students' grievances.

Wu'er Kaixi was born in 1968, and in 1989 was a student at the Beijing Normal University. He had attracted some interest, especially among foreign observers, before his confrontation with Li Peng because he was of **Uygur** origin; his Uygur name is Uerkesh Daolet. After the suppression of the students, he escaped to France and then made his way to the USA, where he studied at Harvard University. Like others who had been prominent in 1989, he found it difficult to settle, and he eventually moved to **Taiwan**, where he now hosts a radio show.

X

Xinhua News Agency
Xinhua tongxun she

The principal news agency serving the **People's Republic of China (PRC)**.

Xinhua News Agency (often formerly referred to by the abbreviation NCNA, for New China News Agency) was established in 1931 as the press outlet of the **Chinese Communist Party (CCP)** and continues to work closely with the Party. It took its present name in 1937. During the **Pacific War** it developed an overseas broadcasting capability and established its first overseas branches. After the Communists gained control of **China** in the country's civil war and established the PRC in 1949, NCNA became the official Chinese news agency, with headquarters in **Beijing** and around 150 domestic and overseas offices. As such, it had and still has considerable influence in the selection and distribution of both domestic news and foreign reports. At times when the PRC had no direct contact with countries or organizations with which it none the less had to negotiate during its early years of comparative diplomatic isolation, NCNA provided a public means of communication. It also performed diplomatic functions for the Chinese government in a number of situations where the PRC did not have formal relations, notably in **Hong Kong**.

Xinhua publishes a number of journals, periodicals and reference works. In 1997 it established its first website, which in 2000 was renamed xinhuanet.com. This now offers news services in seven languages and competes with television companies in providing live coverage of events.

Xinhua News Agency has the status of an institution under the **State Council** of the PRC. Its president, Tian Congming, is a member of the 16th CCP Central Committee.

Leadership: Tian Congming (Pres.); Nan Zhenzhong (Editor-in-Chief)
Address: 57 Xuanwumen Xidajie
  Beijing 100803
  People's Republic of China
Tel: 86-010-6307-1114
Fax: 86-010-6307-1210

E-mail: info@xinhuanet.com
Internet: www.xinhuanet.com (Chinese language)
　　　　　www.chinaview.cn (English language)

Xinjiang

'New frontier' or 'new province', forming the north-west border zone between the interior of the **People's Republic of China (PRC)** and Central Asia.

The area is governed as the Xinjiang Uygur Autonomous Region. Established in 1955, the Region is the largest administrative unit in the PRC and comprises one-sixth of the country's land area, covering more than 1.6m. sq km. Much of it is filled with high mountain ranges or desert, but careful irrigation permits the cultivation of grain, cotton and fruit around the oases, and the northern grasslands support large herds. Xinjiang's small population of 19.25m. (2000 census) is divided between **Han Chinese** and some 14 ethnic minorities, among whom the **Uygur** and the **Kazak** form the largest groups. Eight of these minority nationalities are Muslim. Several—the Kazak, Kirgiz, Tajik, Ozbek and the Uygur themselves—have ethnic and cultural affinities with the populations of the Central Asian republics. These religious and ethnic links are a constant source of anxiety to the Chinese authorities.

Xinjiang is the site of the PRC's nuclear testing ground at Lop Nor and the location of many prison camps. It also has large deposits of oil and natural gas, under exploitation, and reserves of coal and minerals. All these are further factors in determining the PRC's need to keep a firm grip on Xinjiang, despite the measure of self-government implied in the term 'autonomous' and the presence of minority cadres in the Region's administration. The PRC maintains a military presence in Xinjiang, strengthened by the continuing activity of the Xinjiang Production and Construction Corps, a quasi-military organization composed largely of demobilized Han Chinese armymen and resettled Han Chinese, which was set up in the 1950s to assist in the development of the region. A steady flow of Han migration into the area has served to dilute the minority ethnic composition of the population.

China's hold on the region has been very variable since the Qing dynasty first extended its military influence over the area in the 18th century, meeting indigenous and religious opposition. Han settlement started in 1831. The region then passed into Muslim hands as an independent state until 1878, when the Chinese reasserted control and supported large-scale Han immigration into the area. Xinjiang was incorporated into the Qing empire as a province in 1884. After the collapse of the Qing in 1911, the region endured civil war, disturbances and a succession of leaders. From 1933 until 1934, and again from 1944 until 1946, an independent Republic of East Turkestan emerged in the north-western part of the region, representing Uygur and Kazak interests and centred on **Kashgar**. The concept of an independent state has remained to complicate political relations between the Chinese and the indigenous population. In 1949 the Chinese **People's Liberation Army** ousted the Nationalist Chinese troops in the region and seized control. Land reform and renewed Han immigration started immediately. Relations between the Chinese government and the local population have never been smooth. The Chinese have veered between moderate and hardline approaches towards the region. Periods of economic and social upheaval in China, such as the Great Leap Forward (1958) and the **Cultural Revolution** (1966–76), led to disaffection and chaos in Xinjiang. Resentment at Han settlement and what is viewed as preferential treatment for the Han, at the use of Xinjiang territory for nuclear testing and the detention of prisoners, and at the alleged exploitation of the region's resources has erupted from time to time. From the late 1980s what were considered to be religious and racial slights have been added as causes of grievance. In 1990 calls were renewed for the establishment of an East Turkestan state, followed by talk of Uygur liberation movements. The Chinese government has suppressed disturbances and sought to control religious personnel and activities. The PRC remains utterly opposed to any expression of secessionist or pan-Turkic sentiments, while maintaining a conciliatory line on cultural and to some extent religious distinctiveness. It invokes the danger of foreign interference, yet also seeks to use the region's connections with Islamic countries to solicit trade and investment. It was quick to establish diplomatic relations with the new Central Asian republics after 1991, and has joined with four of them and the Russian Federation to set up the **Shanghai Co-operation Organization**, with the aim of combating terrorist and separatist activities.

Y

Yalta Conference 1945

In February 1945, as the defeat of Germany in the Second World War seemed certain, the Allied leaders, Josef Stalin, Winston Churchill and Franklin Roosevelt, met at the Crimean resort city of Yalta to agree the territorial arrangements for post-war Europe, and to map out their strategy for defeating Japan. The Allies secretly agreed that in return for the Soviet Union's undertaking to declare war on Japan, Japan would give up southern **Sakhalin** and the **Kurile Islands**, which would be assigned to the Soviet Union. It was also at this conference that the Soviet Union accepted that, for the purpose of taking the surrender of Japanese forces, the **Korean peninsula** would be divided on a temporary basis between Soviet and US forces.

Yalu river

Amnokgang

The Yalu river forms some two-thirds of the border between the **People's Republic of China (PRC)** and the Democratic People's Republic of Korea (DPRK). The Yalu, which rises on **Mount Paektu**, has always played an important role in relations between north-east **China** and the peninsula, and has been the *de facto* dividing line between them since the 4th century AD. During the **Korean War**, Republic of Korea and US forces reached the Yalu in October 1950, but were then driven back by the PRC's **People's Liberation Army**, which fought as the Chinese People's Volunteers. The Yalu river area was an important centre for prisoner-of-war camps, while its bridges and hydroelectric dams were targeted by the **United Nations** air forces.

Yanan

Town in Shaanxi Province in **China**, where the **Chinese Communist Party (CCP)** and its military supporters regrouped and rebuilt their military base at the end of the **Long March** in 1935. Yanan remained the CCP's main base until **Kuomintang** forces captured it in 1947.

The name has become synonymous with the early days of the CCP, the allegedly simple life led by leaders and followers, and the good companionship of those years. After the **Tiananmen** incident in 1989, some of the older leaders referred to returning to the 'spirit of Yanan' when faced with the hostile international response to what had happened. It was at Yanan that **Mao Zedong** gave his interviews to the US journalist **Edgar Snow** in 1936. These interviews formed the basis of Snow's book, *Red Star over China*, published in 1937, which brought the CCP and its fight against the Japanese to international attention.

Yangzi river

The Yangzi (Yangtse in the Wade-Giles romanization system) river is one of the great rivers of **China**. It rises in **Tibet** and flows some 5,600 km reaching the sea close to **Shanghai**. Although known to foreigners as the Yangzi, or Son of the Ocean, river, the Chinese call it the *Changjiang* or Long river. It forms the natural and linguistic dividing line between northern and southern China, which are sometimes referred to as *Jiangbei* (North of the River) and *Jiangnan* (South of the River). The building of the Yangzi River Bridge at **Nanjing** in 1969 reduced but did not eliminate the river's dividing influence. The controversial **Three Gorges Dam Project** will much affect the river's role in future.

Yasukuni Shrine

Yasukuni jinja

This **Shinto** shrine, established in central **Tokyo** in 1879, played an important role in Japanese 'state Shinto' until the end of the **Pacific War**.

The shrine's original purpose was to honour those killed fighting during the **Meiji Restoration**, and it later came to be the shrine for all war dead. When the **Allied Occupation of Japan** ended 'state Shinto' after 1945, all official funding to the Yasukuni Shrine ceased. The shrine and its museum have remained potent symbols for Japanese right-wing groups and politicians. In 1979 the executed Japanese Class A war criminals were formally enshrined there. This, and the practice of some senior politicians, including a number of Prime Ministers, of visiting the shrine on 15 August, the anniversary of Japan's defeat, has regularly caused controversy both in Japan and in neighbouring countries. Legal rulings on the constitutionality of such visits have been indecisive.

Yellow river

Huanghe

The Yellow river rises in **Tibet** and flows some 4,800 km to reach the sea in the Gulf of Bohai. It takes its name from the heavy deposits of soil that it carries with it, which have been an important contribution to the economic development of northern **China**. Over the centuries the river has changed course several times, causing much devastation and loss of life; hence it is often known as 'China's sorrow'. The need to control the river is thought to be one source of the concept of power based on hydraulics, which is sometimes called 'Oriental Despotism'.

Yi

Ethnic minority group numbering 6,578,500 in the 1990 population census of the **People's Republic of China (PRC)**, living mainly in the mountainous areas of south-west Sichuan Province and north-west Yunnan Province in south-west China. Other Yi settlements are in Guizhou Province and Guangxi Zhuang Autonomous Region. The Yi form the seventh largest minority nationality in the PRC. Their language is a branch of the Tibeto-Burman family. A syllabic writing system, based on a traditional script, was devised for the language in 1958, consisting of 819 syllabic signs. The Yi nationality's preferred name for itself is the Nosu.

Yi Ku

Born in **Tokyo**, Japan, in 1931, Yi Ku is the only son of the last crown prince of the Yi dynasty which had ruled the **Korean peninsula** in 1392–1910. He is thus the formal heir to the Korean monarchy.

His father, Yi Un (1897–1970), who was taken to Japan after the Japanese takeover of Korea in 1919, married the minor Japanese princess, Nashimoto Masako (1901–1989), who is known in Korea as Yi Pangja. Much respected in Korea for her interest in social issues and the arts, she continued to live in **Seoul** after the death of her husband. Yi Ku qualified as an architect at the Massachusetts Institute of Technology in the USA, and practised in Japan, the Republic of Korea, and the USA. He married an American, Julia Mullock, in 1959. They had no children and subsequently divorced. Yi retired to Seoul in 1996. He has shown no interest in reviving a claim to the Korean throne.

Yokohama

Second largest city in Japan, situated in central Honshu, Yokohama is also the capital of Kanagawa Prefecture.

At the time of Japan's opening to the West in the 1850s, Yokohama was a small fishing village, which became one of Japan's **foreign settlements**. From this beginning it developed into the country's principal port and currently has a population of 3.27m. In 1923 the **Kanto earthquake** destroyed much of the old foreign quarter; the city also suffered severely in the Second World War. Since the 1950s it has expanded both as a port and as an industrial centre. The city retains a cosmopolitan air and has a large Chinatown.

Yonhap News Agency

The Republic of Korea's (ROK) sole news agency. Nominally independent, it none the less enjoys official financial support and tends to follow the government line on domestic news and, though somewhat less so, on international stories. Yonhap is the outcome of a long series of mergers, some forced, others determined by financial reasons. It was created in 1980 in the aftermath of President **Chun Doo-Hwan**'s seizure of power in 1979–80. Chun had the two existing news agencies, Hapdong and the Orient Press, disbanded and replaced by Yonhap. The Hapdong News Agency itself emerged in late 1945 out of the short-lived Kukje News that had operated for two months from October 1945 out of the office of Domei, the former Japanese news agency that had functioned in Korea during the Japanese colonial era. Yonhap publishes the *Korea Annual*, the most comprehensive guide to the ROK—and, to a lesser extent, the Democratic People's Republic of Korea (DPRK)—that is available in English.

In 1999 Yonhap News Agency took over the former Naewoe News Agency. Naewoe had been established in the mid-1970s as a government-affiliated organization to give an ROK perspective on news and analysis of the DPRK. Naewoe has retained its own imprint in the merger with Yonhap. Among its regular productions is the monthly *Vantage Point: Developments in North Korea*, and it also publishes books. Yonhap itself signed an agreement with the DPRK's **Korean Central News Agency** in December 2002 to exchange news services, and carries a section of DPRK news in its online service. Yonhap online news is available in Korean, Chinese and English.

Pres.: Kim Kun
Address: 85-1 Susong-dong
         Jongro-gu
         Seoul 110
         Republic of Korea
Telephone: 82-2-398-3114
Fax: 82-2-398-3463/3567
E-mail: english@yonhapnews.co.kr
Internet: www.yna.co.kr

Yu Shyi-kun

Politician, Premier of the **'Republic of China'** on **Taiwan** since 2002.

Yu Shyi-kun was born in 1948 into a poor farming family in Yilan County of Taiwan. His father's death forced him to abandon his schooling at the age of 13 and he did not complete his university education until he was 37. He had already entered politics, having been elected a member of the Taiwan Provincial Assembly in 1981. From 1983 he involved himself in the *Tangwai* ('outside the [KMT] party') movement and was a founder-member of the **Democratic Progressive Party**

(DPP) that evolved from that movement. From 1990 until 1997 Yu served as a county magistrate, during which period he was also a member of the Educational Reform Committee of the **Executive Yuan**, in 1994–96. In 1998 **Chen Shui-bian**, the then mayor of **Taipei**, appointed him as chairman of the Taipei Rapid Transit Corporation. In 1999 he returned to the DPP to become its secretary-general, thus continuing his connection with Chen Shui-bian, the Party's chairman. The two men further shared a similarly humble background. On Chen's election as President in 2000 Yu was appointed as Vice-Premier. He resigned later in that year in the wake of a disaster in which four construction workers drowned in floodwaters; but six months later he was taken back into the administration as secretary-general to the office of the President. In 2002 he was appointed as Premier.

Address: Executive Yuan
      1 Chunghsiao East Rd
      Section 1
      Taipei
      Taiwan
Tel: 886-2-2356-1500/886-2-3356-6500
Internet: www.ey.gov.tw

Yun I-Sang (1917–1995)

The most famous Korean composer of the 20th century.

For most of his life Yun was more honoured in the Democratic People's Republic of Korea (DPRK) than in the Republic of Korea (ROK). Born in Tongyong, in South Kyongsang Province, he studied in Japan before the **Pacific War**, where he became active in Korean revolutionary groups. After his return to the ROK, in 1955, he won a major award from the **Seoul** city government, which allowed him to study music in West Germany. There he acquired an international reputation, but in 1967 he and his wife were among a group of ROK citizens kidnapped by the then Korean Central Intelligence Agency (now the National Intelligence Service). They were brought back to the ROK, where they were accused of spying for the DPRK. Convicted, Yun was sentenced to life imprisonment. Following an international outcry, however, he was released after serving two years of his sentence and allowed to return to Germany.

Thereafter, his music became more political. He visited the DPRK several times, but never returned to the ROK, where his music was banned. After his death, however, the changed political climate in the 1990s led to increased interest in his music, which is now regularly performed in the ROK. He also remains popular in the DPRK. One of **Pyongyang**'s main concert halls is dedicated to his memory, there is an annual series of concerts in his name, in which German orchestras often participate, and a music festival was held in his memory in 1998.

Z

Zaibatsu

The Japanese word *zaibatsu* strictly describes a large, family-controlled business conglomerate, though it has been adopted by English to mean any large business or financial group. The first *zaibatsu* were Mitsui, Mitsubishi, Sumitomo and Yasuda, but later the term was also applied to other large companies.

Until the 1930s these groups were entirely family-owned and dominated, usually via a system of holding companies that gave directions to the various subordinate sections. Even though many of them issued shares in the 1930s, family control persisted, via family members in individual companies and by links to family banks. Such companies had their headquarters in **Tokyo**, which gave them strong political influence, but their operations spread throughout Japan and, from 1895 onwards, into the Japanese empire. By 1945 the four main *zaibatsu* controlled one-quarter of all the paid-up capital in Japan.

Under the **Allied Occupation of Japan** it was believed that the *zaibatsu* had been a powerful driving force behind Japan's decision to go to war, and measures were taken to break them up. In particular, the Occupation authorities dissolved the family holding companies, since these seemed to be the key to *zaibatsu* success. However, by the late 1940s there was much less interest in carrying out such reforms, and the measures against the *zaibatsu* ended. The *zaibatsu* did not formally reappear, but instead regrouped as informal enterprise groups, or *keiretsu*. These still exist, often with the old *zaibatsu* names, but they are no longer the family-controlled groups of the past. Until 1997 holding companies were banned, and the main linkage between the various companies in a *keiretsu* was through a bank bearing the group name. Lending was not confined to the group, however, whose members could seek funds elsewhere if they wished. There is some concern in Japan that the 1997 modifications in the Anti-Monopoly Law might lead to a revival of *zaibatsu*-like groups, but this has not happened so far.

Zhao Ziyang (1919–2005)

Zhao Ziyang was secretary-general of the **Chinese Communist Party (CCP)** of the **People's Republic of China** at the time of the 1989 **Tiananmen** incident.

He was then dismissed from all his posts. However, he remained a member of the CCP.

Born in Henan Province in 1919, Zhao joined the CCP in 1938. He worked in Guangdong Province, disappeared during the **Cultural Revolution**, but reappeared in **Inner Mongolia** in 1971. He moved back to Guangdong in 1972. In 1975–80 he was the Sichuan provincial CCP secretary-general. Elected as an alternate member of the Politburo of the Central Committee of the CCP in 1977, he became a full member in 1979. In 1980, when he moved to **Beijing** to run the **State Council** after the fall of **Hua Guofeng**, he became a member of the Standing Committee of the Politburo. In September 1980 he became Premier. In this role he played a prominent part in the introduction of the economic reforms advocated by **Deng Xiaoping** and the CCP general-secretary **Hu Yaobang**. He did not always agree with Hu, however, and supported the calls for his resignation in 1986. Reluctantly, he took over Hu's party role, but increasingly clashed with his successor as Premier, **Li Peng**. When student demonstrations began in April 1989, Zhao not only tried to negotiate with their leaders, but also failed to endorse Deng's increasingly hard line. Between June 1989 and his death in January 2005 he did not appear in public.

Zheng Qinghong

Vice-President of the **People's Republic of China (PRC)** since March 2003.

Zheng was born in 1939 in Jiangxi Province. His father played an important role in the Communist revolution, and became a minister after the founding of the PRC. Zheng trained as a rocket and missile engineer and joined the **Chinese Communist Party (CCP)** in 1960. He then worked on missiles in the **People's Liberation Army** and in civilian research institutes until he first came to prominence in national politics in 1979 as secretary of the General Office of the State Planning Commission. By 1984 he held senior positions in the **Shanghai** municipal CCP; it was an advantage that his father had been vice-mayor of Shanghai. Zheng worked with **Jiang Zemin** to limit the impact of student activists in 1989, and when Jiang became CCP general secretary after the fall of **Zhao Ziyang**, Zheng followed him to **Beijing**. There he worked in the General Office of the CCP Central Committee. In 1997 he became an alternate member of the Central Committee Politburo and a member of the Central Committee secretariat. He became a full member of the Politburo in 2002. His closeness to Jiang Zemin may benefit him as long as Jiang retains some power, although Zheng has also created his own power base within the Party.

Zhongnanhai

Since 1949 this area of **Beijing**, close to the Forbidden City and once part of the imperial palace, has been the work and residence centre for senior party and government leaders in the **People's Republic of China**. Accordingly, the name is sometimes used as a reference to government thinking or actions.

Zhou Enlai (1898–1976)

Zhou Enlai (Chou En-lai in the Wade-Giles romanization) was Premier of the **State Council** of the **People's Republic of China (PRC)** from 1949 until his death in 1976.

Zhou, from a moderately affluent family, was born in Jiangxi Province. He studied in Japan and in the early 1920s went to France on a work-study programme. While in France he joined the **Chinese Communist Party (CCP)**, but on his return to **China** in 1924 he worked with the **Kuomintang** until it turned against the CCP in 1927. Thereafter, Zhou worked with the CCP. From 1934 he worked with **Mao Zedong** in a partnership that lasted until Zhou's death. During the 1930s and 1940s Zhou proved to be a skilled negotiator, and, after 1949, an equally skilled administrator. For 10 years he combined the role of Premier with that of foreign minister. He was heavily involved in matters relating to the **Korean War**, and led the PRC delegation to the 1954 **Geneva Conference**.

During the political campaigns launched by Mao, Zhou seems always to have acted as a moderating influence, while never formally opposing the chairman. This was particularly true during the **Cultural Revolution** (1966–76), in which Zhou intervened to prevent some of the excesses of the Red Guards. Although he came under attack in the later part of the Cultural Revolution, Zhou survived. He was closely involved with the *rapprochement* with the USA that took place in 1971–72. His death in April 1976, some six months before Mao died, sparked popular demonstrations at **Tiananmen** in **Beijing** that foreshadowed the events of 1989.

Zhuang

The largest among the 55 minority nationalities in the **People's Republic of China**. The Zhuang numbered 15,555,800 in the 1990 population census.

The Zhuang form part of the Thai ethnic group. Their homeland is recognized as the Guangxi Zhuang Autonomous Region, established in 1958, in the sub-tropical zone of southern **China**, with a short border with Viet Nam. Its capital is Nanning. The Zhuang constitute 35%–40% of the population of the Autonomous Region and are also settled in the neighbouring provinces of Guangdong, Yunnan, Guizhou and Hunan. Within Guangxi Zhuang Autonomous Region the Zhuang live mostly in the western mountainous districts. The economy of the Autonomous Region relies mainly on agriculture, practised in the small area of land that is not hilly. The Region's mineral resources have not yet been fully exploited. The Zhuang are traditionally animists and ancestor-worshippers, but include a number of Buddhists, Christians and Muslims. Their language has links with the Tai languages, a group belonging to the Sino-Tibetan family, which also include Thai and Lao. Zhuang formerly used Chinese characters for its written form but now, like Vietnamese, usually employs roman script.